A Revolution in Favor of Government

A Revolution in Favor of Government

Origins of the U.S. Constitution and the Making of the American State

Max M. Edling

OXFORD
UNIVERSITY PRESS

OXFORD
UNIVERSITY PRESS

Oxford University Press, Inc., publishes works that further
Oxford University's objective of excellence
in research, scholarship, and education.

Oxford   New York
Auckland   Cape Town   Dar es Salaam   Hong Kong   Karachi
Kuala Lumpur   Madrid   Melbourne   Mexico City   Nairobi
New Delhi   Shanghai   Taipei   Toronto

With offices in
Argentina   Austria   Brazil   Chile   Czech Republic   France   Greece
Guatemala   Hungary   Italy   Japan   Poland   Portugal   Singapore
South Korea   Switzerland   Thailand   Turkey   Ukraine   Vietnam

Published by Oxford University Press, Inc.
198 Madison Avenue, New York, New York 10016

www.oup.com

First issued as an Oxford University Press paperback, 2008

Oxford is a registered trademark of Oxford University Press

Library of Congress Cataloging-in-Publication Data

Edling, Max M.
A revolution in favor of government : origins of the U.S. Constitution
and the making of the American state / by Max M. Edling
p. cm.
Includes bibliographical references and index.
ISBN 978-0-19-514870-1; 978-0-19-537416-2 (pbk.)
1. Constitutional history—United States.   2. Federal
government—United States—History.   I. Title.
KF4541 .E28 2003
342.73'029—dc21   2002152079

Printed in the United States of America
on acid-free paper

Mark D. Kaplanoff
in memoriam

The year 1776 is celebrated for a revolution in favor of *Liberty*. The year 1787, it is expected, will
be celebrated with equal joy, for a revolution in favor of *Government*.

Pennsylvania Gazette, 5 September 1787

The friends of our country have long seen and de-
sired, that the power of making war, peace and
treaties, that of levying money and regulating
commerce, and the correspondent executive and
judicial authorities should be fully and effectually
vested in the general government of the Union.

George Washington to the president of Congress,
17 September 1787

Money is the sinew of government as well as of
war. To call it forth with certainty—in such quan-
tities and in such only as the public exigencies demand, and in a manner most easy to the people,
is the perfection of legislation.

John Brooks, 4 July 1787

ACKNOWLEDGMENTS

This book began not as one dissertation but as two. I first defended a dissertation on the Federalists and the origins of the American state for a Ph.D. degree in history at Cambridge University, England. Having returned to my native country of Sweden, I presented a revised and expanded version of the dissertation at Stockholm University, as partial fulfillment of the requirements for a doctorate in political science. In the many years of researching and writing this book, I have of course incurred many debts. While it is certainly a great pleasure to acknowledge them here, they go far beyond what I can state in this brief acknowledgment.

Although they are very different universities, I always found Cambridge and Stockholm to be intellectually stimulating places, and I would like to thank everyone who in one way or another made them so. At Stockholm, a few persons deserve special mention. Jens Bartelson, Rune Premfors, and Olof Ruin formed the internal advisory committee that gave the go ahead for the examination of the thesis. They read the complete manuscript and provided many important comments. Björn Wittrock was my supervisor and I owe him a very great debt, both for all that he taught me and for the support he still continues to demonstrate.

Richard Simmons and Daniel Howe acted as my examiners at Cambridge and Gordon Wood did so at Stockholm in his capacity as "Faculty Opponent." They all offered numerous valuable suggestions on how to improve my work, most of which I have heeded. I am also grateful to the latter two for encouraging me to publish the dissertation and for assisting me in my contacts with Oxford University Press. Peter Onuf and Jack Rakove, as well as two anonymous reviewers for Oxford, have read later versions of the manuscript. Their criticisms were always pertinent and appropriate and I have followed many of their suggestions. Had time permitted, I would have followed more of them and the book would have been much the better for it. At Oxford University Press I would like to thank Bob Milks, Jennifer Rappaport, and, especially, Dedi Felman for being at all times supportive and efficient.

I began the revision of my dissertation into a book when I was a fellow at the Swedish Collegium for Advanced Studies in the Social Sciences in Uppsala, Sweden, in the spring of 2000. I would like to thank the Collegium's directors and staff for providing me with that opportunity and the other fellows for making it such a stimulating time. Among the fellows, I must single out Marion Smiley, who took great interest in my work and who offered encouragement and much appreciated help in the revision process. Revision continued after I took up my position in the History Department at Uppsala University. I am grateful to my colleagues in the department and to my fellow Americanists in the university for providing such a warm welcome and such a propitious environment in which to finish the book. I would also like to thank The Bank of Sweden Tercentenary Foundation for providing the pecuniary means to make this possible.

I have saved my greatest debts to last. Susanna Rabow-Edling has read and discussed with me every one of the innumerable versions of this manuscript. Always my harshest critic, she has forced me to sharpen my arguments and to prune my prose. To the extent that the argument presented here is set down with clarity and consistency, it is in great respect due to her. Mark Kaplanoff supervised my dissertation at Cambridge. His knowledge of the period, persons, and issues I worked on never failed to impress me. As a critic he was straightforward but generous and fair. He gave unsparingly of his time and showed great interest in my work. His comments were always constructive and to the point. Indeed, many of my most important insights occurred during—or after—our conversations over drinks in Mark's rooms at Pembroke, and if this book has any value much of the credit belongs to him. It was with great sadness that I learned of Mark's sudden and unexpected death two years ago. He never lived to see the completion of the work to which he was so crucial. It is my hope that he would have approved of the result.

CONTENTS

A Revolution in Favor of Government

INTRODUCTION: BEYOND
MADISONIAN FEDERALISM

On 17 September 1787, the Philadelphia Convention broke its silence to announce the result of its deliberations: the bold plan "to form a more perfect Union." Over the following ten months, the new constitution was ratified by eleven states. In those months, the Constitution's supporters and opponents engaged in a great public debate, which we know as the debate over the ratification of the Constitution. This debate left an extensive record, the full scope of which has only recently become appreciated.[1] It is to this record that scholars, as well as politicians, lawyers, and laymen, have turned to determine the meaning of the founding of the American republic. In the debate over ratification, they have searched for answers as to why the Constitution was adopted and for what purpose it was designed. This book is yet another attempt to do so. Like most other studies, it focuses on the Federalist argument, although it also takes the Antifederalist opposition into account. However, the conclusions reached here deviate sharply from the mainstream interpretation of the Federalist persuasion.

Today, most historians and political theorists agree that the best exponent of the Federalist argument was James Madison. Although there is room for some variation between different interpretations, there is also a broad consensus on what this argument was about. The Federalists, it is claimed, were concerned above all with checking the "excessive democracy" that the Revolution had introduced in the state assemblies, threatening both the common good of the union and the rights of minorities. The essence of the Federalist argument, it is said, was the need to place limits on government action. This study aims to challenge the Madisonian interpretation of Federalism. It does so in two ways. First, it goes beyond the interpretation of *The Federalist* and Madison's pre-Convention writings to analyze a much broader sample of Federalist and Antifederalist writings. Second, based on this broader reading, it provides a new interpretation of what the Constitution and the Federalist argument were about. The major finding presented here is that the Federalist argument was not a proto-liberal call for minority rights and limited government but an argument about state formation, or state building. This work argues that the Federalists tried to create a strong national state in America, a state possessing all the significant powers held by contemporary European states. But it also argues that there were important limitations to state formation in America that had to be taken into account if the Federalists were to secure the adoption of the Constitution and succeed in building an American national state. The Federalist program should therefore be seen as an attempt to combine elements from the European state with respect for limits to state expansion inherent in the American political tradition and American political institutions.

To capture the meaning of the Federalist argument, I have had to pursue my research into fields that have seldom appeared relevant to scholarship on the Constitution. Thus, it has been necessary to look beyond the history and theory of constitutionalism and liberalism to the nature of state building both in early modern Europe and in the United States. By reading the Federalist argument in the context of state formation, I believe we will further our understanding of the meaning and purpose of the Constitution and its role in the political development of the early republic. By adding a comparative element to the study of the adoption of the Constitution, it becomes possible to raise questions about American exceptionalism and to contribute to the general history of state building.

I

Historians and political scientists generally accept the claim that the key to an understanding of the Federalist argument lies in the thought of James Madison.[2] Madison's pre-Convention writings, his notes from the Philadelphia Convention, and his contributions to *The Federalist* provide the Federalist diagnosis of the ills of the union, as well as the prescriptions for its cure. Both of these are well known. The Federalists, it is said, believed that the postwar republic suffered from the "excessive democracy" that had been given free reign in the state legislatures. These bodies repeatedly disregarded both the common good of the union and the rights of minorities. When he reviewed the state of the union before the meeting of the Constitutional Convention, Madison's crucial realization was that if a constitution was poorly constructed, the majority of the citizens in a state could become a "faction," acting to maximize private interests with a complete disregard for long-term public needs and minority rights. To complete the Madisonian analysis, two things have to be added. First, Madison had given up all hope that the states were able to, or would ever be able to, reform themselves. Second, he was convinced that institutional structure rather than formal rules—for example, bills of rights—safe-guarded the public good and minority rights.

This diagnosis provides us with the nature of the Federalist dilemma as Madison saw it. At heart it was a problem of justice: How could minority rights and the public good be made secure in a majoritarian system? Because the states were uninterested in addressing this issue, or unable to do so, the initiative had to come from the union. Hence, the problem became also a problem of federalism and of popular sovereignty. How could the national government be made able to correct the vices of the state governments and still be a government based on the will of the people? Here it should be noted that, according to the Madisonian interpretation, the issues facing the Federalists were of domestic origin. This obvious fact tends not to be much noticed, but it is nonetheless significant. The union's problems, says this interpretation, lay in the relationship between the citizens and the states and between the states and the union. They did not concern the republic's relations with the outside world.

Not only did Madison perceive what was wrong with the American republic, he also knew how these wrongs could be set right. The vices of the existing political system could be corrected by the "extended federal republic," which would "serve the great object of protecting individual liberty against the dangers it faced within the states." It would do so in two ways: first, "by obstructing the formation of factious majorities intent on pursuing private interests in the guise of the public good"; and second, "by encouraging power to pass from the demagogues at the state level of politics into the hands of a better class of men."[3] The use of the large republic to restrict the formation of majority "factions" and the use of representation to refine the will of the majority are the two great ideas that Madison contributed to political theory. By most students of the American founding, these ideas have also been made the core of the Federalist argument in support of ratification.

The concentration on Madison's writings has made analyses of the Federalist argument focus on the institutional makeup, or structure, of the new national government. At the surface level, what matters most is representation. Should Congress represent the states or the people? Who will appoint the Senate and the House of Representatives? What will be the size of the electoral districts? What kind of delegate will be appointed to Congress? What kind of person does *not* stand a chance to be elected to Congress? But at a deeper level, the issue is another one: How can the power of government be restricted? Once again, this point is too obvious to be much noticed. Traditionally, of course, historians have argued that the Constitution was designed to restrict the power of the state legislatures. Recently, it has also been argued that the Federalist concern with government restrictions can be extended to include the national government as well. Although Madison was certainly troubled by the violation of minority rights by majorities, he was equally determined to avoid an "undue concentration of authority in distant, unresponsive rulers."[4] The new-formed American republic, Madison thought, ought to be based on "virtue." But this was not the self-effacing ideal we have come to associate with the tradition of "classical republicanism." Rather, virtue meant "a jealous, vigilant commitment to the public life: continuing participation in a politics that trusted only limited responsibilities to national officials and demanded, even so, that these officials be continuously watched for any signs of an appearance of a separate set of interests."[5] According to this argument, Madison simultaneously made use of the federal government to restrict the citizens from forming majorities that could threaten justice, *and* enrolled the same citizens in guarding against the abuse of power by the federal government. At both state and national level, then, the crucial problem to Madison was how to limit the government's freedom of action.

Because of the emphasis placed on the institutional makeup, or structure, of government, the Madisonian interpretation of Federalist ideas is relatively uninterested in the specific *powers* that the Constitution granted to the new government. Admittedly, leading interpreters say, the question about which powers the union needed, and which powers it could safely be entrusted with, *had* been the central concern *up until* the framing and ratification of the Constitution. There had been recurrent attempts to turn the Confederation Congress into an efficient national government, able to deal with foreign policy, commerce and the disposal of the western lands, but these attempts had all failed. In 1787, the political agenda of the nationalists changed or, more correctly, was enlarged. The issue was no longer whether or not to add a few powers to the national government but instead concerned the way that the union could be used to correct the vices of the state governments. It was this enlargement of the agenda that shifted the focus from the powers of the national government to the institutional makeup of the national government. What is more, this shift was the key to the success of the Constitution. "By placing an entirely new agenda before the American people in 1787," it is claimed, "the framers were able to surmount all the obstacles that in the first years of peace had seemingly consigned the confederation to a condition of 'imbecility.' "[6]

II

The traditional interpretation of the Federalist position has offered important insights into late late-eighteenth-century political thought, insights that in turn have proved very influential in twentieth-century political theory. This interpretation, however, is also problematical. It identifies the core of the Federalist argument by looking at the words of James Madison. Because Madison is defined as the quintessential Federalist, the Federalist argument is all too often believed to be exhausted by his speeches, letters, memoranda, and newspaper contributions. Yet Madison's standing in the

Federalist camp is not altogether self-evident. Although his admirers regard Madison's contributions to *The Federalist* as the fulfillment of his theory of republican government,[7] the collaboration with the nationalist Alexander Hamilton is also compromising. Consequently, there has been an attempt to distance Madison from such supporters of the Constitution who, although they were certainly Federalists, cannot be said to have been Madisonians. In *The Federalist*, it is claimed, Madison wrote not only to answer the Antifederalist opposition. He also wrote to answer fellow Federalists "who sought *more* governmental energy than he considered proper." It is even argued that Madison's contribution to the series was in part an answer to the ideas of his principal coauthor. Indeed, it is said, had Madison fully understood "how Hamilton and others would interpret and employ the Constitution, the Virginia delegation to the Constitutional Convention might have had a third non-signer."[8]

According to Madison scholars, Madison's political position was somewhere in between the Antifederalists and the nationally minded Federalists. Thus, he stood "almost equidistant" from Hamilton and Gouverneur Morris on the one hand, and from George Mason on the other.[9] But if the Federalist side was as heterogeneous as this implies, there is every reason to question if Madison really was the archetypal Federalist. Were his ideas really the same as the ideas of other supporters of the Constitution? This question cannot be answered in any other way than by turning from the political thought of Madison to that vast body of "other" Federalist writings and speeches.[10] This, however, is something that historians of the founding have been reluctant to do. Hence, our knowledge of the Federalists, apart from Madison, is surprisingly limited and far surpassed by our knowledge of their opponents.[11]

Thanks to the publication of *The Documentary History of the Ratification of the Constitution*,[12] it is now possible to investigate the Federalist side of the debate more inclusively than has previously been the case. Such an investigation reveals that to a surprising degree the Federalists and their opponents were busy debating issues that have figured only at the margins of Madisonian Federalism. Two issues of contention stand out as particularly important: first, Congress's power to raise and maintain armies, as well as to command the state militia; and, second, the congressional power to tax and to borrow money. Far from concerning themselves with how to erect barriers to government, the Federalists argued for a national government with the ability to act. In this sense, Madisonian Federalism seems strangely out of tune with the basic thrust of the Federalist argument. Indeed, Madison's main question, how to limit government, is the central concern of the Antifederalists rather than the Federalists. Certainly, it would be going too far to claim that the Federalists had no interests *at all* in placing limits on government action. It is enough to read the many prohibitions on the actions of the state governments in the tenth section of the Constitution's first article to understand that they did. Yet this attempt to limit the state governments does not capture all important aspects of the Federalist persuasion. To gain a full understanding of the Federalist position, the traditional interpretation has to be supplemented by an account of Federalism as an attempt to create a central government with the power to act.

It is tempting to designate such an interpretation "Hamiltonian Federalism." This temptation should be resisted. There is no doubt that the Federalist argument analyzed in this book is stated even more explicitly in the writings Hamilton produced as secretary of the treasury in the new federal government. It can also be found in more coherent form in the correspondence and political writings of Hamilton, Robert Morris, and other nationalists in the early 1780s. The analysis presented here, however, is based on a much broader reading of the ratification debate than the writings of one or two leading politicians. This is a deliberate choice. The fact that the supporters of the Constitution in general held ideas often associated with Hamilton is important to our understanding of both the Federalists and the Constitution. This is true not only for historians but even more so for other fields of enquiry. For, rightly or wrongly, far more than most other commentaries the debate over ratification is held to be crucial to any attempt to establish the meaning of the Constitution.

If we consider what is conventionally regarded as the key elements of the Federalist persuasion, the predominance of military and fiscal questions in the debate over ratification appears strange. How are these issues linked and why were they so prevalent in the debate? The enigma dissolves, however, as soon as we change the interpretative framework used to make sense of the Federalist argument. If the ratification debate is read not as an instant in the history of liberalism and constitutionalism but in the context of state formation, there is nothing mysterious about the fact that the debate over ratification was so largely concerned with military and fiscal matters. In Europe, the early modern era was a period of state formation and state growth. States in this period did little besides waging war and raising money. Consequently, when the state expanded, this expansion was restricted to the growth of armies, taxes, and debts. Although narrowly confined to these areas, the growth of the state nonetheless amounted to a spectacular increase in the ability of the central government to extract resources from society.[13] It is the argument of this work that both Federalists and Antifederalists, although obviously in very different ways, saw the Constitution as the means of creating a national government able to carry out the functions of the contemporary European state. In an important sense, therefore, the Constitution signifies a "Europeanization" of America rather than the beginning of a truly distinct political system. But this, of course, is not the whole story.

In the literature on state formation, the most common explanation for the processes of state building is the pressure of war and the competitive environment of the international system of states.[14] Insofar as the Constitution is seen as the response to problems originating partly in the costs of the War of Independence and partly in the need to safeguard political independence after the war, the American experience may seem to substantiate this claim. Yet further reflection on state formation suggests that external pressure did not determine the development of states in any absolute sense. Early modern states did not differ in their basic aims or functions. Typically, all governments tried to monopolize political power, wage war, form alliances, and extract resources from society. Rather, their differences lay in the institutions and principles they developed to carry out these functions, particularly in the way they went about raising men and money from society. Thus, while both France and Britain developed into strong states that provided similar functions, they did so by radically different paths. France developed into absolute monarchy, whereas the British system was marked by the powerful position of Parliament and far-reaching constitutional rights.

The United States came to differ most from European states precisely in the way that the institutions and principles allowing the government to extract resources from society were organized. Nowhere in the Old World were the stakes against the strengthening of the state raised higher than in the United States. In their own ways, both Antifederalism and Madisonian Federalism were expressions of the extreme skepticism about stronger government that was so widespread in America. A decade or two before the drafting of the Constitution, the ideological struggle against Britain had given vent to the same potent fear of government. Within ten years of the Constitution's adoption, the Democratic-Republicans would organize their resistance against the Federalist administration around the same fear. The Federalists could not choose to ignore this attitude toward the state. Nor could they ignore the other, more "material," limits to state building in America, the principal of which were the nation's geopolitical situation, its political institutions, and the structure of its economy. By taking these limits into account, the Federalists developed a conception of the state that was different from contemporary European states.

The strong anti-statist current in American political culture meant that popular acceptance of a powerful state could only be secured if the Federalists could demonstrate that, in exercising its extractive capacity, the state they wished to establish would not threaten the persons, liberty or well-being of the citizens. In other words, they had to explain that it was possible to create a state that was powerful yet able to respect popular aversion to government. An important step toward the solution of this dilemma was *federalism*, which allowed the centralization of only certain specified government powers. Federalism would create a state focused on the fiscal-military sphere. Recent literature has paid close attention to the way that Madison and other Founders came to terms with this division of power between the national and the state governments. In this literature, federalism has been portrayed both as a means to represent and accommodate sectional interests that threatened the stability of the union and as a means to secure continued popular participation in government as a countermeasure to the centralization of power.[15] However, the central question of this study—a question to which federalism per se contained no answer—has not been addressed by this literature: How was the national government to exercise its newly won fiscal-military powers without exerting undue pressure on the citizens, thereby challenging their anti-statist perceptions? From the perspective of political theory, this may not seem the most profound question, but it was certainly a very pressing one to the Federalists who tried to meet Antifederalist criticism of the Constitution during the ratification debate. On this question, Federalist and Antifederalist conjectures of the future diverged sharply and it was on this question that the Federalist ranks would split a few years after the Constitution's adoption. The Federalist solution to the dilemma of exercising fiscal-military powers in an anti-statist society lay in statecraft. By making the right choices about resource mobilization, it was possible to create a national government that was both light and inconspicuous. It would be *light* in the sense that its demands would not press too heavily on the people and it would be *inconspicuous* in the sense that its actual physical presence would be limited. In this way, the Federalists developed an idea of an American state that possessed powers similar to contemporary European states, yet was shaped by the predominant American mode of anti-statism.

III

Even though a simple comparison between the Articles of Confederation and the Constitution establishes that the latter is a grant of power to the central government, the debate over ratification has not been analyzed before in the context of early modern state formation. Prominent scholars such as Bernard Bailyn, Gordon Wood, and Isaac Kramnick have noted that the Constitution was seen by contemporaries as an attempt to create a powerful centralized state in America, but this has not been a major focus of their writings. In his commentary on *The Federalist*, Kramnick writes that "lost today in the legitimate characterization of the Constitution as bent on setting limits to the power exercised by less than angelic men is the extent to which the Constitution is a grant of power to a centralized nation-state." This loss, he continues, is due to "a persistent privileging" of Madison over Hamilton in interpretations of the Founding. "While posterity emphasizes the Constitution's complex web of checks and balances and the many institutionalized separations of powers," the participants in the ratification debate, "on whichever side they stood, agreed with Hamilton that the Constitution intended a victory for power, for the 'principle of *strength* and *stability* in the organization of our government, and *vigor* in its operations.' "[16]

This book aims to recover this lost characterization of the Constitution. It is divided into three parts. The first four chapters deal with how to interpret the debate over ratification. The book starts with a discussion of the role of the *debate* over ratification in the *struggle* over ratification. I argue that the debate was a necessary part in the decision-making process that led to ratification and that it later became an authoritative source to establish the meaning of the Constitution. The following chapter attempts to identify the ideological disagreement between the Federalists and Antifederalists as expressed in the debate over ratification. It challenges the two dominant interpretations of this disagreement, that is, that the ideological conflict between the opponents and supporters of the Constitution can be described either as a struggle between democracy and aristocracy or as a struggle between liberalism and classical republicanism. Instead, I propose that the debate is best seen as a debate about state formation. The third chapter provides a brief account of what was involved in state formation in continental Europe and Britain in the early modern period. The chapter discusses the conditions for state formation in the newly independent United States and suggests that there were certain obstacles that the Federalists had to overcome if their idea of an American national state was to be accepted by the people. The fourth chapter shows that the European process of state formation had influenced political commentary, giving rise to arguments analyzing and criticizing the growth of the state. In the form of Country thought, these arguments found their way across the Atlantic from Britain to the American colonies.

In the second and third parts of the book, I analyze the debate over the military and the fiscal clauses of the Constitution. The two parts are structured in a similar way. Chapters 5 and 10 provide background accounts of the political development from the War of Independence to the Philadelphia Convention. They establish that, by 1787, Congress was marked by military weakness and financial insolvency. Chapters 6 and 11 lay out the Federalist argument that Congress had to possess an unlimited power to raise men and money from American society without any intervention from the states. Chapters 7 and 12 present the Antifederalist objections to a stronger national government in the "fiscal-military" sphere. Chapters 8 and 13 show how the Federalists responded to these objections, thereby creating an understanding of the kind of state that was proper to American conditions. Chapters 9 and 14 offer a brief sketch of the institutionalization of the military and fiscal powers granted by the Constitution, and the uses made of them, by the Federalists in the 1790s. The book ends with an explication of the Federalists' idea of an American national state.

IV

This book was written with three overlapping audiences in mind. First, it is hoped that the reinterpretation of the meaning and aim of the Constitution and of the Federalists' project will be of interest to political and intellectual historians of the early American republic as well as to political theorists and constitutional scholars working on the American founding and, particularly, on the Federalist-Antifederalist debate. Second, I also hope that the focus on American state formation and the comparative perspective provided in this work will contribute to the study of American political development. Although this vital and expanding field has already produced a number of important works on the American state, they have all dealt with later periods. Often, these works also lack a comparative perspective.[17] This leads to the third audience this book wishes to address. With one important exception, comparative studies of state formation in the eighteenth and early nineteenth centuries leave out the American experience.[18] In view of the economic, political, and cultural success of the United States over the last two centuries, this seems both a strange and an unfortunate lacuna. I hope that the discussion of American state formation presented here may contribute to our understanding of this process by pointing to the way that the development of the American national state both followed and differed from the development of European states.

I

Interpreting the Debate over Ratification

1

LEGITIMACY AND MEANING: THE SIGNIFICANCE OF PUBLIC DEBATE TO THE ADOPTION OF THE CONSTITUTION

A ny study of the ratification debate has to consider precisely *what* such a study is really *about*. On one level, the answer is obvious: A study of the ratification debate is a study of statements made in print or ratifying conventions, which have been handed down to us as texts. Yet at another level the answer is more complicated. Even a quick glance at the many ways scholars have approached the statements made during the ratification debate reveals that there exist very different understandings of what these statements *represent*. This difference leads historians to widely divergent views about the exact way that the *debate* over ratification relates to the *struggle* over ratification and, consequently, about the extent to which the former explains the outcome of the latter. Their perspectives range from economic reductionist accounts, which claim that the debate was completely irrelevant to the vote on the Constitution, to culturalist interpretations, which see the new ideas expressed in the debate as the real transformation of American politics.

This chapter argues that the debate over ratification was significant to the adoption of the Constitution because public debate was a necessary step in the decision-making process leading to ratification. It was a necessary step because adoption would not have been legitimate without the possibility of public debate. But the debate was also significant in another way. It provided the first widely shared and detailed interpretation of important clauses of the Constitution. This original elucidation of the meaning of the Constitution later served as the point of origin for constitutional interpretation in the political life of the early republic.[1]

I

The significance of public debate to the adoption of the Constitution stemmed from the principle of rule by consent of the governed. There was never any question that the adoption of the Constitution had to be a popular act. As the preamble of the Constitution itself clearly states, "We the people of the United States, in order to form a more perfect union . . . do ordain and establish this Constitution for the United States of America." Although occasional Antifederalist voices questioned the existence of a national American "people" able to act in unison to reform its own government, these voices were not very common. The words of the Antifederalist writer "Centinel" are much more representative of Antifederalist views. In America, he wrote, "the people are the sovereign and their sense or opinion is the criterion of every public measure." The Federalist James Wilson specified the nature of the decision on the Constitution early in the ratification debate when he denied that the Philadelphia Convention had transcended its instructions by drafting the Constitution and presenting it to the public for ratification. "I think the late Convention have done nothing beyond their powers," Wilson said.

> The fact is, they have exercised no power at all. And in point of validity, this Constitution, proposed by them for the government of the United States, claims no more than a production of the same nature would claim, flowing from a private pen. It is laid before the citizens of the United States, unfettered by restraint; it is laid before them to be judged by the natural, civil, and political rights of men. By their FIAT, it will become of value and authority; without it, it will never receive the character of authenticity and power.[2]

In the American system of government, the absence of a bureaucracy, a judicial system and a police force independent of popular control made rule by consent as much a practical necessity as a cherished principle. The administrative weakness of the state in fact made it necessary to secure popular support in order for any government measure to work.[3] Any group or individual wishing to realize a political program, therefore, could not simply capture the government and implement policies by means of the state apparatus. Instead, they had to convince the citizenry—or at least the citizens who wielded power locally in towns and counties—that, on balance, it was in their own interest to support the policies proposed. Thus, political legitimacy was not derived from the authority of office but from the consent of the governed. Such consent was achieved by providing arguments in favor of a government measure, thereby collecting as many people as possible behind it.[4]

In the case of the Constitution, the Philadelphia Convention's decision to circumvent the state governments and bestow legitimacy on the Constitution by grounding it on an act of popular sovereignty meant that a broadly based assent became very important. The Articles of Confederation stated that any "alteration" of the compact between the states should "be agreed to in a Congress of the united states, and be afterward confirmed by the legislatures of every state."[5] When Congress called the Constitutional Convention, this principle was maintained. The delegates should meet "for the sole and express purpose of revising the Articles of Confederation and reporting to Congress and the several state legislatures such alterations and provisions therein as shall when agreed to in Congress and confirmed by the states render the federal constitution adequate to the exigencies of government and the preservation of the Union."[6] But when the Convention adjourned, the delegates instead recommended that the constitution they had drafted "be submitted to a Convention of Delegates, chosen in each State by the People thereof, under the Recommendation of its Legislature, for their Assent and Ratification; and that each Convention assenting to, and ratifying the Same, should give Notice thereof to the United States in Congress assembled."[7]

It has been argued that by resting the Constitution on a decision by a sovereign people, the founders tried to invest it with a greater legitimacy than most state constitutions and governments possessed, having been adopted in the same way as ordinary legislation.[8] But the framers were also anxious to restrict the people's choice to either adopting or rejecting the Constitution in its totality. By doing so, they hoped to prevent the ratifying process from giving rise to amendment proposals, and from ending in partial or conditional adoption.[9] This was precisely what had happened in the ratification process of the Massachusetts constitution of 1780, when the towns had been given the possibility to comment on individual clauses and to approve the constitution conditionally. As a consequence, it was impossible to secure a majority for ratification.[10] Considering the Philadelphia Convention's wish to restrict the people's choice to an unconditional adoption or rejection of their plan, the decision to use ratifying conventions seems peculiar, as it was unlikely that a ratifying convention would limit itself to a straightforward adoption or rejection of the Constitution. If the founders sought only to make the Constitution legitimate by grounding adoption on an act by the people, they could have arranged to hold a popular referendum instead. Ratifying conventions were not established practice in the states at the time, and there were no insurmountable technical difficulties to referendums.[11] In fact, Rhode Island ignored Congress's request to call a ratifying convention but held a popular referendum on the Constitution instead. On 24 March 1788, the citizens of Rhode Island voted 2,711 to 243 to reject the Constitution.[12]

It is of course possible to argue that a ratifying convention was nothing more than an indirect referendum, a popular vote by proxy. In the North Carolina convention, the Antifederalist delegate Willie Jones suggested as much when, right after the convention opened, he moved that the question of adoption be put immediately. The delegates, he argued, had had plenty of time to consider the question beforehand and a long debate would only amount to a waste of public money. Seconding Jones, Thomas Person said that he "should be sorry if any man had come hither without having determined in his mind a question which must have been so long the object of his consideration."[13] As we shall see, the Federalists did not agree, and their disagreement provides a clue to the significance of public debate to the Constitution's adoption. To them, the decision to adopt or reject the Constitution had to be based on something more than a mere majority vote.

II

In his study of *The Federalist*, Albert Furtwangler has argued that Alexander Hamilton and James Madison wished for the Constitution to have the "informed" assent of the people. The essays, Furtwangler says, make "a public display of ample discussion of the issues." When they wrote *The Federalist*, Hamilton and Madison worked within a genre that was well established in both Britain and America. Print discourse had become the major form of national communication in eighteenth-century Britain, and it had helped establish the idea that there existed something called "the public opinion," which could, and should, influence the actions of the government. In America, too, the press was the primary means to create a widely shared "public opinion." Indeed, because of the absence of a political center, the importance of the press in America was even greater than in Britain.[14] By the time of the ratification debate, deliberation on public issues in the press was a standard feature of political life. In fact, Hamilton's and Madison's insistence that the question of adoption ought to be preceded by a thorough discussion was a generally shared view among Federalists.[15]

To develop this point, it is helpful to look in some detail at discussions in the ratifying convention of North Carolina as well as at an incident that took place in the Massachusetts convention. A few months before the North Carolina convention met, Federalist Archibald Maclaine published an essay in which he attacked the prevalent practice of constituents to instruct their delegates how to vote on the Constitution. This, Maclaine wrote, would defeat the whole idea of the upcoming convention: to deliberate first and only *then* decide on the question. The people ought to understand that when they elected a delegate, they parted with their right to decide the question themselves and invested that right in their representative. To Maclaine, this was not so much because enlarged societies made it difficult to collect the will of the whole people but because it was a means to arrive at a better decision. "The greatest part of you have not the means of information," he told the freemen of his state, "and being unaccustomed to think of government, few of you are competent judges of it." The decision made by the ratifying convention, then, ought to be not only a *popular* act but also an act of *reason*. If the people insisted on instructing their delegates there would be no room for reasoning: "The members of the Convention would have no more to do than to examine all the different instructions; to *count noses*, and by that summary method, to adopt, or reject." To Maclaine, this was an irrational form of decision making, one he felt was scarcely better than throwing dice. The stipulated procedure—to collect "the united wisdom of the state in order, to *deliberate* and *determine*"—was much to be preferred.[16]

When the Antifederalists in the convention moved that the decision on the Constitution be made without prior debate, Maclaine and other members of the Federalist minority reacted strongly. The Antifederalist suggestion, James Iredell said, amounted to settling the question by "a dead vote."

> Are we to give a dead vote upon it? If so, I would wish to know why we are met together. If it is to be resolved now by dead votes, it would have been better that every elector, instead of voting for persons to come here, should, in their respective counties, have voted or ballotted for or against the Constitution. . . . Shall it be said, sir, of the representatives of North Carolina, that near three hundred of them assembled for the express purpose of deliberating upon the most important question that ever came before a people, refused to discuss it, and discarded all reasoning as useless?

In contrast to Jones's opinion, Iredell claimed that *he* "should be sorry" if he had come "to this house predetermined for or against the Constitution." To the contrary, delegates ought not to have made up their mind before attending the convention. Although Iredell himself was certainly in favor of the Constitution, he claimed that he had "not come here resolved, at all events, to vote for its adoption. I have come here for information, and to judge, after all that can be said upon it, whether it really merits my attachment or not."[17] If the decision to adopt or reject the Constitution were to be a true act of reason, it was necessary that both the people and the delegates in the ratifying conventions were ready to be persuaded by reasoned arguments. Thus, Iredell later said that he presumed "that every man thinks it his duty to hold his mind open to conviction; that whatever he may have heard, whether against or for the Constitution, he will recede from his present opinion, if reasons of sufficient validity are offered."

> Those gentlemen who are so self-sufficient that they believe that they are never in the wrong, may arrogate infallibility to themselves, and conclude deliberation to be useless. For my part, I have often known myself to be in the wrong, and have ever wished to be corrected. There is nothing dishonorable in changing an opinion. Nothing is more fallible than human judgement. No gentleman will say that his is not fallible. Mine, I am sure, has often proved so.[18]

Although the Antifederalist motion not to debate the Constitution was rejected, it was difficult to get the discussion going in the convention. The

Antifederalists adopted a strategy devastating to the ideal of deliberation: They stayed silent. As in the other ratifying conventions, the North Carolina convention debated the Constitution article by article, section by section. After three days of Antifederalist silence, William Davie expressed his "astonishment at the precipitancy with which we go through this business. Is it not highly improper to pass over in silence any part of this Constitution which has been loudly objected to" beforehand?[19] On the previous day, one Antifederalist had complained that faced with the opposition's silence, Maclaine had begun to raise objections to the Constitution, only to answer them himself. Raising hypothetical objections, like Maclaine did, seemed both highly irregular and very time consuming. But Maclaine was not at loss for an answer. It had been decided that the Constitution should be debated by the Convention, he said. If the opposition remained silent, then what could he do? "Are we then to read it only? Suppose the whole of it is to be passed over without saying any thing; will not that amount to a dead vote?" Maclaine was ready to answer any objection raised in the convention, but if he saw "gentlemen pass by in silence such parts as they vehemently decry out of doors, or such parts as have been loudly complained of in the country, I shall answer them also."[20] Right after Maclaine had said this, Jones took to the floor to question the value of reasoned argument once more, saying "he would easily put the friends of the Constitution in a way of discussing it. Let one of them, said he, make objections and another answer them."[21]

It has been argued that the Antifederalists turned their back on reasoned argument, and Jones's comments in the North Carolina convention seem to bear this out. Saul Cornell has recently argued that the majority of Antifederalists did not value rational public discussion and Furtwangler has made the same claim, writing that the Antifederalist opposition to the Constitution was "an outcry against literate civility."[22] On the basis of a speech held in the Massachusetts ratifying convention, Furtwangler claims that the Antifederalists saw their opponents as smooth-talking "lawyers and men of learning, and moneyed men" out to trick the "poor illiterate people" into ratifying the Constitution.[23] According to this interpretation, Antifederalists were not ready to accept the idea that public debate bestowed legitimacy on political decisions. This interpretation of the Antifederalists, however, does not stand up to closer scrutiny.

Toward the end of the Massachusetts convention, Nathanael Barrell delivered a speech that at first seems to support Furtwangler's claim. Barrell opened by saying that he had to speak the plain language of the husbandman as he did not command "the pleasing eloquence of Cicero, or the blaze of Demosthenian oratory." He also noted how insignificant he must appear "in the eyes of those giants in rhetoric, who have exhibited such a pompous display of declamation." Barrell returned to this theme at the close of his speech saying that he had been "cautiously avoiding every thing like metaphysical reasoning, lest I should invade the prerogative of those respectable gentlemen of the law, who have so copiously displayed their talents on the occasion."[24] Yet the actual content of Barrell's speech shows him to be no enemy of reasoned deliberation but a man who lived up to the expectation of Federalists such as Iredell that a delegate to the ratifying convention should keep his mind open to conviction by the force of the better argument. He rose to discharge his duty to his constituents who he knew expected "something more from me than merely a silent vote." But although he stated the objections that he and his constituents had to the Constitution, he also said that some of these objections had been answered during the course of the debate. In fact, his final words were as much a defense of reasoned argument and informed assent as any Federalist speech: "As the greatest good I can do my country at present," he said,

> I could wish for an adjournment, that I might have an opportunity to lay it before my constituents, with the arguments which have been used in the debates, which have eased my mind, and I trust would have the effect on theirs so as heartily to join me in ratifying the same. But, sir, if I cannot be indulged on this desirable object, I am almost tempted to risk their displeasure, and adopt it without their consent.[25]

In the end, Barrell did face the risk of his constituents' displeasure and voted for adoption.

It would be easy to find more examples like this in Antifederalist speeches and writings. Indeed, the incidents in North Carolina are interesting because, with the exception of Rhode Island, this was the only state where the ideal of deliberation was openly challenged. Yet, even in North Carolina, the motion to vote on adoption without prior debate was rejected despite a sound Antifederalist majority in the convention. After Jones had mocked the very idea of deliberation, other Antifederalists rose to say that they wanted the Constitution thoroughly debated.[26] In general, Antifederalists were not averse to public deliberation. In ratifying conventions and in print discourse they proved as willing as their opponents to embrace this ideal.

III

The ideal of public deliberation took as its starting point the assumption that individual reason is fallible but correctable by collective reasoning. This was the idea that Iredell expressed when he said that he had often known himself to be in the wrong and had then "ever wished to be corrected," knowing as he did that "nothing is more fallible than human judgement." The best known expression of the idea is probably Benjamin Franklin's call to the nonsigners in the Constitutional Convention to bow to the will of the majority. The call was made to convey an impression of unanimity to the public, but it is also interesting for the light it sheds on the contemporary understanding of individual reasoning and deliberation between enlightened minds:

> I confess that I do not entirely approve of this Constitution at present, but Sir, I am not sure I shall never approve it; For having lived long, I have experienced many Instances of being oblig'd, by better Information or fuller Consideration, to change Opinions even on important Subjects, which I once thought right, but found to be otherwise. It is therefore that the older I grow the more apt I am to doubt my own Judgement and to pay more Respect to the Judgement of others.

Franklin's speech was reprinted, in whole or in part, in no less than forty newspapers and pamphlets, suggesting that the point he made was widely accepted.[27] In fact, one of the nonsigners, Edmund Randolph, later came to change his mind and endorsed the Constitution. When George Mason, the other Virginia nonsigner, publicly challenged Randolph to explain why he had changed his mind on certain crucial clauses of the Constitution, Randolph defended himself by saying that he had changed his opinion after "further consideration of the subject," but also after paying "attention to the lights which were thrown upon it by others."[28]

The statements by Franklin, Randolph, and Iredell suggest that they all championed the idea that reasoned deliberation required "impartiality," that is, a readiness to keep one's mind open to conviction by the force of the better argument.[29] These examples could easily be multiplied, but only two more will be offered here. Toward the end of the Virginia convention, when many of the delegates rose to state their grounds for supporting or rejecting the Constitution, James Innes told the convention that "I came hither under a persuasion that the felicity of our country required that we should accede to this system; but I am free to declare, that I came in with a mind open to conviction, and a predetermination to recede from my opinion, if I should find it to be erroneous." In the New York convention, John Jay made a similar declaration. "We did not come here to carry points," he said. "If the gentlemen will convince me I am wrong, I will submit. I mean to give my ideas frankly upon the subject. If my reasoning is not good, let them show me the folly of it. It is from this reciprocal interchange of ideas that the truth must come out."[30]

The principle of impartiality and the acceptance of the better argument found its ultimate expression in the practice of anonymity in print discourse. In the first number of his "Philadelphiensis" essays, the Antifederalist Benjamin Workman addressed the argument put forward by some Federalists that the newspapers should not publish opinions on the Constitution unless the author was willing to publish his name. On matters of such great importance as the Constitution, Workman wrote, "it is as plain as any axiom in geometry, that it is of no importance whether or not a writer gives his name; it is with the illustrations and arguments he affords us, and not with his name, we have any concern: Besides this practice would tend to draw off the mind of the writer from the calm investigation of the subject, to recriminations and personal invective."[31]

Historians have sometimes argued that the Federalists did not share the ideal of anonymous print discourse. Although it is true that some printers and writers held the view criticized by Workman, all but a handful of the Federalist writers published anonymously. Sometimes Federalists also accused their opponents of ignoring the principle of impartiality by circulating their criticisms of the Constitution privately or by publishing it under their own names. When George Mason circulated his objections to the Constitution in manuscript, he was charged with disseminating them "in such a manner as to gain partizans to his opinion, without giving them an opportunity of seeing how effectually his sentiments may be controverted, or how far his arguments might be invalidated." Because Mason tried to avoid submitting his objections "to the test of public investigation," his accuser arranged for the objections to be published and followed up by a point-by-point rebuttal two weeks later. Richard Henry Lee, another prominent Virginia Antifederalist, drew criticism from Federalists because he published his objections under his own name, thereby trying to influence the public not with reasoned argument but with his own social position. A *"great name,"* his critic said, "on many occasions, makes up for a deficiency of argument."[32]

It is significant that Workman came forward to defend rational deliberation. His passionate rhetoric was very far from the calm reasoning found in *The Federalist*. Indeed, one historian has claimed that he failed to provide any reasoned arguments against the Constitution at all and that his "feverish diatribes" were unmatched by anything written during the ratification debate. But no matter how correct this assertion is, even a writer like Workman apparently subscribed to the idea that the question of adopting the Constitution ought to be settled by the force of the better argument. In later numbers of his "Philadelphiensis" series, Workman claimed to write to "inform" and not to "inflame" his readers' minds, and in one essay he explained the scurrility and abuse he had suffered from his Federalist opponents by pointing out that *"nothing cuts like the truth."*[33] Indeed, because the Federalists argued that the decision on the Constitution should be preceded by rational discussion, the Antifederalists repeatedly charged their opponents with failing to live up to their own ideals. In doing so, they came to offer a full defense of the ideal of impartial reasoned deliberation.

Thus, the "Centinel" series began by criticizing the thousands of Philadelphians who had attended public meetings and signed petitions to show their support for the Constitution. Addressing himself to "the freemen of Pennsylvania," "Centinel" wrote that "it behoves you well to consider" the Constitution "uninfluenced by the authority of names. . . . Instead of that frenzy of enthusiasm, that has actuated the citizens of Philadelphia, in their approbation of the proposed plan, before it was possible that it could be the result of a rational investigation into its principles; it ought to be dispassionately and deliberately examined, and its own intrinsic merit the only criterion of your patronage." In later essays, coercion rather than passion was the object of "Centinel" 's censure. He claimed that the Federalists had tried to stifle debate by destroying "the free and independent papers" by "withdrawing all the subscriptions to them." In the same way, the "Dissent of the Minority of the Pennsylvania Convention" noted that "every measure" had been attempted by the Federalists "to intimidate the people against opposing" the Constitution. "The public papers teemed with the most violent threats against those who should dare to think for themselves, and *tar and feathers* were liberally promised to all those who would not immediately join in supporting the proposed government be it what it would."[34]

Some Antifederalists also complained about the closed-door policy of the Constitutional Convention, not only because it suggested conspiracy but also because it prevented the delegates from entering into dialogue with informed public opinion. Because most of the delegates were well respected men—none more so, of course, than Washington and Franklin—direct criticism of the Convention's decision was a dangerous tactic. Luther Martin's description of the decision to deliberate in secret, which he published in his "Genuine Information" essays, is the best-known example of such critique. Martin claimed to have opposed the decision because he "had no idea that all the wisdom, integrity, and virtue" of the United States "were centered in the convention." Rather than closing the doors to the public, Martin wished to be allowed to correspond "freely, and confidentially, with eminent political characters" in his own state of Maryland and elsewhere in order "to give their sentiments due weight and consideration." "Centinel" argued that because the Convention met for the purpose of reforming the old government, not to develop a new one, the delegates simply could not have informed themselves of the wishes and views of their constituents. Instead, they "seem to have been determined to monopolize the exclusive merit of the discovery, or rather as if darkness was essential to its success they precluded all communication with the people, by closing their doors." Unable to consult either "public information or opinion," the "well disposed" members of the Convention were fooled into giving "their sanction to this system of despotism."[35]

IV

The Federalists valued debate as a way to overcome the fallibility of the individual mind and to reach a well-grounded opinion. But they did not believe that the capacity to reason was evenly distributed among the citizenry. The Philadelphia Convention was often praised in terms that stressed how it had collected men of outstanding capacity for reasoning. The Convention's ability to rightly determine the needs of the union was therefore far greater than that of any individual person. For this reason, if a person "even of great capacity" came to the conclusion that the Constitution ought to be rejected, it was much more likely that he was mistaken "than that so respectable a body as the Convention, with minds equally enlightened, and more unbiased, should, after the freest and fullest investigation of this important subject, be wrong."[36] As Maclaine had reminded the freemen of North Carolina, most members of the public were not able to reason well on matters of politics and ought to defer to the greater ability of their betters. An example of such deference can be found in a resolution adopted by the tradesmen and mechanics of Boston in January 1788. "From the first appointment of the late Continental Convention," the resolution said,

> they looked up to that honourable Body, as to the *enlightened* and *distinguished patriots* of their country, from whose deliberations and decisions they had EVERY THING to hope—nor have they been disappointed.— The CONSTITUTION which they have proposed to the UNITED STATES, they consider as the result of much wisdom, candour, and those mutual concessions, without which America cannot expect ever to harmonize in any system of COMMERCE or GOVERNMENT.[37]

But even if this resolution shows the lower and middling orders of the American public in the act of deferring to the great men of the Convention, it does not suggest that the Constitution should be accepted only because it was drafted by "enlightened and distinguished patriots." The tradesmen and mechanics of Boston had also judged the plan and, in their minds, found it to be not only the result of much wisdom, candor, and a spirit of compromise but also necessary to establish an adequate national government.

As soon as the Constitution was published, Federalist writers invited the people to read and reflect on it. A well-known example of this invitation is found in the opening number of *The Federalist*, in which Hamilton said that "it seems to have been reserved to the people of this country, by their conduct and example, to decide the important question, whether societies of men are really capable or not, of establishing good government from reflection and choice, or whether they are forever destined to depend, for their political constitutions, on accident and force." It has been estimated that within six weeks of the Philadelphia Convention's adjournment, the Constitution had been printed in its entirety in every newspaper known to have existed in the United States. Only five days after the Convention had ended, the *Pennsylvania Packet* described a Philadelphia street scene where a five-year-old and an elderly man—"whose head was covered with hoary locks"—both pored over the new constitution. "The unthinking youth, who cannot realize the importance of government seems to be impressed with a sense of our want of union and system; and the venerable sire, who is tottering to the grave, feels new life at the prospect of having everything valuable secured to posterity." A letter from Salem County published in the *Pennsylvania Herald* told that "nothing is talked of here, either in public or private, but the new Constitution. All read, and almost all approve of it. Indeed it requires only to be read, with attention and without prejudice, to be approved of."[38]

Although the correspondent from Salem County may have been ready to approve of the Constitution merely after reading it, many Federalists believed that the people required more information in order to reach the right decision on the Constitution. Although they stressed that the adoption of the Constitution should be an act of reason, they never questioned that it should also be an act of the people, which required the active assent of the majority of the citizens. "The people always mean right; and, if time is allowed for reflection and information, they will do right," the arch-Federalist Fisher Ames said in a statement that reveals his faith both in popular sovereignty and in reason. "I would not have their first wish, the momentary impulse of the public mind, become law; for it is not always the sense of the people, with whom I admit that all power resides." In the same way, Oliver Ellsworth declared that "the people at large generally determine right, when they have had means of information." Simeon Baldwin said the same thing in his Fourth of July oration of 1788: "The great bulk of mankind, when they have the means of knowledge, and time to deliberate, in general adopt right political sentiments."[39]

But even if the people at large were invited to reflect on and to judge the Constitution, there existed a division of labor in this process in which those with better education or more developed faculties for reasoning produced the arguments that the majority of the public consumed or reproduced. The Federalists were certainly elitist, although membership in the elite was determined not by birth but by education and ability. Those who did belong to the elite had a duty to address those who were "in quest of information" and to refute the sophistry of their opponents, which prevented the public from arriving at a proper understanding of the Constitution.[40] Antifederalist writers did not reject the Federalist understanding of a division of labor in public deliberation on the Constitution. "Centinel" embraced the same idea when he wrote that "those who are competent to the task of developing the principles of government, ought to be encouraged to come forward, and thereby the better enable the people to make a proper judgement; for the science of government is so abstruse, that few are able to judge for themselves." One of the most frequent accusations Antifederalists levied against the Federalists was their promotion of "aristocratic" principles and policies. Yet this accusation did not challenge the idea that some people were better able to reason than others. Instead, the Federalists were criticized for failing to make use of their education and knowledge to further public debate. Federalists, "Centinel" wrote, shied away from reasoning. From the instant the Constitution was made public, they had instead "exerted all their power and influence to prevent all discussion of the subject, and when this could not be prevented they have constantly avoided the ground of argument and recurred to declamation, sophistry, and personal abuse, but principally relied upon the magic of names."[41] Indeed, Antifederalists believed that *they* upheld the ideal of public reasoning, while the Federalists were abandoning it. The critics of the Constitution, then, were hardly enemies of reason but, rather, reasoning skeptics.[42]

V

In the summer of 1788, when the adoption of the Constitution was secured, the Federalists looked back at the ratification struggle and took great pride in the achievement of the American public. It seemed to them that, by their example, the people had indeed demonstrated to the world that good government *could* be established through reflection and choice rather than violence and chance. "While the revolutions of government, in other countries, have given rise to most horrid scenes of carnage and bloodshed," the *Pennsylvania Mercury* reported in words echoing Hamilton's, "America alone can boast of a constitution framed by her chosen sages, and, after the most mature deliberation, approved of by the people at large, without tumultuous disorders, or intestine broils, notwithstanding the industrious efforts of a few desperate incendiaries." It seemed as if a new era had dawned in politics. "Justly may it be said," Enos Hitchcock declared in his Fourth of July oration, that "the present is an age of philosophy, and America the empire of reason."[43]

In the ratification debate, both Federalists and Antifederalists repeatedly claimed that reasoned argument was the best ground for political decisions. It is not necessary, however, to accept such claims as expressions of sincerely held opinions, in order to argue that the ideal of public deliberation mattered to the ratification of the Constitution. All political systems possess rules that determine legitimate behavior. What I have attempted here, although only in a very cursory fashion, is to lay bare those rules in order to assess the role played by the debate over ratification in the decision-making process leading to the adoption of the Constitution. In many ways, the political culture of 1787–1788 was different from that of the early twenty-first century. It was a culture that did not regard the open pursuit to realize group interest as legitimate.[44] It was a culture in which a majority vote did not suffice to make a political decision legitimate. For this reason, both Federalists and Antifederalists had to accept, and work with, the ideal, ultimately classical in origin, that the common good was revealed through public deliberation. In this sense, public debate was a necessary part of the ratification process. Popular ratification meant more than a popular vote: It also meant that the people had the opportunity to reason about the decision they were about to make. It is important to stress here that the fact that public deliberation was a source of political legitimacy does not necessarily mean that the participants in the debate saw it as anything more than a means to an end. It certainly does not mean that the participants were at all detached from partisan motives. The point is, rather, that even actors who entered the debate over ratification, only to realize self- or group interests, had to accept that the rules of the political game made reasoned argument crucial. Superior arguments, persuasion by reason, were also a legitimate ground for the delegates to ratifying conventions to change their minds, even to the point of disregarding the instructions of their constituents. Yet again, it should be pointed out that this does not necessarily say anything about the ulterior reasons a delegate may have had for doing so.[45]

It would, of course, be possible to argue that the ideas presented by the Federalists in the debate over ratification actually persuaded citizens to vote in favor of the Constitution. Regardless of how likely or unlikely this may appear, it is a claim that is difficult either to substantiate or falsify. However, it is doubtful if we really need the answer to this question in order to assess the significance of the debate to the outcome of the ratification struggle. This is because the true importance of the debate lies not as much in getting the people to adopt the Constitution, as in determining *what* it was that the people adopted, that is, in determining the *meaning* of the text the American people made the fundamental law of the United States. After more than two centuries of continuous constitutional interpretation, no one can credibly claim that the meaning of the Constitution is transparent in all details. In fact, conflict over constitutional interpretation began with the very first Congress. This conflict, however, did not emerge out of nowhere but continued the struggle over interpretation started by the debate over ratification. This is where the real significance of the debate over ratification can be found: It provided the first publicly shared understanding of what central clauses of the Constitution meant. Furthermore, this original interpretation later became authoritative in shaping political institutions and political life in the new republic. Obviously, this point needs to be elaborated, although it can only be done in a very superficial way here.

The Constitution was a grant of power from the people of America to the national government. But, in contrast to the delegation of power establishing the state governments, it was a grant that was understood to be specific and delimited. Congress's authority was "to be collected, not from tacit implication, but from the positive grant expressed in the instrument of union." In the Constitution "every thing which is not given" to

Congress "is reserved" by the people.[46] If adoption is understood in this way, the crucial issue naturally becomes to determine the exact limits of this grant of power, that is, what the Constitution allowed the new government to do and, perhaps more important, what the Constitution did not allow it to do. As I will point out in chapter 2, the Constitution radically challenged the American political tradition of anti-statism and it became the task of its supporters to calm the fears, and answer the objections, of the opposition. But, in doing so, the Federalists did not resort to opportunist arguments. Although they argued that Antifederalist worries were unfounded, they also stressed that every grant of power entailed in the Constitution was necessary to the preservation and well-being of the union. Thus, Federalists did not hesitate to argue that the national government might have to pursue unpopular policies: that the power of the local courts might be restricted; that direct taxation might one day be needed; and that a peacetime standing army might prove a benefit to society. If all the Federalists wanted was to secure adoption, this appears a strange strategy. It would have made more sense to pretend to concede to Antifederalist demands in order to secure adoption and a majority in the first Congress, only to disregard whatever had been promised during the ratification campaign. The reason for not doing this lies in the structure and tradition of Anglo-American government, which made it necessary to rule through the consent and cooperation of the people. Whatever the Federalists promised before adoption that the new government would not do, they could not legitimately do after adoption. And, because it lacked a coercive apparatus, the government simply could not do what the people found illegitimate.

Clearly, the need to rule by the consent of the governed does not in itself mean that the government was somehow "bound" by what had been said in the debate over ratification. Once the people stopped worrying about high taxes and standing armies and declared themselves willing to accept them—or, more realistically, once they stopped protesting against piecemeal increases in taxation and the peace establishment—the government was free to introduce them. But this did not happen. Instead, the political agenda shows a strong continuity between the struggle over ratification and the party conflicts of the 1790s. During the decade following the Constitution's adoption, the basic issue was still the expansion of central power. This issue was fought over by essentially the same people who had faced each other during the ratification struggle, employing essentially the same arguments they had used in the ratification debate. What is more important, the debate over ratification played an important part in this struggle.[47]

After the movement for a second constitutional convention had disintegrated, the Antifederalists were transformed from the Constitution's greatest critics to its greatest defenders. Because the first ten amendments did not answer the central objections that the Antifederalists raised against the Constitution—that is, that it was absolutely necessary to provide clear restrictions on Congressional power—politics in the new republic continued to be a struggle about the extent of the powers of the national government. In their opposition to the Federalists, former Antifederalists gathered behind the charge that the administration tried to force through unconstitutional measures. Their principal weapon in this struggle was a literal interpretation of the Constitution. When they developed this interpretation, the opposition turned to the debate over ratification to find the original meaning of various clauses of the Constitution. Essays and ratifying conventions were consulted to provide arguments for or against the constitutionality of government measures. Naturally, this hermeneutic endeavor neither aimed at, nor resulted in, bipartisan agreement on the meaning of the Constitution. Nevertheless, because original intent became an important way to justify an interpretation of the Constitution, the arguments from the ratification debate were kept alive in the critical decades following ratification, when the text of the Constitution was transformed into the policies and institutions of the new national state.[48]

2

THE ELUSIVE MEANING OF THE DEBATE OVER RATIFICATION

The publication of the Constitution sparked a political debate of unprecedented scope. The new plan of government was publicly debated in ratifying conventions and in print, mainly in newspapers but also in pamphlets and broadsides. Yet although Federalists and Antifederalists engaged in a war of words that was prolonged, extensive, and often bitter, it has proved difficult to define the precise nature of their disagreement. At times it has even been questioned if any serious discord existed at all. "Their disagreements," one of the debate's most prominent interpreters has written,

> were not based on different premises about the nature of man or the ends of political life. They were not the deep cleavages of contending regimes. They were the much less sharp and clear-cut differences within the family, as it were, of men agreed that the purpose of government is the regulation and thereby the protection of individual rights and that the best instrument for this purpose is some form of limited, republican government.[1]

Still, we are faced with the fact that no matter how much they agreed on fundamental principles, Federalists and Antifederalists wrote thousands of pages and made thousands of speeches stating their differences. As has been pointed out, the difficulty is how to "capture the essence of these differences with appropriate terminology."[2] An important reason for this difficulty lies in the rhetorical structure of the debate over ratification. Neither Federalists nor Antifederalists articulated a positive political program during the ratification controversy. On the contrary, the Antifederalist argument was characterized by "extreme negativity." Naturally, this followed from their opposition to the Constitution and their fear of what it would bring about. What is more strange is that the Federalist argument was "almost equally" negative.[3] In fact, attempts to merely summarize the bulk of the Federalist campaign tend to be disappointing, as most of the writing appears "rather shallow and routine." Indeed, a quantitative content analysis of the ratification debate concludes that 20 percent of Federalist rhetoric consisted of "cheers for the campaign."[4] It seems that the majority of Federalist statements do not have anything important to tell us either about the meaning of the Constitution or about the polity the Federalist wished to create. This, of course, is the reason why historians and political scientists tend to rely so heavily on *The Federalist* for information on the political ideas held by those who backed the Constitution. Of all the statements in support of the Constitution, only the collective effort of Hamilton, Jay, and Madison seems to contain anything worth close study.[5]

The reason for the intellectual poverty of the Federalist contribution to the debate over ratification is that it was overwhelmingly a response to Antifederalist attacks on the Constitution. It is striking, Herbert Storing has noted, "how much of the Federalist effort was directed to mere explication of the Constitution or to criticizing the opposition." Among "the 'front line' debaters, the Anti-Federalists criticized the Constitution, and the Federalists criticized the Anti-Federalists."[6] In fact, this holds true for much of *The Federalist* as well. In the first number, Hamilton told the people of New York that he would "endeavour to give a satisfactory answer to all the objections" that had been raised against the Constitution "that may seem to have any claim to your attention."[7] But, far from being a cause for despair, the dialogic character of Federalist rhetoric in fact provides the key to the Federalist position in the debate over ratification. The Federalists were not writing timeless political theory. They were promoting the adoption of the Constitution by answering the objections of its critics. Because the Federalist argument was a response to Antifederalist criticism of the Constitution, we can only hope to make sense of the Federalist argument if we first make sense of their opponents. Hence, any attempt to find out what the Federalists were for has to start with the question what it was, exactly, that the Antifederalists were against. What I will attempt in this chapter, therefore, is to take the first step toward an understanding of the Federalists by trying to make sense of the Antifederalists.

One may, of course, question if this strategy really captures the Federalist position. Is it not rather the case that in the ratification debate the Federalists were caught up in a situation they would have preferred not to have been in: on the defensive, forced to meet the challenges of their opponents, and lacking control over the issues that became the leading subjects of debate? A positive statement of the Federalist persuasion, surely, must be sought somewhere else: somewhere where an author laid out his or her political principles with system and order and of his or her own accord. The answer to such an objection, I think, is that the issues that dominated the ratification debate continued to dominate the political life of the early republic for decades. It would seem, therefore, that the Federalists were never able to control the political agenda. For this reason, an analysis of the Federalist response to the challenges of the Antifederalists provides us with their stance on the most important and persistent political questions of their day. Nonetheless, the stated objection serves as a useful reminder of the necessity to keep open multiple avenues to the analysis of Federalist social and political thought.

In the first two sections of this chapter, the two main approaches to the analysis of the ratification debate are discussed. Until the late 1960s, the predominant interpretation described the debate over ratification as a conflict between "aristocratic" and "democratic" ideals and interests.[8] At about that time, scholars began the shift to the terms "liberalism" and "classical republicanism" to account for ideological differences during the revolutionary era. This shift was also accompanied by a change in the interpreters' concerns away from social struggle toward the study of the development of political ideas. The argument presented here is that the terminology so far favored by historians and political scientists has obscured important aspects of the ideological differences between the Federalists and their opponents. This is so because the terminology has drawn attention away from the actual issues debated during the ratification struggle. This claim can be supported in different ways. The approach I use here is to look closely at what prominent interpreters themselves say about the limits of their own interpretation. Although this approach is economical, it risks being unfair to the perspectives reviewed. It is important to note that my aim is not to give a full account of the interpretations that are discussed here; rather, the purpose is to show why they are of limited use to the *present study*, which aims to make sense of the ideological differences expressed by the parties in the ratifying debate. The struggle over ratification can certainly be approached with different, equally important, questions in mind. The fact that the major interpretations of the ratification struggle are rejected for the purposes of this work therefore does not mean that they are false or without value.

The third section of this chapter presents an approach that promises better to capture the essence of the ideological disagreement between the Federalists and the Antifederalists as presented in the debate over ratification.

I

The idea that the Federalists were an aristocratic party, whereas the Antifederalists represented the people, lies at the heart of the so-called progressive interpretation of the framing and ratification of the Constitution. Although this interpretation originated with Charles Beard, his economism made the distinction between aristocrats and democrats merely a superstructural adjunct to more basic class identities.[9] Hence, it was left to Merrill Jensen to express the progressive understanding of the Constitution's role in the history of American democracy. To Jensen, the revolutionary era was dominated by the struggle between "radicals" and "conservatives," which followed on "the democratization of American society by the destruction of the coercive authority of Great Britain and the establishment of actual local self-government within the separate states under the Articles of Confederation." Jensen's radicals were democrats and supporters of state sovereignty, while his conservatives were aristocrats and nationalists. Whereas the Declaration of Independence and the confederation articles were the institutional manifestations of radical ideals, the Constitution was the work of the conservatives. The Federalists, said Jensen, "engineered a conservative counter-revolution and erected a nationalistic government whose purpose in part was to thwart the will of 'the people' in whose name they acted." The Constitution was nothing short of "the culmination of an anti-democratic crusade."[10]

Jensen's analysis was never supported by any systematic study of Antifederalist rhetoric and writings. In the mid-1950s, Cecelia Kenyon undertook such a study but reached conclusions that seriously challenged the progressive interpretation. Judged by their own words, the Antifederalists "were not latter-day democrats" and they certainly did not wish for simple majoritarianism to be the reigning principle of government. "Above all," Kenyon wrote,

> they consistently refused to accept legislative majorities as expressive either of justice or of the people's will. In short, they distrusted majority rule, at its source and through the only possible means of expression in governmental action over a large and populous nation, that is to say, through representation. The last thing in the world they wanted was a national democracy which would permit Congressional majorities to operate freely and without restraint.[11]

There have been two major attempts to save the progressive interpretation from Kenyon's critique. Jackson Turner Main tried to do so by refining the definition of the class struggle identified by Beard and by introducing a distinction between the political *interest* and the political *rhetoric* of Antifederalism. It is only the second aspect of Main's contribution that is of interest here. In short, his solution to Kenyon's challenge was to argue that Antifederalist rhetoric sounded undemocratic, because it was produced by a minority of Antifederalists belonging to the social and political elite, while the grassroots majority remained silent. This claim is important because Main also argued that the ideas held by the leadership were not representative of the attitudes of the majority of Antifederalists. The leadership, Main wrote, "frequently defended views somewhat less democratic than those of the constituents, and they were often out of sympathy with the economic demands of the rank and file. . . . As a result, Antifederalism as formulated by its most prominent spokesmen sometimes lacks the democratic overtones we have attributed to it."[12]

The idea that Antifederalist leaders and their constituents encompassed different, and even conflicting, political ideals has proved persistent. But the idea has also proved persistently difficult to demonstrate because of the difficulties of reconstructing the political ideals of the nonelite. To an economic determinist, this can, of course, be inferred from the position of the nonelite in the American economy. Most historians, however, have been reluctant to fall back on economic determinism and so have faced the empirical problem of recovering the political ideals of a segment of American society that left very few records. One instance when this "silent majority" *did* speak out was during the Carlisle Riot in western Pennsylvania, in late December 1787. This riot has been the object of detailed study by Saul Cornell. Cornell supports Main's distinction between the Antifederalist majority and the Antifederalist leadership. Even the most "plebeian" figures among the Antifederalist leaders, he claims, were part of the social and political elite. They feared what they called "excessive democracy" and endorsed the idea of elite rule. The majority of Antifederalists, at least in the backcountry, held a vision of popular democracy, calling for broad political representation reflecting the actual composition of society.[13] To the majority of Antifederalists, as opposed to their leaders, the struggle over ratification really was a struggle over democracy.

The other major attempt to salvage the progressive interpretation was made in the pages of Gordon Wood's seminal *Creation of the American Republic*. More than three decades after its publication, it still dominates the analysis of state and national constitution making in the early republic more than any other work. More than most works, too, its complex argument has lent itself to different readings and uses.[14] Wood denied that the conflict over the Constitution was a struggle between economic classes, although he did maintain that it was fundamentally a social conflict. Its backdrop was the popular challenge to the right of the elite to govern the common people without their participation, which followed on the Revolution. As in the progressive account, Wood saw the Constitution as an attempt by the elite to restrict the power of the people and, consequently, the struggle over ratification is best regarded as a struggle over democracy. Like Main, Wood saw a split in the Antifederalist movement between the elite and the majority. The most famous Antifederalist leaders, he wrote, "scarcely represented, either socially or emotionally, the main thrust of Antifederalism. Such aristocratic leaders were socially indistinguishable from the Federalist spokesmen and often as fearful of the excesses of democracy in the state legislatures as the Federalists."[15] For this reason, "many of the *real* Antifederalists . . . were never clearly heard in the formal debates of 1787–88."[16]

Wood saw "real" Antifederalism as a challenge to the Federalists' ideas about elite rule and as an argument in favor of more popular representation. Much more than the Federalists, it is the Antifederalists who are the real origin of American pluralism and interest group politics, that is, of modern American democracy.[17] But to prove this claim, Wood defines Antifederalism as a political tradition that is much broader than the criticism of the Constitution made during the ratification debate. Having discredited the most articulate critics of the Constitution as unrepresentative of real Antifederalism, Wood in fact finds that the best expression of the Antifederalist position was not made in the debate over ratification at all. Rather, it can be found in the context of the conflict over the rechartering of the Bank of North America, an event that took place in the Pennsylvania assembly a full year before the Constitutional Convention met.[18] This criticism of Wood's definition of Antifederalism is not meant to question the existence of strong continuities in the political thinking of the revolutionary period. The existence of such continuities is beyond doubt. Nevertheless, for a study that addresses the ideological differences between Federalists and Antifederalists during the ratification debate specifically, it is of course problematical to define the ideology of Antifederalism by an analysis of arguments made before the Constitution appeared.

The problem that has faced scholars who have interpreted the struggle over ratification as a struggle over democracy is that it does not accord with what Antifederalists said in newspapers, in pamphlets, and at conventions during the ratification debate. For this reason, progressives have argued that Antifederalist rhetoric was produced by a small and well-defined group: members of the social and political elite whose views were not representative of the vast majority of those who opposed the Constitution, that is, the "real" Antifederalists. But no matter what the *struggle* over ratification was about, the progressive account itself makes clear that the *debate* over ratification was not an explicit debate about democracy. Indeed, the progressive perspective has very little to say about the ideological differences that the opponents and the supporters of the Constitution expressed in the debate. This is because, to progressive historians, the debate does not reveal anything significant about the conflict between Federalists and Antifederalists. To them, the ratification debate was merely a conversation among members of the elite, who by definition—or, rather, by social and economic determination—composed the antidemocratic element in American society. A focus on elite discourse is therefore a focus on only one side in the struggle over ratification. As far as this study is concerned, it is not important if the progressive interpretation squares with the historical evidence or not.[19] What matters—and this is in fact admitted by the progressives themselves—is that the progressive interpretation cannot account for the ideological differences expressed by Federalists and Antifederalists in the debate over ratification.

II

Progressive interpreters never accepted Wood's work as a study of social conflict.[20] Instead, the great impact of *Creation of the American Republic* was its contribution to the reorientation of academic interest that had begun at the time of its publication. Increasingly, students of eighteenth-century American politics shifted their attention away from the world of social and political conflict toward the realm of political ideas. Wood's book fitted well into this context. His work is not only an analysis of the democratic challenge to aristocratic rule but also an account of the changes in political thought that occurred between the Revolution and the ratification of the Constitution. Wood describes how "an essentially classical and medieval world of political discussion" was transformed into an understanding of politics "that was recognizably modern." The Constitution marks this crucial break. It was the "end of classical politics."[21]

Whereas the "modern" conception of politics could be translated as "liberalism," it was originally less clear how to describe the classical "world of political discussion." Wood's teacher, Bernard Bailyn, had first drawn attention to the prominence in revolutionary rhetoric of a body of thought distinct from the natural rights theories of the Enlightenment, which had conventionally been regarded as the major intellectual influence on the revolutionary generation. The political pamphlets written during the struggle against Britain revealed the influence of "a group of early eighteenth-century radical publicists and opposition politicians in England who carried forward into the eighteenth century and applied to the politics of the age of Walpole the peculiar strain of anti-authoritarianism bred in the upheaval of the English Civil War."[22]

Bailyn and Wood called this tradition "Opposition thought" but sometimes also employed the terms "Country" or "radical Whig" thought.[23] Their findings were soon appropriated and placed in a broader context by the efforts of John Pocock and some of his followers. In a review of Wood's work, Pocock described the American Revolution "less as the first political act of revolutionary enlightenment than as the last great act of the Renaissance."[24] It was so, Pocock argued, because it was informed by a "classical republicanism" that traced its roots via James Harrington and Algernon Sidney to Niccolò Machiavelli and, ultimately, to Polybius and Aristotle. The central concept in the classical republican ideology, sometimes also called "civic humanism," was "virtue." In the eighteenth-century Anglo-American world of ideas, writes Pocock, there existed "a line of thought which staked everything on a positive and civic concept of the individual's virtue." It presented "an image of the human personality, at once intensely autonomous and intensely participatory, entailing a *vita activa* and *vivere civile* which carry us back to the beginnings of humanism."[25] In short, the civic ideal of classical republicans was "essentially Greek."[26] Treating Opposition or Country thought as an instance of classical republicanism, Pocock writes that it "was founded on a presumption of real property and an ethos of the civic life, in which the ego knew and loved itself in its relation to a *patria, res publica* or common good, organized as a polity, but was perpetually threatened by corruption operating through private appetites and false consciousness."[27] Classical republicanism held that "the furthering of the public good" was "the exclusive purpose of republican government," and that this "required the constant sacrifice of individual interests to the greater needs of the whole."[28] Clearly, this was an ideology profoundly at odds with liberalism. But if Pocock believed that Wood was right in stressing the importance of classical republican thought to the revolutionary generation, he did not agree that the Constitution marked a break between the old ideology and a new one. Seconded by Lance Banning, Pocock argued that the classical republican vision survived into the 1790s and the early nineteenth century.[29]

The claim that the American revolutionary generation adhered to classical republicanism has not gone unchallenged. In a critique of Wood's *Creation of the American Republic*, Gary Schmitt and Robert Webking have exorcised all traces of an ideology postulating the primacy of the common good from the American founding. Americans of all hues, they claim, were primarily concerned with the protection of private rights, and any differences between them concerned minor points about means rather than ends.[30] But, whereas Schmitt and Webking follow Bailyn and Pocock in presenting an account of the revolutionary period as essentially ideologically homogeneous, the works of Joyce Appleby and Isaac Kramnick have reintroduced the theme of political and social struggle. They have argued that the era was characterized by a striving for individualism, pluralism, and competitive capitalism: in other words, by an attempt to realize liberal ideals. Liberalism was the ideology of the men on the make, the "bourgeoisie," who challenged the classical republican ideals of the aristocratic elite, first during the Revolution and later in the struggle against the Federalists. But, contrary to the progressives, Appleby and Kramnick see the market as conducive to a development toward democracy and intimately linked to values such as egalitarianism and liberty.[31]

Today, the historiographical controversy over the character of the revolutionary era's rhetorical universe has ended in an agreement that neither the notion of a sharp distinction between a liberal and classical republican tradition, nor the idea that the former replaced the hegemony of the latter in a clear-cut shift in political thought, have stood up in the light of conflicting evidence. When Bailyn first questioned the conception of American political culture as primordially liberal by drawing attention to the prominence of Opposition thought, he never claimed that this tradition was incompatible with liberalism. Rather, he found it "interwoven with, yet still distinct from" other influences from Enlightenment thought, the common law, religion and classical literature.[32] Recently, Bailyn has declared that there was in revolutionary rhetoric "no singular application of something scholars would later call 'civic humanism' or 'classical republicanism,' nor were these ideas felt to be incompatible with what would later be described as 'liberalism.'" Wood, too, has criticized the idea that the period was characterized by a conflict between liberalism and classical republicanism. Such a view "assumes a sharp dichotomy between two clearly identifiable traditions that eighteenth-century reality will not support." He reminds historians that they "ought to remember that these boxlike traditions into which the historical participants must be fitted are essentially our own creations, and as such are distortions of past reality."[33]

The denial of any inherent incompatibility of liberalism and republicanism now seems to be the received wisdom. As Knud Haakonssen puts it, "the opposition between liberalism and republicanism, while a source of inspiration for the recent revival of the latter, is more an invention of this revival than ascertainable historical fact."[34] Former contestants now agree that there was no ideological hegemony during the revolutionary era, that there was no incompatibility between liberalism and republicanism, and, finally, that neither the adoption of the Constitution nor any other event marks a clear shift from a classical republican to a liberal conception of politics.[35] Instead, Bailyn's original suggestion that revolutionary rhetoric bears traces of diverse intellectual influences has been accepted and extended to the debate over ratification. In the ratification debate, Kramnick writes, varied intellectual traditions were present, such as the Protestant ethic, reason of state doctrine, natural and common law arguments, and French as well as Scottish Enlightenment thought, in addition to liberalism and classical republicanism. Hence, there "was a profusion and confusion of political tongues among the founders. They lived easily with that clatter; it is we two hundred years later who chafe at their inconsistency."[36]

What was once a bitter contest has now ended in a draw. But it is a draw that frustrates any attempt to apply the distinction between liberalism and classical republicanism to capture the ideological differences between the participants in the debate over ratification. If the distinction between liberalism and republicanism is analytical rather than something apparent to the debaters themselves, and if the analytical distinction does not follow the division between Federalists and Antifederalists, then the terms cannot be used to define either the parties' ideological position or the nature of their disagreement. Put another way, if there was no apparent conflict between liberalism and classical republicanism, and if both "languages were heard on both sides,"[37] these terms cannot serve as a meaningful way of distinguishing between the ideological differences that the Federalists and the Antifederalists expressed in the debate over ratification.

III

At the time of the Constitution's bicentennial, both the progressive and the liberalism-republicanism interpretations were dead. Yet there was no sign of an interpretative framework to replace them. Indeed, the special issue of the *Journal of American History* devoted to "the Constitution and American life" did not include a single article on the founding because "experts on the drafting and ratification of the Constitution suggested that there was little fresh thinking in their field."[38] Nor has this changed in the fifteen years since the bicentennial.[39] Today we are as puzzled as ever about the true character of the ideological disagreement between Federalists and Antifederalists. Although historians have failed to establish much common ground on this point, there is at least a common patch. It is in this consensus that any attempt to make sense of the ideological disagreement between Federalists and Antifederalists has to begin.

Both progressive scholars and intellectual historians have noted the similarity in Antifederalist rhetoric and the rhetoric employed to oppose Britain during the Revolution. Thus, while Jensen pointed to a "remarkable continuity" between Antifederalists and revolutionaries, Bailyn writes that the "identity between antifederalist thought and that of the most fervent ideologists of '76 is at times astonishing." Many scholars have come to the same conclusion as Jensen and Bailyn, and others have demonstrated that the Revolution's rhetoric survived into the 1790s and beyond. There is agreement, then, about a strong continuity in American political thought, and it is also agreed that the Antifederalists were the carriers of this tradition during the ratifying struggle. Furthermore, there is also a consensus that the immediate source of this type of rhetoric was a group of political writers active in late seventeenth- and early eighteenth-century England.[40] The agreement ends when historians attempt to define the ideological content of this rhetoric. If, as it appears, this tradition of political thought, which here will be called "Country thought," was neither about democracy nor about liberalism, what was it really about?

To Country thinkers, the world was locked in a conflict between power and liberty. Only two actors were cast in this drama: the rulers, who were the agents of power, and the ruled, who were the agents of liberty. Power was regarded as by nature expansive and aggressive, with an inherent tendency to encroach on liberty. Significantly, the preferred metaphor to describe the workings of power was the act of trespassing. Because popular liberty was the natural victim of power, the people had to take care not to entrust their rulers with more than a minimum of power. But such precaution was not enough. It was also essential that the people kept their rulers under close guard to make sure that they did not abuse popular trust. For just as power always tended to expand and to threaten liberty, so it tended always also to corrupt those who wielded it. In the Country tradition, the relationship between the people and the government ought to be characterized by "jealousy," that is, the distrust of power. The people had to keep up a constant watch on the actions of their rulers. This was so much more important, as power made inroads on popular liberty only gradually, at an almost imperceptible pace, rather than by bold and open actions.[41]

Central to the defense of liberty were popularly controlled institutions that acted as counterweights to the power wielded by the rulers. Institutions such as the jury trial, the militia, or the colonial or state legislature were invariably referred to as "palladiums of liberty" or "bulwarks of freedom," and so on.[42] These institutions were not only popularly controlled; they were also, to a varying degree, locally controlled. Obviously, this was more so with the jury and the militia than with the assembly. As long as the central government, whether Parliament or Congress, remained administratively weak, these popular and local institutions allowed the people to veto any attempts by the central power to interfere in their lives. Through the jury, the militia, and the state legislature, the people could give or withhold their consent to the acts of the rulers simply by enforcing or not enforcing the law.[43]

In the debate over ratification, one aspect of the Antifederalist critique of the Constitution sprang out of their fear that if adopted it would undermine the power of, if not even abolish or destroy, important local and popular institutions. Thus, Antifederalists feared for the future of the jury trial and the militia if the Federalists would come to power. But they were also very concerned about the future of the state governments, and especially about the future of the legislatures, which after the Revolution had become the most important branch of government. In their eyes, the Constitution made the national government supreme and reduced the states to subordinate governmental bodies. What they called the "consolidated" national government, introduced by the Constitution, would take over many important government functions from the states. Consequently, the significance of the states would diminish steadily until eventually they withered away altogether.[44]

Many of the Antifederalist objections to the Constitution, then, consisted of fears that it would subvert popularly controlled local institutions, the primary function of which were to preserve liberty against the encroachments of the power of the rulers. Another side to the same coin was their concern with the centralization of power in the national government. Antifederalists worried both about the structure of the new government and about the powers granted to it by the Constitution. Their claim that the Constitution did not provide for adequate representation of the people is of course well known. Constituencies of 30,000 inhabitants ensured that the electorate would only return men of a certain stature in the electoral district, if not even in the state or nation. Consequently, Congress would be recruited from the social elite. This meant that the popular element in society would be unrepresented at the national level of government. Obviously, if they were unrepresented, the people could neither consent to, nor dissent from, government actions, and it could hardly be said that this government would rule by the consent of the governed. Instead of relying on popular consent to legislation and on popular administration of the law, this government would rely on force. It would be a government independent of the people—a despotism.[45]

But it was not only the composition and appointment of Congress that appeared troublesome to the critics of the Constitution. The new government was also granted powers that Antifederalists believed threatened the future of liberty. The right to raise and maintain standing armies in peacetime was one of these. In the Country ideology, "standing armies" carried strong and ominous connotations as a certain bane to liberty. In all nations in which standing armies had been created, slavery had followed. Another dangerous power granted to Congress was an almost unlimited right to tax. Money could easily be transformed into soldiers. In this respect, the Constitution compared unfavorably to conditions in Britain. There, the House of Commons had managed to keep the executive from encroaching on popular liberties by controlling the revenue. The Constitution, by contrast, granted the national government the right to tax the people regardless of the say of the state legislatures. Because Antifederalists denied that Congress represented the American people, it followed that they saw the state legislature as the only institution capable of collecting the popular will. But if the legislatures had no means of controlling the national government, there was no institution to stop Congress from introducing heavy and arbitrary taxes. With a large revenue at its back, Congress would have every means to make itself independent of the people.[46]

Antifederalists, in short, feared that the centralization of power would create a government both arbitrary and powerful. As Bailyn has written, Antifederalists saw in the Constitution "the construction of what could properly be seen, and feared, as a *Machtstaat*, a central national power that involved armed force, the aggressive management of international relations, and, potentially at least, the regulation of vital aspects of everyday life by a government superior to and dominant over all other, lesser governments."[47] Late eighteenth-century Americans believed themselves to be fortunate in being free of the demands on society resulting from heavy government. In writings intended to promote European emigration, as well as in other European accounts of America, it was pointed out that American government was cheap and American taxes "inconsiderable." This was in marked contrast to conditions in Britain, where, it was claimed, the "many Taxes, Rates, Assessments, and other Disbursements" ate up from half to two thirds of the annual income of the industrious man.[48]

In the rest of the Old World, all the major nations were governed by absolute princes. Although contemporary commentators in the Anglo-American world did not use the term *Machtstaat* to describe the systems of government in continental Europe, their recurrent talk of the introduction of "Turkish despotism" in Europe meant something even worse: A government that deprived the subjects of their inherent rights and left their lives, liberty, and property to the caprice and will of their rulers.[49] To the revolutionary generation, it seemed that the recent history of Europe could be written as a history of the expansion of arbitrary power and the decline of liberty. France was now as despotic as Spain. The same was true of the papacy, Austria, and the German states, and only recently Venice, Sweden, and Denmark had lost their liberties. Finally, to many Americans, as well as to many Englishmen, it seemed as though liberty was being destroyed in Britain, too.[50] It was widely accepted that sooner or later all free peoples would succumb to their rulers. This would happen when the rulers became independent of the people. Crucial to this contingency would be the executive power's ability to raise a standing army and secure revenue independent of the will of the people. Thus, the creation of a standing army and fiscal independence were not only objectionable in themselves but also a definite sign that power was expanding and liberty was threatened.[51]

With Britain's policies toward the colonies in the wake of the Seven Years' War, the struggle between power and liberty reached the New World. As noted, the colonists knew that America was different from Europe because no absolute prince and no "big government" pressed on the nation or threatened its liberties. When they took up arms against king and Parliament, they demonstrated that they believed this difference worth fighting for. A year later, they even accepted that to preserve America from the dangers of an expanding government they had to declare independence.[52] In 1787, Antifederalists were no less aware, nor less appreciative, of American difference than the revolutionaries had been. This time, however, the enemy was not Britain but their own countrymen. These men, who had wrongly claimed the name "Federalists," intended to undermine American difference by imitating Europe in building a great and expensive state.

Europe and other parts of the Old World often served as points of reference when the Antifederalists talked about the Revolution or the Constitution. "The banners of freedom were erected in the wilds of America by our ancestors," wrote Mercy Otis Warren. There had been "reason to hope they would continue for ages to illumine a quarter of the globe, by nature kindly separated from the proud monarchies of Europe, and the infernal darkness of Asiatic slavery."[53] But this was not to be. The Federalists had devised a plan for a new government that claimed powers similar, too—or even greater—than those claimed by Britain, "which we lavished our blood and treasure to separate ourselves from, as a country of slavery." In the same way, and in his characteristic style, "Centinel" wrote that the admiring world lately beheld the sun of liberty risen to meridian splendour in this western hemisphere, whose chearing rays began to dispel the glooms of even trans-atlantic despotism: the patriotic mind, enraptured with the glowing scene, fondly anticipated an universal and eternal day to the orb of freedom; but the horison is already darkened and the glooms of slavery threaten to fix their empire.

An anonymous poem in the State Gazette of South Carolina made the same point:

> Tho' British armies could not here prevail
> Yet British politics shall turn the scale;—
> In five short years of Freedom weary grown
> We quit our plain republics for a throne;
> *Congress* and *President* full proof shall bring,
> A mere disguise for Parliament and King.[54]

The Constitution, the Antifederalists said, would introduce a standing army, and by this means the American people were destined to suffer the same fate as the nations of Europe. As the prominent Antifederalist writer "Brutus" noted, standing armies were a feature of despotic governments as well as of "all the monarchies of Europe." They were "kept up to execute the commands of the prince or the magistrate," but they "have always proved the destruction of liberty, and is abhorrent to the spirit of a free republic." "If it was necessary," he said in a later essay, "the truth of the position might be confirmed by the history of almost every nation in the world." Warren was of the same opinion, writing that "standing armies have been the nursery of vice and the bane of liberty from the Roman legions, to the establishment of the artful Ximenes, and from the ruin of the Cortes of Spain, to the planting the British cohorts in the capitals of America." In his list of "curses" of the Constitution, another Antifederalist put "1st. A *standing army*, that bane to freedom, and support of tyrants, and their pampered minions; by which almost all the nations of Europe and Asia, have been enslaved."[55] But not only would there be a standing army in America; the new government would also levy heavy taxes like the governments of Europe. The cost of maintaining the "emperor," the "well-born" Congress, and the standing army would necessitate an "immoderate revenue" that had to be squeezed out of the people. Americans would become as poor as their European brethren, who struggled under heavy and oppressive taxes. "Do I exaggerate here?" one writer asked. "No truly. View the misery of the poor under the despotic governments of Europe and Asia, and then deny the truth of my position, if you can."[56]

To the Antifederalists, it seemed that the liberty enjoyed by the American people was the result of the absence of the sort of "big government" that prevailed in contemporary Europe. To the extent that America was a social experiment and a source of hope for the oppressed in Europe, the Federalists betrayed America when they tried to build a strong centralized government, complete with all the trappings of the European state.[57] As "Brutus" said:

> The European governments are almost all of them framed, and administered with a view to arms, and war, as that in which their chief glory consists; they mistake the end of government—it was designed to save men's lives, not to destroy them. We ought to furnish the world with an example of a great people, who in their civil institutions hold chiefly in view, the attainment of virtue, and happiness among ourselves. Let the monarchs in Europe, share among them the glory of depopulating countries, and butchering thousands of their innocent citizens, to revenge private quarrels, or to punish an insult offered to a wife, a mistress, or a favorite: I envy them not the honor, and I pray heaven this country may never be ambitious of it.[58]

IV

The Antifederalists' opposition to the Constitution was an opposition to the creation of a central government, which they feared would become as heavy and as powerful as the governments of contemporary European states. The best way to make sense of the ideological differences expressed in the debate over ratification is therefore to regard it neither as a debate about democracy nor liberalism, but as a debate about *state formation*.

In the social sciences, the "state" is usually defined by a mixture of institutional and functional terms. Thus, it is typically seen as a differentiated set of institutions and personnel, possessing a center from which political relations radiate outward to cover a territorially demarcated area. Over this territory the state holds a monopoly on authoritative binding rule making, backed ultimately by a coercive apparatus.[59] To an understanding of the issues debated in the ratification struggle, however, the functional aspects of the state, that is, what the state *does*, is much more relevant. It has been suggested that all states are involved in four basic, or minimum, activities. First, the state attacks and checks competitors and challengers to its authority within the territory over which it claims jurisdiction. In other words, it strives to monopolize political power by eliminating or subordinating other centers of authority. Second, it wages war against rivals outside its claimed territory. Third, it protects the ruler's principal allies by attacking or checking their rivals both inside and outside the territory claimed by the state. Finally, the state is involved in extracting resources from society to make possible these three activities. Essentially, this means that the state raises soldiers and money from its subject population.[60]

It is clear that the extractive capacity is of central importance to a state's ability to perform its other basic functions. Given this, "state building" or "state formation" can be understood as the building up of military force by the extraction of men and money from society. In order to strengthen the extractive capacity of the state it is necessary to eliminate, subjugate, coopt, or in other ways pacify other actors laying claim to such resources. State building is therefore characterized by three elements: an increase in military capacity, an increase in extractive capacity, and a centralization of authority. As I have shown in the previous discussion, these were precisely the points on which the Antifederalists opposed the Constitution. The Antifederalist fear was that the Constitution would create a state that would bring about a growth of armies, taxes, and public debts, as well as the concomitant strengthening of centralized power.

The start of this chapter asserted that the Antifederalists' critique of the Constitution is the key to the Federalist argument in support of the Constitution. If this is true, we would expect the Federalist argument to be a defense of the imitation of a European-style state in America. The match between Antifederalist and Federalist rhetoric is not perfect, however. To a large extent, Antifederalists did not believe, or pretended not to believe, the words of their opponents. Hence, they deliberately misconstrued the Federalist argument and attacked a straw man. Nevertheless, it is certainly true that the Federalists defended the strengthening of the national government, but the type of state they advocated was both similar to and different from the states in the Old World. Thus, while they drew extensively on European, especially British, experience to develop an idea of a state suitable to American conditions, the end result was in important respects unique. To understand why this was so, it is necessary to look closer at the European early modern state as well as at some characteristics of American society and political institutions.

3

EUROPEAN STATES, AMERICAN CONTEXTS

In order to interpret the debate over ratification as a debate over state formation, it is necessary to know something both about the development of the European state in the early modern period and about the ideological response this development generated. The aim of this chapter is therefore to provide a historical sociology of state building whereas the aim of the next chapter is to review the eighteenth-century discourse on the state. In this chapter I will proceed by means of a discussion of the development of the British state after the Glorious Revolution. Although it is true that Britain was by far the most common point of reference in the ratification debate, this is not the primary reason for concentrating on Britain rather than other states. The reason is rather that no other government was nearly as successful as the British when it came to raising taxes and mobilizing resources and men. It should be noted at the outset that the discussion of Britain is not meant to imply that the Constitution was adopted in order to introduce a British "fiscal-military state" in America. On the contrary, the aim is to demonstrate that there were certain limits to the expansion of the central government in the United States that did not apply in Britain. Precisely for this reason, the state created by the Federalists was very different from the contemporary British state.

I

In recent decades, there has been a resurgence of interest among historians and social scientists in European state formation.[1] Despite different theoretical and methodological approaches, they have tended to support the claim that the early modern European state was the result of war. As Charles Tilly puts it, "over the long run, far more than other activities, war and preparation for war produced the major components of European states."[2] This, of course, is not a new insight. It repeats conclusions reached by social scientists such as Otto Hintze, Gustav Schmoller, Joseph Schumpeter, Max Weber, and others who were active in the early twentieth century.[3] Because the state was made for war, the growth of the state in the early modern era consisted mainly in the growth of armies and navies. But because soldiers and battleships cost vast amounts of money, the growth of the state also consisted in a growth of taxes and public indebtedness. This change in the state's military and fiscal capacity has been treated by historians as respectively the "military revolution" and the emergence of the "tax state." It resulted in a type of state that British historians have called the "fiscal-military state," which is the term used in this work to describe the European state in the period from around 1500 to 1800. In the following discussion, the "fiscal-military state" may be understood as a state primarily designed for war.[4]

There is considerable disagreement among researchers both about the precise meaning of the "military revolution" and the precise date of its occurrence.[5] What has not been contested, however, is that it brought about an increase in the size of navies and fleets. The terms "tax state" and "financial revolution" refer to the great increase in the revenue of the central government, which accompanied the "military revolution." This occurred partly by the transformation of extraordinary levies to annual taxation, partly by innovations in public finance, which allowed governments to run up long-term debts. The importance of loans to the state building process cannot be stressed strongly enough. Loans offered a ready way to mobilize social resources far beyond what the fiscal basis would allow. But the state's ability to borrow money was not unlimited. Public credit was a function of the proportion of the present debt to the present revenue, on the one hand, and an assessment of the political and economic limits to further increases in taxation, on the other. Because of its importance to the mobilization of resources, public credit became a measure of state strength and governments did what they could to keep track of the debts and revenues of their adversaries.[6]

By themselves, increasing military and extractive capacities do not necessarily amount to state building. This growth has also to be controlled and induced by the central government or at least the central government's control and influence have to be on the increase. Although the traditional picture of European absolutism has to be modified, it appears that the trend during the sixteenth to eighteenth centuries was nevertheless for European central governments to strengthen their control over social resources. This took the form of a transition from indirect to direct rule, both in terms of government administration and in terms of the legitimate demands that the state was able to make on its subjects. In this context, it may be useful to follow the historical sociologist Michael Mann in distinguishing between two meanings of state power: on the one hand, "despotic power," which signifies the actions that the government "is empowered to undertake without routine, institutionalized negotiation with civil society groups"; and, on the other, "infrastructural power," which is "the capacity of the state to actually penetrate civil society, and to implement logistically political decisions throughout the realm."[7] It appears that the "despotic power" of the absolutist state was less extensive than has sometimes been thought to be the case.[8] The absolute monarchies of continental Europe ruled not by the application of blunt force, but by means of "bargaining," or negotiation, with local elites.[9] With regard to the "infrastructural power" of continental states, however, there was an increasing trend, although it was limited to the sphere of fiscal and military activities.

Before the seventeenth century, large states ruled through powerful intermediaries, who possessed significant autonomy in their relation to the prince. Increasingly, rulers gained a direct control over the resources of the nation by imposing a direct rule by the state over the population. On a legal level, the transition to direct rule established an unmediated relationship between the state and the subjects and limited the importance of the corporate bodies that had previously regulated the relationship between the subjects and the ruler. However, there was also a change to direct rule in the actual administration of basic state functions.[10] In the military sphere, the trend was toward conscription, which advanced the claim that the state had the right to demand military service from all its subjects. States also relied less on mercenaries and more on soldiers recruited from their own populations, and their military administration relied less on entrepreneurs and more on a state-controlled administrative apparatus.[11] In the fiscal sphere, it became legitimate for the state to make regular, direct and growing demands on part of the subjects' property. The administration of the revenue saw a development toward state-controlled and state-supervised collection rather than tax-farming and locally controlled administration.[12] The expansion of the state generated resistance from many groups. We may note, however, that the increase of the infrastructural power of the state went hand in hand with a decline in violent resistance to state demands. When the states first increased the fiscal pressure and reformed fiscal administration in the wake of "the military revolution," it triggered protests all over Europe. But, although the sixteenth century witnessed many large-scale tax rebellions, the eighteenth century was relatively calm—although state growth continued unabated.[13]

II

The traditional view of the English, later British, state has been that it followed a different path of development from the states on the Continent.

The German constitutional scholar Otto Hintze argued that there was a specific English type of state formation, characterized by the principle of constitutionalism, the power of the House of Commons, and the local and nonprofessional nature of public administration. The English experience was very different from that of the continental states, which were characterized by the principle of absolutism, the centralization of power in the monarch, and a bureaucratic system of administration. To Hintze, the reason for the different trajectories of the English and the continental states was found in geopolitics. The Channel allowed the English state to rely on a navy to protect its national interest. By this means, England avoided the fate of the states on the Continent, where constant warfare urged rulers to create standing armies, establish bureaucratic and absolutist rule, and to undermine the power of representative assemblies.[14]

Recent work on the creation of a "fiscal-military state" in Great Britain has made the idea of English exceptionalism problematical.[15] From the end of the Hundred Years' War to the Glorious Revolution, England was on the periphery of European power politics. But, from 1689 to 1783, the nation fought five major conflicts, gained an empire, and became a world power. Almost half of those years were war years. As a consequence, Britain, like its continental neighbors, experienced a sharp increase in the size of its military forces, its revenue, and its public debt. In fact, it outdid them all. In the last quarter of the seventeenth century, the English army counted no more than 15,000 men. By the turn of the eighteenth century, it had grown fivefold. In 1713, the army stood at 144,650 men. Between the Nine Years' War and the American War of Independence, the navy doubled in size. In addition to the army and navy, Britain also subsidized foreign troops. In 1710, during the War of the Spanish Succession, the British state had an army of 139,000 men and a navy and marine corps employing another 48,000 men, as well as 105,000 foreign troops in its pay. In that year, Britain managed to field almost as many men as France, although it possessed only half the population.[16]

The revenue and the debt followed a similar pattern of steep growth. In constant terms, taxes increased about eight times between 1670 and 1790. This increase cannot be explained by the growth of either the economy or the population. In the same period, national income increased about three times in constant terms. Calculated on the basis of *English*, rather than British, population, per capita taxes increased seven times in current terms and five times in constant terms during this period.[17] On per capita basis, taxes were almost three times higher in England than in France, although the greater prosperity of Britons compared to the French meant that the real burden of taxation was about twice as high in Britain as in France.[18] Yet it was the government's ability to borrow money rather than to raise taxes that impressed Britain's rivals more than anything else did. In 1697, the public debt stood at £16.7 million. At the end of the War of American Independence, it had reached £242.9 million, an elevenfold increase in constant terms. In 1785, the debt was almost eighteen times the size of the annual tax revenue.[19]

Far from following a different path, then, Great Britain experienced precisely the same growth in armies, taxes, and public indebtedness that characterized state expansion in the rest of Europe. In some respects, it did so even more. Nor did the Hanoverian state differ in terms of its priorities. As much as any other eighteenth-century state, it was made for war. Indeed, as Paul Langford notes, by the middle of the eighteenth century Britain had "become the supreme example in the western world of a State organized for war-making."[20] This priority is revealed by the structure of expenditure. For all the royal splendor associated with the *ancien régime*, the expenses of the French court made up no more than a tenth of the budget during the second half of the eighteenth century. The cost of the civil administration was about the same. The truly significant items in the French budget were the military and debt servicing, which together amounted to about 60 to 70 percent of total state expenditure.[21] The structure of expenditure in Britain was even more extreme. Over the century, civil spending increased modestly in real terms but declined relative to total government spending. Normally, it amounted to less than 15 percent of expenditures. By contrast, the government spent from 60 to 75 percent of its income on the military during war years. This sum was much reduced in peacetime, but in years of peace the cost of debt servicing increased sharply. After 1707, debt charges never absorbed less than 30 percent of the tax revenue. During most of the middle part of the century, it hovered around 40 percent. The costs peaked toward the end of the American war, when two thirds of tax income was reserved for debt servicing.[22]

III

The growth of the extractive capacity of the eighteenth-century British state surpassed that of its archrival France as well as all other continental powers. We have to ask which elements of the British state or British society made this possible. There is general agreement in the recent literature that the truly crucial factor was the existence of a strong and centralized representative assembly at the very core of government. But, in a twist on Hintze's argument, the House of Commons is now regarded as an asset rather than an impediment in the government's attempts to increase the tax on its subjects. This constitutes a revision of the traditional view that the degree of autonomy of the state in its relations to dominant social groups and classes determines the strength of the state.[23] It is this traditional view that has led to the erroneous belief that absolutist regimes were strong because they concentrated legitimate authority in the monarch and allowed no, or only limited, representation of social groups, classes, or estates. With the realization that Britain was in fact the most powerful state in the eighteenth century—in terms of the ability to field soldiers, equip navies, and collect taxes—scholars have begun to argue that a representative assembly improved the capacity of the early modern state to mobilize social resources.[24]

As the French case demonstrates, absolutism could also allow for an impressive growth in army and navy size, public indebtedness, and taxation. The insulation of the state from powerful groups in society had one important drawback, however. When the government wished to expand its extractive capacity—thereby canceling privileges and laying claims to the property of individuals, groups, and corporations—far-reaching state autonomy meant that there were no institutions in which a renegotiation of state-society relations could take place. The failure to establish an institutional arrangement whereby society could influence the state eventually proved fatal to the regime. Contrary to what is often maintained, therefore, state autonomy is often a sign of weakness rather than strength. As Mann points out in his revision of theories of the state, "states are simultaneously centralized actors *and* places where civil society relations are coordinated."[25] In contrast to French state autonomy, the permeation of the gentry into the British state made it possible to deal with pressures on society emanating from the state, and vice versa, by ordered negotiation that did not threaten the stability of the regime. Obviously, this does not mean that there were no conflicts between the state and society, or between different social classes and groups, in Britain, but, rather, that these conflicts could be settled by means of parliamentary majorities.[26]

The representation of the gentry class in Parliament does not mean that the British state was in any sense democratic. In fact, the House of Commons represented a mere fraction of the total population of Britain, voted into office by no more than 10 to 15 percent of the adult male population. Essentially, Parliament represented the landed gentry class and, to a lesser extent, richer merchants, tradesmen, and professionals. The vast majority of the British population did not possess any direct access to the state.[27] The Commons' most important power was its control over taxation. But even though the lower house possessed the power to withhold resources necessary to British state building, its eighteenth-century record is one of compliance with executive demands. Executive influence in the Commons was one important reason for this, and it was certainly the most frequent explanation in contemporary laments over legislative corruption. But a more important cause was that the restricted franchise, the class-character of Parliament, and the fiscal control of the Commons allowed the gentry and the merchant classes to shift the cost of building a "fiscal-military state" onto the economically and politically powerless.

The sharp increase in British taxes during the eighteenth century affected industry and trade, whereas for most of the century the land tax actually declined relative to the income the land generated. In 1790, duties on manufactures and trade made up about 80 percent of the total tax revenue and land and property taxes a mere 20 percent. This is significant because the latter fell on the landholders and the wealthy, whereas the excise and the customs duties were increasingly levied on articles of mass consumption. In terms of tax incidence, this development of British taxation meant that the "middling" rather than the upper classes in society carried an increasing part of the fiscal burden. Obviously, the advanced state of the British economy was a prerequisite for duties on consumer items to contribute so much to government income. Yet the structure of the economy did not determine the preference for one type of tax rather than another. Within the confines of what the economy allowed, this was instead a political choice. The policy followed was the effect of the efficient opposition by the House of Commons to all attempts to increase direct taxation. As Patrick O'Brien writes, "by default excises and stamps provided successive administrations down to the early nineteenth century with the only effective instruments for extracting extra revenue from the nation's slowly evolving tax base." For this reason, the House of Commons fiscal policy "might be depicted as a holding operation against the introduction of an income tax—or, what was in effect the same thing, a reform of the land tax."[28]

The injustice of the British fiscal system did not pass unnoticed to contemporaries. During the reign of George III, radicals criticized the discrepancy between political influence and tax incidence and made taxes a primary reason for their demand for a broadening of the electorate.[29] In his *Essay on the First Principles of Government*, Joseph Priestley wrote that

men of equal rank and fortune with those who usually compose the English house of Commons have nothing to fear from the imposition of taxes . . . but persons of a lower rank, and especially those who have no votes in the election of members, may have reason to fear, because an unequal part of the burden may be laid upon them. They are necessarily a *distinct order* in the community, and have no direct method of controlling the measures of the legislature.[30]

In the same way, James Burgh noted that "ministers, to curry favour with the house of commons are tempted to burden commerce with taxes for the sake of easing the landed interest."[31]

Whereas contemporaries such as Priestley and Burgh were aware of the inequities of British taxation, the system was very difficult to reform for outside groups. The groups affected by the tax policies lacked the direct influence over government actions that the landholding and, to a lesser extent, merchant classes possessed. There were certainly other ways to protest and promote policies than through parliamentary representation, such as petitioning and the formation of associations, but they demanded greater organizational effort and carried less certain results. Consequently, groups that were not represented in the legislature faced difficulties protesting against the distribution of the tax burden. Another difficulty arose from the domination of the gentry not only in the central government but in local government, too. The Commons in effect constituted a direct link between local and central politics. Furthermore, the lower house was the only representative assembly in Britain. Whereas most central governments in Europe had to negotiate with many different corporate bodies and regional assemblies to secure their revenue, the British government secured the consent of the political nation by means of a single vote in the House of Commons. In England, therefore, there were no local or regional institutions that could serve as rallying points for resistance against the policies of the central government. The significance of this circumstance is best revealed in the political development of the parts of the British Empire where the link between local institutions and Parliament did not extend. Effective resistance against the impositions of the British state could be formed in the American colonies and in Ireland precisely because in these places there existed institutions such as representative assemblies, militias, and law courts controlled by an elite that was *not* represented in the House of Commons.[32]

In their attempt to shift the cost of state expansion to politically excluded groups, the House of Commons was even prepared to accept that the gentry's control over the administration of taxation decreased and that fiscal administration came to be carried out by government officials under executive supervision. Land tax administration was locally controlled by the county elite and carried out by part-time amateur officials. The growth sectors of Britain's fiscal machinery, the customs and the excise, by contrast, were bureaucratic administrations firmly controlled by the state through a hierarchical and professional organization.[33] In the military sphere, direct rule had been established before the start of the eighteenth century. Before the French Revolutionary War, there is only one major instance when the Commons promoted the expansion of the government's right to demand military service from its subjects. The Militia Act of 1757 stipulated that if chosen by lot, every able-bodied man between the age of eighteen and forty-five had an obligation to serve in the militia. Again, this act may be seen as a way for the gentry class to increase the military capacity of the state while avoiding the costs this entailed. Previous militia regulations had made militia service a duty primarily for the landowners. The new law extended militia service to all subjects equally. For the general population, the Militia Act represented a dramatic increase in the state's ability to exercise a direct influence on their lives. Although the act affected most people as a new tax rather than as actual military service, at the level of principle it represented an important change in the relation between the state and the people. In contrast to continental governments, the British system of government was characterized by the very low demands it made on the active support of the subjects. As long as the people paid their taxes, they were left largely alone. In this context, the Militia Act signified an ominous new beginning. As Eliga Gould points out, it "came dangerously close to undoing the limited military obligation that had represented one of the mainstays of Britain's matchless constitution since the Glorious Revolution."[34]

IV

In the mid-1770s, the thirteen colonies on the American mainland created a common government to take charge of the struggle with the mother country, which would soon develop into the War of Independence. As will be shown in chapters 5 and 10, the national government created by the Articles of Confederation was too weak in extractive and military capacity to pursue the war efficiently. To a great extent, the reason for this weakness was that fiscal and military power rested with thirteen sovereign state governments rather than with Congress. These problems did not abate when the war was won and independence was achieved; rather, independence gave rise to new problems, as Congress proved unable to defend the union's territorial integrity and commercial interests. To the Federalists, these were serious problems and the Constitution was intended to solve them by creating a stronger national government.

As was pointed out in chapter 2, the Antifederalists objected to elements in the Constitution that they feared would allow for the creation of a "fiscal-military state" in America. Thus, they objected to the centralization of authority when they accused the Federalists of wanting to create a "consolidated" government and to subvert the role of local institutions. They objected to the extractive capacity of the Federalist state when they attacked the Constitution's taxation clauses, but they also worried about the coercive capacity of the new state when they protested against Congress's right to raise and maintain armies. To the Antifederalists, it seemed that these new powers would create a government that would be tyrannical and that would press heavily on the people. Given this, it makes sense to see Antifederalism as an anti-statist argument against the formation of a "fiscal-military state" in America. The Antifederalists' anti-statism was probably no different from contemporary popular opinion of government in Britain and continental Europe. In an age when the central government gave little in return for the subjects' tax money, dislike of the state was common and widespread.[35] There were important reasons, however, why the American tradition of anti-statism represented by the Antifederalists had to be taken as a serious impediment to state building. These reasons have to do with specific American circumstances that did not exist in other nations. They are brought out clearly if we compare the socioeconomic and political conditions in America with those prevailing in Britain.

State formation depends on the mobilization of social resources. Consequently, the state has to be successful in taxing wealth accumulated in society. In Britain, a diversified and commercialized economy made sure that there were plenty of taxable objects apart from land. The American economy, by contrast, was characterized by the production and exportation of agricultural products and the importation of consumer items. There was very little large-scale manufacturing of consumer items. Thus, whereas excise duties could generate a substantial income in Britain, the structure of the American economy left state governments with two main fiscal options: direct taxes on lands and polls, or indirect taxes on trade. Potentially, customs duties were a good source of government income. The problem was that trade was unevenly concentrated to a few busy transit ports—in the postwar period, above all, New York. To the great majority of states, which lacked important ports, there was no other option than to resort to direct taxes on lands and polls in order to raise a revenue.[36]

In sharp contrast to the situation in Britain, however, landownership in America was widely dispersed. This meant that in America, a tax on land fell on the majority of the population and not on a small minority. In the United States, therefore, the incidence of the land tax was similar to the incidence of duties on consumption in Britain. But Britain and the United States differed not only in the distribution of property among the population. Another important difference was that political influence was also much more evenly dispersed in America than in Britain. The comparatively equal distribution of property in turn made the American franchise much broader than the English franchise. Before the Revolution, around 50 to 60 percent of the white adult male population possessed the vote, although there was considerable difference between the colonies. The reformation of government during the Revolution broadened the electorate even further, to include around 60 to 90 percent of white adult males. The Revolution also broadened representation in the lower houses of assembly, bringing previously excluded groups into the legislatures. Yet another difference between America and Britain was that the terms of office in America were much shorter than in Britain. After 1716, the House of Commons was elected for seven years, whereas elections to the American state assemblies were typically annual. Together, these differences meant that the state legislatures responded to the wishes and demands of a far broader segment of society than the House of Commons did, while short mandates ensured that this response was more or less immediate.[37]

The differences in political institutions, in the structure of the economy, and in the distribution of property and political power in Britain and America meant that there was no possibility in the United States to follow the example of the House of Commons and to shift the tax burden on to politically impotent groups. This was not for want of trying. In the prewar period, political majorities did what they could to ensure that the tax incidence fell mostly on the minority. As Robert Becker writes, "control over the tax laws was both a prize bestowed for victory at the polls and a weapon designed to ensure reelection."[38] When taxes rose sharply after the War of Independence, such practices continued. In *Federalist* 10, James Madison observed that "every shilling with which" the majority "over-burden the inferior, is a shilling saved in their own pocket."[39] Because taxes increased five to ten times and because they were levied predominantly on polls and land, however, it was inevitable that the tax rise would have to be borne by the political majority, no matter how much they tried to avoid it. Contrary to conditions in Britain, in America the men who paid taxes were the men who voted governments into—and, more important, out of—office. As will be described in greater detail later, the American people made use of this power over the vote when they responded to the heavy taxes levied by some of the states in the postwar period.

V

The combination of an agrarian economy, widespread property and suffrage, responsive legislatures, and a political culture dominated by anti-statist sentiments had important consequences for any attempt to create a "centralized nation-state" in America. To begin with, such a state was not likely to be created at all without widespread popular acceptance. If it were created, it would only be tolerated as long as it acted in ways that the people found acceptable. The Federalists argued that America had to possess a stronger national government. For this reason, they wished to give the national government direct control over military and fiscal matters, in order to ensure that the union had a sufficient income, sound finances, and an adequate defense. According to the Federalists, this was necessary if the United States was to be able to defend its territory and interests against the ambitions of other states. These goals may seem quite modest, and in a comparative perspective they certainly were modest. Nevertheless, there were formidable barriers against state formation in America that did not apply to Europe. In America, state growth had to be paid for by people who possessed political power. If these men were unwilling, or unable, to pay for the costs of government, they had the means to put an end to state expansion. As both the War of Independence and the postwar period had shown, the will, or ability, to contribute to the costs of government was limited. The dilemma faced by the Federalists was therefore how to create a state possessing sufficient strength to withstand the "fiscal-military states" of Europe, despite the widespread aversion to a strong central government among the American people. In the debate over ratification, they faced two specific Antifederalist charges made against the Constitution: first, that the Constitution would create a "consolidated" government that would reduce the states and locally controlled institutions to insignificance; and, second, that the Constitution would create a tyrannical government that would make heavy demands and press hard on the people. The Federalists met the first of these accusations with the concept of a federal government, that is, the idea that only certain specified powers were to be centralized. They met the second charge by showing how, despite the creation of a national government possessing sufficient military and fiscal capacity, friction between state and society could be reduced by building a state that was both inconspicuous and light.

Parts II and III show how the Federalists answered the Antifederalist charges in the debate on the military and fiscal clauses of the Constitution. Before I turn to that analysis, however, another issue has to be addressed: To what extent were contemporaries aware of the rapid expansion of the fiscal and military capacity of central government in the early modern period?

4

THE IDEOLOGICAL RESPONSE TO
STATE EXPANSION

It would be a fundamental mistake to assume a priori a complete correspondence between the historical sociology of state formation and the conceptual history of the "state," or, in more general terms, between institutional and intellectual development, between political reality and political rhetoric. But it would be an equally great mistake to assume that there is no relation whatsoever. As a prominent historian of ideas has said, "political life itself sets the main problems for the political theorist, causing a certain range of issues to appear problematic, and a corresponding range of questions to become the leading subjects of debate."[1] It would certainly have been remarkable if the great expansion of the fiscal and military capacity of central government in the early modern period had gone unnoticed by contemporaries, so as to leave no mark on historical, political and social reflection. In fact, it did not. As this chapter will show, there existed in the Anglo-American world of political discourse a complete vocabulary with which to respond to the growth of the British fiscal-military state.

I

Military historians have pointed to the French invasion of Italy in the late fifteenth century as the "catalyst" for the military revolution, which in turn provided the impetus for early modern state formation.[2] The invasion also prompted contemporary political writers to consider its significance and, indeed, modern political thought is commonly held to have originated in the period. To Niccolò Machiavelli, France's invasion seemed an event of profound importance and it brought about his call for the reformation of the Italian city-states. Although his belief in the ability of the citizen-soldier and in the possibility for city-states to survive in a world of emerging nation-states was fundamentally mistaken, Machiavelli certainly perceived, and wrote about, the political consequences of mobile siege-guns, new military tactics, and nationally recruited standing armies. Significantly, Machiavelli's only work on political theory published in his own lifetime was his *Art of War*.[3] Indeed, it soon became a commonplace that the inventions in statecraft as well as in military organization and technology—introduced by the French monarchs and soon imitated by other princes—caused the transformation of European political organization.

Two and a half centuries after Machiavelli, the celebrated Scottish historian John Robertson singled out the late fifteenth century as a critical period to the formation of the European state and the introduction of standing armies as the crucial factor bringing it about.[4] By Robertson's time, it was in fact generally accepted that the recent centuries had witnessed a sharp growth in armies, taxes, and public debts. Commentators saw this as a novelty and as a clear break with earlier conditions. In *The Spirit of the Laws*, Baron Montesquieu gave an account of recent European developments that included all the elements contained in the present-day accounts of state formation by historical sociologists:

> A new disease has spread across Europe; it has afflicted our princes and made them keep an inordinate number of troops. It redoubles in strength and necessarily becomes contagious; for, as soon as one state increases what it calls its troops, the others suddenly increase theirs, so that nothing is gained thereby but the common ruin. Each monarch keeps ready all the armies he would have if his peoples were in danger of being exterminated; and this state in which all strain against all is called peace. Thus Europe is so ruined that if individuals were in the situation of the three most opulent powers in this part of the world, they would have nothing to live on. We are poor with the wealth and commerce of the whole universe, and soon, as a result of these soldiers, we shall have nothing but soldiers and we shall be like the Tartars.
>
> . . .
>
> The consequence of such a situation is the permanent increase in taxes; and that which prevents all remedies in the future is that one no longer counts on the revenues, but make's war with one's capital. It is not unheard of for states to mortgage their lands even during peace and to ruin themselves by means they call extraordinary, which are so highly extraordinary that the most deranged son of a family could scarcely imagine them.[5]

In the debate over the ratification of the Constitution, one has to look no further than *The Federalist* to find the impact of these accounts of European history. In number 41, James Madison described the fifteenth century as "the unhappy epoch of military establishments in time of peace." A standing army in time of peace was first introduced by Charles VII, and every other nation was soon forced to follow the French example or else wear "the chains of a universal monarch."[6] In number 17, Alexander

Hamilton gave an account of the centralization of power and the creation of the nation-state by describing the transformation of Europe from a "feudal anarchy" to a system of "royal authority" brought about by a union between the common people and the monarch to break the power of the barons, who were each "a kind of sovereign within his particular demesnes."[7] In number 45, Madison explained this transformation in terms of external pressure on the nation-states. "Had no external dangers enforced internal harmony and subordination," Madison wrote, "and particularly had the local sovereigns possessed the affections of the people, the great kingdoms in Europe would at this time consist of as many independent princes as there were formerly feudatory barons."[8]

The Federalist, like the rest of the ratification debate, is sprinkled throughout with references to European experiences of standing armies, taxes, and public indebtedness. These statements reveal an awareness of the basic mechanisms of the state-building process and of the differences between the early modern state and its predecessor. Indeed, when the *Norfolk and Portsmouth Journal* advertised the second volume of the pamphlet version of *The Federalist*, the paper noted that the work offered "dispassionate reasoning, and the most liberal and candid discussion" derived not only from prominent political commentators but also from "the theory and practice of the different Sovereignties in Europe."[9]

As the quotation from Montesquieu suggests, the expansion of state power was regarded as an evil by many political commentators. When the rulers came to see the people as "their property" and the people's possessions as "a common stock from which they have a right to take what they will," Richard Price wrote, governments became oppressive.[10] It was often claimed that the many wars and the heavy demands by government imposed such hardship on the common people in Europe that the continent was being depopulated. For this reason, Jean-Jacques Rousseau could claim in *The Social Contract* that the surest mark of good government was population growth. In his *Discourse on Political Economy*, Rousseau was more explicit, saying that the inventions of artillery and fortifications had made the monarchs of Europe return to the practice of ancient Rome to keep up regular troops. As a consequence, Rousseau claimed, it would be "no less necessary than formerly to depopulate the country to form armies and garrisons; it will be no less necessary to oppress the peoples; in a word, these dangerous establishments have increased of late years with such rapidity in this part of the world, that they evidently threaten to depopulate Europe, and sooner or later to ruin its inhabitants."[11]

II

It has been noted that the Antifederalists criticized the Constitution by drawing on arguments from English "Country" writings. As in other parts of Europe, the growth of the state provided the agenda for political debate and reflection also in England. To a large degree, contemporary writers occupied themselves with criticizing the growth of standing armies, public indebtedness, and heavy taxes, as well as the increase of executive power and the undermining of the independence of the House of Commons. The question that concerned these writers was whether or not the growth of the state and executive power would destroy English liberties. To Englishmen and foreigners alike, more than anything else it was "liberty" that distinguished the British system of government, or constitution, from the states on the Continent.[12] Indeed, Montesquieu was far from original when he noted in a well-known passage that there was only one nation in the world "whose constitution has political liberty for its direct purpose."[13]

"Liberty" is a polysemic word and it is not always easy to determine its precise meaning in the early modern Anglophone world. Typically, the liberty of Englishmen was praised in terms such as "this inestimable blessing" or "the root of our felicity," without being further specified. Explicit definitions are easier to find negatively, in the catalogues of monarchical abuse of liberties that can be found in documents such as the English Bill of Rights or the Declaration of Independence. Nevertheless, despite the problem of delimiting the exact meaning of the word, it is clear that central to liberty was limited government and the rule of law, as well as the preservation of the Protestant faith.[14] It is useful to follow William Blackstone's influential *Commentaries on the Laws of England* in defining English liberty with reference to the "absolute rights of individuals." To Blackstone, the existence of such rights made the British constitution "very different from the modern constitutions of other states, on the continent of Europe, and from the genius of the imperial law; which in general are calculated to vest an arbitrary and despotic power, of controlling the actions of the subject, in the prince, or in a few grandees." Although the absolute rights of Englishmen had once been the common rights of all humankind, they had been retained by the people only in Britain and its colonies. They consisted of three basic rights and five subordinate auxiliary rights. In the first category were the rights to personal security, personal liberty, and private property. In the second category were the rights of Parliament and the restrictions on the royal prerogative. This category also included the right to apply for a redress of injuries to the courts, the right to petition Parliament and the sovereign, and, last, the right to possess arms for self-defense.[15]

The rights of Parliament and the restrictions on the royal prerogative made Britain a limited monarchy. They are the two rights mentioned by Blackstone that are of greatest concern here. Under the British constitution Parliament was "the supreme and absolute authority of the state," invested with the legislative power. Parliament was composed of the king, the lords temporal and spiritual, and the commons. Although the executive power therefore formed part of the legislature, the British constitution still avoided placing the right to make and to enforce laws in the same hands, that is, the formula for establishing tyrannical government.[16] This was because power was not evenly distributed among the composite parts of the legislature. The formal power of the king in the legislature was restricted to "the royal negative" on legislation. The truly significant powers over legislation were held by the Commons. Foremost among these powers was the need for the Commons' consent in order to raise revenue through taxation and to create and maintain armies and navies.[17] As Richard Price noted in his *Two Tracts on Government*, "as long as that part of a government which represents the people is a fair representation, and also has a negative on all public measures, together with the sole power of imposing taxes and originating supplies, the essentials of liberty will be preserved."[18] But not only was the Commons superior to the monarch in the legislature; the legislative branch of government was also superior to the executive branch. The royal prerogative was restricted by the subordination of the king under the law. According to Blackstone, the "principal duty" of a British monarch had always been to govern his people according to law. This was a duty prescribed no less by nature and reason than by ancient Germanic practice and the common law. In the eighteenth-century, the terms of this "original contract between the king and people" were expressed in the coronation oath when the monarch promised "to govern according to law; to execute judgement in mercy; and to maintain the established religion."[19]

If the British nation seemed singularly blessed with a free system of government, contemporary political thought was neither triumphant nor complacent but full of anxiety. Far from reveling in England's achievements, political commentators feared for the future of liberty. These writers agreed that Britain was markedly different from the rest of Europe. Although there was certainly some variation, there was also a basic agreement on the reasons for this difference and the reasons why British exceptionalism was precarious. It was generally held that, under the Stuarts—both prior to and after the English Revolution—England was well on its way to follow the states on the Continent on their path toward absolutism. The Glorious Revolution, however, put an end to the increase of executive power and laid the basis of England's exceptionalism. Had this growth not been checked, it was claimed, the king of England would have become "as arbitrary as the king of France."[20] Liberty would have been extinguished and Britons would have found themselves "groaning under the infamy and misery of popery and slavery."[21]

But for all its importance, the Glorious Revolution failed to make liberty safe from the encroachments of executive power. The restriction and definition of executive power, which was the very essence of the Revolution, also marks the turning point when executive power began to expand in less obvious and noticeable ways, to once more become a threat to liberty. Thus, while the Glorious Revolution may have stopped the growth of the royal prerogative, the accession of William and Mary accelerated the growth of the state. To the government's Country critics, it was evident that William's creation of a peacetime standing army aimed to introduce the "French fashion of monarchy, where the king has power to do what he pleases, and the people no security for anything they possess."[22] Looking back at William's reign some seventy years later, William Blackstone and Tobias Smollet both described it as the time when England for the first time acquired a standing army and a permanent debt. To Blackstone, it was "the fashion of keeping standing armies," which "had of late years universally prevailed over Europe," that forced Parliament "to maintain even in time of peace a standing body of troops," both in order to defend Britain and to maintain the balance of power in Europe. The costs of such an active policy forced William to introduce what Smollet described as "the pernicious practice of borrowing upon remote funds." William, Smollet wrote, "entailed upon the nation a growing debt, and a system of politicks big with misery, despair and destruction." This change of policy was never reversed, but the army, the public debt, and the tax pressure continued to grow. By the time Blackstone wrote, the bulk of the tax revenue was no longer used to pay for war, but "first and principally, to the payment of the interest on the national debt."[23]

To contemporaries, the expansion of the state appeared threatening to the preservation of liberty. This was a prevailing theme that persisted throughout most of the eighteenth century. Quoting from Bolingbroke's *Dissertation on Parties*, James Burgh wrote that while "the power of prerogative was more open and more *noisy* in its operations" the powers that the crown had acquired after the Glorious Revolution were "more *real*."[24] Foremost among these "more *real*" powers were the increased tax revenue and the public debt. The expanded fiscal administration, said Blackstone, gave rise "to such a multitude of new officers, created by and removable at the royal pleasure, that they have extended the influence of government to every corner of the nation." This great strengthening of the Crown surely went against the intentions and spirit of the Glorious Revolution. By "an unaccountable want of foresight," Blackstone noted, the men who had "gloriously struggled for the abolition of the then formidable parts of the prerogative" had unintentionally brought about stronger executive power. By the 1770s, the growth of the state had become very visible and was watched with alarm by many writers. "Witness the commissioners, and the multitudes of dependents on the customs, in every port of the kingdom," Blackstone wrote in a passage that was later quoted by Burgh,

> the commissioners of excise and their numerous subalterns, in every inland district; the post-masters, and their servants, planted in every town, and upon every public road; the commissioners of the stamps, and their distributors, which are full as scattered and full as numerous; the officers of the salt duty, which though a species of the excise and

conducted in the same manner, are yet made a distinct corps from the ordinary managers of that revenue; the surveyors of houses and windows; the receivers of the land tax; the managers of lotteries; and the commissioners of the hackney coaches; all which are either mediately or immediately appointed by the crown, and removable at pleasure without any reason assigned; these, it requires but little penetration to see, must give that power, on which they depend for subsistence, an influence most amazingly extensive.[25]

The vast patronage power was important mainly because it gave the Crown influence in the House of Commons. The executive branch employed its power to distribute places and pensions to Members of Parliament and their clients and to interfere in elections with a view to secure a legislative majority in the Commons. Thus, according to Smollet, the opposition to the excise scheme of 1732 were largely driven by the conviction that an expanded Excise Department "would produce an additional swarm of excise-officers, and warehousekeepers, appointed and paid by the Treasury, so as to multiply the dependants on the Crown, and enable it still further to influence the freedom of elections."[26] Such practices gave rise to criticism of executive "corruption" of the legislature. In the scholarly literature of recent decades, such critique has been interpreted as an essentially moral argument about the depreciation of civic "virtue," both of the individual subject and of the body politic. But, on the surface at least, the critique of corruption seems more concerned with the balance of power between the different branches of the government than with the decline of virtue.[27]

By means of the corruption of the Commons, the executive undermined the independence of the legislature. The strength and independence of the legislature was regarded as crucial because this was the institution that had a principal duty to protect liberty by checking executive encroachments. In the rest of Europe, absolute rule had been erected on the ruins of popular assemblies. All the "*Gothic* states," Burgh argued, had once been characterized by strong legislative assemblies, limited monarchies, and, as a consequence of this, a respect for the rights to personal security, liberty, and private property. It should be remembered, Burgh said, quoting Voltaire, that France "was once governed as *England* is now."[28] Burgh was not alone in identifying the growth of executive power and the destruction of liberty as the major theme of European history. The "absolute rights of individuals," Blackstone wrote, "were formerly, either by inheritance, or purchase, the rights of all mankind; but, in most other countries of the world being now more or less debased and destroyed, they at present may be said to remain, in a peculiar and emphatical manner, the rights of the people of England."[29] But these rights would remain the property of Englishmen only for as long as the House of Commons possessed enough strength to protect them from executive encroachments. Montesquieu's words are perhaps the best-known statement of this idea: "Since all human things have an end, the state of which we are speaking will lose its liberty; it will perish. Rome, Lacedaemonia, and Carthage have surely perished. This state will perish when legislative power is more corrupt than executive power."[30]

To writers as different as Thomas Paine and David Hume, it seemed that the erosion of the independence of the Commons in relation to the Crown meant that Britain was becoming more like the states on the Continent. Although the British government was sometimes described as a "republic," Paine wrote, it had in fact become "as monarchical as that of France or Spain."[31] In his *Essays*, Hume posed the question whether the British government inclined more to absolute monarchy or to a republic. His conclusion was that "unless there happen some extraordinary convulsion, the power of the crown, by means of its large revenue, is rather upon the encrease." He also famously suggested that absolute monarchy was "the easiest death, the true *Euthanasia* of the BRITISH constitution."[32] It is significant that Hume singled out the revenue as the most important element of government power, whereas political thinkers of an earlier generation were certain to have placed more stress on the army. It was the increased revenue that allowed the government to create and distribute more offices. To Paine, the British government did not deserve to bear the name of "republic" precisely "because the corrupt influence of the crown, by having all the places at its disposal hath so effectually swallowed up the power and eaten out the virtue of the House of Commons." "Why is the constitution in England sickly but because monarchy has poisoned the republic, the crown has engrossed the commons?"[33]

III

There is no doubt that eighteenth-century Britons possessed concepts and arguments with which to analyze and assess the effects of the unparalleled growth of state power after the Glorious Revolution. Indeed, the major dividing line in politics, no less than in political thought, was between the Court defenders of state expansion and their Country critics.[34] Country ideologists focused on the novel features of the post-Revolutionary state. The standing army and fiscal institutions such as the Bank of England and the excise were favorite targets of attack. But they also worried about the Commons' ability to act as a counterweight to executive power and as a guardian against government abuse. To them, the power of the lower house was being undermined by the executive's distribution of places and pensions and by its interference in elections. All these aspects of Country thought are too well known to need further elaboration here.[35] Even a quick glance at the predominant Antifederalist arguments suggests the affinity with Country ideas. If other aspects of the Country persuasion are taken into account, this affinity will appear even stronger.

Like Antifederalism, the Country ideology was an attempt to make sense of history. It presented the basic historical trend as the victory of despotism over liberty. Yet, although it saw history as tragedy, it was not a fatalistic perspective. Despotism could be resisted and the historical trend contained; sometimes even broken and reversed. This was the case in Britain and its empire. Nevertheless, even a free people such as the British lived always under the threat of impending tyranny and despotism could be held in check only as long as the people maintained an active supervision of government actions. This was a duty made both harder and more urgent and difficult by the belief that power subdued liberty by gradual, almost imperceptible, encroachments. Fortunately, Country supporters knew the mechanisms by which tyranny was introduced, and these mechanisms served as signs of warning showing that liberty was endangered. Some of the most important mechanisms, all of which triggered an immediate response in America both before the Revolution and after the publication of the Constitution, were taxation without consent and the creation of standing armies.[36]

Seen from a distance of two or three centuries, Country rhetoric appears peculiar. It is characterized by a "logic of escalation" by which it tended to see in every limited act of government a larger plan aiming to subvert popular liberty. It is this peculiarity that gives Country rhetoric its invariable tone of urgency. A proposal to add more regiments to the peace establishment was interpreted as an attempt to introduce military rule. A proposal for a new excise law was interpreted as the first step toward the introduction of a general excise in order to secure the fiscal independence of the Crown, which was certain to usher in absolute monarchy. To Country spokesmen, no matter how limited a government act may have been, liberty was always in the balance. It is this aspect of Country thought that accounts for its exaggerated tone. The rhetorical response often seems disproportionate to the act that provoked it.[37]

As noted, the Antifederalist response to the Constitution is very similar to the Country critique of the "fiscal-military state." This, of course, is because of a direct influence on Americans from English political commentators.[38] But this influence would never have been so strong—nor would the Country argument have proved so persistent in Britain—unless it was felt that it made sense of what was happening in political life. The critics of the Constitution took to Country rhetoric so easily because the Constitution seemed to threaten liberty by strengthening executive power beyond popular control. Like Country spokesmen, Antifederalists voiced concerns about executive influence and the corruption of the legislature. They feared the expansion of centralized power and stressed the need for the people to be vigilant and suspicious of their rulers. They attacked standing armies and praised the militia. They feared the introduction of heavy and arbitrary taxation. They insisted on annual elections. The list could easily be continued.[39] As parts II and III will show, Antifederalist rhetoric resembled Country rhetoric not only in content but also in form. There is the same basic concern for liberty and the same propensity for exaggeration. There is the same tendency to proceed from a seemingly harmless clause of the Constitution to unwrap a sinister plan for the suppression of liberty. More than anything else, it is this affinity with the form of Country thought that has induced some interpreters of the ratification debate to write off their critique as "trash based on hysterical assumptions or on political calculations intended to deceive and incite fear of the Constitution."[40]

IV

Although it does not appear problematic to describe Antifederalism as an expression of Country thought, it cannot be claimed that Federalism was merely a repetition of central Court arguments.[41] This is because many Court arguments simply were not useful to the defense of the Constitution. Such is the case, for instance, with the Court demand that in order to uphold the balance of the constitution the Crown had to possess some influence in the House of Commons and the claim that septennial elections were necessary to secure political stability.[42] The Constitution contained both a place act and a provision for biannual elections to the House of Representatives.[43] Rather, the similarity between Federalism and Court thinking lies on a much more general level—in their attitude to the relationship between power and liberty. In contrast to Country thinkers and Antifederalists, Federalists and Court thinkers shared the view that government strength may be less a threat to, than a prerequisite for, the preservation of liberty. Court apologists tended to date the introduction of liberty to 1688. This was more than a historiographical quibble because the Glorious Revolution introduced the state apparatus that the Country tradition protested against. To the Court, such a state was necessary for the defense of the liberties of Englishmen, mixed government, and the Protestant religion. Although they may not have liked high taxes, a growing debt, and peacetime standing armies, they presented them as necessary means to the preservation of Britain's free constitution. As one Court supporter wrote, "the national debt was contracted in the defence of our liberties and properties and for the preservation of our most excellent constitution from popery and slavery." In the same way, a peacetime standing army and a navy were necessary to protect Britain from France and the Stuart threat.[44]

To the Antifederalists, the Constitution resembled the British system of government against which they had rebelled. Although the Federalists did not deny that similarities existed between the Constitution and its British counterpart, they emphatically denied that the Revolution had been directed against the English constitution. Antifederalists, the Federalists said, ought to remember that "the quarrel between the United States and the Parliament of Great Britain did not arise so much from objections to the form of government . . . as from a difference concerning certain important rights resulting from the essential principles of liberty, which the [British] Constitution preserved to all the subjects actually residing within the realm." No one in America had then believed that the British constitution made Englishmen "slaves." On the contrary, what they had objected to was that Americans were refused the same degree of freedom as the inhabitants of the mother country.[45] Should the Constitution "remind you of a Government, once justly dear to us," one Federalist wrote,

> then let us enquire, where, among foreign nations, are the people who may boast like Britons? In what country is justice more impartially administered, or the rights of the citizen more securely guarded? Had our situation been sufficiently contiguous; had we been justly represented in the Parliament of Great-Britain; to this day we should have gloried in the peculiar, the distinguished blessings of our political Constitution.[46]

English liberty was so much more remarkable as it had thrived under an energetic government. As John Dickinson pointed out, Britain was unique among European powers in sustaining "a gradual advancement in freedom, power and prosperity" with frequent warfare. No other nation had "so perfectly united those distant extremes, *private security* of life, liberty and property, with exertion of *public force*."[47] Although Federalists found great flaws in the British constitution, and even more in the policies of the executive, in several of their comments during the ratification debate the British system of government did not serve primarily as an example of despotism but of the possibility of combining government strength with the preservation of freedom.

A basic line of division between the Federalists and the Antifederalists consisted in their different opinions about the amount of power that the central government could possess without endangering liberty. The Antifederalists found Congress's power to raise armies and taxes especially troublesome in this respect. By this means, Congress would make itself independent of the people and would come to resemble the governments of Europe. The Federalists, as we shall see, argued that it was crucial that Congress was granted powers similar to those of European governments. The Antifederalists claimed that such a development would mean the end to popular liberty in America. According to the Federalists, this development was a prerequisite for liberty's preservation. Antifederalists hoped that America would provide the world with an example of a government designed for other purposes than war. The Federalists presented their opponents as hopelessly naive. As long as the United States was part of an international system of states, the choice whether or not to be involved in war was not for Americans to decide on their own. No matter how "moderate or unambitious we may be," they said, "we cannot count upon the moderation, or hope to extinguish the ambition of others." The history of mankind suggested that "the fiery and destructive passions of war" were much stronger than the wish for peace. Hence, "to model our political systems upon speculations of lasting tranquility is to calculate on the weaker springs of the human character."[48] The Antifederalist position, their opponents said, turned on the "supposition:—*We shall always have peace, and need make no provision against wars. Is this not deceiving ourselves? Is it not fallacious? Did there ever exist a nation which, at some time or other, was not exposed to war?*"[49] In the modern era, no nation could hope to remain free, independent, and prosperous unless protected by a sufficiently strong state. A good government, therefore, should be "formed with all those powers, those checks and balances, which may be necessary to give it energy, on the one hand, and to secure the liberties of the people, on the other."[50]

II

Military Powers

5

AN IMPOTENT CONGRESS

Military power has always been central to the state. One of the state's basic functions is to wage war on other states and to check competitors to the government's authority within the territory over which it claims jurisdiction. In fact, until the early twentieth century, war making and preparation for war dominated the state's activities. In the United States, the Articles of Confederation had divided the power over war making between Congress and the states.[1] Whereas Congress was responsible for the defense of the union, the power over mobilization remained in the hands of the states. This division of power between the national and the state governments hampered the war effort during the struggle against Britain. After independence, it prevented Congress from acting forcefully in defense of the union's commercial and territorial interests.

In the Constitutional Convention, there was little disagreement about the need to strengthen the military and fiscal powers of the union. Nor was there disagreement about the need to grant Congress the power to regulate commerce and to enforce treaties. Because of this consensus, little debate on the fiscal and military clauses took place in the Convention.[2] This does not mean that military and fiscal powers were regarded as unimportant. The Virginia plan opened by drawing attention to the inability of Congress to preserve the union against internal and external enemies and to its failure to honor its creditors. The second article of the New Jersey plan gave Congress the right to raise revenue from import duties and stamp taxes as well as the right to regulate trade.[3]

In the Convention, taxation was discussed primarily in relation to representation. At an early stage, the issue was whether or not representation ought to be proportionate to the contributions made to the federal treasury. After the principle of representation had been settled, the question arose again with regard to taxes on, and representation of, slaves. There was also debate over whether or not to prohibit export duties. But there was no direct discussion about the type of taxes the national government would levy, nor about the need to impose restrictions on the government's fiscal power apart from the well-known concessions to the southern states. The assumption, nevertheless, was that the main part of the revenue would come from tariffs. Occasionally, an aversion to direct taxation came to the surface in the Convention's debates. Luther Martin at one point said that "direct taxation should not be used but in case of absolute necessity." At another point, Gouverneur Morris objected to the ban against the taxation of exports. "Taxes on exports are a necessary source of revenue," he argued. "For a long time the people of America will not have money to pay direct taxes. Seize and sell their effects and you push them into revolts."

The delegates were aware that the powers granted to the new national government were far greater than those possessed by the Continental Congress. James Madison noted that "according to the views of every member, the Genl. Govt will have powers far beyond those exercised by the British Parliament, when the States were part of the British Empire. It will in particular have the power, without the consent of the State legislatures, to levy money directly on the people themselves." Yet, of all the delegates, only Martin tried to restrict the government's fiscal power by proposing an amendment that would recur often in the ratification debate. According to the proposal, Congress would only have the right to levy and collect direct taxes after a state had first failed to comply with a requisition from the federal government. The proposal, however, was soundly defeated by the Convention. There were to be no restrictions on Congress's power to levy taxes directly on the American people.[4]

The debate on Congress's right to organize and discipline the state militias and to raise standing troops in peacetime was brief, but it introduced some of the objections to the military clauses of the Constitution that would later figure prominently in the ratification debate. The most important were Elbridge Gerry's warnings that the people would regard a nationalized militia "as a system of despotism" and that they would protest against any attempt to create a standing army in time of peace. Gerry also "proposed that there shall not be kept up in time of peace more than _____ thousand troops. His idea was that the blank should be filled by two or three thousand." Backed by Martin, Gerry continued to offer this proposal, but to no avail. In the responses he drew from Charles Pinckney, John Langdon, and Jonathan Dayton can be found some of the arguments later used to defend Congress's military powers against Antifederalist attacks.[5]

Out of doors, however, the military and fiscal powers of the national government figured more prominently. Public debate was dominated by a concern with the political and economic difficulties that sprang from the union's weakness in diplomatic and commercial relations. Furthermore, it was accepted that in order to come to terms with these difficulties, Congress had to possess greater powers in the fiscal-military sphere. In late July 1787, the Charleston *Columbian Herald* published a letter from "a Gentleman in Philadelphia," relating news gathered from "some of the first informed men in this city" about the work of the Constitutional Convention. The letter was dated July 4. At this time, a committee in the Convention had just begun the work that would lead to "the great compromise." Yet this Philadelphian reported neither about the formation of the Convention committee nor about its work. He had nothing to say about the Senate or the representation of small and large states. What he believed to be the "leading points" of the Convention's debate were altogether different matters. His report told that the Convention worked to establish import and export duties in addition to a poll tax. The poll tax was to be used for bounties on shipbuilding and fishing. The import duty was earmarked for payment of the public debt, foreign and domestic, and the export duty would go to "the expences of keeping up a small land force and navy." According to the Philadelphia gentleman, the Convention further considered how to put pressure on Spain to open the Mississippi River to American trade and made plans for a build-up of military force. Three frigates were to be constructed and "five hundred troops" were to be "raised and kept up in each state; one half on the seacoast, and the other half on the frontiers."[6]

The difference between the report of the anonymous Philadelphia gentleman and what went on in the Constitutional Convention is characteristic of the difference between the public debate and the secret deliberations of the Convention during the summer of 1787. Examples could easily be multiplied,[7] but only one more will be offered here. One of the most prolific writers in this period was Nicholas Collin, who published twenty-nine essays in the *Independent Gazeteer* of Philadelphia, addressing the need to reform the national government. Like the Philadelphia correspondent just quoted, Collin—who wrote as "Foreign Spectator"—was remarkably quiet about the structure of the new government. Instead, the essays dealt with various means to raise the patriotic spirit among Americans and with the need to build a stronger union. By mid-September, Collin devoted a couple of essays to the need for the United States to create "a solid military union" that would include "a few thousand standing troops" in addition to extensive national control over the state militias. On the very day the Constitution was made public, Collin had arrived at a discussion of the need for the federal government to possess an independent power over taxation in order to secure the peace and interests of the union: "The federal government must have a *fixed and ample revenue to be furnished by certain taxes in every state, and collected by officers of its own appointment, and under its own direction*," he wrote. "Without this we shall either have foreign soldiers or our own Shayses for collectors." The next day, Collin declared that in time of war the fiscal powers of Congress had to be unlimited, saying that "it will not be possible to limit them but in very general terms."[8]

To the Federalists, military and fiscal powers as well as powers to regulate commerce and enforce treaties were interdependent: An income was a prerequisite for the creation of a defense establishment. Military strength was needed in order to enforce commercial regulations, which would secure treaties. Treaties, in turn, would promote trade, which would be the major object of federal taxation and therefore the national government's main source of income.[9] Although much of the Federalist call for a stronger military establishment was couched in geopolitical terms, it was also interwoven with broader concerns about the economic advantages that would fall to the American nation from a stronger national government.

This chapter provides a background to the conflict between the Federalists and the Antifederalists over the military clauses of the Constitution, which is analyzed in chapters 6 to 8. The debate over the fiscal clauses is analyzed in part III of this book. In this chapter, I argue that two principles frustrated the ability of the Confederation Congress to provide the union with the military capacity it needed to function: first, the sovereignty of the states; and, second, the strong aversion in the American political tradition to a peacetime standing army. In the end, these principles led Congress to become passive in foreign affairs. I end this chapter with an attempt to locate the Federalist demand for an improved military capacity of the national state not in the context of militarism but in the context of the promotion of commerce.

I

On 14 June 1775, the second Continental Congress took command of the forces the British troops in Boston. This act nationalized a conflict that had begun as the concern of Massachusetts and its New England neighbors. It also placed Congress in charge of the struggle against Britain. In the early stages of the conflict, Congress and the states relied on traditional ways to recruit the army rather than to invest Congress with the full powers over mobilization. There were three main reasons for this decision. First, there was a general expectation that the showdown with Britain would be a short-lived affair. Second, there was awareness among American officeholders in the newly created state governments that the legitimate claims they could make on the property and the personal service of the citizens were very limited. Third, and perhaps most important, Congress preferred to do things the way they had been done in the past.

Late at night on 18 April 1775, British troops set out from Boston to capture American-held arms and ammunition at Concord. In response to this "aggression," some 20,000 men mobilized more or less instantaneously in their local militia units. After the British regulars had retreated to Boston, the Americans began to lay siege to the city. The militia, however, was not an institution organized for wartime and the militiamen had neither the equipment nor the inclination to remain encamped outside Boston for any extended period of time. Rather than attempt to recruit or draft an army for the duration of the conflict, the Provincial Congress of Massachusetts chose to recruit volunteers from the militia, who agreed to serve to the end of the year. This volunteer force was augmented by similar contingents from the neighboring states. In 1775, American political leaders expected a political rather than a military solution to the conflict with Britain. Under such circumstances, the recruitment of a permanent army might be counterproductive to American interests. Furthermore, even if the delegates and officers of the state and national governments had wished otherwise, it was doubtful if they could have claimed, much less enforced, obedience to demands made on the people's time and money. In 1775, the sole source of legitimacy for actions undertaken either by the Continental Congress or the state governments was popular consent. As Pauline Maier remarks in her discussion about the Declaration of Independence,

> nowhere in America was there an institution that, like Parliament, could claim the right to speak for the "whole community" without its specific authorization. Surely the Continental Congress had no such right: it was new and wholly dependent on grants of power from the states, where the effective authority of government was in all but a handful of cases exercised by extra-legal congresses or conventions that were themselves obliged to measure their acts against the will of those who elected them.

Consequently, Congress and the states had to rely on voluntary contributions by the people to pursue the struggle against Britain. Nevertheless, the recruitment of volunteers, enlisting only for a short period of time, was not an invention born by necessity. This was the form that wartime contingents had for a long time taken in colonial America.[10]

Apart from the occasional handful of border guards, the colonial governments possessed no professional troops of their own. However, the colonists did have some experience of raising and equipping troops for the wars between Britain and its European enemies. In the Seven Years' War, several colonies had raised soldiers by means of voluntary enlistment, normally for a short period of time and for a specific campaign. The number of men raised in this way could be substantial. In 1758, more than 20,000 Americans were under arms. As the short enlistment periods suggests, these men did not see enlistment as a career choice. Instead, they were mostly young men who enlisted for compensation in money or land that would allow them to buy a farm and start a family. In the words of one historian, military service "was a risk of life in the pursuit of a more encouraging future." The volunteer force was not a permanent army, contrary to the British army, nor was it an institution separated from the population at large. As soon as their enlistment periods were over, these "one-time" soldiers drifted back into civilian life.[11]

When in October 1775 a congressional committee suggested that an army of 20,000 men be created by means of voluntary one-year enlistments, it merely followed colonial practice. The committee believed that the main part of the army could be got simply by reenlisting the troops encamped outside Boston. These men, however, turned out to be unwilling to serve another term and marched home at the end of the year. Meanwhile, new recruits were slow to come forward and George Washington, commander-in-chief, found himself in an exposed situation, forced to form a new army before the eyes of the British. The eagerness of soldiers to return to civilian life and the reluctance of civilians to volunteer for army service left gaps in the ranks. These gaps were filled by militia units, which served for a specified and very short period of time, anything from two weeks to a few months, and only within a certain area—they normally refused to march beyond their own state. Within the first six months of the conflict with Britain, a pattern of recruitment was established that would plague Congress and the army leadership throughout the war. There would always be too few volunteers and the men who came forward were only ready to serve for short periods. Consequently, the army became dangerously undermanned, which left commanders no choice but to rely on the militia, a force they generally despised. In September 1776, Congress authorized an army of 75,000 men, but at no time during the war did the Continental Army contain even half that number.[12] Often enough, Washington's own command in the middle department was pitifully small. The actions at Trenton and Princeton, in the last few days of 1776, for instance, were undertaken because enlistment terms for most of the soldiers were coming to a close. Washington knew that on New Year's Day, no more than 1,500 men would remain in camp.[13]

The lack of recruits may lead one to believe that the American people were unwilling to contribute to the war effort at all. This conclusion, however, has to be qualified. According to one estimate, as much as half the male population capable of bearing arms may have served in some capacity and at some point during the War of Independence.[14] But the vast majority of these men were not willing to serve as long-term professional soldiers. In Europe, men did not volunteer for armed service primarily out of patriotic fervor but because limited options made the army a sufficiently attractive career choice. In this respect, America's relative prosperity left its government at a disadvantage. In a comparative perspective, America's "surplus" population of economically marginal men, the traditional source of army recruits, was not very large. Because there were other alternatives, there were few incentives to enlist. As Charles Royster writes, "able-bodied young men who sought their own material well-being above all else had alternatives better than service in the Continental Army. Privateering, farm labor, brief service as a militia substitute all offered more money, food, and physical comfort than regular army duty did."[15] But even if the root of the problem of mobilization was demographic and economic, the structure of government under the Articles of Confederation made the situation worse.

Although the Articles gave Congress the power to decide on the number of troops to be raised and to direct the states to mobilize them, it was the state governments that were responsible for recruitment. When a state received a congressional requisition for troops, it assigned the number of men to be raised by each county or town. This decentralization of mobilization was one factor that clogged recruitment. Two other elements were the existence of different terms and conditions of service and the reliance on voluntarism rather than coercion as the principle of recruitment. In addition to the demographic and economic aspects mentioned earlier, these factors made it difficult to mobilize enough men for the Continental Army.

Congress learned more or less immediately that patriotism alone would not procure an adequate supply of men to the Continental Army. In theory, Congress and the states had the option to rely on compulsory and universal conscription, but this was never a real alternative. As Thomas Jefferson said about conscription, it "ever was the most unpopular and impracticable thing that could be attempted. Our people even under monarchical government had learnt to consider it as the last of all oppressions." Instead, the guiding principle was to make armed service as far as possible a voluntary act. Hence, even when the states turned to drafts to fill their quotas, draftees were always offered the choice of finding a substitute or of paying a fine rather than serve in person. Obviously, this choice was only open to men of means, which had consequences for the social composition of the Continental Army. Significant as this may be, the most important consequence was that the draftee's option created a market where men willing to enlist could sell their services to men looking to hire a substitute. Inflation, poor pay, and lack of money meant that Congress could not offer soldiers attractive terms once they had enlisted. For this reason, the compensation earned when enlisting, the "enlistment bounty," was the only payment a recruit could be certain to receive. Obviously, the rational thing to do under such circumstances was to maximize the bounty and to minimize the term of enlistment. The different terms of service and the competition between buyers made it possible for potential volunteers to maximize the benefits of enlistment in precisely this way. Counties, towns, recruitment officers, draftees, and entrepreneurs were all bidding against each other for recruits. Whereas a volunteer enlisted for three years, a draftee, or his substitute, served only for one year. To make things worse for the Continental Army, there were also plenty of men anxious to avoid militia service on the lookout for substitutes. In this situation, a man willing to serve his country in arms had an excellent opportunity to make a good deal out of his patriotic commitment.[16]

Royster has aptly described the history of mobilization during the struggle for independence as an attempt by the people to buy "freedom from the demands of their own government." This observation has led historians to argue that the American people's apparent lack of political virtue was an issue of concern at the time.[17] A few years after the war had ended, however, when Federalists and Antifederalists clashed over the Constitution's military clauses, neither party appeared troubled by the lack of enthusiasm for armed service demonstrated by the American people. The Federalist concern was rather with the way that the structure of government made efficient recruitment impossible. Given the stress sometimes put on the influence of classical republicanism in America, it is well to remember that when writing the Constitution and struggling for its adoption, it was government, not the moral character of the American citizenry, that the Federalists hoped to reform.

Drafts did not help the states to raise the men demanded by Congress. Throughout the war, the divergence between the designated and the actual strength of the Continental Army continued to be great. Short enlistment periods meant that the army lacked permanence and experience. As noted, its numerical weakness forced the army command to rely on militia, a force still more transient and inexperienced. Inexperience affected the battlefield performance of the American soldier and, especially, the performance of the militiaman, and provided the Federalists with another important lesson when contemplating the future peace establishment of the union. Lack of experience may have mattered less if American commanders had been more imaginative and less orthodox in their tactical thinking. As it were, the army command never contemplated anything but a conventional campaign and consequently the experience of the British and German regulars paid off.[18] This in turn meant that the American army had to become more like the enemy army or perish. While the record of the Continental Army is unimpressive, its battle performance nevertheless improved as the army became more permanent and professional. This is not true of the militia. With the notable exception of Bunker Hill and Saratoga, the militia proved inefficient and unreliable in the pitched battles of the War of Independence.[19] As early as the Battle of Brooklyn Heights, Washington had come to the conclusion that the war could only be won by a "permanent standing army," dismissing the militia as a burden more than an asset. This was a position Washington would maintain throughout the war. A year before the decisive victory at Yorktown, he wrote that "I most firmly believe that the Independence of the United States will never be established till there is an Army on foot for the War."[20] Indeed to most of the officers who had served in the Continental Army, and to many of the Congressmen who had been involved in the administration of the war effort, the most important lesson from the War of Independence was that only a regular army could be relied on to do battle with regulars.[21]

II

No matter how obvious this conclusion may seem, this was a lesson that ran counter to the American political tradition. From the seventeenth century onward, English Country thinkers and politicians had warned about the danger of professional armies to the preservation of popular liberty. The colonists were familiar with such antiarmy rhetoric, but as long as no regiments were permanently posted in North America there was little reason to employ it. The deployment of troops in the colonies after the Seven Years' War changed this situation and from the "Boston massacre" until well after the adoption of the Constitution, the antiarmy argument was an integrated part of American political rhetoric. In fact, most military historians agree that antiarmy sentiments drawn from Country thought dominated popular attitudes toward military institutions in revolutionary America.[22]

According to the most influential treatment of Country thought, this tradition encompassed a classical, "essentially Greek," conception of citizenship, which saw the true citizen as a man of property standing free from all forms of dependence. One of the most important elements of this conception of the citizen was his readiness to appear in arms for the defense of his country. In practice, this ideal was realized through service in the militia, "whereby the public defence is exercised directly by the independent proprietors appearing in arms at their own charge."[23] Even if Country thought dominated American political rhetoric, actual military institutions did not conform to the principles of the Country tradition. Starting in the late seventeenth century, the militia began to be replaced by volunteer forces in military campaigns. These forces were not made up of freeholders but of men with little or no property. In this respect, the Continental Army was no different.[24]

The fact that military forces in America were not made up of citizen-soldiers has led some scholars to conclude that they had more in common with the standing armies of Europe that Country thinkers feared so much than with the citizen-army they cherished.[25] Implicit in this argument is the idea that the American people and their governments had come to accept a reliance on professional troops. Such a conclusion, however, disregards what the Country ideology took as the defining feature of the standing army. The crucial point about the standing army was not that it was composed of socially marginal men but that it was a force "permanently embodied and kept 'standing' even in time of peace."[26] With the establishment of the standing army in *peacetime*, soldiering became a profession. Soldiers were set apart from the rest of society and were governed by a separate law, which disregarded many important rights held by British subjects.[27] The most problematic aspect of this development, however, was that soldiers were molded into creatures who owed allegiance only to the Crown. By this means, the executive power was greatly strengthened at the expense of the other parts of the British government. In short, the problem with the standing army was not that it brought about the moral corruption of the citizen but that it upset the balance of power between the prince and the people.[28]

With independence, the duty to provide for American peacetime defense devolved from the British government to the union. But, rather than provide for a peace establishment, Congress dissolved the Continental Army and relied on ad hoc solutions to meet the union's military needs. Hence, at one point in 1783, the military strength of the United States was down to some eighty men, commanded by a captain. A state without military power appears an anomaly. Yet in the American context it can be argued that complete demobilization was no more than a return to normality. Except for a few border guards, colonial governments had not kept up troops in peacetime. The wars against France, Spain, and the Indian nations had begun as surprise attacks, followed by mobilization, perhaps also British involvement, and retaliation. There were no troops kept up as a deterrent to potential aggressors.[29] In the long perspective, the British regulars posted in America after the Seven Years' War could be regarded as no more than an unfortunate parenthesis.

Nevertheless, it was obvious to the delegates to Congress that the independent United States had military needs, however limited. In 1783, a congressional committee presented a plan for a peace establishment. Had it been accepted, it would have provided the United States with a small permanent army. Instead, disagreement among the states combined with traditional Country fears of centralized power and standing armies to kill the plan. Even so, delegates to Congress did agree that some troops had to be raised at least to guard against the Indian nations along the Ohio River. But, rather than attempt to create a long-term plan for the union's defense, Congress opted for a temporary solution. It created the First Regiment by requesting altogether 700 men from Connecticut, New York, New Jersey, and Pennsylvania. Soldiers were recruited through voluntary enlistment and the term of service was a mere year.[30]

It can be argued that the First Regiment was a success and that the system of requisitions now allowed Congress and the states to answer the defensive needs of the union in a concerted effort. The postwar economic slump and the resumption of emigration meant that it was possible to fill the ranks and when enlistment periods were up, a surprising number of soldiers chose to reenlist for a three-year period.[31] When the Constitutional convention met in May 1787, these 700 men made up the United States army. To the men who convened in Philadelphia and to the men and women who would later support the Constitution, Congress's military weakness was one of the issues that appeared most critical to the future of the union. Their reasons for thinking this may seem a natural reaction to the diminutive size of the army. Admittedly, 700 appears small for an army protecting a nation as large and populous as the United States. It is also true that the army was too weak either to appease the Indians or to keep out squatters in the Northwest territory. Even so, this was years before Arthur St. Clair's army was destroyed by an Indian confederacy on the banks of the Wabash River and there was no acute danger of invasion from either Spain or Britain. If the colonial tradition not to maintain peacetime armies is also considered, it seems necessary to ask precisely why it was so important for the union to increase its military capacity.

III

The traditional question regarding the military clauses of the Constitution has been whether or not the Federalist believed in "militarism." Antifederalists and, later on, Democratic-Republicans accused the Federalists of wishing to establish a standing army in peacetime and to base government on coercion rather than consent. These accusations have been picked up by historians who view Federalists as elitist and undemocratic.[32] As far as the debate over ratification goes, however, the first Antifederalist claim can be accepted only with qualifications, whereas the second has no support at all. It is necessary to enter a caveat here. Obviously, it would be naive to expect Federalists to openly profess their wish to govern by military coercion. There is simply no way to reach final certitude about what individual Federalists privately thought about this matter.[33] But Federalists were nevertheless ready to make a number of claims during the ratification debate that challenged the strong antiarmy sentiment prevailing in America. They spoke about the need to possess professional troops in peacetime; they criticized the militia; and they defended the use of military force to put down domestic disturbances. However, they also rejected the claim that the Constitution would establish a government of force and they never suggested anything other than that the peacetime army would be very small and garrisoned out of sight of the people. But if greater military power was not needed to strengthen the position of the national government vis-à-vis the people, what was it for?

Federalists answered this question in part with talk of national pride. Stronger government would make the United States "a great and respectable nation,"[34] restoring "that consequence and respectability abroad, which have been lost since the days of Saratoga and York."[35] But most of their rhetoric pointed to more material benefits that would follow from a stronger position in international relations. A stronger state was important in this context, because economic prosperity and government strength were closely interdependent. During their struggle against Britain, Americans had been told that "peace and independence would reward your toil, and that riches would accompany the establishment of your liberties, by opening a wider market, and consequently raising the price of such commodities as America produces for exportation."[36] Yet it was the case "that being free by the rights of independence, from the constraints, fetters and prohibitions, which the metropolis used to impose on our agriculture, our industry and our commerce," America was nevertheless "really more unhappy" than when she formed part of the British Empire.[37]

It is difficult to arrive at a certain verdict on postwar economic performance, in part because the period is little researched but also because there is too little reliable data and considerable regional variations.[38] Nevertheless, economic historians now tend to believe that something "truly disastrous" happened to the American economy between 1775 and 1790.[39] It is certainly the case that the Federalists presented the situation as an economic crisis and stronger government as its solution.[40] This argument is best seen as a reaction to the expulsion of the newly independent states from the British common market, which straddled the Atlantic. This market was upheld by the Navigation Acts dating from the seventeenth century, which regulated trade within the first British Empire in three ways: First, the Navigation Acts reserved the carrying trade to British vessels, excluding all other nations; second, they "enumerated" certain goods, such as tobacco and sugar, which meant that these items had to be sent to Britain before being shipped to the Continent; and third, they made sure that the imports into the different parts of the empire came mainly from other parts of the empire. Thus, for instance, Britain imported goods from the colonies and vice versa. Although the Navigation Acts were criticized in the colonies when employed to raise revenue, trade regulations were otherwise accepted. The Acts were beneficial to the colonists because they treated Americans as Englishmen and therefore shielded American merchants from foreign competition. Hence, there seems to have been no indication before 1776 that the colonists wished to become economically independent from the mother country. As one commentator notes, "Americans willingly accepted the British mercantilist system under which they had prospered and were content to continue living within its confines."[41]

No matter how much the colonies benefited from their participation in the imperial common market, the promotion of colonial prosperity was never the primary purpose of Britain's commercial regulations. Rather, these aimed at enhancing the position of Great Britain in the European power struggle. Britain's mercantilist policies responded to a system of trade organized on the understanding that international relations were a "zero-sum" game: Relations between states could be reduced to a competition for advantage and what one nation gained, another lost. Britain's mercantilist policies therefore at the same time aimed at promoting the wealth of Britain and at reducing the wealth of other nations. The function of colonies in this system was to enhance the wealth and power of the mother country by providing it with markets and raw materials.[42]

When the War of Independence ended, Americans acted as if exchange between America and Britain would resume the prewar pattern. The basic structure of American trade has of course long been recognized: The colonies exported raw materials and foodstuffs, and imported consumer goods, both manufactures and eat- and drinkables.[43] Although this picture remains true, recent research has added two important particulars to our knowledge of the early American economy. First, market integration in the second half of the eighteenth century was far more extensive than has previously been appreciated. It is now believed that fluctuations in international trade left virtually no American unaffected. This of course meant that the regulation of commerce was one of the most important ways in which the government influenced the well-being of its citizens.[44] Second, even though the annual value of colonial imports exceeded the value of exports by more than a million pounds, or well over a third of the total value of exports, it is no longer believed that the colonies suffered a deficit in their balance of trade. Rather, balance of trade was achieved through the extensive involvement of American merchants and ship owners, primarily from the northern and middle states, in providing shipping and commercial services in the Atlantic economy. In other words, the carrying trade contributed a significant share of overall American income.[45]

While Americans resumed importation from Britain as soon as the war ended,[46] other commercial activities were more difficult to revive. This was because America was no longer a full member of the "interdependent multilateral trading system" that made up the Atlantic economy. There had always been much bilateral trade between Britain and the colonies, but important incomes also came from the triangular trade where the American mainland made up one angle; the West Indies, the Wine Islands, and the Iberian peninsula the second; and Britain the third. The need for carriers and other commercial services that arose from this trade provided New Englanders, Pennsylvanians, and New Yorkers with much needed incomes.[47] After independence, however, Britain restricted American access to the trading system of the empire. American products that were strategically important to Britain's economic and maritime interests continued to be favorably treated. Products that the remaining British colonies or Britain itself could supply, by contrast, were banned from entering Britain. Thus, the British West Indies was closed to American ships and to some American products, while American trade with Canada, Nova Scotia, and Newfoundland was also restricted. Finally, British subjects were prohibited from buying ships in America, where one-third of the British merchant marine had been built before the war.[48] The policies pursued by Britain were all the more important as Spain and France, far from offering Americans new markets, pursued similar restrictive policies.[49]

Britain's policies may or may not have made economic sense. Their purpose, however, was not to promote the British economy for its own sake. Before the era of free trade, commercial advantage was inseparably intertwined with military strength. Britain's position both as a commercial and a military world power rested on its command of the seas. The maintenance of a navy that could secure this command cost immense sums, while at the same time the skills required to construct and operate a man of war were not very different from the skills required in the merchant marine. For this reason, Britain's merchant sailors and civilian shipyards can be aptly described as the nation's naval reserve, allowing the sharp shifts between the Royal Navy's peacetime and wartime capacity. When the American colonies were lost to the British Empire, it became necessary to replace that part of Britain's prewar naval capacity that now belonged to the United States. This was done by discriminating against American ships and shipyards.[50]

American troubles did not end with Britain's Navigation Acts. A struggle over the expansion of the United States into the trans-Appalachian West also underlined Congress's need to defend the integrity and interests of the union against European ambitions. Western Pennsylvania, Kentucky, and Tennessee were rich and expanding, but the area suffered from one major drawback. Because of the mountains, the trading routes followed the waterways in a north-south direction. This meant that American trade had to pass through British-held Quebec or Spanish-held New Orleans. That trade also had to move on rivers exposed to attack from the Indian nations north and west of the Ohio River. It is important to realize that access to markets was no superficial aspect of western settlement. Because market integration was well developed, access to markets determined the future of the region. Without markets, there would be no American settlements west of the mountains. This, of course, was precisely what Spain and Britain wished to achieve. In the 1780s, neither of them had given up their ambitions in the American interior. Hence, they posed a threat to the sovereignty of the United States both by inducing their Indian allies to attack American settlers and by encouraging those settlers to secede and become subjects of Spain or Britain. When Spain closed the Mississippi River to American trade in 1784, the future of the union's presence in the region became precarious. Three years later, this issue still awaited its resolution.[51]

IV

Clearly, Britain no less than Spain had important economic and military reasons to squeeze American trade out of existence. Consequently, the United States failed to make Britain open her markets to American trade, just as it failed to make Spain open the Mississippi River to American navigation. To the Federalists, America was still kept "under the slavery" of Europe's "prohibitive laws" in 1787.[52] To change this, two structural deficiencies in the confederation had to be rectified. First, as long as Congress could not enforce treaties, neither Britain nor anyone else was likely to treat with the United States. The Constitution dealt with this by making treaties "the supreme Law of the Land" and by creating a federal judiciary.[53] The second deficiency consisted in the weakness of the national government, which prevented it from retaliating against the adversarial policies of other states. There was no incentive for foreign powers to make commercial treaties with the United States as long as "the imbecility of our Government enables them to derive many advantages from our trade, without granting us any return."[54] When American envoys had approached the British government to secure a commercial treaty, they had been told that Britain "derived greater profits from the present situation of our commerce than we could expect under a treaty; and you have no kind of power that can compel us to surrender any advantage to you." Another British insult came from Lord Sheffield who, in his widely circulated *Observations on the Commerce of the American States*, had said that the United States was not and "should not be, for a long time, either to be feared or regarded as a nation."[55]

First and foremost, retaliation demanded that Congress be able to direct the policies of the union and to keep recalcitrant state legislatures in line. But ultimately any attempt at retaliation also had to be backed by military strength. This was especially true if not only a future army but a navy, too, was taken into account.[56] If the United States could only "unite under one head, and bring to one point, the resources, strength and commerce of this extensive country,"[57] it would gain "respectability abroad in the eyes of foreign nations,"[58] for the geopolitical situation of the United States offered not only risks but also opportunities. The possessions of European states on the American continent and, especially, the vicinity to their profitable colonies in the West Indies made Spain, France, and Britain vulnerable to American attack. When arguing about the Mississippi question, Federalists were explicit about the interconnection between military strength and commercial advantage. As George Nicholas pointed out, because the national government under the Constitution would be "more powerful and respectable, it will be more feared; and as they will have more power to injure Spain, Spain will be more inclined to do them justice, by yielding it, or by giving them an adequate compensation."[59]

But the connection between commerce and military capacity also existed in another and more roundabout way. Federalists did not argue in favor of aggressive warfare, but they did suggest that in a future conflict between European powers—and in all likelihood it was only a question of time before such a conflict would erupt[60]—the support of the United States would be decisive to its outcome in the Western hemisphere. "While they contend for their American possessions," David Ramsay said, "those whom the United States favor will be favored, and those whom they chuse to depress will be depressed."[61] If America could only stand united and strong, therefore, foreign nations would be "much more disposed to cultivate our friendship, than provoke our resentment."[62] Indeed, could this be achieved a "price would be set not only on our friendship, but upon our neutrality."[63] In such a position, there would be no difficulty securing trade concessions through treaties. "The respectable figure you will make among the nations," one Federalist promised, "will so far command the attention of foreign powers, that it is probable you will soon obtain such commercial treaties, as will open to your vessels the West-India islands, and give life to your expiring commerce."[64]

In 1787, nominal political independence may have been won, but the national government created by the Articles of Confederation was too weak to defend American interests abroad. This was especially true about overseas trade, with significant consequences for the vast majority of the American people. By the late 1780s, it had become clear to many Americans that the national government was too feeble to ensure the well-being of the people. To some, the nation now appeared more dependent on Europe than before the break with Britain. "Once we were dependant only on Great Britain," Oliver Ellsworth wrote, "now we are dependant on every petty state in the world and on every custom house officer of foreign ports."[65] As another Federalist asked: "Where is the port worth visiting from whence we are not utterly excluded or loaded with duties and customs sufficient to absorb the whole?"

> Where is the port in the British dominions which deigns to receive a wandering American? Wandering I say, because full of enterprise and yet unable to find an asylum from the storm of bankruptcy. Have we fought and bled, have we conquered and loaded ourselves with the trophies of this potent king, and yet shall we be by him condemned to beg our bread; while his subjects, in full sail, are entering every port, choosing their own market, and carrying away the fat of the land? They are growing rich by our industry, and we poor, because unable to withstand their power.[66]

6

INDEPENDENCE, COMMERCE, AND MILITARY STRENGTH

The Constitution redistributed military power between the states and the national government. Under the Articles of Confederation, Congress had to raise armies by means of requisitions on the states, whereas the Constitution gave the national government the means to do so directly and on its own authority.[1] The Constitution also extended the power of the national government over the militia, by giving it the right to "provide for organizing, arming, and disciplining, the Militia, and for governing such Part of them as may be employed in the Service of the United States," as well as the right to use it "to execute the Laws of the Union, suppress Insurrections and repel Invasions."[2] As in the Confederation articles, the Constitution prohibited the states from keeping up troops without the consent of Congress.[3] Congress's power to raise and maintain armies was unrestricted and more than anything else, it was the right to establish a standing army in *peacetime* that provoked the greatest opposition to the Constitution's military clauses. If Congress established an army and used its power over the militia to disarm the people, it would in effect hold a monopoly on armed force in the nation. By altering the distribution of military strength between the government and the people in this way, the national government could make itself independent of the people. Ultimately, this would lead to the end of liberty in America.

Chapter 7 will look more closely at Antifederalist objections to the military clauses of the Constitution. Here, the concern is only with the proposals for amendments to the Constitution, which Antifederalists suggested, or which Federalists suggested as concessions to Antifederalist objections. The purpose of this chapter is to address the question of why the Federalists refused to accept limits to the Constitution's army clauses. When the first Congress presented the states with the proposal for what would become the Bill of Rights, this contained a guarantee against the disarmament of the people, as well as a specification of what was involved in Congress's power to govern state militias. It also contained a restriction on the right of the national government to quarter troops in private houses. The first ten amendments, however, made no attempt to restrict the national government's right to raise an army. This, of course, was not because of oversight. Neither James Madison, nor anyone else present at the first Congress, could have been unaware of the strong reservations Antifederalists had expressed against the unlimited power to raise and maintain armies, which the Constitution vested in Congress. This power was central to the national state that the Federalists attempted to form, and in the debate over ratification they made clear why no limits could be placed on Congress's power of military mobilization.

I

The Antifederalists accepted that the defense of the union was a duty belonging to Congress rather than the states. They also accepted that all nation-states had to have the power to raise and maintain regular troops. "In the present state of mankind, and of conducting war," one of them wrote, "the government of every nation must have power to raise and keep up regular troops."[4] They even accepted the need for troops to garrison frontier posts and to guard arsenals.[5] Nevertheless, their antipathy to standing armies in time of peace was very strong and the belief that they threatened liberty was regarded as "a kind of axiom."[6] In the Constitutional Convention, Elbridge Gerry had drawn attention to the absence of any restriction on the establishment of peacetime standing armies in the Constitution and he had warned that "the people were jealous on this head, and great opposition to the plan would spring from such an omission."[7] Once the Constitution became public, Antifederalists tried to amend it in order to place limits on Congress's power to raise armies and also to restrict its command over the militia. These amendments were of two kinds: either proposals for a bill of rights to be added as a whole to the Constitution, or proposals for amendments to the actual body of the Constitution itself. With regard to restrictions on the establishment of peacetime armies, these stipulations in the bills of rights were recommendatory rather than outright prohibitions, typically using the word "ought" where the amendments used "shall."[8] The declaration of rights proposed by the Virginia convention, which was based on Virginia's own Declaration of Rights, may serve as an example of the first type of proposal. It was followed by New York and North Carolina, whereas a slightly different version had earlier been provided by Antifederalists in the Pennsylvania convention. Section seventeen of the Virginia proposal declares

> That the people have a right to keep and bear arms; that a well regulated militia composed of the body of the people trained to arms, is the proper,

natural and safe defence of a free state. That standing armies in time of peace are dangerous to liberty, and therefore ought to be avoided, as far as the circumstances and protection of the community will admit; and that in all cases, the military should be under strict subordination to and governed by the civil power.[9]

The second type of proposal, which comprised true amendment proposals, originated in individual Antifederalist writers, as well as in ratifying conventions. Among them were suggestions to continue the system of requisitions and to allow a fixed quorum of the state legislatures the right to disapprove of them; to stipulate the exact number of troops that could be raised through direct levy;[10] and to define precisely the purposes for which regular troops could be lawfully employed in peacetime.[11] In some of the ratifying conventions, Antifederalists tried to limit the period of enlistment to avoid creating a permanent class of soldiers,[12] and demanded that no soldiers be quartered in private houses in peacetime without the consent of the owner.[13] By far the most common suggestion for amending the Constitution, however, was that a qualified majority of members present in both houses be necessary to raise an army in time of peace. Thus, the Virginia convention's ninth amendment proposal was that "no standing army or regular troops shall be raised, or kept up in time of peace without the consent of two-thirds of the members present in both houses."[14] Such proposals reflected the requirement under the Articles of Confederation that the consent of the delegations of nine states be necessary for Congress to make requisitions for troops.[15]

Although it may be argued that had this amendment been accepted, Congress's power over mobilization would have been similar to that of the Confederation Congress, this would not be quite true. Contrary to the Confederation Congress, the members of the House of Representatives would not be appointed by the state legislatures. Senators, admittedly, would and so could be held to be more liable to control by the state legislatures. But the Senate, as is well known, was the object of intense dislike on the part of most Antifederalists.[16] The Antifederalist proposal therefore seems to run counter to their frequent rejection of the Federalist claim that Congress would represent the American people. Nevertheless, it would seem that a qualified majority in Congress could serve as a stopgap measure until such time as representation could be increased. Even if constituencies of thirty thousand inhabitants would only rarely be able to return representatives possessing "similar feeling, views and interests" as the common people, a two-thirds majority would give the "democratic members" in Congress "some tolerable chance of a reasonable negative, in behalf of the numerous, important, and democratic part of the community."[17]

When it came to the militia, the Antifederalist attempt to restrict Congress's power had two different goals. On the one hand, they wished to restrict Congress's use of the militia. The importance of such restrictions stemmed from the fact that for white men the duty to serve in the militia was more or less universal. For this reason, the government commanding the militia in effect commanded all white males between the age of sixteen and sixty. As one Antifederalist noted, the militia "when properly formed, are in fact the people themselves."[18] Specifically, Antifederalists wanted service outside the militia's home state, at least for any extended period of time, to be dependent on the consent of the state legislature. They ascribed great weight to this question.[19] In effect, it would give the states a veto on the national government's employment of the militia. They also tried to achieve restrictions on the extension of martial law to the militia,[20] and protection for conscientious objectors.[21] On the other hand, Antifederalists sought to establish a prohibition on Congress's right to disarm the people,[22] and at the same time also to provide protection against Congressional *neglect* to organize, arm, and discipline the militia.[23] The purpose of these amendments was to retain a military capacity in the states and in the citizenry in order to counterbalance the coercive power of the national government.

As the federal Bill of Rights suggests, the Federalists could accept many of the proposed restrictions on Congress's power over the militia, something that reflects their belief that this institution was of only limited importance to the national state they wished to create. When it came to the power to raise and maintain armies, however, their only concession concerned the quartering of soldiers. Yet a reader of the ratification debate looks in vain for a discussion and dismissal of the Antifederalist demand that the decision to raise an army ought to require the support of a qualified majority of Congress. Instead, the Federalists argued as if the Antifederalists had demanded an absolute prohibition against standing armies in time of peace. Although in part this may well have been a tactical choice, one may also note that the important early Antifederalist responses to the Constitution could be read as a complete ban on peacetime troops.[24] Furthermore, as has been pointed out earlier, the aversion to standing armies was an ingrained principle in American political thought and institutional arrangements. Regardless of the reason, however, it is clear that the debate over the Constitution's army clauses differed from the debate over the taxation clauses in that the Federalists neglected to address the real Antifederalist amendment proposal.

To the Federalists, the question of a peacetime standing army was simple. Congress was responsible for the union's defense and therefore had to possess the means to secure that end.[25] They dismissed the Antifederalist objection to peacetime standing armies as a mistaken attempt to apply a restriction on the executive power in the British system of government to the legislative branch in the American system. Clearly, it was an adequate safeguard against any encroachments on liberty that the power to raise a peacetime army, and to vote the appropriations needed to support it, was vested in Congress, a body that the Federalists claimed was popularly appointed and dependent on the people. In Britain, Oliver Ellsworth said, it was necessary to contain the power of the hereditary monarch by vesting the "sword" in the king and the "purse" in Parliament. "But does it follow," he asked,

> because it is dangerous to give the power of the sword and the purse to a hereditary prince, who is independent of the people, that therefore, it is dangerous to give it to the parliament, to congress which is your parliament, to men appointed by yourselves, and dependent on your-selves? This argument amounts to this, you must cut a man in two in the middle to prevent his hurting himself.[26]

In order to provide for the nation's security against foreign aggression the "powers requisite for attaining it, must be effectually confided to the federal councils."[27] This would be achieved by the Constitution through the es-tablishment of direct rule of the national government over the individual citizens of the United States.

Federalists were extremely critical of the system of requisitions that Congress had relied on during the struggle against Britain. To them, gov-ernment under the Articles of Confederation provided ample and "mel-ancholy" testimony of the inability "to obtain by requisitions supplies to the fœderal treasury or recruits to the fœderal armies."[28] During the War of Independence, the system had proved to be equally wanting in justice, economy and efficiency. Thus, whereas states threatened by the enemy did what they could to comply with federal requisitions, those distant from the theatre of war ignored Congress's call.[29] Because the states rather than Congress were responsible for recruitment, a competition ensued between the states for men who were willing to serve, which forced the states to "outbid each other, till bounties grew to an enormous and insupportable size." Potential soldiers delayed their enlistment in the hope of greater gain, and the hope of reenlisting for an additional bounty encouraged enrollment for the shortest possible period. Finally, the system repeatedly led to inefficiency and friction, resulting in

> slow and scanty levies of men in the most critical emergencies of our affairs—short inlistments at an unparalleled expence—continual fluc-tuations in the troops, ruinous to their discipline, and subjecting the public safety frequently to the perilous crisis of a disbanded army— Hence also those oppressive expedients for raising men which were upon several occasions practiced, and which nothing but the enthusiasm of liberty would have induced the people to endure.[30]

In fact, the structural deficiency of the national government had prolonged the war at great expense and suffering, and had ultimately jeopardized its very outcome.[31] The conclusion was obvious: the "fallacious scheme of quotas and requisitions" ought to be discarded "as equally impracticable and unjust."[32]

Federalists found "a manifest inconsistency" inherent in the Articles of Confederation in that they devolved "upon the Fœderal Government the care of the general defence" but left "in the State governments the *effective* powers, by which it is to be provided for."[33] For this reason, it was necessary to reform the federal system by transferring the power to provide for the defense of the union from the states to Congress. Although Congressional requisitions were constitutionally binding under the Confederation articles, in practice the states were free to disregard them.[34] Many states responded to requisitions with contempt or neglect and they would continue to do so "as long as their consent and inclination would be the only criterion of their grants."[35] The reason was obvious. "A bare sense of duty, or a regard to propriety is too feeble to induce men to comply with obligations," James Marshall noted. "We deceive ourselves if we expect any efficacy from these."[36] Edmund Randolph stated this objection with even greater force. "No government can be stable," he said, "which hangs on human inclination alone, unbiassed by the fear of coercion."[37] What was needed, therefore, was to equip the national government with the means to sanction its decisions. There were two ways in which this could be done. The states could retain the control over the mobilization of men if the national government was granted the right to coerce delinquent states. This option, however, was likely to lead to bloodshed and social discord. The alternative, which was the option favored by the Federalists, was to grant Congress the right to raise an army independent of the states by giving it the power to "extend the authority of the union to the persons of the citizens."[38]

On paper the introduction of direct rule by the national government might have consisted "much less in the addition of NEW POWERS to the Union, than in the invigoration of its ORIGINAL POWERS" through "a more effectual mode of administering them."[39] Yet, it seems clear, and it certainly seemed so to the Antifederalists, that this was a complete change in the allocation of power between the states and the national government. To the Antifederalists, peacetime standing armies might be necessary in certain cases, but as far as possible they should be avoided as the bane of liberty. In Antifederalist rhetoric, the conceptual link between standing armies and absolutist rule remained intact. To the Federalists, by contrast, the United States appeared in need of adequate military strength, both to ward off external and internal threats and to assert America's place as a commercial republic in a hostile world. Federalists therefore had to adopt a different position than their opponents regarding the relationship between military power and free government. In a way similar to the development of the Court argument in Britain, the Federalists transcended the Country view that standing armies meant the end of liberty. In the end, the Federalists came to see standing armies as a necessary means to safeguard the independence and liberty of the United States rather than as a threat to free government.

II

The accession of William and Mary after the Glorious Revolution led to England's entry into European power politics. Although the Revolution was a reaction against the growth of royal power and state expansion, paradoxically the engagement on the Continent led to rapid state growth. British foreign policy in this period was far more aggressive than it had been in earlier periods, yet it was perceived as, or at least presented as, a defense of English liberties and the Protestant religion against the threats of slavery and popery. The perception that Britain's religion and system of government were threatened originated in the weak dynastic claims of the late Stuarts and the Hanoverians to the English Crown. Parliament's decision to depose James II and disinherit his son was made on doubtful constitutional grounds. Things did not improve when both Mary and her sister Anne failed to produce an heir and it seemed that the Crown would pass to a Catholic prince. In order to ensure Protestant succession, Parliament passed the Act of Settlement, settling the right to the English Crown with Sophia of Hanover, a granddaughter of James I. In doing so, more than sixty relations to Anne, all with a stronger dynastic right than Sophia, were passed over. Although the grounds for deposing James and for adopting the Act of Settlement were overtly religious, they may with equal justice be regarded as political. In the minds of most Englishmen, Catholicism and absolutist rule were inseparable. Thus, it was generally believed that the restoration of a Catholic prince to the throne of England would lead to absolute monarchy.[40]

It is doubtful if the dynastic right of the Stuarts was a threat to Britain's postrevolution political order in itself. But the dynastic quarrel became part of power politics when France backed the Stuart claim. At the Treaty of Ryswick, Louis XIV had to recognize William III as the rightful ruler of England, but France nevertheless continued to give support to the Stuart pretenders. In 1708, 1715, and 1745, expeditionary forces landed in Scotland with the aim to restore the Stuart monarchy. In 1717, 1719, 1720–21, 1743–44, and even as late as 1754, rumors circulated in Britain about an impending Jacobite invasion. These invasions and invasion scares, coupled with the recurrent wars against France, served as a reminder to Britons that their political system and established religion could not be taken for granted.[41]

It is against this background that the Court party's reformulation of the relationship between the military strength of the state and the preservation of liberty has to be seen. For some Englishmen, it came to seem that it was in fact the development of a "fiscal-military state" that had preserved Protestantism and English liberty against the ambitions of the Stuart pretenders and the French Crown. Contrary to what the Country argument held, heavy taxes, large armies, and a growing public debt were not so much a threat as a necessary price to pay for freedom. Thus, when the establishment of a peacetime army was attacked by Country writers and politicians after the War of the League of Augsburg, Court writers could respond by asking, with reference to James II, "whether 'tis not more certain, considering all things, that HE will Invade us, or attempt to Invade us, if we have no Land-Force for our defence, then that the Land-Force we may provide for that purpose will Invade our Privileges and Liberties?"[42] The state and its impositions was still regarded as an evil by Court sympathizers, but it was a necessary, or lesser, evil, intended to ward off a greater one. As one Member of Parliament said in 1690:

> Our dear bought experience has taught us what Vast Taxes are absolutely necessary to maintain the armies and Fleet, which are requisite for our security; and for the defence of our religious and civil rights; and provided that we attain those ends, it will not be thought, at long run, we have bought them any too dear. In this case we may say, *diminium plus toto.* A wise and good man will rather chuse (if it comes to that pass) to enjoy one half of his estate, with the liberty of his conscience and the preserve of his birthright, than to possess a double or treble proportion of his riches, whilst his mind must be enslaved to superstition, of knavish and interested priests, his innocent friends and countrymen sacrificed to the idol of arbitrary power (as we have seen lately practiced) and the title that is left him in his own possession and Liberty, only precarious and during pleasure.[43]

By the middle of the eighteenth century, the broad majority of the political nation had reached an accommodation with the understanding that an army could be the defender rather than the destroyer of independence and liberty. Thus, in a sermon on "Britain's happiness" in 1759, even a radical like Richard Price could speak of the glory and virtue of British soldiers and sailors and hold up their sacrifice as an example to be emulated by all true patriots.[44]

It should be noted that even though the Court party always defended the need for the British state to possess a powerful military and fiscal capacity, this did not mean that they were eager for war. War tapped a state's strength. Hence, a powerful fiscal-military apparatus served its purpose not only when a state went to war but perhaps better when it deterred attack and when it was used to threaten other states into making commercial concessions. Robert Walpole, the primary example of a Court politician, established the sinking fund to reduce the public debt and introduced his excise scheme to reduce the tax pressure on the landed classes. Walpole also aimed to keep Britain out of war and, when trouble arose with Spain, he went to war only reluctantly. Had his policies been successful, the growth of the British state would have slowed down. By contrast, a politician like the elder Pitt, who often took a Country stance, pursued the Seven Years' War with great energy and immense sums of money. The war almost doubled the public debt and it increased the peacetime army by 10,000 men. The need for fiscal reforms to cover increased costs led the British state to expand its fiscal power to the American colonies, with well-known results.[45] Finally, it should also be noted that far from always opposing aggressive policies and large-scale war, the broad layers of the population often demonstrated their support for them, although they would inevitably lead to state expansion.[46]

III

To the Federalists, it was obvious that if the national government had the duty to defend the union and its interests, it also had to possess the right to raise and maintain armies. The power to raise and keep up armies was essential to governments and Federalists regarded a "government without the power of defense" as "a solecism."[47] In *The Federalist*, Madison noted that a standing army had become an intrinsic part of the modern state. "If one nation maintains constantly a disciplined army ready for the service of ambition or revenge, it obliges the most pacific nations, who may be within the reach of its enterprizes, to take corresponding precautions."[48] The Antifederalists, as we have seen, had no difficulty with granting Congress the right to establish a regular force in time of war. To the Federalists, however, this was not sufficient. They also pointed to the necessity to maintain an "appearance of strength in a season of the most profound tranquility,"[49] that is, to keep up a standing army in peacetime.

The notion, expressed in the state bills of rights as well as in Antifederalist amendment proposals, that the American republic could trust its defense solely, or even primarily, to the militia appeared plainly unrealistic and dangerous to the Federalists. "This doctrine in substance had like to have lost us our independence," wrote an incensed Alexander Hamilton. "It cost millions to the United States, that might have been saved. The facts, which from our own experience forbid a reliance of this kind, are too recent to permit us to be the dupes of such a suggestion."[50] Ordinary citizens, who made up the militia, were "unacquainted with the hardships, and unskilled in the discipline of war." It could hardly be expected that "men only inured to the peaceable occupations of domestic life, encounter with success, the most skilful veterans, inured to the fatigues and toils of campaigns."[51] In fact, as the war against Britain had demonstrated beyond all doubt, they did not. In the Virginia convention, General Henry Lee recalled the militia's record at the Battle of Guilford Courthouse. Whereas the Continentals "behaved there with the most gallant intrepedity," the militia broke and ran, abandoning the regulars and causing American defeat. Had the militia stood their ground at Guilford, said Lee, that battle would have ended the war. Nor was Guilford the only instance when the militia broke before the British and the German veterans. Lee could have enumerated "many instances" offering "incontrovertible evidence that the militia cannot always be relied on."[52] In the modern age, amateur soldiers simply could not stand up to professional soldiers. War, said Hamilton, was now "a science to be acquired and perfected by diligence, by perseverance, by time, and by practice." Hence, "the steady operations of war against a regular and disciplined army can only be successfully conducted by a force of the same kind."[53] The choice whether or not to rely on regular troops or on militia was simply not for Americans to make. It had already been made for them centuries ago by the monarchs of Europe. A nation could no longer expect to survive unless it possessed a proper peace establishment. Therefore, the American republic faced the stark choice between accepting dependency on a peace establishment of regulars or risk its independence.[54]

The Federalist analysis of the European state system, of which the newly independent United States formed a part, suggested that a weak state was destined to become the victim of the stronger members of the system. There were nations "whose interest is incompatible with an extension of our power and who are jealous of our resources to become powerful and wealthy," Madison argued. These "must naturally be inclined to exert every means to prevent our becoming formidable." Oliver Ellsworth, too, described the nations of Europe as "not friendly" toward the United States. "They were pleased to see us disconnected from Great Britain; they are pleased to see us disunited among ourselves." Others believed that Europe's aversion stemmed not only from the material and demographic strength of the United States but also from the nation's "spirit of liberty," with its promise of popular freedom and an end to tyrannical government. Threatened by this spirit, the monarchs of the Old World would consider ending the republican experiment by partitioning the union. "It is certainly the interest of the powers of Europe to suppress that spirit of liberty which their subjects began to imbibe from America, where it has been the glorious instrument of a revolution which they have heard of with admiration and envy," wrote "A Freeholder." "The partition of America would undoubtedly establish the monarchies of Europe in their thrones and deter any nation from ever making another attempt to bring about a revolution."[55] The hostile nations Federalists were talking about had dominions to the north and south of the union, while in the west they fuelled the animosity of the Indian nations.[56] There was, then, a real, if limited, threat to the territorial integrity and political existence of the United States. As James Wilson pointed out, "we are not in the millennium. Wars may happen."[57]

Without the existence of a defense establishment and a complete power to mobilize the resources of the nation invested in Congress, in time of war as well as peace, Federalists believed that the American people exposed their "property and liberty to the mercy of foreign invaders," inviting them by a self-imposed weakness "to seize the naked and defenceless prey."[58] It is symptomatic that when Federalists tried their hand at allegory, European powers were described as "robbers" and "pirates."[59] The monarchs of Europe reportedly watched the political development in America closely and should the Constitution be rejected in favor of the "present weak, unenergetic federal government,"[60] they would join together and form a plan "to canton us out among them, as they did the Kingdom of Poland."[61] Given the Federalist theory of international relations—a theory that of course was, had been, and still is the conventional one—the Federalists quite naturally adhered to the ancient maxim that the best defense is preparation for war.[62] Consequently, there could be no compromise on the national government's right to raise and maintain standing armies in time of peace. If the Constitution were amended to prohibit peacetime standing armies, the United States would in fact "exhibit the most extraordinary spectacle, which the world has yet seen—that of a nation incapacitated by its constitution to prepare for defence, before it was actually invaded."[63]

America's fortunate geopolitical situation meant that the size of the peacetime army could be very limited. According to the Antifederalists, there was no doubt that the Federalists wished to establish a large standing army. This is hardly a correct depiction of the Federalist argument. Despite Federalist acceptance of a small peacetime army, however, the Antifederalists were right in claiming that the Federalists wanted to give, and that the Constitution did in fact grant, Congress an *unlimited* power to raise and maintain armies. To the Federalists, this was necessary because the adequate means for the defense of the United States were not determined by Americans but by the strength and policies of the states of Europe. Therefore, the future needs of the union could not be determined in advance and therefore could not be limited. Any attempt to do so would merely lead to a situation in which Congress would have to exceed its authority. As Madison put it, "it is in vain to oppose constitutional barriers to the impulse of self-preservation."[64] A basic principle of a proper system of government, often expressed in Federalist writings and speeches, was that the means of government had to be proportionate to the ends. Because Congress had been entrusted with the defense of the republic, and because it was impossible to foresee the needs that this required, it followed that the "means ought to exist without limitation."[65]

IV

Federalists did not regard military strength, including a standing army in time of peace, as a threat to American independence, liberty and happiness. On the contrary, a professional army and an unlimited power over mobilization were prerequisites for the preservation of the union's independence and therefore also of liberty and property. The power to raise armies and taxes were the "powers by which good rulers protect the people,"[66] but military strength was also a precondition for material prosperity. Through their own weakness, Americans had become "slaves to Europe" in commercial relations.[67] If the weakness of a government prevented it from protecting the lives, liberty, and property of the citizens, then that government failed to fulfill its part of the social contract. This was what had happened in the United States. "We combine in society, with an expectation, to have our persons and properties defended against unreasonable exactions either at home or abroad," Oliver Ellsworth said. If the government cannot do so, "we do not enjoy our natural rights."[68]

Independence, liberty, and the safe enjoyment of property demanded self-determination, which in turn required that a nation possessed the means to defend its territory and interests. With a weak national government, Americans in effect trusted their lives, liberty, and property to luck, or to the benevolence of foreign governments and nations. As one Federalist remarked, "without a ship, without a soldier, without a shilling in the federal treasury, and without a nervous government to obtain one, we hold the property we now enjoy at the courtesy of other powers."[69] Through the adoption of the Constitution and the creation of a stronger national government, this would change. "If we mean to have our natural rights and properties protected," Ellsworth wrote, "we must first create a power which is able to do it."[70]

7

A GOVERNMENT OF FORCE

The opponents of the Constitution never accepted the Federalist claim that the independence, liberty, and prosperity of the American republic depended on the creation and maintenance of a peace establishment consisting of regular troops. They did not believe that the union faced as serious threats as the Federalists claimed,[1] but kept to the view that standing armies in time of peace were a threat to liberty. Both ancient and modern history had taught that "almost all" nations in Europe and Asia had lost their liberty because of the establishment of a standing army.[2] Obviously, if other nations had been "enslaved" by means of their standing armies, it hardly made sense for Americans to imitate them.[3] To Antifederalists, it seemed "pretty obvious" that the "*standing army* will have *other fish to fry* than fighting a foreign enemy."[4] If the Constitution was adopted and the Federalists realized their plan to raise a standing army, the people of America would soon find that the Constitution's supporters would make use of it on the domestic—not international—scene. The Antifederalist criticism of the army clauses therefore said little about commercial treaties and the importance of military strength in international relations. Instead, they approached the issue from the traditional Country perspective, claiming that standing armies in time of peace posed a threat to liberty.

In continental Europe in the early modern period, state formation largely consisted of the creation and rapid growth of professional armies. Although it occurred somewhat later, this development took place in Britain as well, accelerating after the Glorious Revolution. This development gave rise to a strong dislike among many political commentators in England, who opposed the growth of the British state. It was on the work of these men that the Antifederalists drew to formulate their critique of the Constitution. The fact that the Antifederalists took their arguments against the Constitution from this source suggests that they saw Congress's right to establish standing armies as part of an attempt to form a national state in America, possessing powers similar to those of the states in Britain and Europe. Although they could agree with the Federalists that a standing army was an important feature of most contemporary states, the critics of the Constitution did not agree that an American standing army would make the people safe in their enjoyment of life, liberty, and property. Rather, it would make them unfree, just as it had the peoples of the Old World.

I

A persistent theme running through British opposition writings in the eighteenth century was an energetic denunciation of the peacetime standing army. The argument was stated coherently for the first time during the great debate over the introduction of a peace establishment in 1697–1699.[5] Although the aversion against the army had abated somewhat toward the end of the eighteenth century, the antiarmy argument still formed a part of the opposition's attack against the British political system.[6] To these men and women, the army was an institution alien to society. It was made up of aristocratic officers, on the one hand, and soldiers recruited from the bottom of society and brutalized by military discipline, on the other. Such men did not form a part of society but were the blind tools of their commanders and ultimately of the monarch.[7]

According to Country thought, the creation of an army meant that the king's position was strengthened and when this happened the balance between the rulers and the ruled was upset. If the monarch possessed control over a standing army, the people would not be able to oppose any breaches against the "contract" between the ruler and the subjects, but would be left to their sovereign's caprice and will. In this way there was a direct link between the establishment of a standing army and absolutism.[8] This connection was widely accepted and even a moderate writer like William Blackstone worried about the consequences that "the force of a disciplined army" at "the absolute disposal of the crown" would have on the future of the British constitution. Similarly, David Hume believed that the monarch's preference for a standing army and his neglect of the militia was "a mortal distemper in the BRITISH government, of which it must at last inevitably perish."[9]

Although the eighteenth-century British army never attempted a coup to overthrow the constitution, other activities in which it engaged offered cause for concern. Throughout the century the army was increasingly used for domestic purposes as a police force. Soldiers suppressed smuggling by enforcing the Navigation Acts and the fiscal laws. They also maintained and restored public order.[10] In peacetime approximately 15,000 regulars served on the British mainland. Mostly these were mobile troops, widely dispersed in small contingents in order to allow them to assist in maintaining the public peace. The well-known instances when the army was called in to restore public peace and caused civilian casualties, such as the Porteus, Wilkes, and Gordon Riots, represent only the tip of an iceberg of army intervention in social and political conflicts during the eighteenth century. In the vast majority of cases, these actions did not even result in violence. But the importance of the army as a law enforcing institution is not fully appreciated even if these interventions are taken into account, for its most significant function was most likely preventive; it safeguarded law and order simply by maintaining a presence in society.[11]

The increasing use of the army as a law enforcement instrument was accompanied by changes in constitutional theory. The use of the army against civilians had originally been regarded as deeply problematical and even unconstitutional. By the middle of the eighteenth century, however, new conceptions of constitutionalism fully accepted the use of soldiers as a police force. Military support was now seen as necessary to the civil magistrates' ability to maintain the peace and enforce laws, although there was often reluctance on the part of local magistrates and military commanders to make use of it against civilians. In the words of one legal historian, this change meant that an "old constitutionalism of law by consensus or popular custom" was replaced by a "new constitutionalism of coercive power."[12] Even if such changes were taking place, however, the use of the army against civilians was still carefully circumscribed by law in the Anglo-American system of government. In Britain as well as in the colonies, regular troops could be employed to restore order only if the civil magistrates called them out. Normally this meant a justice of the peace, an amateur official drawn from the local elite. But, while there was usually a sufficiently strong union of interest between the local magistrates and army officers in Britain, this link was most often missing in America.[13] With a few exceptions, therefore, colonial justices of the peace did not ask for the backing of the army in order to quell disturbances and, as a consequence, the army was rendered largely impotent as a police force in America.[14]

Yet it was the exceptions that mattered. On 5 March 1770, soldiers opened fire on a Boston crowd, killing five civilians. The colonists readily made the connection between the "Boston massacre" and the "massacre" at St. George's Fields, which had taken place in London two years before, and they interpreted it as a deliberate assault on liberty. To them, it seemed as though the government in London was introducing a new principle in the relationship between the army and society both in Britain and America.[15] The events in Boston brought about a marked change in American political rhetoric. Whereas antiarmy sentiments had been relatively rare in America before the "massacre," they became a staple argument afterward.[16] This is hardly surprising considering the colonists' inexperience with peacetime standing armies. There had been regulars in America during the wars against France, but it was only after the Seven Years' War that Britain decided to retain a substantial number of troops in time of peace.[17] In 1763, fifteen regiments—some 6,000 men—were posted in frontier posts from the mouth of the St. Lawrence River to the Gulf of Mexico. By the late 1760s, however, the British government transferred most of the troops to the Eastern seaboard, at first stationing them at Halifax, New York, Philadelphia, and St. Augustine. In the autumn of 1768, the army's police duties in America began in earnest when more than four regiments were sent to Boston with the express purpose of suppressing resistance to tax laws and customs regulations. Although they were withdrawn after the "Boston massacre," they returned in greater number after the Tea Party on 16 December 1773. By early 1775 there was one soldier to every five inhabitants in Boston. This time the soldiers were protected from the civil power by the Administration of Justice Act, which made it possible for a soldier or royal officer charged with killing a civilian in the line of duty to have his trial in another colony or in England.[18]

Stationing troops among civilians in order to police them seemed an ominous act to the colonists. In the context of traditional English constitutional theory, their resistance to the Stamp Act, the Townshend Acts, and the Tea Act could be interpreted as lawful because these acts, and the attempts to enforce them, were *un*lawful. Although Britain came to encompass a modern understanding of law as the command of a sovereign legislature in the eighteenth century, the colonists subscribed to the traditional conception that an act of Parliament was lawful only when it had the consent of the governed. Because the colonies were not represented in Parliament, popular consent was granted not by enacting legislation but by complying with the administration of the law. When the British government tried to enforce legislation by means of the army and without the consent of the governed, their action could be seen as an attempt to enforce an act of power rather than a law, and in this situation resistance was legitimate.[19] Against this background it was "evidently" the case, as James Warren said, that troops were sent to America "for the purpose of effecting *that*, which it was the principal design of the founders of the [British] constitution to prevent (when they declared a standing army in time of peace to be AGAINST LAW) namely, for the enforcement of obedience to Acts which, upon fair examination, appeared to be unjust and unconstitutional."[20] When the colonists drew up their indictment of George III in the Declaration of Independence, they therefore gave prominent place to the role of the army in the king's attempt to establish "an absolute Tyranny" over the American states against the laws and the constitution.

He has kept among us, in times of peace, Standing Armies without the Consent of our legislatures.—He has affected to render the Military independent of and superior to the Civil power.—He has combined with others to subject us to a jurisdiction foreign to our constitution, and unacknowledged by our laws; giving his Assent to their Acts of pretended Legislation:—For Quartering large bodies of armed troops among us:—For protecting them, by a mock Trial, from punishment for any Murders which they should commit on the Inhabitants of these States . . . He is at this time transporting large Armies of foreign Mercenaries to compleat the works of death, desolation and tyranny, already begun with circumstances of Cruelty & perfidy scarcely paralleled in the most barbarous ages, and totally unworthy the Head of a civilized nation.[21]

After the war, neither Congress nor the state governments posted regulars among the people. No soldier enforced legislation and in several of the state bills of rights there were explicit warnings about the danger of standing armies.[22] In this context, the Federalists' stubborn insistence on the need to create a peacetime army in America seemed to their opponents a betrayal of an important principle of free government. It also cast doubts on their ultimate motives. To the author of "The Federalist's political creed," the Constitution came across as an attempt to roll back the achievements of independence and as an attempted revival of the "old *tory system* . . . by different hands." To this writer, the Federalists tried to do what Parliament and the king had failed to achieve, that is, to divest the people of their liberties by erecting "an absolute Tyranny." As with George III, the standing army played a crucial role in their plans:

1. They maintain that the *revolution* and the *declaration* of *independence*, however important at those periods, are now to be considered as mere farces, and that nothing that was then done ought to be any bar in the way of establishing the proposed system of arbitrary power.

2. That as most of the European nations are in a state of vassalage and slavery, the Americans easily may be brought to a similar situation, and therefore ought to be reduced to the same abject condition.

3. That to encompass this end, a large standing army should be kept up in time of peace, under the specious pretence of guarding us against *foreign* invasion and our frontiers against the savages; but in reality to overawe and enslave the people, who, if provoked at the violation of their rights, should at any time dare to murmur or complain, the military should be employed to *bayonet* them for their arrogance and presumption.[23]

II

Antifederalist critique against the Constitution's army clauses centered on the transfer of military power from the states to Congress. To them, the centralization of power brought about by the Constitution threatened the continued existence of two institutions, which they believed to be vital to the preservation of liberty: the militia and the state assemblies. These provided the people with the means to withstand the possible abuse of power by the central government. Should the militia and the state governments be swallowed up by Congress, this would tip the balance of power decisively in favor of the national government, which would then be able to pursue whatever actions it chose regardless of popular opposition.

Antifederalists accused the Federalists of transforming the union from a confederation of sovereign states to a "consolidated" nation-state. In Antifederalist rhetoric, "consolidation" could mean either that the Constitution brought about a transfer of crucial powers from the states to Congress or that the Constitution would unavoidably lead to a total concentration of power in the national government and the destruction of the states at some future date.[24] Although there would still be a division of the objects, or duties, that would fall within the respective jurisdictions of the states and the national government, all the fundamental government duties would belong to the latter. Independent of the states, the national government would have the power to raise revenue and an army. It would control the militia and establish a national judiciary. Congress would no longer be an assembly of sovereign states working on, and through, the member states, but a government ruling individual citizens directly without making use of the state legislatures as intermediaries. Within this system of government, the role of the states would diminish. "What shall the States have to do?" bewildered Antifederalists asked. "Take care of the poor—repair and make high-ways—erect bridges, and so on, and so on."[25] "I am, sir, at a loss," Melanchton Smith confessed to the president of the New York convention, "to know how the *state legislatures* will spend their time."[26]

To the Antifederalists, it was unclear how "any writer of sense" could argue, as the Federalists did, that the states retained their sovereignty even if they were deprived of the power over the revenue, the command over the militia, the regulation of elections and the payment of representatives.[27] In a reply to James Wilson's argument that the states retained their sovereignty under the Constitution because their legislatures appointed presidential electors and senators,[28] "Cincinnatus" retorted that Wilson had reduced state sovereignty merely to "electing the members of a sovereignty." But "to make laws—preside over the administration of justice—command the militia, or force of the state—these I suppose, do not constitute its sovereignty, for these are totally taken away, and yet you are clear the sovereignty remains."[29] To any sensible person, it was plain to see that under the Constitution the state governments would be "not only destitute of all sovereign command of, or controul over, the revenue or any part of it," but also "divested of the power of commanding, or prescribing the duties, wages, or punishment of their own militia, or of protecting their life, property or characters of the rigours of martial law." And, as Robert Whitehill said, "that government which possesses all the powers of raising and maintaining armies, of regulating and commanding the militia, and of laying imposts and taxes of every kind must be supreme and will (whether in twenty or in one year, it signifies little to the event) naturally absorb every subordinate jurisdiction."[30]

If the Constitution was adopted, the national government would possess "unlimited power to establish systems of taxation, armies, navies, model the militia, and to do everything that may essentially tend soon to change, totally, the affairs of the community." State representatives and senators, by contrast, would be left with making "fence laws, and laws to regulate the descent and conveyance of property, the administration of justice between man and man, to appoint militia officers, &c."[31] Although these tasks were certainly necessary functions for a government to carry out, from an eighteenth-century perspective they were hardly the most important ones. Would it not be better to abolish the state legislatures "at once" as Patrick Henry suggested? "What purposes should they be continued for?"[32] Above all, it could be asked if the people would accept to pay for a government that carried out such few and such unimportant tasks. For how long would the people "retain their confidence" in representatives "who shall meet once in a year to make laws for regulating the height of your fences and the repairing of your roads"? The answer, clearly, was that the state governments, "without object or authority, will soon dwindle into insignificance, and be despised by the people themselves."[33]

Among the important powers that the Constitution transferred from the states to Congress was the control over the militia. This transfer reduced the state governors to "the quality of *drill sergeants* only to discipline the militia, and fit them for the President of Congress."[34] Yet, the real danger from a national control over the militia was not that Congress would turn the militia into an efficient military force but that Congress would choose to neglect it. This could happen through the establishment of a select militia, which had been proposed by a congressional committee in 1783. A select militia was made up by only a part of the total militia. It trained more frequently than the ordinary militia and the men were committed to extended service in case of war or the threat of invasion. In modern terms, the select militia amounted to an army reserve.[35] To the Antifederalists, the creation of such an institution seemed only an excuse for putting the ordinary militia "upon a plan that will render them of no importance." Thus, whereas the ordinary militia would then be "defenceless," the select militia would "answer all the purposes of an army."[36]

Whether or not Congress decided to form a select militia, it was clear that it possessed "the powers, by *which only* the militia can be organized and armed, and by the neglect of which they may be rendered utterly useless and insignificant, when it suits the ambitious purposes of government."[37] To the critics of the Constitution, "ambitious purposes" was precisely what characterized the Federalists. As soon as they gained power, they would erect a standing army "to deprive" the "citizens of freedom, and reduce them to slavery," while at the same time they would reduce the militia to insignificance, "*least they might oppose its arbitrary designs.*"[38] With soldiers at their command and the citizens disarmed, Congress could make itself independent of the people. In this position, the national government could pass whatever oppressive laws it wished. Elections could be abolished and petitioning disallowed if Congress drew its strength from the army rather than the people.[39] With a military force "to back their despotic decrees," Congress might "laugh at the people,"[40] because the army was "so forcible, and at the same time so terrible an instrument, that any hand that wields it may, without much dexterity, perform any operation, and gain any ascendancy in human society."[41] The independence of the rulers from the people, and their superior strength, challenged the important principle in a free government that the power of the people ought to be paramount to the power of the executive.[42] If the army was "the strongest force in a State," that government "must be a military government."[43]

It was therefore in its role as an institution capable of resisting government abuse that the militia was regarded as "a bulwark of freedom."[44] The militia was "the last resource of a free people,"[45] because as long as the people were organized and trained to arms oppressive laws could not be executed against their will. It "would be a resource against great oppressions," one Antifederalist said. "The laws of a great empire are difficult to be executed. If the laws of the Union were oppressive, they could not carry them into effect, if the people were possessed of a proper means of defence."[46] If the militia fell into neglect, by contrast, there would be no ultimate protection against oppression by a government possessing an army, for when "against a regular and disciplined army, yeomanry are the only defence—yeomanry unskillfull and unarmed, what chance is there for preserving freedom?"[47] Speaking in the Virginia convention, Patrick Henry made no secret of where the real importance of the militia lay. "My great objection to this Government is, that it does not leave us the means of defending our rights; or, of waging war against tyrants," he said. "Have we the means of resisting disciplined armies, when our only defence, the militia is put into the hands of Congress?"[48]

III

The Antifederalists, then, did not object to the decline of the militia and the creation of a standing army, because they held on to a classical republican ideal of the citizen-soldier. What they feared most was not the moral consequences of the decline of the "Greek conception of citizenship," but that the army would make it possible for the national government to deprive the people of their property without their consent, by levying and collecting arbitrary taxes.[49] This fear reveals the Antifederalists' awareness that one important purpose of the Constitution was to ensure the national government sufficient revenue.[50] The state-run fiscal administration, they believed, would be replaced by "a continental collector assisted by a few faithful soldiers," who would make sure that taxes were paid "however grievous or improper they may be."[51] Under the new government, said the dissenting members of the Pennsylvania convention, "the people will have but this alternative, either to pay the tax, or let their property be taken, for all resistance will be vain. The standing army and select militia would enforce the collection."[52]

The argument that the Constitution would allow the national government to create a standing army in order to expropriate the people's property shows that Antifederalist objections to the Constitution were grounded in traditional Anglo-American individual rights. But the argument also reveals their conception of rule by consent, as well as their view on the proper role of government coercion in the American republic. In the American system of government, the bureaucratic apparatus in the hands of the state was weak or even absent. This meant that the administration of government was carried out by amateur officials with strong local attachment. Obviously, this arrangement limited the government's ability to enforce laws that were not accepted by the people who were affected by them. As a consequence, the consent of the governed was given not only when representatives passed legislation but also just as much when the people accepted or rejected the administration of the law. In this way, popular consent was given continually and locally.[53] If the government possessed an army to force through legislation, this would reduce the people's ability to withhold consent through their control of local institutions. This was the meaning of the Antifederalist charge that the Constitution would introduce "military rule" and that the American political system would no longer rest on the principle of rule by consent.

The degree to which Antifederalists accused their opponents of *deliberately* attempting to introduce military rule varied, sometimes with the same author. Some said that the Constitutional convention had been "sensible that no dependence could be placed on the people for their support: but on the contrary, that the government must be executed by force."[54] Hence, the army would be employed to "compel the submission of the people to the arbitrary dictates of the ruling powers." This charge was often repeated. The army, said the Constitution's opponents, would "carry the arbitrary decrees of the federal judges into execution." It would be used to "ensure the submission of the people" and "rivet the chains of perpetual slavery upon the American people."[55] But the more intriguing argument claimed that regardless of Federalist intentions, a military execution of the laws was the only possible form of administration under the Constitution, "however wise and energetic the principles of the general Government might be."[56]

The reason for this was size. The American people would not recognize the legitimacy of Congress because it failed to provide for an adequate representation, the only means by which a government could win popular confidence. In a free republic, "Brutus" said, the faith that the people placed in their rulers stemmed from "their knowing them, from their being responsible to them for their conduct, and from the power which they have of displacing them when they misbehave." The proposed republic of the Federalists, however, would be so extensive while the representatives were so few, that these conditions could not be met. The vast majority of the citizens would not know their representatives; they would find it difficult to keep themselves informed of Congress's doings and they would have little chance of keeping track of how their representatives behaved. Furthermore, the many constituencies throughout the union would have no real chance of concerted action to remove the government should the need arise.

> The consequence will be, they will have no confidence in their legislature, suspect them of ambitious views, be jealous of every measure they adopt, and will not support the laws they pass. Hence the government will be nerveless and inefficient, and no way will be left to render it otherwise, but by establishing an armed force to execute the laws at the point of the bayonet—a government of all others the most to be dreaded.[57]

"Federal Farmer" also believed that the government would fail to secure the obedience of the people because the distance to the representatives was too great to instill the necessary affection for, and confidence in, the government. Hence, Congress would have to make itself "feared and respected" by enforcing the laws by means of "a multitude of officers and military force." In the South Carolina convention, Patrick Dollard testified to the pertinence of such fears, when he spoke of his constituents' feelings about the proposed system of government. "They say they will resist against it," he said, "that they will not accept it unless compelled by force of arms, which this new Constitution plainly threatens; and then, they say, your standing army, like Turkish janizaries enforcing despotic laws, must ram it down their throats with the points of bayonets."[58]

Antifederalists believed that it "ought to be laid down as a principle that free states should never keep a standing army for the support of its laws."[59] In a free republic, the government should never rely on a standing army to ensure compliance with the laws but on the willingness of the citizens to obey and execute them. To ensure this, the government had to be constructed so as to have "the confidence, respect, and affection of the people."[60] If this was not the case, the laws would have to be executed by "the military," which could mean either the standing army or a militia controlled and commanded by Congress.[61] But the military execution of the law would be incompatible with "every idea of liberty; for the same force that may be employed to compel obedience to good laws might, and probably would, be used to wrest from the people their constitutional liberties." Or, as John Smilie put it, "in a free government there will never be need of standing armies; for it depends on the confidence of the people. If it does not so depend, it is not free."[62] To "Brutus," however, the problem was not so much that soldiers would enforce legislation but that the citizens would obey and assist the government not from consent but from fear of retribution.

> Men who, upon the call of the magistrate, offer themselves to execute the laws, are influenced to do it either by affection to the government, or from fear; where a standing army is at hand to punish offenders, every man is actuated by the latter principle, and therefore, when the magistrate calls, will obey: but, where this is not the case, the government must rest for its support upon the confidence and respect which the people have for their governments and laws. The body of the people being attached, the government will always be sufficient to support and execute its laws, and to operate upon the fears of any faction which may be opposed to it, not only to prevent an opposition to the execution of the laws themselves, but also to compel the most of them to aid the magistrate.[63]

Government acts, which were ultimately backed by coercive power, were simply illegitimate acts. In the words of one Antifederalist, "*that government* and *those laws* which require a standing army to enforce them ought not to be supported in any nation under Heaven."[64]

IV

So far, the Antifederalist objections against the right of Congress to create a standing army in time of peace have been described as an objection to the centralization of power at the expense of the people's ability to withhold consent through their control of strong local institutions. It has also been noted that what the Antifederalists feared from the establishment of the new government was not the loss of popular influence in itself but the consequence of such a loss—the government's confiscation of the people's property through arbitrary taxation. In their attempt to maintain what they perceived to be a proper balance of power between the people and their rulers, the Antifederalists gave special attention to the role played by the militia. But even though they supported the militia, the Antifederalists did not believe that the citizens were very eager to sacrifice their time and effort, much less their lives, for the benefit of the public good. This is made clear by an Antifederalist objection to the federal control over the militia that is significantly different from their other strictures on the Constitution.

This objection has nothing to do with the danger of neglect and disarmament of the militia, but instead with the fear that Congress would rather make *too much* use of the militia. This further underlines the Antifederalists' wish to protect individual rights by reducing Congress's power over the militia. They resisted the growing power of the state both when it allowed the national government—through the standing army and the disarmament of the militia—a greater reach into the lives of the citizens in areas such as tax collection, *and* when the national government sought to mobilize men for service in the militia. There is, of course, a contradictory element to this reasoning, and the Federalists were quick to point this out. For instance, Oliver Ellsworth accused Luther Martin of oscillating between incompatible positions in the Philadelphia Convention. "One hour you sported the opinion, that Congress, afraid of the militia resisting their measures, would neither arm nor organize them: and the next, as if men required no time to breathe between such contradictions, that they would harass them by long and unnecessary marches, till they wore down their spirit and rendered them fit subjects for despotism."[65] But, rather than pointing to the muddled character of Antifederalist thought, we should see their objections as different expressions of the same fear: the fear for the future of liberty under a strong central government.

Early modern political theory had established the connection between the rise of absolutism and the professionalization of soldiering through the creation of standing armies and the marginalization of the citizen-soldier. In actual practice, the struggle for domination in Europe steadily increased the state's need to mobilize society's resources. Toward the end of the seventeenth century, this need led to the reappearance of the idea of military service as a universal obligation of all male subjects. Throughout Europe, militias were reorganized from a local to a national force. This time, however, the militia was not primarily intended for war duty but functioned as a reserve for the regular army, moving militiamen into the regular troops in order to fill out the ranks as the need arose. Prussia, of course, was the state that went furthest in imposing military duties on its subjects. There, boys were registered at the age of ten, underwent military training for eighteen months to two years on reaching adulthood, and were thereafter compelled to serve for two to three months every year for the rest of their lives.[66] Britain reorganized its militia in 1757 in order to strengthen home defense so that regular forces could be freed for service abroad. Although there were many political commentators who praised the militia, the institution was unpopular among the people. The burden of militia service tended to fall disproportionally on the poor and it was often resisted as a government intervention in the private lives of the subjects.[67]

There was a trend in Europe, then, for rulers to improve their military capacity by mobilizing their subjects in the militia. Part of the Antifederalist objection against the federal control over the militia focus on the way that militia service might become a way to deprive the people of their liberty, rather than a means to guarantee liberty's preservation. Thus, among the "*blessings* of the new-proposed government," one Antifederalist mentioned "a Prussian militia,"[68] implying the idea of compulsory military service. In the same way, "Brutus" wrote that if "the general legislature deem it for the general welfare to raise a body of troops, and they cannot be procured by voluntary enlistments, it seems evident, that it will be proper and necessary to effect it, that men be impressed from the militia to make up the deficiency."[69]

But other encroachments on individual rights than involuntary enrollment into the armed forces could also follow from Congress's power over the militia. By law, the American militia consisted of all men between the age of sixteen and sixty. Congress's unlimited power over the militia therefore gave it power over the vast majority of adult men, which meant that the entire political nation was within the reach of the government's command. By subjecting the militia to martial law, Congress could "inflict the most ignominious punishments on the most worthy citizens."[70] All militiamen "from the *lowest* to the *greatest* [could] be *subjected* to *military law*, and *tied up* and *whipped* at the *halbert* like the *meanest* of *slaves*."[71] The idea that Congress would subject the militia to martial law in peacetime appears fanciful, but at its heart lay the fear that the national government might deprive the citizens of the protection against government abuse, which was provided by the common law. This was in grim contrast to Britain, where it was "contrary to magna charta to punish a freeman by martial law in time of peace, and murder to execute him."[72] The concern that military duty might endanger private rights was expressed in other contexts regarding the militia as well. Thus, for instance, Antifederalists often claimed that conscientious objectors would not be allowed the right to hire a substitute. On a more general level, they argued that, when serving under Congress, militiamen might be forced to act in ways that they found morally repugnant.[73]

This concern with the government's ability to make undue demands on the citizens also came to the fore in one of the most common objections to federal control of the militia: that Congress might march the militia out of its home state and keep it in service for an undetermined period of time. This challenged what had been earlier practice, even during the War of Independence. When England reformed its militia through the Militia Act of 1757, it was stipulated that the militia could not be moved outside its home county in time of peace and not outside the kingdom in times of war or rebellion.[74] There was no such limit on the power of Congress according to the Constitution, and the Antifederalists warned the people that "you may be dragged from your families and homes to any part of the continent and for any length of time, at the discretion of the future Congress."[75] As amateur soldiers, the militiamen had other occupations; the vast majority—of course—were farmers, and they could not afford to leave their farms for long stretches of time.[76] It was against this background that the Antifederalist minority in the Maryland convention believed it to be "essential" to restrict the national government's right to march the militia out of the state. To "march beyond the limits of a neighbouring state, the general militia, who consists of so many poor people that can illy be spared from their families and domestic concerns, by power of congress, who could know nothing of their circumstances" was bound to result in grievances.[77]

The problem with the restrictions proposed by the Antifederalists was that while they might offer protection to the militiamen, they also made it difficult to make much use of the militia. An efficient fighting force could not make concessions to the ethical considerations of the soldiers and it had to maintain discipline by means of martial law. Nor could there be restrictions on the time during which it would serve or where it would march. The War of Independence had repeatedly demonstrated that the existing organization of the militia was inefficient. If the militia was to make up the union's defense, it simply had to be reformed. But the Antifederalists refused to accept classing of the militia, which would have made possible the creation of a select militia, while at the same time they objected to giving Congress the power to reform the ordinary militia. In this way, they effectively blocked any chance of making the militia the main force of American defense.

The Antifederalist stance on the militia can be explained by returning to their understanding of the citizens' limited readiness to sacrifice their resources to promote the public good. For, just like their opponents, Antifederalists knew that the people were not very keen on militia service. Should such service become a heavy burden, the citizens would rather not do it. Faced with the choice between submitting to the hardships of soldiering, on the one hand, or with leaving the care for military duties to professional soldiers, on the other, most people would choose the latter. Division of labor had made the majority of citizens more concerned with their private affairs than with public matters. Hence, Antifederalists feared that Congress would deliberately harass the militiamen, "subjecting them to unnecessary severity of discipline in time of peace, confining them under martial law, and disgusting them so much, as to make them cry out, *Give us a standing army.*"[78] The power of Congress would thereby "increase by those very means that will be adopted and urged as an ease to the People."[79] Having been "freed from the burthen of militia duties," the citizens would then be contentedly "left to their own private occupations or pleasures."[80]

8

GOVERNMENT BY CONSENT

In their defense of the Constitution's military clauses, the Federalists argued for the need to maintain a peace establishment of regulars. They also argued that the national government had to possess an unrestricted power over mobilization. In their minds, both military professionalism and the unlimited power over mobilization were necessary to preserve the independence, liberties, and interests of the American nation. The Antifederalists, by contrast, raised objections to Congress's right to create and maintain a standing army in time of peace. They were also concerned about the unrestricted nature of Congress's military powers. Their objections can be subsumed under three headings. First, the Antifederalists believed that the new system of government would change the administration of the laws from an administration based on the consent of the governed to an administration based on coercion or the threat of force. Second, they believed that the national government would create a large army while neglecting the militia. This would upset the balance of power between the rulers and the ruled, the government would be strong and the people weak. As a consequence, the national government would become independent of the people and be able to establish tyrannical rule. Third, the critics of the Constitution believed that Congress had been granted too much power to interfere in the private lives of the citizens through its command over the militia. Through service in the militia, the national government could subject citizens to martial law, force them to take part in actions abhorrent to their conscience and religion, and also remove them from their homes and occupations for undetermined periods of time.

In the debate over ratification, the Federalists answered these objections. In doing so, they argued that it was possible to create a strong state without abandoning traditional Anglo-American ideals about free government. Their answer is the subject of the present chapter.

I

Antifederalists had accused their opponents of wanting to establish a "Government of force" in America. To the Federalists, such sweeping accusations made little sense. There "never was a Government without force," as James Madison said. "What is the meaning of Government? An institution to make people do their duty. A Government leaving it to a man to do his duty, or not, as he pleases, would be a new species of Government, or rather no Government at all."[1] Charles Pinckney declared that

> he could not conceive that either the dignity of a government could be maintained, its safety insured, or its laws administered, without a body of regular forces to aid the magistrate in the execution of his duty. All government is a kind of restraint. We may be told, a free government imposes no restraint upon the private wills of individuals which does not conduce in a greater degree to the public happiness; but all government is restraint, and founded in force. We are the first nation who have ever held a contrary opinion, or even attempted to maintain one without it.[2]

But, even though force, or coercion, was a necessary part of every government, it did not follow from this that the federal government would depend on coercion in its day-to-day administration of the laws. Nor did it follow from the national government's possession of the means of coercion that liberty was in danger.

"Liberty," according to the Federalists, amounted to the citizen's subordination under just laws. The selfish character of man meant, however, that such subjection did not come natural to humankind. Man was a creature, the Constitution's supporters said, "in the gross, blind and inconsistent—naturally averse to government."[3] For this reason, if there was no "social government," there would be no "individual government." Hence, "our very being depends on social government."[4] Given such presumptions, the realization of man's subordination under just laws demanded that the government possess the means to enforce legislation. For to "what purpose should a legislative enact laws if nobody is obliged to obey them?"[5] Laws that went unheeded were in fact worse than no laws at all, "because they weaken the government, expose it to contempt, destroy the confidence of all men, both subjects and strangers, in it, and disappoint all men who have confided in it."[6] Ultimately, it was force that secured submission to the laws.[7] There was nothing new with this idea. The states had "ever made the military power their last resort for executing their laws." Although there was seldom need to use it, "on some occasions it is indispensably necessary." Rather, what was controversial was that the *national* government would now possess such power. This was really nothing more than a corollary to Congress's right to legislate for individuals rather than states, however. For, if "Congress is invested with power to make laws, the power of executing laws in the most ample and effectual manner ought to be lodged there also. Without this, there would have been an inconceivable absurdity in the Constitution."[8]

Yet even though the Federalists were ready to defend the national government's need for coercion, as far as the ordinary enforcement of the laws was concerned they denied that the government would have need for a coercive apparatus independent of the states. Rather, Congress would "employ the ordinary magistracy of each [of the states] in the execution of its laws."[9] Should opposition to federal laws arise "from the disorderly conduct of refractory, or seditious individuals, it could be overcome by the same means which are daily employed against the same evil, under the State governments."[10] Nor were there grounds to assume that the people would distinguish between the different sources of the law, federal or state.[11] The local magistracy would uphold the law of the land; no matter if it originated in Congress or the state legislatures, they were in fact "bound by Oath or Affirmation" to do so. No doubt they would "be as ready to guard the national as the local regulations from the inroads of private licentiousness."[12] In enforcing the law, the Federalists wished to avoid the construction of dual sets of *administrations*, one federal and one state, in favor of employing the same officers in dual *capacities*. This idea of how the federal administration would work is also present in the debate over the judiciary and the revenue administration. Merging the federal and the state officer in the same person would avoid the popular aversion that would result from saddling the American nation with the agents of a distant central government. As Alexander Hamilton said, the "Legislatures, Courts, and Magistrates of the respective members will be incorporated into the operations of the national government, *as far as its just and constitutional authority extends;* and will be rendered auxiliary to the enforcements of its laws." It followed that there was "good ground to calculate upon a regular and peaceable execution of the laws of the Union; if its powers are administered with a common share of prudence."[13]

As we have seen, Antifederalists had been especially concerned that the peacetime standing army would allow the national government to enforce heavy and arbitrary tax laws without the consent of the governed. To the Federalists, there was no reason why the people would not realize the "salutary consequences" that would follow from an adequate federal revenue. For this reason, the idea that taxes would be collected at the point of bayonets "must eventually prove the mere effusion of a wild imagination, or a factious spirit."[14] The Antifederalists had also claimed that the people would only have faith in their representatives if they knew them well. If they did not, the people would be suspicious and likely to ignore or resist government measures. To Hamilton, this argument was simply false. Because the people's acceptance of government measures depended on the nature of these measures, the need for coercion depended on how well the government governed. As the national government would attract better men than the state governments, it would in all likelihood be better administered than the states. Therefore, "there can be no reasonable foundation for the supposition, that the laws of the Union will meet with any greater obstruction from [the people], or will stand in need of any other methods to enforce their execution, than the laws of the particular members."[15]

The Federalists, then, denied that a special national military force would be needed for the daily administration of government, although coercion might in extraordinary instances be needed to ensure compliance with acts of Congress. This did not mean that a national force had no domestic function at all. In case of large-scale insurrections and threats of secession, the national government might have to use force. The military forces of the republic would thus perform only one of the two basic tasks of the British Army. It would be used in situations corresponding to the Jacobite risings of 1715 and 1745 but not to suppress the frequent petty riots of the socially distressed. It was with this in mind that the Constitution declared that the union should protect the member states "against domestic Violence."[16] When state governments used force against violent protests it did not give rise to controversy. Massachusetts had put down Shays's Rebellion and Pennsylvania had sent a force to suppress rioters in Luzerne County. As Hamilton wrote, this showed that military force of one kind or other might at times be "essential to the security of the society." In his response to Hamilton, "Brutus" denied that these forces could be compared to standing armies, but he did not object to the use they had been put to. About Luzerne County he wrote merely that "a number of armed men had levied war against the authority of the state, and openly avowed their intention of withdrawing their allegiance from it," thus certainly suggesting that he found the actions of the Pennsylvania legislature legitimate.[17]

If the insurrection was limited to only a part of a state, there would be no need for federal intervention, as "the militia of the residue" would then suppress it. But if the rebellion should "pervade a whole State, or a principal part of it," it would be necessary to resort to "a different kind of force." In order to "preserve the peace of the community, and to maintain the just authority of the laws" it might even be necessary to make use of the army against civilians.[18] Preferably, however, this task should be left to the people themselves rather than to the army. The Constitution made this possible by granting Congress the right to "nationalize" state militias by calling them out to execute federal law. "If insurrections should arise, or invasions should take place," said Madison, "the people ought unquestionably to be employed to suppress and repel them, rather than a standing army. The best way to do these things, was to put the militia on a good and sure footing, and enable the Government to make use of their services when necessary."[19]

Obviously, government use of military coercion against the people is always problematic to justify in a political system grounded in popular sovereignty. In *The Federalist* 43, Madison asked if a majority of the citizens in a state had not always the right to subvert the government. He also asked if a minority of the citizens in a state could ever have the means to subvert the government against the wishes of the majority.[20] The Federalists answered the second of these questions easily. Congress, Oliver Ellsworth wrote, had to possess the power to raise armies because it was "necessary to restrain the violence of seditious citizens. A concurrence of circumstances . . . frequently enables a few disaffected persons to make great revolutions, unless government is vested with the most extensive powers of self-defence."[21] Differences in economic resources and military capacity as well as foreign aid made it more than possible that the minority might be stronger than the majority. As Madison noted, nothing "can be more chimerical than to imagine that in a trial of actual force, victory may be calculated by the rules which prevail in a census of the inhabitants, or which determine the event of an election!" Besides, there might be an influx of aliens or a substantial presence of resident noncitizens within a state. In other words, with suitable allies, a minority of citizens might well make up a majority of men. As the slave population of the South demonstrated, and Madison made explicit reference to it here, this was more than hypothetical reasoning.[22]

The question if a majority of citizens had not always the right to subvert the government Madison answered in the negative. There might well be "illicit combinations for purposes of violence" made up by majorities in a state as well as in a county or district within a state. Madison's reasoning suggests that the Federalists defined "the people," in which they had invested sovereignty, as a national, not a state, body. If a factious majority was formed in a county, the state government had a duty to aid the local magistrates. If a factious majority was formed in a state, the union had a duty to assist the state government.[23] To other Federalists, this appears to have been something of a quasi-problem. Edmund Randolph merely noted that "it would afford some consolation, if when rebellion shall threaten any state, an ultimate asylum could be found under the wing of Congress."[24] To Hamilton, seditions and insurrections were simply a consequence "of civil society upon an enlarged scale." They were "as inseparable from the body politic, as tumours and eruptions from the natural body." There was no doubt that established governments of any kind, state or national, had the right to suppress them by means of any force necessary.[25]

The Federalist argument may seem to delimit popular sovereignty by making "the people" a body constituted on the national rather than state level, and by denying violence as a legitimate political means. But, leaving aside the question of the extension of the franchise, this hardly amounts to more than the "domestication" of popular sovereignty necessary for the development of any ordered system of representative government at the national level. It is important to note, however, that the Federalists never advocated, although their opponents sometimes suggested this, the "absurd and slavish doctrine of non-resistance," that is, the idea that whatever the circumstances, the people never had the right to resist government with violence. On the contrary, in this respect the Federalists, no less than their opponents, were faithful Lockeans. "If the representatives of the people betray their constituents," Hamilton wrote, "there is then no source left but in the exertion of that original right of self-defence, which is paramount to all positive forms of government."[26]

Much more important in practice, however, was the fact that the balance of strength between the people and the government would always be to the advantage of the former. The Federalists, in other words, subscribed to the idea that the power of the people ought to be greater than the power of Congress, and they repeatedly stressed that the national government would never be strong enough to subdue a majority of citizens or an alliance of the state governments.[27] Because of this distribution of power, it could well be argued that any exertion of force by the national government against civilians took place at least with the tacit consent of the majority of citizens. The most important reason why the balance of strength would remain in favor of the people and the states was that the national government would not create a large standing army.

II

Antifederalists accused their opponents of wanting to establish a large standing army as a necessary means to erect their "government of force." Thus, "Cincinnatus" claimed that James Wilson wanted the United States to pursue aggressive warfare, for which nothing less than "the Prussian number," or 200,000 men, would suffice. Other Antifederalists suggested that the army would consist of 100,000 men. Most of them, however, were content with claiming merely that the Federalist army would be "numerous."[28] They also believed that the army would be widely dispersed in order to pursue police functions similar to those carried out by the British army in England. "Centinel" wrote of how only "cantonments of troops in every district of America" would ensure submission to "the arbitrary dictates of the ruling powers." In order for the new system of government to work, said another Antifederalist, the standing army "must and will be garrisoned in every district through the whole."[29]

Although the Federalists argued that the United States needed a peace establishment of regular troops, they never discussed the details of this institution during the debate over ratification. James Madison at one time argued that under no circumstances could America support more than 25–30,000 soldiers, while Alexander Contee Hanson noted in passing that not even 10,000 men would be able to subdue the people of America.[30] Both men certainly implied that the peace establishment planned by the

Federalists would be much smaller. Although they did not present any plan during the ratification debate, nothing that the Federalists said suggests that their plans differed from the proposals offered by the congressional committee on the peace establishment a few years earlier. These suggestions were realized in the 1790s when the Federalists came to power. There was, then, a strong continuity in Federalist thought on the peace establishment. When they left office in 1801, comments the foremost historian of Federalist military institutions, "they had succeeded in creating the very peacetime establishment many of them first envisioned at the close of the Revolution."[31]

After hostilities with Britain ceased, Congress put Alexander Hamilton in charge of a committee to investigate the matter of a suitable peacetime establishment for the republic. This committee also included Oliver Ellsworth, James Madison, and James Wilson, all of whom would come to play a prominent part on the Federalist side in the struggle for ratification. The committee of Congress on the peace establishment also solicited opinions from George Washington, Henry Knox, Friederich von Steuben, and other leading officers. When Hamilton drew up the committee's report, he was well aware that neither public opinion nor public finances would accept a large standing army. Hence, he suggested that Congress establish a small force of about 3,000 men. Part of the force would be made up of a corps of engineers, which in turn would include an artillery regiment. Attached to the corps of engineers would be instructors in mathematics, chemistry, natural philosophy, and civil architecture.

This 3,000-men-strong peacetime establishment had two major functions. The first was to police the western frontier to defend American interests against the ambitions of Spain and England and to preserve the peace with the Indian nations. Consequently, the army would not be posted among the people but would be garrisoned out of sight of the vast majority of the citizenry. The other major function was to ensure a future military capability of the United States. This it would do in two ways. First, it would preserve the military skills and traditions acquired by the Continental Army. The instructors would train prospective officers in the military sciences, and would serve as a substitute for a military academy. Second, the peace establishment would be organized as a "skeleton" force designed for swift expansion. It would have more officers and companies than wartime regiments, in order to allow for a doubling of manpower without the need for reorganization. If there was a need to mobilize an army, the peace establishment would constitute the nucleus around which the wartime army could be formed.[32]

Most of the elements of the proposals in the report by the committee of Congress on the peace establishment turned up in the ratification debate. Thus, Pelatiah Webster argued that the peacetime troops would serve as a military academy to preserve "the knowledge and habits of military discipline and exercise." It was also pointed out that the nation was too poor to support a large army. For this reason, there was no danger to the liberties of the people from a standing army in time of peace.[33] When Madison and Hanson mentioned troop figures, they did so in order to demonstrate that Congress would never be able to maintain an army strong enough to overcome the people or the states. When Hamilton wrote about the duties of the peacetime standing army in *The Federalist*, he said that the soldiers would be garrisoned in posts on the western frontier. Their duty was to guard "against the ravages and depredations of the Indians" as well as to act as a deterrent to Spain and Britain. Troops were needed in the northwest in order to man military posts of great strategic importance; additionally, as James Wilson pointed out, troops were needed to "secure our interest in the internal navigation of that country."[34] Congress's existing contingents on the Ohio River were not there only to protect the settlers but also to ensure a rise in the value of land.[35]

The idea that the national government would be able to develop the West by pacifying the Indian tribes in the Ohio country through war or treaty was a very common theme in Federalist rhetoric. So, too, was the claim that Britain and Spain had interests in the American interior and that they supported and stirred up the Indian nations against American settlers. "Hostile tribes of Indians make daily incursions upon our frontier, and are supplied by Spaniards and Englishmen, with the apparatus of modern war," Harrison Gray Otis noted. "Thus the horrours of savage ferocity are increased by the contribution of civilized malice." Another writer claimed that Britain was unhappy with the loss of the thirteen colonies and anxious to recapture America. Britain intended to "buy the *Indians*" and use them to force Americans to accept a tyrannical government. Similarly, a Pittsburgh meeting noted that British possession of the northern posts made the western settlements "liable to the incursions of the savages."[36] But even if the peacetime standing army would perform an important duty, it would not only be small, the nature of its duties ensured that the only civilians it would come into contact with, would be western settlers.[37]

By any comparison, an army of 3,000 men was a pitiful force. By European standards, the British peacetime army of 45,000 men was small. Frederick the Great inherited an army of some 83,000 men in 1740 and brought the number up to 180,000 at the time of his death. In terms of the number of soldiers to civilians, the British army was more than four times the size of the peace establishment proposed by the Federalists. In Prussia in 1786 there was one soldier to every twenty-nine civilians. Measured in this way, the Prussian army was about ten times the size of the British, and more than forty times the size of the suggested American army.[38] The United States could manage with a Lilliputian peace establishment thanks to the nation's fortunate geopolitical situation. In Europe, the Federalists noted, Britain was the only nation in which liberty had not succumbed to peacetime standing armies. This was because the Channel and a strong navy made a large military establishment unnecessary; for this reason, the people had refused to accept one.[39] Similarly, the "distance of the United States from the powerful nations of the world gives them the same happy security." The British and Spanish possessions were unlikely to pose a great military threat. "Extensive military establishments cannot, in this position, be necessary to our security," Hamilton wrote.[40] To an even greater extent than was the case with Britain, geography had provided the American nation with the chance of doing without "big government" in the form of a large army and heavy taxes. But this opportunity depended on the preservation of the union, because the union prevented the development of a competition between states that had been the engine of the state building process in Europe.

> A dangerous establishment can never be necessary or plausible, so long as they continue a united people. But let it never for a moment be forgotten, that they are indebted for this advantage to their union alone. The moment of its dissolution will be the date of a new order of things. The fears of the weaker or the ambition of the stronger States or Confederacies, will set the example in the new, as Charles VII. did in the old world. The example will be followed here from the same motives which produced universal imitation there. Instead of deriving from our situation the precious advantage which Great-Britain has derived from hers, the face of America will be but a copy of that of the Continent of Europe. It will present liberty every where crushed between standing armies and perpetual taxes.[41]

III

When it came to the militia, the congressional committee that Hamilton chaired in 1783 went against the solicited opinions of the generals. In his sentiments on a peace establishment for the United States, which he offered to the committee, Washington had noted that "we are too poor to maintain a standing Army adequate to our defence." For this reason, it was necessary "to put the National Militia in such a condition that it may appear truly respectable in the Eyes of Friends and formidable to those who would otherwise become our enemies." Washington suggested that the entire militia be reformed so as to ensure uniformity in organization, training, and equipment. But he also expressed his "private sentiment" that it would be useful if one militiaman in every eight was "inlisted or drafted from the best Men for 3, 5, or 7 years" into special light infantry companies. These companies would train more than the rest of the militia and would always be ready for action. Washington, however, did not advocate the creation of a "Continental Militia." Hamilton suffered no restraint in this respect. Although he, too, suggested a reorganization of the general militia, the truly important force would be an 8,000-men-strong select militia. It would be made up of young, unmarried men from the cities and incorporated towns. The men would be volunteers rather than draftees from the state militia and they would be paid and equipped by the national government rather than the states. In other words, Hamilton's select militia would form a Continental militia.[42]

The report presented by the committee was never realized but met with stiff opposition in Congress. In no small part this was because of the plans for the select militia. In 1786, Henry Knox offered his *Plan for the General Arrangement of the Militia*, which was more in accord with the Country tradition of universal militia service. Indeed, Knox borrowed heavily from a true Country classic: Andrew Fletcher's *A Discourse of Government with Relation to the Militia*. Knox's plan called for all men between the age of eighteen and twenty to attend "Camps of Discipline," military training camps that would turn them into fully-fledged citizen-soldiers. These camps promised a break from the modern world, providing for forty-two days of spartan simplicity. All frivolous activities—apart from running, swimming, wrestling, and listening to edifying discourses on civic duties—would be banned, so that a martial spirit could develop in America's youth. Although Knox's militia plan was a point of reference for discussions of militia reform well into the 1790s, it, too, failed to materialize.[43]

In the debate over ratification, the Federalists pointed out that one of the best ways to make sure that a large standing army was never created in the United States was by granting Congress the means to turn the militia into an efficient force. "If standing armies are dangerous to liberty," Hamilton wrote, "an efficacious power over the militia, in the body to whose care the protection of the State is committed, ought as far as possible to take away the inducement and the pretext to such unfriendly institutions." If the national government could make use of the militia to support the civil magistrate, it could avoid using the army. If it had no access to the state militia, by contrast, the government would have no choice but to rely on the army. This was a much more efficient means to circumscribe the national government's ability to make itself independent of the people than any constitutional barrier. "To render an army unnecessary will be a more certain method of preventing its existence than a thousand prohibitions upon paper." "If you deny the General Government the power of calling out the militia," George Nicholas said in the Virginia convention, "there must be a recurrence to a standing army.—If you are jealous of your liberties, confide in Congress"[44] Other Federalists made a similar claim and pointed also to the militia's role in limiting the size of the army by providing for the defense against foreign aggression.[45]

But of all the Federalists, it was only Hamilton who spoke out about the specific way to reform the militia. When doing so, he repeated the view he had held when he wrote the report on the peace establishment in 1783. To Hamilton, "the project of disciplining all the militia of the United States is as futile as it would be injurious, if it were capable of being carried into execution." It would also be very costly. Rather, what the national government should do was to direct its attention to "the formation of a select corps of moderate extent upon such principles as will really fit them for service in case of need. By thus circumscribing the plan it will be possible to have an excellent body of well trained militia ready to take the field whenever the defence of the State shall require it." To the Antifederalists, the political consequences of a select militia were similar to those of a standing army. Hamilton presented it differently. The select militia would reduce the need to raise a large army. But should there ever arise a need to mobilize an army large enough to threaten popular liberties, the select militia would be able to offer effective resistance, because it would be almost as well trained and disciplined as the regular army. The Antifederalists had taken their suspicions too far when they made a force drawn from the political nation itself the object of republican jealousy.

> Where in the name of common sense are our fears to end if we may not trust our sons, our brothers, our neighbours, our fellow-citizens? What shadow of danger can there be from men who are daily mingling with the rest of their countrymen; and who participate with them in the same feelings, sentiments, habits, and interests?[46]

IV

In general, the critics of the Constitution accepted that, in the event of war, the defense of the union ought to be left to a regular army. Yet, on occasion, Antifederalists vented a different view. Despite the experiences of the War of Independence, these Antifederalists maintained that the war had been won by the efforts of the people and the militia rather than by the Continental Army. If the American nation would ever find itself in danger, Patrick Henry said, he "would recur to the American spirit to defend us;—that spirit which has enabled us to surmount the greatest difficulties." What Henry expressed was a belief in the spontaneous and immediate mobilization of the nation in the face of danger. Henry's Federalist opponents sneered at his naive remark. "If the American spirit is to be depended upon," Edmund Randolph responded, "I call him to awake, to see how his Americans have been disgraced: But I have no hopes that things will be better hereafter. I fully expect things will be as they have been, and the same derangements will produce similar miscarriages."[47]

Other Antifederalists declared that the citizen-soldiers of the militia would have no trouble overcoming regulars on the battlefield. Professional soldiers, wrote Benjamin Workman's "Philadelphiensis," lacked "that amour patriæ, that love of virtue, that noble love for the welfare and happiness of their fellow men which animates the man of courage and constitutes him the soldier." Hence, regulars "would either flee ere the battle commenced or submit on the first charge." Looking back at the war against Britain, some Antifederalists believed that it was the "generous rustics" rather than Washington's Continentals who had saved America from "Britain's bloody hand."[48] Surely, it is no coincidence that men who argued like this had had little direct experience of battles or war administration in the late war. Workman only arrived in America from Ireland in 1784 and Henry held neither an army commission nor a congressional office during the war.

But even those Antifederalists who praised the militia did not address the question how it could be made an efficient fighting force. Only one plan was presented during the ratification debate, published pseudononymously in the *Virginia Independent Chronicle*. The author, "Denatus," suggested that academies be established to educate America's youth in useful arts, among them "the art of defending and conquering nations, in battle." By merging the soldier and the citizen in the same person, such academies would allow the republic to build up strength sufficient to overcome any enemy:

> Our people educated in this manner, at stated times, would put the theory of fortification, gunnery, and manouvering of armies into practice. We would march, encamp, have mock battles and sieges, go through every part of the military duty as if in real war, then return home, prepare our arms for a moments warning, and each man fall to his occupation as before. This would guard against effiminacy: It is the natural way to enjoy the sweets of society, and to prevent any nation, or people from disturbing our quiet.[49]

Here "Denatus" faithfully reproduced the Country view on the proper military establishment of a republic. A republic ought to be defended by its citizens in arms. But, as we have seen, Antifederalists had no monopoly on these ideas. Knox, who was certainly a Federalist, had presented very similar ideas about militia reform. What is most interesting in "Denatus"'s suggestion for reform is his awareness of the demands that the development of military technology and tactics placed on the citizen-soldier in modern war. These advances in military art meant that it took long practice for soldiers to master the skills of their craft. Consequently, as "Denatus" pointed out, the "great art in this business would be to regulate the militia in such a manner that neither agriculture, industry, commerce, nor the military spirit should suffer."[50] To most Federalists, this equation could not be solved. What they set about to do instead was to argue for a division of labor between the citizen and the soldier.

As "Denatus" noted, the militia was neither adequately trained nor disciplined to be able to engage a regular army. The trouble was that ordinary militiamen could not be counted on either to train for, or serve in, a militia of the kind "Denatus" and Knox proposed. In fact, the amount of training required to entitle the citizens "to the character of a well regulated militia" would be so time-consuming as to constitute "a real grievance to the people." Furthermore, the militiamen would refuse to do garrison duty in frontier posts. As Alexander Contee Hanson pointed out, "there are always honest purposes, which are not to be answered by a militia. If they were, the burthen on the militia would be so great, that a free people would, by no means, be willing to sustain it." This unwillingness to serve in the militia obviously challenged the classical conception of republican citizenship according to which soldiering was an integral part of citizenship. To the Federalists, such a merging of functions in the same person was neither rational nor desirable in the modern republic. The modern age was characterized by a more efficient employment of labor brought about by specialization. "The industrious habits" of modern men, wrote Hamilton, "absorbed in the pursuits of gain, and devoted to the improvements of agriculture and commerce are incompatible with the condition of a nation of soldiers, which was the true condition of the people of [the classical] republics."[51]

In the modern era, society was best organized by implementing the division of labor. The survival of the republic did not depend on the willingness of the citizens to appear in arms for the defense of their country. Rather, it depended on their willingness to toil in agriculture, for if agriculture "be neglected, every thing else must be in a state of ruin and decay. It must be neglected if those hands which ought to attend to it are occasionally called forth on military expeditions." No wonder, then, that Edmund Randolph could reject the idea that the militia ought to defend America because the "militia of our country will be wanted for agriculture." In *The Federalist*, Hamilton repeatedly criticized the use of the militia for military duties by pointing to the aggregate economic loss to society that followed from employing the militia to do the job of regulars. Even if militiamen could be prevailed on to garrison the western posts, "the increased expence of a frequent rotation of service, and the loss of labour and disconcertion of the industrious pursuits of individuals, would form conclusive objections to the scheme." Similarly, the time taken to train the citizens to become adequate soldiers would amount to a serious "annual deduction from the productive labour of the country." And to "attempt a thing which would abridge the mass of labour and industry to so considerable an extent would be unwise."[52] As Hamilton summed up the Federalist position, depending on the militia for peacetime defense "would be as burthensome and injurious to the public, as ruinous to private citizens."[53]

Much better, then, to accept the division of labor. If part of society was occupied with seeing to its defense and the rest was employed in agriculture, the result would be that "the arts of war and defence, and of cultivating the soil, will be understood. Agriculture will flourish, and military discipline will be perfect." But if the militia were entrusted with the re-public's defense, the result would be ignorance in arms and negligence in farming. Therefore, one could argue for a peacetime standing army in terms of cost efficiency. If the farmers were often called out to serve in the militia, they might lose their crops. This could be avoided "by a trivial expence, if appropriated to the purpose of supporting a part of the community, exclusively occupied in the defence of the whole."[54]

V

The Federalist response to Antifederalist fears denied that the Constitution would create a government of force, depriving the people of their property by means of a military execution of unjust tax laws. It also denied that the Constitution would lead to the establishment of a large standing army. The Federalists never retreated from their conviction that the United States had to possess an army of professional soldiers in time of peace. They believed, however, that this army could be of limited size and deployed so as not to come into contact with the majority of citizens. Most significantly, it would not be employed in the daily administration of government. For such purposes, the civil arm of the magistrate would be sufficient. In this context, the Federalists rejected the Antifederalist argument that the people would not regard acts of Congress as legitimate. To the contrary, good administration and a merger of federal and state administration would bestow legitimacy on the new national government. This legitimacy would be increased by the reduction of government demands on the citizens. Apart from Hamilton, no Federalist seriously addressed the question of militia reform. From what they said on the use of a standing army, however, we can see that the Federalists accepted a division of labor between the soldier and the citizen. In fact, Federalists and Antifederalists converged in their opinion that the people of America were not likely to accept demands for extensive public service but were more interested in their private pursuits. The difference between them was that the Federalists fully accepted this fact and formed their ideas of government accordingly.

9

THE FEDERALISTS AND THE
USES OF MILITARY POWERS

On 8 December 1795, in a confident tone, George Washington addressed the Fourth Congress. "Fellow-Citizens of the Senate and the House of Representatives," the president began. "I trust I do not deceive myself, when I indulge the persuasion, that I have never met you at any period, when more than at the present, the situation of our public affairs has afforded just cause for mutual congratulations."[1] The period following the adoption of the Constitution had been a difficult time for the new federal government. Toward the end of 1795, however, many of the problems that had plagued the young republic ever since it gained its independence in 1783 were either resolved or in the process of being resolved. In retrospect, this moment in Washington's second administration seems but a temporary respite before the Federalists had to deal with domestic and international crises arising from deteriorating relations with revolutionary France. But 1795 seemed a year that both called for expressions of gratitude to "the Author of all good" and provided cause for the branches of the federal government to offer mutual congratulations.

In a convenient way, the president's message sums up the achievements of the administration. Washington began by drawing attention to the pacification of the Indians in the Ohio country and to the recently concluded Treaty of Greenville. To the tribes in the Northwestern territory—and, indeed, to North American Indians in general—the army's victory at the Battle of Fallen Timbers and the subsequent treaty signed at Greenville were the opening stages of a tragedy. To the United States, by contrast, it meant that one of the most serious impediments to western expansion—an expansion pursued as eagerly by Federalists as by Republicans, although by different means and driven by different visions of the territory's future—had been removed. By 1795, peace had also been secured with the Indian nations in the Southwest. Of equal importance to the future development of the trans-Appalachian West was the conclusion of negotiations between the United States and the European powers that held neighboring possessions in the area. From the court of Madrid, Washington reported, news had arrived that the American envoy, Thomas Pinckney, was about to sign a treaty "securing amicably, very essential interests of the United States." Although the treaty with Britain had been publicly known for months, the president also took the opportunity to disclose officially that John Jay had concluded "a Treaty of Amity, Commerce and Navigation" with the former mother country. Pinckney's Treaty reopened the Mississippi River to American trade—thereby bringing to an end a conflict between the United States and Spain that began in 1784 when the river was closed—providing for the realization of the full economic potential of the West. Jay's Treaty was of no less importance to the future of the West. The treaty forced the British to evacuate the strategic military posts they occupied in breach of the 1783 peace treaty. These posts controlled the fur trade and the transport routes in the Old Northwest and therefore held the key to the pacification of the Indian nations living there. Without American possession of the posts, the Treaty of Greenville would have been no more than a dead letter. "This interesting summary of our affairs," Washington concluded

> with regard to the foreign powers between whom and the United States controversies have subsisted, and with regard also to those of our Indian neighbours, with whom we have been in a state of enmity or misunderstanding, opens a wide field for consoling and gratifying reflections. If by prudence and moderation on every side, the extinguishment of all the causes of external discord, which have heretofore menaced our tranquillity, on terms compatible with our national rights and honor, shall be the happy result; how firm and how precious a foundation will have been laid for accelerating, maturing and establishing the prosperity of our country!

In fact, by 1795, the economic prosperity of the United States was already well under way. The primary reason for this was the government's success in keeping the nation out of the wars of the French Revolution. Neutrality had saved the country from the hardships of war and the domestic turmoil suffered by European powers. "Agriculture, Commerce and Manufactures, prosper beyond former example," Washington noticed. The population was growing rapidly and "every part of the union displays indications of rapid and various improvement." What is more, this improvement had taken place "with burthens so light as scarcely to be perceived." Even the "misled" Whiskey Rebels had now "abandoned their errors" and paid "the respect to our Constitution and laws which is due from good citizens." Surely, the president had every right to wonder if it was "too much to say, that our country exhibits a spectacle of national happiness never surpassed, if ever before equaled?"[2]

But although the state of the nation offered cause for celebration, this state was precarious. Washington urged Congress to unite with the administration "to preserve, prolong and improve, our immense advantages." To do so, Congress was urged to consider a number of issues ranging from relations with the Indian nations to the state of the militia and the military and naval establishment, as well as the revenue and the public debt. The careful management of these matters was the source of the present happy state of the nation no less than the guarantee for its continued well-being.[3]

In the preceding chapters, I have analyzed the arguments used to attack and defend the Constitution's military clauses. In light of how the Federalist position and the meaning of the Constitution have often been interpreted, these arguments are important in themselves. Yet, any judgment on the political achievement of the Federalists obviously hinges on the extent to which they managed to translate their principles into action. Unfortunately, a full investigation of the development of the federal government in the years following the Constitution's ratification is beyond the scope of this book. All that I can attempt here is a brief sketch of the uses made by the national government of the military powers it was granted by the Constitution.

This attempt must start with the question of whether the achievements listed by Washington in his message to Congress really can be credited to the new modeling of the federal government. The First Congress had not been convened even six months when a Parisian crowd stormed the Bastille, thereby ushering in a quarter century of political upheaval, social change, and warfare on a scale never before seen. During this quarter century, the United States had to respond repeatedly to events originating in Europe far beyond the federal government's control. Overall, the United States drew advantage from the warfare that engulfed Britain, France, and Spain, but the question remains if the federal government had any part in making this possible. This is not an easy question to answer. In fact, it can only be answered, if at all, by investigating the perceptions held by the leading actors responsible for formulating and implementing the foreign policy of Britain, France, and Spain of the capacities and intentions of the federal government. Such investigations have long been out of fashion. Nevertheless, a cautious answer based on works of diplomatic history would be that the reform of the federal government did make a difference to the actions of European governments. Certainly, the United States remained peripheral to these governments and it posed no threat to any of them on its own. Yet the evidence suggests that Spain and Britain concluded treaties with the United States because they did not wish to see the American republic allied with their enemies.[4] With war raging in Europe, the United States was approaching, at least temporarily, the point Alexander Hamilton had dreamed of in *Federalist* 11, when "a price would be set not only upon our friendship, but upon our neutrality."[5]

In the end, however, the question of whether or not the Constitution ought to be credited with the republic's diplomatic, military, and economic successes in the decade after its adoption is of less importance to the argument presented here than it may at first seem. This is because the significant issue is less the effect achieved by the federal government when it used its new military and fiscal powers than the *way* in which the government used these powers. The Federalists believed that the federal government could only be successful if it avoided making heavy demands on the citizens and visible intrusions in their lives. The Antifederalists, by contrast, believed that the new federal government would be heavy and oppressive. The true test of the Federalists' political achievement was therefore whether or not they followed their principles when they transformed the articles of the Constitution into the policies and institutions of the new national government.

I

As Washington's address suggests, the administration had achieved two important things: economic prosperity and the belated consolidation of the peace treaty of 1783. The president did not exaggerate when he described the improvement of the American economy. Even before the First Congress met, the economy had begun to recover from the postwar depression. Exact figures are difficult to establish, but there is general consensus that the struggle for independence and the postwar years were a period of economic downturn.[6] A moderate assessment claims that, in per capita terms, the wartime depression "knocked the economy back to the level it had been at a half-century earlier."[7]

Although economists argue about the long-term significance of foreign trade to the development of the American economy, there is no doubt that both exports and imports declined substantially during the War of Independence and the postwar period.[8] After the war, trade failed to recover because of the commercial restrictions that Britain and other powers imposed on American ships and goods.[9] With the onset of the wars of the French Revolution, the situation changed radically for the better. British restrictions to trade with the West Indies now became so riddled with exceptions as to become almost ineffectual. It was in the interest of belligerents to shift their shipping to neutral carriers and, as a consequence, American exports and shipping experienced an extraordinary upsurge. The value of American exports doubled from $20 million in 1790 to $40 million in 1795 and the value of reexports rose from zero to $10 million.[10] Meanwhile, the tonnage of U.S. vessels in foreign trade entering U.S. ports increased from 354,767 tons in 1790 to 580,277 tons in 1795, whereas the tonnage of British vessels entering U.S. ports declined from 216,914 tons to 27,079 tons. By the end of 1795, more than 90 percent of American trade was carried in American ships. Altogether, earnings from shipping increased four times between 1790 and 1795.[11]

Economic prosperity was based on political neutrality. Challenged both by domestic critics and international threats, the Federalist administration strove hard to keep the United States from being dragged into the European war. The Democratic-Republican demand for commercial discrimination against Britain was easily fought off with reference to the rapid expansion of American trade.[12] The actions of Britain and France, however, were a greater threat to the administration's aims. Because U.S. merchantmen carried goods to and from both British and French possessions in the Americas, it was inevitable that they would be attacked by the other side. In March 1794, news of a campaign of British seizures in the West Indies caused an outrage in the United States. In Congress, Federalists and Democratic-Republicans vied with each other to come up with forceful countermeasures. In terms of actual legislation, however, little came out of these congressional debates. Meanwhile, leading Federalists worked to convince Washington to attempt a diplomatic solution to the crisis before initiating hostilities. Washington agreed and, on 18 May 1794, sent John Jay to negotiate with the British.[13]

Jay has often been accused of negotiating a poor treaty for the United States. Even a diplomatic historian generally sympathetic to the Federalists concludes that "except perhaps for the right to trade with British India, Jay did fail to win anything more than what Americans were obviously entitled to."[14] If the Treaty of Amity, Commerce, and Navigation is regarded only as a commercial treaty, this is a fair conclusion. By agreeing to the treaty, the United States at least temporarily abandoned the struggle, in which it had been involved since the Revolution, to create a more liberal commercial order and accepted Britain's interpretation of the rights of neutral traders in wartime. The treaty also prohibited both parties from employing commercial discrimination against the other party, thereby depriving the United States of a weapon Democratic-Republicans believed to be formidable. But presenting the Jay Treaty as no more than a commercial treaty misrepresents Jay's mission. Jay's instructions reveal that he was sent to Britain first of all to avoid war by demanding compensation for British seizures. His second objective was to settle a number of outstanding differences over the Treaty of Peace and Independence from 1783. Only if these two objectives were settled to the satisfaction of the United States should Jay proceed to consider a commercial agreement.[15]

If Jay's instructions are compared to the Federalist arguments in defense of the Constitution during the ratification debate, it is noteworthy that a commercial treaty ranked so low compared to the mission's other objectives. In 1787 and 1788, a commercial treaty was believed to be essential to the recovery of the American economy. But, when war broke out in Europe, Britain and France needed American carriers and American goods with or without a treaty. As a consequence, in 1794, a commercial treaty seemed relatively unimportant. If the agreement is therefore seen not primarily as a commercial treaty but is judged according to the priorities of Jay's instructions, his mission must be counted a success. To the Federalists, the treaty achieved two crucial things: First, it kept the United States out of the war and thereby made sure that the economy would continue to prosper; second, it succeeded in finally making Britain comply with the peace treaty of 1783. Britain now transferred the important military posts in the Northwest Territory to the United States.[16] With the posts in American hands, the United States could control the Indian nations that inhabited the Ohio country. Together with the military victory at the Battle of Fallen Timbers, this ensured that the first of two main impediments to western expansion was removed. Soon after the signing of the Jay Treaty, the Treaty of San Lorenzo would remove the second by reopening the Mississippi River to American trade.[17]

The importance of the reopening of the Mississippi and the conquering of the Indian nations to the subsequent development of the West is perhaps seen most clearly in the region's rapid growth in population. In 1790, there were 74,000 people living in Kentucky and 36,000 in Tennessee. Ten years later, the population of both states had almost tripled. By 1800, an additional 45,000 settlers lived in Ohio and another 6,000 in Indiana. Of the total population growth of the United States between 1790 and 1800, a full 20 percent took place in the four states mentioned.[18] But the region was not only growing; the ties between the federal government and the West were now safely established. In the future, the region would advance its interests within the union and not through threats of secession. Western expansion also raised the value of the national land in the Northwest Territory and, from Thomas Jefferson's presidency onward, land sales yielded a substantial income to the federal government. As Andrew Cayton sums up the Federalist achievement in the West, "in a decade and a half, they had transformed trans-Appalachia from a potential source of revenue, disunion and chaos, into a region of genuine revenue, growing external security, and increasing loyalty to the United States of America."[19]

II

When the federal government acted to safeguard and promote the territorial and commercial interests of the United States in the 1790s, it made use not only of diplomacy but also of the military powers it had been granted by the Constitution. In the ratification debate, Antifederalists expressed fear that the national government would use its military powers to deprive the people of their liberties. Specifically, they claimed that the Federalists would establish a large army, that they would use this army to implement illegitimate and unpopular policies, and, finally, that the Federalists would either disarm the militia or make service in the militia odious.

The Federalists, by contrast, ensured that they would create only a very small peacetime army that would be used to police the frontier and therefore be garrisoned out of sight of the vast majority of Americans. They also protested against the charge that their rule would rest on military force, and, finally, they presented an argument in favor of a division of labor between the citizen and the soldier that suggested that military service ought not to be a duty inherent to citizenship. In the end, Federalist policies proved every Antifederalist prediction wrong. Before the crisis with France toward the end of the decade, Federalists made no attempt to expand the army beyond very narrow confines. Nor did they use regulars against civilians with the one exception of Fries's Rebellion in 1799, which occurred in the midst of an undeclared war with France. When it came to the militia, finally, every reform proposal that promised to turn the militia into an efficient force stumbled on the refusal of Congress to impose burdens on the citizenry. In the ratification debate, Federalists had been vague about how they envisioned the future peace establishment. The small regular army they advocated would perhaps be adequate as a border constabulary, but it would not be sufficient to secure the United States against attack. In the end, beyond its very limited regular army, the Federalists failed to develop military institutions that both worked and were acceptable to the American people. As the War of 1812 demonstrated, their successors fared no better.

The Federalists made use of armed force against civilians on two occasions, when subduing the Whiskey Rebellion in 1794 and Fries's Rebellion in 1799. On both occasions, coercion was used to secure the implementation of tax legislation. The response to the Whiskey Rebellion is sometimes believed to epitomize Federalist attitudes toward the common people. Heavy and regressive duties on whiskey provoked just protests that the administration callously put down by force of arms. Some historians even claim that the Federalists "followed the example of the British ruling class in aggressively suppressing domestic dissent."[20] This description of Federalist policy seems exaggerated. Routine administration under Washington and John Adams did not meet with resistance and did not rest on force any more than did later administrations. In fact, a closer look at how Washington handled protests against the whiskey excise shows that the administration knew well that it could not rest its authority on coercion.

When they answered Antifederalist attacks during the ratification debate, Federalists openly declared that the national government would have both a right and a duty to suppress insurrections. But they also said that should suppression be necessary, the government would rely on the law-abiding citizenry rather than the army. When the excise on whiskey was introduced in 1791, it gave rise to protests almost immediately. Yet the federal government did not respond with coercion but with an amendment to the excise law that reduced duties and facilitated payment of the tax. Nevertheless, the protests continued. At this point, there was disagreement within Washington's cabinet whether or not to employ force. The president, however, settled on issuing a warning to the protesters as part of his fourth annual message to Congress. But after the protests had escalated further and a mob attacked the district excise inspector in early 1794, Washington decided that the protests had gone too far.[21]

By early August, Supreme Court Justice James Wilson had declared that federal excise laws were obstructed "by combinations too powerful to be suppressed by the ordinary course of judicial proceedings" in several counties in western Pennsylvania. Under the Militia Act, this gave the president the right "to call forth the militia" to suppress the protests.[22] Despite the fact that the administration now had lawful right to use armed force against the Whiskey Rebels, it proceeded with caution, sending negotiators and a further warning to the protesters. In his proclamation of 7 August, Washington tried to secure the support of public opinion for the actions of the government. He stressed that the government had so far acted with leniency because it expected that the rebels would mend their ways. Washington also stated his intention to mobilize the militia and explained that he had the legal right to do so by quoting at length from the Militia Act. Finally, he called on "the patriotism and firmness of all good citizens" to aid the government in reducing the rebellion. Later the same month, the secretary of the treasury, Alexander Hamilton, tried to gain further public support by publishing a detailed letter in which he explained the advantages of excise duties compared to other forms of taxation and outlined the attempts made by the administration to remove the grounds for the distillers' discontent. In particular, Hamilton stressed that the government had tried to avoid "the ultimate resort, till all milder means had been tried without success."[23]

When the government commissioners sent to western Pennsylvania reported that negotiations had failed and that they therefore recommended "military coercion," Washington finally ordered the militia to mobilize. It should be noted that the administration never contemplated the use of regulars against the excise protests. The careful publication of the protesters' actions and the emphasis on the patience and leniency of the government now paid off. The Philadelphia militia responded with enthusiasm and even the primary Republican paper supported coercion. Leading Democratic-Republicans in Pennsylvania such as William Findley, Albert Gallatin, and Hugh Henry Brackenridge all condemned the rebels.[24] But the most striking proof of the government's successful handling of the rebellion was the declarations of support emanating from the Democratic-Republican Societies, usually the administration's harshest critics. The Democratic Society of Chittenden, Vermont, presented the president "with their unfeigned thanks for the lenient proceedings he in the first instance adopted, against the Western insurgents, by deputing commissioners to treat with them, and for the spirited and effectual measures he afterwards pursued, for enforcing a due submission to the laws." Its sister society in

Philadelphia told the public that, in response to the president's call, "many members of this Association voluntarily stepped forward to maintain the legal authority, and joined those patriotic bands of Citizen-soldiers" who marched to restore order in western Pennsylvania.[25]

Compared to the volunteer force of more than 10,000 men sent to coerce the Whiskey Rebels, the suppression of Fries's Rebellion was a minor affair. Adams sent only 1,500 men to deal with the rebellion. Probably because Fries's Rebellion was a smaller event than the Whiskey Rebellion, and because it took place in the midst of the conflict with France, Adams seemed less hesitant than Washington had been to use force against the protestors. In retrospect, the most significant aspect of Adams's handling of the rebellion is that the federal government used regular troops in addition to militia to suppress protests. This gave the Republican charge that the Federalists aimed to establish a military despotism some credibility and it is likely that it affected the outcome of the presidential election of 1800.[26]

Despite Republican protests against Adams's actions, the trend toward increasing reliance on regulars in domestic disturbances continued during Jefferson's presidency. Jefferson found the militia unable to deal both with the Burr Conspiracy and with the protests against the Embargo Acts. At the president's request, Congress passed a law in March 1807 declaring that "in all cases where it is lawful for the President of the United States to call forth the militia for the purpose of . . . causing the laws to be duly executed it shall be lawful for him to employ, for the same purposes, such part of the land and naval force of the United States, as shall be judged necessary." Two years later, another law gave the president the right to use the army to enforce the Embargo Acts. Commenting on the latter law, one historian has written that it represents "the only time in American history that the President was empowered to use the army for routine or day-by-day execution of the laws." In fact, Jefferson called out the army only in Vermont and New York and relied for the most part on the militia to suppress protests. His presidency cannot be said to have rested on force any more than the Federalist administrations before him. By extending the right of the federal government to use the regular army as a police force, however, Jefferson helped to blur the distinction that the Federalists had tried to draw during the ratification debate between the proper response to large-scale insurrections, on the one hand, and to minor cases of disobedience to federal legislation, on the other.[27]

Until the Civil War, the federal government continued to make use of a mixed force of regulars and militia whenever it employed coercion against civilians. Quite apart from the use of the Union Army during Reconstruction, there was a marked change in policy after the Civil War. Between 1867 and 1957, there is no incident when a president called on the militia to deal with civil disturbances. Instead, the federal government came to rely solely on the service of regulars. In the last quarter of the nineteenth century, one of the most important duties of the army was to break up strikes that only rarely involved any challenge to federal legislation. According to one estimate, the army was employed in more than three hundred labor disputes in this period. During the Pullman strike in 1894, of the army's nominal 25,000 men, 16,000 were made available against the strikers. Admittedly, the army's intervention in labor disputes was merely the tip of an iceberg of National Guard interventions in response to calls from state governments. But, given the widespread fear of a standing army a century earlier, it is striking that the government could now use regulars for such purposes. There were certainly critics of the government's use of force, but it seems reasonable to conclude that during the century following Washington's suppression of the Whiskey Rebellion, the federal government felt increasingly confident about using regular soldiers against civilians as a means to maintain order and to realize its policies.[28]

III

By comparative standards, the American republic possessed an exceptionally small army well into the twentieth century. For a brief period in the immediate postindependence period, the United States even tried to manage without any army altogether. Conflict with Indian nations in the Northwest Territory soon forced the Continental Congress to recruit a force of 700 men, which became the First American Regiment. Despite the fact that Federalists saw the republic's military weakness as one of the major defects of the Confederation, the army grew only slowly after the adoption of the Constitution. The First American Regiment was augmented to 1,216 men in 1790 and another regiment was added the following year. The army was increased to 5,100 in 1792 and to 5,800 in 1794. At this point, the army had reached its zenith and it was reduced to 3,100 in 1796. A peace establishment of around 3,000 would then be the norm under both Adams and Jefferson. Jefferson increased the army to 9,300 in 1809 and James Madison maintained a peace establishment of 10,000 men, not counting officers, after the War of 1812. In 1821, the army was again reduced to 5,600 and the peace establishment fluctuated between this low point and a high of 11,804 until the war with Mexico. Both during the Quasi-War and the War of 1812, the nominal strength of the army was much greater, although in the former case the troops were never mobilized, whereas there was a wide discrepancy between actual and nominal numbers in the war against Britain.[29]

Although the army was small and although recruitment was sometimes difficult, in comparison to the record from the War of Independence it is still noteworthy that the nation now managed to keep 3–6,000 men permanently under arms. The intermittent expansion of the army also shows that the federal government could use military force as a policy instrument. The Federalists responded to crises with the Indians in the early 1790s, with England in 1794, and with France in 1798 by increasing, or preparing to increase, the republic's military potential. But it was not the Federalists but the Republicans who put the federal government's military powers to greatest use. In 1812, they went to war to realize U.S. policy objectives relating to free trade and neutral rights.

A peacetime army of 3,000 men hardly lived up to Antifederalist fears of an American standing army of Prussian proportions. Yet it is symptomatic of the persistence of antiarmy sentiments that even this tiny force gave rise to political resistance. In fact, the army increased only as a response to immediate crisis. The Second Regiment was raised in 1791 after an expeditionary force under Josiah Harmar had suffered defeat from a confederation of Indian tribes in present-day Ohio. The American Legion was formed in 1792, as a direct consequence of the annihilation of Arthur St. Clair's expedition by the same foe. During the crises with France and Britain, the army also grew. The normal pattern, however, was for the army to return to its low precrisis level as soon as the crisis appeared to be resolved. In this way, wartime increases of the army never became permanent. Thus, Anthony Wayne's successful use of the Legion at the Battle of Fallen Timbers also proved the Legion's undoing. After the Greenville and the Jay Treaties had been concluded, Congress cut the strength of the army by half. After war with France had been aborted in 1800, the Federalists reduced the army and Jefferson then reduced it even further after he gained the presidency. In the same way, Monroe could not maintain the military build up initiated by Madison after the War of 1812 because Congress saw no need for a large army. This resistance to permanent increases of the army shows no consistent partisan pattern. Congress acted in much the same way regardless of whether it was dominated by Federalists or by Republicans.[30]

Despite the fact that the Federalists never created a substantial standing army, they are sometimes portrayed as supporters of a large military establishment. According to this argument, the military build up during the Quasi-War reveals the Federalists' true colors. Under the pretext of preparing for a war with France, the Federalists raised an army in reality intended to suppress their political opponents. Yet, Richard Kohn, the most careful student of Federalist military thought and policy, has found no evidence that more than a fraction of the Federalist party, the followers of Hamilton, "wanted the army precisely for the reasons most Americans rejected it: its ability to suppress dissent and intimidate the population." This portrayal of Hamilton as a militarist has recently been challenged, and Kohn's interpretation is at least open to doubt. But what must surely be more important is that, even if this description should be correct, there were forces *within* the Federalist party strong enough to stop the use of the army against political opponents. Even if Hamilton really was "the personification of American militarism," his stance in 1799 cannot be made to represent the Federalists and the age of Federalism anymore than Madison's position in 1815 can be made to represent the Republicans and the rule of the Virginia dynasty.[31]

The fact that the Federalists never created a large military establishment does not mean that the army they created was unimportant. But its importance in the development of the nation was confined mainly to the gradual expansion of the western frontier. The Washington administration's policy in the West aimed to secure the peaceful and ordered settlement of federal land in what is today the state of Ohio. This land was owned, inhabited, and controlled by a number of Indian nations, among them the Miami and Shawnee. Despite its commitment to western expansion, the administration also wanted to avoid war. An Indian war would be costly and, even should the United States be victorious, that victory would be of limited value as long as the British controlled the military posts commanding the supply and transportation routes to Canada. The federal government therefore tried to keep settlers from provoking war, while attempting to make the Indians give up their land by treaty. The administration had no problem realizing that the interests of the settlers and the Indians were incompatible and that the government had to be the arbiter of this conflict. In the end, however, the government never managed to reconcile these clashing interests but used the army to destroy the Indian tribes, thereby setting a pattern that would often be repeated as the republic pursued its westward course.[32]

When the Indian nations that inhabited the Ohio area refused to give up their land but instead insisted on maintaining the Ohio River as the western limit to United States settlement, negotiations broke down. The Washington administration decided to put pressure on the Indians by using military force. However, the failure of Harmar's campaign in the fall of 1790 meant that what had been intended as a show of force became a demonstration of weakness. To remove the stain of failure, a new campaign was mounted the following fall. It fared no better than the previous one. To this day, St. Clair's defeat remains one of the greatest setbacks ever in the history of the U.S. Army. The destruction of St. Clair's force led to the reorganization and expansion of the army into the American Legion. Under the command of Anthony Wayne, the Legion defeated the Indian confederacy at the Battle of Fallen Timbers on 20 August 1794. Together with the transfer of the British posts as a result of the Jay Treaty, the defeat broke the military power of the tribes and demonstrated that the federal government possessed both the will and the power to assert its sovereignty in the West. The new situation was reflected in the Treaty of Greenville, signed in the summer of 1795, by which the Indian nations made peace with the United States and gave up most of present-day Ohio and part of what would become the state of Indiana.[33]

The army had been brought into existence to deal with western expansion and to coerce the Indians. With the conclusion of the Jay Treaty and the Treaty of Greenville, its rationale for existence was therefore removed. Hence, by 1795, the army was at a critical juncture. In 1783, Congress had demobilized the remains of the Continental Army when reached by news of the peace treaty with Britain. In 1795 and 1796, however, no one suggested that the United States could manage without a regular army in time of peace. Antiarmy sentiments had not disappeared completely, but most of the opposition consisted in attempts to weigh the costs of the army against the military needs of the republic. With peace secured, the expense of retaining the army at full strength could not be justified. But the traditional fear for the future of liberty no longer held first place in a debate about the peacetime standing army. Even a leading Republican such as Gallatin could claim that "the present question was merely a money bill. If there was no occasion for five thousand men, it was better that they should only have three, because it would save money." Less than a decade after the adoption of the Constitution, the opposition had come to share with the Federalists the belief that a small standing army in time of peace was a guarantee for rather than a threat to popular liberties. In the history of the U.S. Army, as well as in the history of the conception of the military needs of the republic, this was certainly an important turning point. As Kohn notes, the 1796 Act to Ascertain and fix the Military Establishment "marked the beginning of America's peacetime army."[34]

When they created the peace establishment, the Federalists were true to the promises they had made during the ratification debate. The army was not used as a police force the way that regulars had long been used in Britain. It was deployed in small contingents along the western frontier and it remained exceptionally small by comparative standards. For this reason, the army was never a presence in American society the way that regular soldiers were in Europe. Apart from the settlers on the frontier, the citizenry was unlikely to ever come into contact with regulars. The army also fulfilled the rather precise and limited role that the Federalists had claimed it would. It was essentially a border constabulary that policed the frontier and kept the Indians in check.[35]

Jefferson came to power the avowed enemy of standing armies. But the often-quoted words from his first inaugural address that "a well-disciplined Militia" was the republic's "best reliance in peace and for the first moments of war till regulars may relieve them" did not signal an intention to abolish the small army he inherited from Adams.[36] Temporarily, Jefferson reduced the army before international tension forced him to increase it again, but he left the organization, deployment, and function of the Federalists' peace establishment essentially intact. His main contribution to the military establishment was the creation of a military academy at West Point, something that had proved politically impossible for the Federalists to achieve. In fact, the army established by the Federalists remained the peace establishment of the United States throughout the nineteenth century. As the century wore on, the army grew in real numbers but shrank relative to the population. The ratio between military force and population never reached the level of the 1790s in any peacetime year of the nineteenth century. It was only with the advent of the Cold War that the United States came to create a powerful peacetime army. Relative to the total population, the armed forces in 1970 was fifteen times greater than in 1800.[37] The army's function as a frontier constabulary also remained unchanged throughout the nineteenth century. Its primary role was to prepare the way for settlers by policing and eventually destroying the Indian nations.[38]

IV

The army created by the Federalists and inherited by the Republicans was designed neither for defense against invasion nor for deterrence against invasion. In his first inaugural address, Jefferson said of the Federalists' army that "for defence against invasion, their number is as nothing." The extent of the republic meant that "the only force that can be ready at any point" to oppose an enemy was "the body of neighboring citizens as formed into a militia." Almost two decades earlier, Washington had said the same thing when drawing up his "Sentiments on a Peace Establishment," designed for the newly independent United States. Although in favor of creating a small regular army, Washington was also convinced "that the only probable means of preventing insult or hostility for any length of time and from being exempted from the consequent calamities of War" was "to put the National Militia in such a condition as that they may appear truly respectable in the Eyes of our Friends and formidable to those who would otherwise be our enemies."[39] For deterrence and defense, the United States would look to the militia.

If the militia were to serve as the first line of defense in the event of invasion, it had to be radically reformed. Seven years after Washington had written his "Sentiments," he repeated the call for militia reform in his first annual message to Congress, noting that "a free people ought not only to be armed but disciplined; to which a uniform and well digested plan is requisite." Congress did not agree. When Jefferson assumed the presidency, the militia remained unreformed. In *his* first annual message, Jefferson asked Congress to renew work on "the laws regulating the militia, until they are sufficiently perfect. Nor should we now or at any time separate, until we can say we have done everything for the militia which we could do were an enemy at our door."[40] But Jefferson was as unsuccessful as the Federalists. Regardless of whether the reform proposal originated with a Federalist or a Republican administration and regardless of party strength in Congress, reform was always rejected.

There were two basic alternatives for militia reform. The first was to form a select militia much smaller than the ordinary militia, something that Hamilton had proposed to the Continental Congress in 1783 and had repeated during the ratification debate in *Federalist* 29. The other was to do something about the general militia. For political—if not principled—reasons, both Federalist and Republican administrations decided on the second alternative. But this choice had its own difficulties, for it ran up against a persistent unwillingness in Congress to let the federal government place any burdens on the citizens. No matter how much the citizens may have disliked a standing army, the army was never more than a *potential* threat to their liberty. Militia regulation, by contrast, affected them directly. As one Congressman said, militia legislation was "a law that affects every individual, touches the whole community."[41] This was in marked contrast to the border constabulary that passed for the republic's army.

During the ratification debate, the Federalists had argued for a division of labor between the soldier and the citizen when they defended the creation of a regular army. They had also showed their awareness of the American people's unwillingness to submit to arduous militia service. Yet, when Secretary of War Henry Knox presented his militia plan in January 1790, these ideas were conspicuously absent. Knox's plan was a plan to reform the general militia. True, because he suggested classing by age, military service was primarily a duty for young men. Still, it was a universal duty, and Knox even sought to significantly reduce the number of persons eligible for exemption from service. Had Knox's plan been accepted, the federal government would have controlled the training and organization of the militia; it would have supplied its arms and equipment; and it would have had the right to draft men for military service from the militia in times of emergency. The plan had the potential to turn the militia into an efficient force, but it would do so only by laying claim to the citizens' property and labor. Congress thought the price too dear.[42]

Surprise and disbelief greeted the plan. Senator William Maclay even suspected that Knox's real aim was to stir up resistance to militia reform so as to make pending proposals for expanding the regular army easier to swallow.[43] Only with the news of St. Clair's defeat did Congress take any action. On 8 May 1792, Congress passed "An Act more effectually to provide for the National Defence by establishing an Uniform Militia throughout the United States." Reform had been debated on and off since December 1790 and the main result of these deliberations was that Congress had stripped Knox's plan of all the measures that promised to turn the militia into a working force. The Militia Act had no provision for classing militiamen by age; federal control over training, organization, and equipment was removed; and Congress's right to draft men from the militia was removed as well. The Militia Act ensured that every aspect of the militia's organization and training would remain the concern of the states but it did nothing to make sure. With good reason it was described as a "milk-and-water law," to all effects not a reform but a preservation of the status quo.[44]

When Congress debated Knox's plan—and, later, when reform proposals were debated in Congress—arguments that had figured in the ratification debate reappeared, thus demonstrating the persistence of the belief that the federal government had no right to demand burdensome service from the citizens. Knox's requirement that the men in the youngest class would train for a full month each year was regarded as "a great and unnecessary tax on the community." Nor was it the case that families and employers could afford the loss of income and labor that would be the consequence of such training. These young men, it was said, "would be journeymen; others newly married. They would be forced to leave their employment, and lose their customers, who in their absence would employ others." In the midst of the Quasi-War, a number of prominent Republicans—Findley and Gallatin among them—opposed a proposal for militia reform by saying that "to take young men away from their business which they might be just commencing, for ten or twelve days at a time, would ruin them."[45]

When the Federalist Theodore Sedgwick calculated the costs of a reform proposal presented in 1795, he included the cost of labor lost to society. "The value of the time was not, indeed to be paid out of the Treasury," he conceded, "but it was a loss to the productiveness of the public." Sedgwick did not hesitate to compare military service to "all the necessary and useful occupations of labor" and noted that it was particularly unfortunate that so much labor of persons "in the most profitable and productive period of life" would be lost to the community. But too much military service would also corrupt the character of the American citizen. "In Sparta," Sedgwick said, "the only country where an attempt has been effectually made to create a whole community of soldiers, the existence of slavery rendered labor disgraceful to citizens." This was in marked contrast to America where labor was equally necessary "to promote the happiness of our country" and to continue the "virtuous habits" of "the yeomanry of America."[46] In contrast to the citizen of Sparta, the duty of the American citizen was to be a farmer, a mechanic, or a tradesman, not a soldier.

Although the Federalists tried several times to reform the militia and although Jefferson did so repeatedly and Madison tried both before and after the War of 1812, Congress never acted. Instead, the militia continued to suffer the neglect of both the federal and the state governments throughout the nineteenth century. Despite its shortcomings and despite the many attempts to repeal it, the militia legislation passed by the second Congress proved to be long-lived. Only with the Dick Act of 1903—which provided for the standardization of the arms, equipment, organization, and discipline of the National Guard with those of the regular army and that gave the federal government the responsibility for providing arms and equipment—did Congress finally repeal the Militia Act of 1792.[47]

V

The War of 1812 is often referred to as a second war of independence, a war that proved the Jeffersonians right in their belief that the American republic could successfully defend its rights and interests without replicating the fiscal-military machinery of contemporary European states. But, in fact, the United States did not emerge from the war with Britain confident of its own strength. It emerged from the War of 1812 with the belief of the political leadership in Jeffersonian principles fundamentally shaken. After the war had come to a close, the Madison administration proposed several reforms that were incompatible with cherished Jeffersonian ideals. The strength of the peacetime army was increased to 10,000 men, more than three times the size of the Federalist peace establishment but no more than half the strength for which the president had asked. Faith in the militia was abandoned and reliance placed in the regular army. A new national bank was chartered and wartime internal taxes retained. The contemporary Republican and government critic John Randolph complained that the administration's program "*out-Hamiltons* Alexander Hamilton," while historians have argued that Madison's proposals signifies his realization that "Hamilton had been right, at least in significant part." In a hostile world, the American republic could not maintain its independence unless it emulated the fiscal and military institutions of contemporary European states.[48] Commentators are surely right to point out that this was a remarkable development of the position held by the Republican executive leadership. One historian has even claimed that Madison's reform package marked "the advent of a very different age."[49] But while it is true that Madison's postwar policies signified a radical break with established practice, those policies were of short duration. The military build-up as well as the retention of internal taxation were the result of a pressing international situation. Once that situation had changed, the legitimacy of these novel fiscal-military measures disappeared.

In 1815, it was far from certain that the European war would not flare up again. From the perspective of the United States, the Treaty of Ghent had left several issues unresolved and there were also questions outstanding with Spain. For the first time in the history of the United States, it was the republic's own expansionist policies that threatened to trigger war with Britain or Spain. In this situation, and with the failures of the recent war in fresh memory, it proved possible to secure a congressional majority for the creation of a military establishment that could serve as an instrument of foreign policy. This entailed expanding the role of the army beyond that of a frontier constabulary, to include preparation for war with European states.[50] But this new understanding of the role of regular troops in the military establishment and of the role of the military establishment in foreign policy proved to be short lived. Five years after Madison's reform proposals were presented to Congress, the international situation giving rise to them had been radically transformed. The danger of war in Europe no longer seemed imminent. By means of treaties concluded with Britain in 1818 and Spain in 1819 the tension in the republic's relations to its immediate neighbors had subsided. With the toning down of expansionist ambitions among the political leadership, there was reason to believe that relations to Spain and Britain would continue to be peaceful. With the rationale for the expanded army thus gone, the Monroe administration was defeated by a Congress that saw no need for military preparedness. The size of the army was reduced to its pre-1812 level and its duties again confined to policing the frontier.[51]

With the administration's failed attempt to retain a peacetime army sufficiently strong to allow the United States to be prepared for war, and with the continued failure to reform the militia, the question of military preparedness remained unresolved. As Europe and the Atlantic world entered the era of free trade and free security after the end of the Napoleonic War, the American republic came to rely for its security on the weakness of its neighbors and on the vastness of the Atlantic Ocean.

III

Fiscal Powers

10

CONGRESSIONAL INSOLVENCY

A government's ability to extract money from society lay at the very heart of the state-building process in early modern Europe. The national government created by the Articles of Confederation experienced serious difficulties in this respect, and in the end it failed to raise sufficient money to meet its expenses. In this short chapter, it is impossible to give a complete account of the history of public finance and taxation during the War of Independence and the Confederation era. Nor is it possible to go into the technicalities of the public debt, which resulted from the war against Britain, in all its bewildering detail. In a very general way, the focus of the chapter is instead on the means by which Congress raised money from the outbreak of war up to the Philadelphia Convention, and also on how, one by one, these means were lost. By 1787 the insolvency of the national government was total. The problem had to be addressed—and the Constitution was by no means the only way to do so—or the Confederation was in danger of passing into oblivion.

Although the first and the second parts of this chapter describe at greater length Congress's attempts to raise money through loans and taxes, the basic outline can be readily summarized here. Congress fought Britain on credit, raising the necessary resources by making use of the printing press, supply certificates, and loans. As far as public finance is concerned, the history of the war is a history of the gradual decline of the public's faith in Congress's ability to honor its obligations. As faith in the government gradually dissipated, the various means of raising money on government credit were destroyed. With its credit deteriorated, the federal government tried to raise money by requisitions on the states, demanding that the state legislatures tax the people on its behalf. Nationalists in Congress also tried to amend the Articles of Confederation in order to grant the national government an independent revenue in the form of customs duties, the so-called impost. Although the states did pay part of the requisitions, they failed to raise enough money to cover congressional expenses. Meanwhile, the impost proposals did not come through. In 1787, Congress had debts and obligations but no money. The problem lay partly in the structure of the federal government. The Articles of Confederation granted Congress the right to borrow money but not the means to pay its debts. But the problem lay also in the inability, or unwillingness, of the American people to contribute to the costs of the national government.[1]

I

Under the Articles of Confederation, Congress did not possess an income independent of the states. Instead, the power to tax remained with the state governments and the federal government had to raise money through requisitions on the states. When the conflict with Britain created a demand for money, however, Congress did not at first ask the states to tax their citizens. Political prudence suggested that the new state governments would do well not to press their right to levy taxes on a people suffering the hardships of war, in particular as the war was brought about by resistance to taxation in the first place.[2] But regardless of such concerns, an attempt to finance the war with taxes would have been anomalous. In the modern era, wars were fought with borrowed money.[3] To take the most pertinent example, the other party to the conflict in America, the British government, financed the war by increasing its national debt by £58 million. Similarly, the cost of the French participation in the conflict added almost a billion livres to France's public debt.[4]

Still, the Americans funded their war effort in a very different way from their enemy. In Britain, a system by which the government raised money by selling interest-bearing securities had developed since the accession of William III. The government took great pains to service the debt religiously and it was a care that paid off. The ability of the British government to borrow huge amounts of money for long terms at low interest was the marvel of the world.[5] Congress, however, chose to rely on another expedient: fiat money. But printing money was not a desperate act by a government devoid of other means to make ends meet. The American experience of financing a sustained and large-scale war effort was limited to a single case: the Seven Years' War. The pecuniary means to fight that conflict was created by emissions of paper currency, which had proved a successful strategy. In 1775, political leaders in America simply attempted to repeat that success.[6] This time, however, "currency finance" was tried out on a vastly greater scale and, which was worse, without meeting the conditions necessary for it to work.

By creating a continental currency alongside the Continental army in 1775, Congress made sure that the responsibility not only for directing the war but also for financing it came to rest with the federal government. Fiat money gave Congress an independent income and a freedom of action in relation to the states, which the Articles of Confederation had denied it. Even so, there appear to have been no protests against the decision. The continental currency held its value until the autumn of 1776, after which inflation set in, leading eventually to the collapse of the currency in the spring of 1781 when it passed out of circulation.[7] It is not hard to see why this happened. Just like selling securities, emitting paper money was a means for governments to finance extraordinary expenditures by anticipating tax returns. But, just as the interest on securities had to be paid, so fiat money had to be managed in order to avoid depreciation. When issuing the currency, the government had to pledge to withdraw the paper within a specified and not too distant time. It did so by taxing it out of existence, something that required a tax rise. In fact, the primary use of the paper to the recipients was as a means to pay taxes, although it was also often made legal tender. Finally, there was a limit to the amount of paper that a colony's economy could absorb before the market became glutted. In short, a government emitting paper had to control the size of the emission and the means to withdraw it from circulation through taxation. If it did, the system had a fair chance to work. The problem that Congress faced during the War of Independence was that it controlled neither.[8]

Although the federal government controlled the printing press, the actual demand for money was determined by the war rather than by Congress. When hostilities with Britain began, there was no anticipation of a lengthy conflict, but as the war and the emissions of money continued, the critical point where the economy was no longer able to absorb the paper was soon reached. During the Seven Years' War the colonies successfully emitted £1.7 million of paper money. By comparison Congress printed $226 million—equivalent in value to $45.5 million, or £10.2 million specie—between the start of the War of Independence and 1780. Neither did Congress control withdrawals. It tried doing so by pledging the faith of the state legislatures to the redemption of the very first emission but without making a formal requisition for money. There existed no means by which the federal government could guarantee that the states would tax away the paper, and it possessed no sanctions with which to secure compliance. In fact, the states did not levy any taxes at all during 1775 and 1776. When inflation threatened the continental currency, Congress put pressure on the states and, in November 1777, the first formal requisition was adopted. But, as the states failed to respond sufficiently, depreciation could not be halted. Eventually, the currency became worthless and passed out of circulation. No attempt was ever made to compensate its holders. Although the states were hard pressed during the war and may have been unable to tax the continental currency out of existence, this does not alter the crucial fact that after 1779 it was no longer possible to finance the war or the administration of the federal government by printing money.[9]

The continental currency may be regarded as a failure of public finance, but it may with equal justice be counted a success. In the end, Congress got $45.5 million worth of spending power through the paper. The decline in the value of the currency to worthlessness can be—and by some contemporaries indeed was—regarded as a form of tax, extracting from the people of the United States by means of inflation what the states could, or would, not raise through taxation.[10] Yet, there was one obvious drawback. Any attempt to finance future extraordinary expenditures by emitting paper backed by nothing but the faith of Congress was doomed from the start. Without an amendment to the Articles of Confederation granting Congress the power to tax, "currency finance" was no longer an option to the federal government. In contrast, Congress could successfully issue $36.7 million in treasury bills during the War of 1812 because it now had the tax power to back the issue.[11]

In addition to printing money, Congress also attempted to float a loan through its Loan Office. In augmented form, the loan certificate debt survived the war to become the public debt that provided the subject for so much discussion during the struggle over ratification. A tiny part of the loan certificate debt, the "first generation" certificates, in fact resembled the securities that the British government sold to finance its many wars. These securities bore interest paid in foreign bills of exchange, literally as good as gold, from funds earmarked for this purpose. Even so, the loan did not prove popular and the money it generated was dwarfed by other incomes. Congress also issued "second generation" loan certificates to a nominal value more than eight times the nominal value of the "first generation" certificates. These bonds carried interest only in paper currency and were not regarded as an attractive form of investment by moneyed men. The $60 million worth of certificates were actually not issued to buyers but to merchants who accepted them as payment for supplies in preference to paper currency. Whereas the "first generation" bonds held their value until Congress discontinued interest payments in 1782, the "second generation" certificates depreciated heavily and rapidly. After the war, the total loan certificate debt was scaled down to $11 million by substituting the nominal value for the specie value at the date of acquisition. During Robert Morris's administration as superintendent of finance, the debt increased by another $11 million when Congress issued "final settlement certificates," rather than pay, to the soldiers of the continental army. To this was added a further $3.7 million in final settlement certificates issued to the holders of the revalued and unredeemed "supply certificate" debt, which is discussed later. Together with a few other minor debts, this brought the sum total of the public debt to $27 million by 1783.[12]

As with the paper money, the certificate loan gave Congress purchasing power although it did not control any source of specie income. The major part of the debt cannot be regarded as a voluntary contribution to Congress. Merchants preferred bonds to currency and soldiers preferred them to nothing at all. But both groups would much rather have been paid in gold or silver. Their skepticism soon proved well founded. Even when the debt was revalued in order to correspond to specie value, certificates depreciated fast as there was universal doubt that Congress would ever be able to redeem them. Loan certificates traded at twenty to twenty-five cents on the dollar from the end of the war to the ratification of the Constitution, whereas final settlement certificates went for ten to fifteen cents on the dollar.[13] They avoided the fate of the currency solely because it was hoped that the Articles of Confederation would be amended so as to provide Congress with a hard money income, thereby allowing for interest payments in specie, or else that the state governments would accept responsibility for the debt. As with the currency, the loan certificate debt was a measure that could not be repeated. Given the choice, no one would subscribe to a loan floated by the federal government if it had no guarantee of payment other than Congress's word. This claim does not rest on mere conjecture. In October 1786, Congress tried to borrow $500,000 to increase the federal army in the wake of Shays's Rebellion and asked the states to pledge money for repayment by voting tax funds. The result was dismal. Only Virginia bothered to take any action at all, but did so insufficiently, whereas the other states did nothing. Not surprisingly, the loan failed to attract a single subscriber.[14]

Congress also had the option of raising money by foreign loans. Thanks to mismanagement, however, this option, too, was slipping away by 1787. Up to 1780, the federal government received subsidies and loans amounting to $2.2 million from France in addition to a minor loan and subsidy from Spain and small private loans in Holland. Later, mostly during the Morris administration, Congress borrowed another $6 million from the French and opened loans for a total of $2.8 million in Amsterdam. As with its other obligations, however, Congress failed to honor the foreign debt. It never paid any interest to the Spanish and defaulted on the French loan in 1785. Although credit was retained with the Dutch, this was done only at the price of taking up a new loan to pay interest on the old one. It was not a measure that could be sustained in the long term and, unless Congress was granted the means to honor the claims of its foreign creditors, it could not count on further loans.[15]

As the loan certificate debt suggests, the extent to which the American people freely chose to volunteer their money, goods, or services to the federal government was limited. With the "supply certificate" debt, however, there was hardly any voluntary element at all. This debt was run up as the Continental Army took from the people what the people would not offer to sell. Admittedly, there were instances of voluntary sales, but in the vast majority of cases the supply certificate was a receipt for goods and services impressed by the army. The certificates were used extensively; one estimate places the nominal amount issued in the region of the entire sum of the continental currency. Quartermaster and commissary officers often did what they could to compensate not only for the value of what they impressed, but also for taking goods without the consent of the owner. However, given the strong likelihood that Congress would never realize this compensation, it is hard to describe the use of the supply certificate as anything but mass expropriation.[16]

The lesson of the supply certificate debt was that a cornered government would adopt whatever measures it took to secure its own survival. As Alexander Hamilton pointed out in *The Federalist*, a government without the legitimate means to procure an income faced the choice of perishing, by sinking "into a fatal atrophy," or of impressing resources from the citizens without their consent.[17] The latter alternative, of course, amounted to a challenge to a right much cherished by Englishmen, that there could be no taxation without the consent of the taxed.[18] There is no doubt that in the context of the Anglo-American political tradition, expropriation was an extreme measure. If the Continental Army fought to preserve the birthrights of Englishmen, then the demands placed by the army on the citizens violated those very rights.[19]

II

Early modern governments, like their present counterparts, financed extraordinary expenses, such as wars, with loans rather than taxes. Nevertheless, underpinning the capacity to borrow was the ability to pay interest and mortgages on the public debt, and this money was normally derived from tax incomes. Taxation, however, was a measure not open to the Confederation Congress, which instead had to rely on the state governments to tax the American people on its behalf. The period between Yorktown and the Philadelphia convention showed that this arrangement could not produce the necessary means to cover government expenditures. This period also saw the failure of the attempt to amend the Articles of Confederation in order to provide Congress with an independent income. The latter of these failures can be disposed of quickly, while an account of the breakdown of the requisition system requires more space.

The history of the impost proposals of 1781 and 1783 is well known. The first proposal asked the states to amend the Articles so as to grant Congress the right to levy a 5 percent impost, the income of which was to be used toward paying the interest and the principal on the national public debt. To Robert Morris, the superintendent of finance, the amendment proposal was only a first step toward more extensive federal taxation, which would include a land tax, a poll tax, and an excise on spirits. Because the Articles of Confederation could only be amended by unanimous ratification, the Impost of 1781 was killed when Rhode Island refused to ratify and Virginia repealed its earlier ratification. The Impost of 1783, regarded by leading nationalists as completely inadequate, proposed that Congress be granted the right to levy a 5 percent *ad valorem* duty on all imports, in addition to specified duties on certain articles. To make the amendment less objectionable to state rightists, the proposal limited the grant to a twenty-five-year period. In addition to the impost, the states were asked to contribute $1.5 million annually to the continental treasury, also for a twenty-five-year period. This time both Rhode Island and Virginia ratified, but New York did not. Its refusal to do so is hardly surprising, considering that duties on imports through New York City provided the state government with its major income. By the spring of 1787, the Impost of 1783 was to all effects dead.[20] Yet, although the amendment proposals failed, they signaled a widespread approval of an independent Congressional income in the form of an impost, an approval that only stumbled on the Articles of Confederation's extreme demand for unanimous ratification of amendments. As we shall see, in the debate over ratification the Antifederalists would repeatedly state that even though they strongly disapproved of an unlimited federal fiscal power, they had no objections to a federal impost.

The record of federal requisitions is equally dismal. Congress's six requisitions between 1781 and 1787 netted $5,071,237. Although a substantial sum, it was only a little more than a third of what the national government had asked the states to contribute. The real problem, however, was that the returns on the requisitions decreased rapidly during the period. In the spring of 1787 the states had paid two thirds of the requisitions of October 1781 and April 1784, but only 35 percent of the September 1782 requisition, 20 percent of the September 1785 requisition, and a mere 2 percent of the requisition of August 1786. At this time, the national government's financial situation was critical. In the six months before 31 March 1787, the treasury received no more than $663 to meet current expenses. Congress was able to pay neither its troops nor its few civil servants.[21]

There is a prevalent belief that the national government found itself in financial difficulties because the states ignored its calls for money. The state legislatures, it is claimed, were "localist" in outlook and not very interested in national concerns once the War of Independence was over. As has recently been demonstrated, however, this view is incorrect. Not only did the states raise tax levels dramatically in the postwar period; they also levied them in specie rather than paper or farm products. In addition, they enforced harsh collection measures. Persons who failed to pay taxes had their property taken and sold at public auction. If the tax delinquent's possessions did not raise enough to cover his debt to the public, he was jailed. By making tax administrators at various levels personally responsible for the collection of taxes, legislatures made sure that an essentially local tax administration obeyed the commands of the state government and enforced heavy tax laws.

Despite heavy taxes and harsh law enforcement, the returns on taxation in the states declined throughout the first half of the 1780s. In all but four states, the same pattern of development can be discerned. When returns diminished, the state governments put pressure on the tax administrators, who increased the pressure on the taxpayers. In response, the people resisted. They petitioned the legislatures, refused to pay their taxes, formed no-bid covenants to counter tax auctions, and obstructed court proceedings. When nothing else helped, they employed violence or the threat of violence.

Resistance went furthest in Massachusetts. Historians now accept that the primary cause for the outbreak of Shays' Rebellion was the heavy taxation and tax enforcement pursued by the Bowdoin administration. Although the government suppressed the rebellion with force, it also relaxed its tax policy. But the retreat came too late to appease the people, who voted Bowdoin out of office, effectively putting an end to heavy taxation. Massachusetts was more typical than is sometimes appreciated. In most states there was popular resentment toward taxation and violent resistance to tax administration. But in these states, tax relief came sooner than in Massachusetts. In some states, such as South Carolina, the governing elite backed down and offered relief; in others, such as Pennsylvania and Rhode Island, hardliners were voted out of office and the new governments passed relief measures. Such relief took the form of relaxed fiscal administration, tax postponements, and, most important, emissions of paper money, which was loaned out to cash-starved farmers, thereby allowing them to settle public and private debts. Connecticut, New York, North Carolina, and Georgia did not experience the cycle of heavy taxes, government pressure, resistance, and relief. This was not because the people there were more complacent than in other states, but because relief-oriented majorities controlled the legislatures and prevented heavy taxes from being levied in the first place.[22]

Congress's attempt to extract money from society through state taxation failed because the people were unable or unwilling to pay the taxes the governments demanded. It is, of course, difficult to judge whether the farmers were merely putting on the poor mouth or if they were in genuine distress. Yet there is good reason to believe that the taxes levied and collected brought hard times on the people. More important, however, is that the comparatively widespread franchise ensured that the state governments could not continue policies that caused resentment among the population. In other words, the system of government created by the Articles of Confederation and the resources of the nation did not allow Congress to raise the money it needed through taxation. Although this adequately sums up the crucial issue, it will be useful for an understanding of the clash over federal taxation in the debate over ratification to possess some further knowledge of taxation in late eighteenth-century America.

Before the War of Independence, Americans were very lightly taxed in peacetime. In Britain, taxes were several times higher.[23] Indeed, in the literature promoting British emigration to America, the absence of heavy taxation to service public debts and standing armies was pointed to as something peculiar to America.[24] The Seven Years' War, the only military campaign engaging the resources of all the colonies before the War of Independence, demonstrated that although the colonies were willing to finance extraordinary expenses through borrowing, they refused to be saddled with a permanent public debt. Contrary to Britain and the rest of Europe, this feature of the early modern state had not found its way over the Atlantic by 1787 and in fact a perpetual debt was strongly condemned in America. Instead, the debt arising from the Seven Years' War was paid off within a mere five to ten years after hostilities ended. Hence, in order to return to a normal state of low taxation, the colonists were willing to accept heavy taxes for a limited period of time. This performance, it has been argued, influenced the actions of the state governments before, during, and after the war against Britain. It instilled in them an inflated belief in their own capacity to finance military operations and to reduce debts swiftly. The cost of the War of Independence was more than twenty times higher than the cost of the Seven Years' War, however.[25] The demand on the people after the war against Britain was therefore a good deal greater than after the war against France. In the end, it was a burden that the people were unable, or unwilling, to bear.

The burden of taxation was increased by the structure of American taxation. In the debate over ratification, both sides often claimed that oppressive taxation arose from the *mode* by which a tax was raised rather than from the *amount* of money levied. What they were mainly concerned with was whether the taxes levied were direct or indirect. In late eighteenth-century Britain, indirect taxes in the form of the impost, that is, customs duties, and the excise, that is, a tax on the production and retail sale of consumer articles, contributed about four fifths of the total revenue. The American economy, however, made sure that yields from excises would be insignificant. The impost had the potential of generating a substantial income, but in the Confederation era this potential was not realized. Furthermore, the proceeds from the impost went only to states possessing busy ports. New York in particular derived a great part of its revenue from this source. Hence, in predominantly agricultural America, the most important taxes by far were direct taxes. These took two basic forms: the land tax and the tax on polls. The fact that governments taxed farmers rather than industrialists and merchants, as was the case in Britain, in itself generated hardships. Whereas the latter groups had ready access to specie, American farmers were chronically starved for cash. They might well have assets in land, tools, livestock, and buildings, but they found it troublesome to find the gold or silver with which to pay taxes. This fact explains the frequent clamor for a "circulating medium," that is, the demand that the government emit paper money and loan it out to farmers to allow them to pay taxes. Another problem with direct taxes was their regressive nature, that is, that they hit the lower and middle ranks relatively more than those who were better off. The poll tax, which was much used in New England, was levied at a flat rate regardless of income. Similarly, the land tax tended not to discriminate sufficiently between lands of various degrees of productivity.[26]

The important conclusion to draw from the history of taxation between Yorktown and the Philadelphia convention is that the Confederation Congress could not extract money from society through taxation, even when the states were ready to comply with requisitions. In fact, the money could not be had even when the governments pressed the people to the verge of rebellion. What followed instead was a popularly propelled backlash, ending in an offer of relief to the taxpayers and a postponement of all attempts to pay Congressional requisitions. By 1787, the system of requisitions was as dead as the impost proposals.

It has been argued that as a consequence of this failure, the Federalists wanted to create a government strong enough, and independent enough of the people, to withstand the demands for tax relief. This argument, as will be readily recognized, is essentially the application to fiscal policy of the traditional argument that the Constitution was an attempt by the social elite to stem the tide of popular politics. The Federalists, it is claimed, felt that all taxes levied by the state governments in the 1780s ought to have been collected and that the key to do so was to apply more, not less, government pressure on the taxpayers. Citizens who failed to pay their taxes had only their own indolence and profusion to blame. The industriousness and frugality to which they would now be forced in order to meet the demands of the national government would therefore be the means to their moral improvement. Thus, in one stroke, heavy taxes would create a solvent Congress and better citizens.[27] As will be seen, my own reading of the Federalist argument points in another direction. It is my contention that the Federalists accepted existing restrictions to taxation and formed a tax system that would be able to generate a sufficient income for the national government, without putting undue pressure on the American people.

III

In the end, the reason why the states exerted such heavy pressure on the citizens was because money was needed to pay interest and installments on the public debts run up by Congress and the states during the War of Independence. According to a recent calculation, 90 percent of taxes levied in the postwar years were earmarked for debt payment.[28] Considering that the debt was the ultimate cause of much political turbulence, one has to ask why Congress and the state legislatures persisted in the attempts to pay interest on the debt rather than declare a public bankruptcy. After all, the war against Britain had been won and independence had been recognized.

Historians who address this question have generally done so in the context of the federal assumption of state debts, which was engineered in 1790 by Alexander Hamilton, secretary of the treasury in the first Federalist administration. Through federal assumption, the sum total of the domestic and foreign debt reached $74 million. No pledge was made to pay the principal of the domestic debt. Instead, it was turned into long-term interest-bearing bonds, thereby creating a "funded" debt. Despite the growth in the size of the debt, Hamilton managed to service it with a lot less effort than the states and the Confederation Congress. The interest rate on the loan was cut, and an income secured from the impost rather than from regressive direct taxes. The effect was dramatic. Relieved of their single largest expense, the states could cut direct taxes by as much as 85 percent in a few years and the political unrest created by heavy taxes subsided. The value of the securities rose to par or above as Congress started making punctual interest payments.[29]

Progressive historians have seen the assumption of state debts as part of a struggle over democracy, a view that fits their understanding of the Constitution as first and foremost an attempt to reduce popular influence in politics. According to this view, at the heart of the question whether the states or the federal government should service the debt, and whether or not Congress should be granted an income independent of the states, was the issue of where sovereignty ought to reside in the republic. Both nationally minded politicians and their opponents, it is claimed, "believed that national payment of the war debt would mean the supremacy of the central government," whereas "state payment would mean the retention of ultimate power in the hands of the states." Those who opposed assumption did so, the argument goes, in order to retain power in the hands of the state governments. Retaining power in the state governments was of utmost importance because only the state legislatures could collect and realize the will of the people. The Federalists, by contrast, sought a "refuge from democracy" by transferring state power to a strong national government able to withstand the pressure from popular opinion.[30]

Other historians have disregarded democracy as the key to an interpretation of federal assumption, in favor of an economic interpretation of the Constitution very different from Beard's. According to this view, the founders wanted the national government to promote exports and shipping, support domestic manufactures, develop the West, protect property against domestic unrest, and create a stable medium of exchange. The Federalists tried to make use of the debt to meet some of these challenges, primarily to increase the supply of money. In doing so, they would turn the debt from a liability to an asset. If Congress started to make punctual specie payments on the interest charge, securities would appreciate. Thus, appreciation would mean the creation, or perhaps rather the re-creation, of capital. Because the debt to such a large extent had been bought up by merchants and moneyed men, this capital could be counted on to be invested in America rather than squandered on the importation of British consumer goods.

But there were further advantages to be had from the appreciation of securities. Once the bonds had reached par, or at least a stable specie value, they could serve as a security or an exchange medium in large-scale transactions. Yet another use for the bonds was as securities in banking, thereby further multiplying capital. The bonds would also increase the money supply by being an attractive investment in which to ply down profits. This would free money that would otherwise have been invested in assets that were harder to liquidate, such as land.[31] Finally, it has been suggested that the Federalists wished to fund and assume the public debt in order to buy the loyalty of the public creditors. Influenced by English precedents, it is claimed, the nationalists around Robert Morris and later the Federalists tried to create "a vested interest in the new regime." If the debt was serviced impeccably, this would sever the ties between the powerful group of creditors and the state governments, replacing them with an allegiance to the union.[32]

Before these attempts to account for the motives behind the funding and consolidation of the public debt are tested against the evidence provided by the debate over ratification, it is necessary to offer a few words of caution. Obviously, it would be naive to draw conclusions about an actor's motive from public statements. For this reason, one is for instance unlikely to find anyone openly canvassing the idea that debt payment would buy the loyalty of creditors. Still, this study has argued that the public debate over the Constitution was important in providing legitimate reasons for the American people to support or reject adoption. Hence, what was said about the reasons for making payments on the public debt must have been regarded as convincing arguments aimed at influencing people's stance on ratification. Interestingly, these arguments were seldom openly opportunistic. Yet what was said did not conform to any of the interpretations historians have offered.

Thus, the idea that the debt was a pawn in a battle over the future of democracy in America is not supported by what was said in the debate over ratification. Although it is certainly true that Congress's power over taxation was seen as a challenge to state sovereignty, this is not the case with the public debt. No Antifederalist argued that the states ought to hold on to, or enlarge, their part of the public debt. During the 1780s, some states had assumed part of the federal debt in addition to their own debts.[33] What little was said about this part of the federal debt was said by Federalists. They promised that once the Constitution was adopted, the obligations assumed by these states would revert to Congress and thereby offer relief to the states.[34] No Antifederalist offered any objections to such a scenario. Neither was the prospect of federal assumption of state debts much mentioned. In fact, federal assumption of state debts was not widely anticipated even after the Constitution was adopted.[35] One of the few persons who did mention it was none other than Hamilton, but what he said did not support the idea. In *The Federalist* 34, Hamilton objected to the idea that the states' revenue be limited to cover the costs of running their governments, because "it would have been inadequate to the discharge of the existing debts of the particular States, and would have left them dependent on the union for a provision for this purpose."[36]

But the economic interpretation is no less problematic. There is simply no discussion at all of the idea that appreciated securities would give a much-needed boost to the economy. One may of course question whether it was politically possible for Federalists to argue publicly on behalf of merchants and moneyed men in a nation dominated by farmers. Nonetheless, they did in fact repeatedly declare in public that the creditors' claims were legitimate and ought to be honored by the government. Nor did they shy away from promising payment on adoption of the Constitution. Pelatiah Webster, to take one example, claimed that it was "only from a federal treasury that the public creditors, of all descriptions, can expect substantial and permanent justice."[37] What casts most doubt on the economic interpretation of debt servicing, however, is that there was no attempt among the participants in the ratifying struggle to discriminate between the domestic and the foreign debt. Economic benefits flowing from debt payment could come only from an appreciation in the value of domestic securities, not from money paid out of the country. Had the Federalists' primary incentive been to promote the economy, Congress might as well have extended its policy of nonpayment toward France and Spain to include the Dutch creditors.[38] Yet there was never any suggestion that the foreign debt should be handled differently from the domestic debt.

What, then, were the reasons given by the Federalists as to why Congress had to resume payment on the debt? First, they argued that the claims of the creditors were just and that the union was bound to honor its engagements with Americans and foreigners alike. Defaulting on the debt was both dishonorable—it was noted with pain how in Europe "American faith" had "become a proverb"—and a symbol of Congress's complete impotence.[39] Second, they pointed out that the aggrieved creditor nations had the right to take by force what Congress was not ready to give to them. Thus, American ships would be seized and port towns ransacked.[40] Most of all, however, the Federalists worried about the fact that the union was no longer credit-worthy. In fact, the Federalists did not talk so much about present problems as about future exigencies. Hence, they worried less about paying the national debt than about the union's future ability to borrow. By far the most important publicly stated motive for debt servicing was *the restoration of public credit.*

Public credit, Oliver Ellsworth wrote, "is as necessary for the prosperity of a nation as private credit is for the support and wealth of a family." But the actions of the federal government had made sure that the people had no faith in the republic. The way Congress had treated the Continental Army and the public creditors meant that, in the event of a future crisis, the United States would be unable to mobilize either men or money from American society. "What man will any longer take empty promises of reward from those, who have no constitutional power to reward or means of fulfilling them," Ellsworth asked. Promises had worked their toll, the "delusive bubble has broke, and in breaking it has beggared thousands, and left you an unprotected people; numerous without force, and full of resources but unable to command one of them."[41]

11

UNLIMITED TAXATION, PUBLIC CREDIT, AND THE STRENGTH OF GOVERNMENT

The Constitution redistributed fiscal power between the states and the national government. The Articles of Confederation made Congress dependent on requisitions on the states, whereas the Constitution gave the national government a right to tax the American people independent of the states. Furthermore, the plan for the new national government did not grant a limited and specified right but a general and unlimited power to "lay and collect" taxes of all kinds, together with the power "to borrow money on the credit of the United States."[1] It was precisely the unlimited character of Congress's power to tax that provoked such strong resistance from the Antifederalists. What their opposition boiled down to was the belief that the Federalists strove to create a government that would exact such heavy pressure on American society that it would stifle cherished individual rights. The next chapter will look in greater depth at Antifederalist objections to the federal fiscal powers. Here the concern is solely with the restrictions to this power that they suggested in the form of amendments. This chapter discusses the reasons why the Federalists refused to accept these Antifederalist amendments, and indeed any restrictions on Congress's fiscal power other than those already written into the Constitution. Unlimited taxation was an important issue to them, just as it was to the Antifederalists. When James Madison drafted the first ten amendments, he made a token gesture to calm Antifederalist worries about the future of the militia, but he would not compromise on the question of the national government's power over taxation. In the debate over ratification, the Federalists repeatedly and forcefully made clear why it was crucial that no restrictions be placed on Congress's right to extract money from society by means of taxation.

In the following sections, I will argue that the need for an unbridled federal right to raise tax revenue arose from the conviction that Congress had to have full command over all the resources of the nation in times of crisis. Primarily, this was needed in order for the government to be able to borrow money abroad and at home, which suggests that the Federalists designed the Constitution as much for future challenges as for present problems. For this reason, they refused to let the powers of the national government be defined by the demands on the union existing in the late 1780s, but instead strove to create a government with powers sufficiently extensive to safeguard the union's future existence, in peace as well as in war.

I

Antifederalists accepted that it fell to the national government to look after the common interests of the states. They also accepted that this would cost money and that the Articles of Confederation had created a flawed system of government in this respect. Under the Articles, Congress had not been able to raise the money it needed to carry out its duty. To correct this, Antifederalists were quite willing to grant Congress an independent revenue in the form of the impost, something that most state legislatures had already shown themselves willing to do when they voted on the impost proposals of 1781 and 1783. But this was where their generosity ended. Thus "Centinel" wrote that the "delegation of the power of taxation to Congress, as far as duties on imported commodities, has not been objected to," whereas the seceding delegates from the Pennsylvania assembly claimed that had the Constitution left "the exercise of internal taxation to the separate states, we apprehend there would have been no objection to the plan of government."[2] The power to lay and collect any and all kinds of internal taxes was regarded as "a very unjust and improper one." To the Antifederalists, the defining feature of a "federal republic," as they understood the term, was that the general government was "dependant on, and kept within limited bounds by, the local governments."[3] In other words, power had to be retained in the state legislatures as far as convenience allowed. It was with this in mind that they formed their campaign to amend the Constitution.

When they proposed amendments to the military clauses of the Constitution, the Antifederalists demanded only that a qualified majority of both houses be required for Congress to raise an army in peacetime. When it came to the federal revenue, they tried to drive a harder bargain.[4] Obviously, this was a reasonable course of action considering that control over the purse strings meant control over the army. What the Antifederalists wanted was that "a true line of distinction" be drawn between Congressional and state authority in matters of taxation. Commonly, it was suggested that this line distinguish between external taxes, which Congress should be allowed to levy, and internal taxes that should be restricted to the states.[5] Pennsylvania held the first convention where a strong opposition to the Constitution made itself felt. Here the Antifederalist stance on the federal revenue was an uncompromising one, demanding that "no taxes, except imposts and duties upon goods imported and exported, and postage on letters shall be levied by the authority of Congress."[6]

In the following conventions the Antifederalist position softened. First, Congress was given the power to levy excises. Although this power was rather insignificant because of the structure of the American economy, it is of course interesting in the light of the later opposition to the federal whiskey excise. By permitting Congress to levy excises, the line of distinction between national and state power was redrawn between direct and indirect, rather than external and internal, taxes.[7] Second, Antifederalists gave to Congress a "suspended" right to lay and collect direct taxes. Congress would indeed have the right to raise direct taxes, but only when the impost and the excise was insufficient and then only after the states had first been given the chance to comply with a federal requisition. This was the form that the amendment on the federal revenue took in each of the eight states where one was proposed by ratifying conventions.[8] The fourth amendment proposed by the Massachusetts convention thus recommended

> That Congress do not lay direct taxes, but when the moneys arising from the impost and excise are insufficient for the public exigencies, nor then, until Congress shall have first made a requisition upon the states, to assess, levy, and pay their respective proportion of such requisitions, agreeably to the census fixed in the said Constitution, in such a way and manner as the legislatures of the states shall think best, and, in such case, if any state shall neglect or refuse to pay its proportion, pursuant to such requisition, then Congress may assess and levy such state's proportion, together with interest thereon, at the rate of six per cent, per annum, from the time of payment prescribed in such requisitions.[9]

South Carolina, New Hampshire, and New York offered identical, or next to identical, proposals. Antifederalists in Maryland also suggested a "suspended" power over direct taxation, but their proposal was defeated by the Federalist majority. Like the Constitution's opponents in New York, they also added a prohibition against a federal poll tax, together with the highly unfederal demand that the incomes from imposts and duties levied by Congress "shall be placed to the credit of the state in which the same be collected, and shall be deducted out of such state's quota of the common or general expences of government." North Carolina copied Virginia's proposal, which differed from the other states only in adding the excise to the "suspended" powers. New York also proposed restricting the power of the federal excise by prohibiting excises on everything but "ardent spirits."[10] Quite in line with the Antifederalist definition of a federal republic, the states would hold the ultimate power over direct taxation, by far the major source of government income in the 1780s.

The deal offered by the Antifederalists would not have been all that bad had the major concern of the Federalists been to raise enough money to pay for the national debt, the civil government, and a small border constabulary. As the Federalists themselves repeatedly pointed out, the impost together with an excise on distilled spirits and the sale of the western lands would be adequate to cover these costs.[11] Yet they were not interested. They directed a heavy critique against the idea that the state legislatures should have anything whatsoever to do with raising the federal revenue. Basically, their argument was that if the federal government was to function properly there could be no restrictions on its power to extract money from society. Neither restrictions to certain kinds of taxation nor institutional restrictions in the form of state participation in raising federal revenue were allowed to stand in the way of Congress. Given the strong Antifederalist opposition on this point, it was not a demand likely to win over opponents for adoption. But the Federalists were consistent in their demand, and they believed that the experiences from the War of Independence demonstrated that they were right.

To the Federalists, the system with states paying their quota of congressional requisitions had proved to be inefficient and cumbersome. In fact, it was the source of the republic's debility and a serious threat to its future existence. It had been tried and found wanting. As James Madison said, "the utter inutility" of requisitions was "too well known" for anyone to credibly argue that they could ever work. Federalists poured a torrent of scorn over requisitions, claiming that they "had been in vain tried every year since the ratification of the old Confederation, and not a single state had paid the quota required of her." One Federalist described them as "pompous petitions for public charity," making much noise but bringing little cash into the federal treasury. "Have we not sported with the bubble long enough to discover its emptiness?"[12]

The problem with requisitions, then, was that regardless of the reason the states did not pay them. When that happened, Congress had "no powers to exact obedience, or punish disobedience to their resolutions."[13] During the war against Britain, the states wore a "very federal complexion" whenever the enemy was near, but as soon as the British withdrew, payment to the federal treasury stopped. "Necessity of circumstances, which operates with almost physical energy, alone procured any tolerable supplies."[14] It was this poor record of federal requisitions that made the Federalists reject their opponents' suggestion that Congress receive only a "suspended" right to lay and collect direct taxes. Was it likely, they asked, that a state that had refused to meet the demands of Congress would accept the intervention of federal revenue officers? Rather, this was a system that would invite state resistance against federal taxes and maybe even lead to civil war. Nor could it be expected that the people would acknowledge the legitimacy of federal taxation when the state government had failed to acknowledge the requisition from Congress. They were far more likely, Robert Livingston pointed out, to "resist it as they would a foreign tribute, or the invasion of an enemy." Hence, Congress would only be able to collect money by employing force against delinquent states, certainly a most costly, despotic, and unfair fiscal policy.[15]

The solution was to allow the national government the right to extract money from society by "the same process" that was employed by all other governments, that is, by direct application on the individual citizens of the states.[16] Instead of collecting taxes with the assistance of armed force, Congress could then make use of the gentle arm of the magistrate to punish delinquent individuals rather than delinquent states. If the people were really in earnest about the need to strengthen the national government, it was necessary to "extend the laws of the Federal Government to the individual citizens of America," as this was the only means to make the law effective. The federal government had to circumvent the states, to "operate directly upon the individual constituents of it without the intervention of local, or subordinate legislatures."[17]

The supporters of the Constitution, then, strongly rejected the Antifederalist demand that the states play a key role in raising the federal revenue. The reason was that the state governments had repeatedly demonstrated their incompetence in this respect. But it remains to be seen why it was necessary for the federal government to have an absolute command over the resources of the nation. There were strong Antifederalist objections on this point and, had the Federalist argument been opportunistic, or had the issue been of less importance, one would have expected them to compromise, or evade the issue. Yet they did not, and the reason for this was their strong urge to restore public credit.

Early in the eighteenth century, Daniel Defoe compared public credit to a wary and coy lady and noted that those wishing to "entertain this Virgin" had to act with tact and delicacy. According to Defoe's counsel,

> you must act upon the nice Principles of Honour, and Justice; you must preserve Sacred all the Foundations, and build regular Structures upon them; you must answer all Demands, with a respect to the Solemnity, and Value of the Engagement; with respect to Justice and Honour; and without any respect to Parties—if this is not observ'd, Credit will not come; No, tho' the Queen should call; tho' the Parliament shou'd call, or tho' the whole Nation should call.[18]

But, as we have seen, the Confederation era saw the systematic and persistent abuse of public creditors, when Congress failed to secure the money to cover interest charges and defaulted on the public loans. Consequently, in the harsh words of one historian, "the public had earned a credibility rating of zero."[19] The unreliability of the state legislatures to produce the money needed by the federal government was the very root of the problem. If federal income would depend on state cooperation, any attempt to woo credit was doomed from the start.

Public credit lies at the heart of the controversy over the federal revenue. But to better understand the importance ascribed by the Federalists to the ability of the national government to borrow money, it is useful to know something about eighteenth-century public finance. When eighteenth-century Americans tried to make sense of the intricacies of public finance, they turned to European, and above all English, precedents. To understand the concerns of these men and women, we will do the same.

II

It appears to have been the common practice of antiquity, to make provision, during peace, for the necessities of war, and to hoard up treasures before-hand, as the instruments either of conquest or defence; without trusting to extraordinary impositions, much less to borrowing, in times of disorder and confusion. . . .

On the contrary, our modern expedient, which has become very general, is to mortgage the public revenues, and to trust that posterity will pay off the incumbrances contracted by their ancestors: And they, having before their eyes, so good an example of their wise fathers, have the same prudent reliance on *their* posterity; who, at last, from necessity more than choice, are obliged to place the same confidence in a new posterity.[20]

These words, written by David Hume, describe a system of public finance that had been in use in Britain since the accession of William III, and which allowed the government to augment the state's resources through long-term indebtedness. The tone of Hume's essay "Of Public Credit" is symptomatic of the heavy and sustained criticism that the system attracted from political commentators of various hues throughout the eighteenth century. Nevertheless, it was this system that helped bring about Britain's rise from a small state on the European periphery to a world power. This change in status was brought about by frequent engagement in war. These recurrent wars were extremely costly and to pay for them the government took up loans from British subjects and foreign nationals on a large scale. The English—later British—state was unusually successful in raising money in this way, but the practice of borrowing money to pay for the costs of war was common to almost all European states.[21]

It is important to bear in mind how completely military spending dominated the budgets of early modern states. The court at St. James might have seemed extravagant to Americans, but civil expenditures remained stable and minor compared to military expenditure throughout the eighteenth century. It increased from £1 million to £1.5 million annually, which on average amounted to less than 15 percent of government costs. The rest of government spending went to the military and debt servicing. Furthermore, this cost increased proportionally much more than did the costs of civil government. A comparison between the top-spending years of the Nine Years' War and the War of Independence, for instance, shows that costs increased from £11 million to almost £30 million annually.[22]

As noted, the government relied on loans rather than taxes to pay for wars. This practice made public finance flexible. As with any loan, money could be got quickly when the need for it arose and the costs distributed over a period of time. It may be true that the government merely made a virtue out of necessity, as the strong opposition against an income tax in the House of Commons made it politically impossible to finance war by raising large sums of money through taxes.[23] But it is difficult to see which revenue administration would have been able to adjust swiftly and easily from low peacetime to high wartime taxes. Nor is it likely that the British people would have accepted a tax raise of several hundred percent as an accompaniment to the hardships of war. The urge to cut tax rates in peacetime, by contrast, made the policy of "hoarding," that Hume seemed to advocate, impossible to realize. Given these conditions, public borrowing was a rational response to frequent and costly wars. Borrowing was also something the British government became extremely good at. The national debt grew with every new war, increasing from £16.7 million in 1697 to £245 million at the end of the American War. The immediate effect of this policy was that the part of government income spent on debt servicing increased as well. After 1707, this figure was never less than 30 percent and at most as much as 66 percent of the total expenses.[24]

An obvious precondition for borrowing on the scale engaged in by the eighteenth-century British state was the availability of surplus capital. Apart from this, there were two things that made extensive borrowing possible. First of all, the government paid the interest punctually and in hard cash. For every new loan specific funds were set aside as a security for interest payments. As a result of such prudence, government bonds became perhaps the safest, and therefore one of the most attractive, forms of investment available at the time. Second, early in the century a market for securities developed. Because the bonds were freely alienable, as well as an attractive investment, public creditors could liquidate their assets by selling their claims on the state to a third party. The market in securities thereby removed pressure on the government to redeem the debt, allowing it to perpetuate, and freed it to direct income toward interest charges rather than installments. The creation of the huge national debt was also helped by a low and sinking general interest rate, which kept down the cost of the debt. Taking all these factors into consideration, it is not difficult to see how Britain's funded debt allowed her to raise money far beyond the amounts generated by taxation. Assuming a 5 percent interest charge and no installments, a £1 million revenue could be transformed into a £20 million loan.[25]

Nevertheless, we should never lose sight of the crucial role of taxes in this equation. If public credit depended on punctual payment of the interest on the debt,[26] then payment obviously depended on the income derived from taxes. In the end, it was the power to levy taxes and the ability to collect them that determined the government's credit rating. Conversely, any limits to the government's right to levy taxes or any inefficiency in tax administration eroded public credit. As has been pointed out, the "capacity of the English government to levy taxes underpinned and was the prerequisite for Britain's 'funding system.' "[27]

The "funded debt" may have been an ingenious solution to the problem of public finance, but to contemporaries it also carried great dangers. When a government is spending 66 percent of its income on debt servicing, it is approaching the point where all income is mortgaged and its future depends on the ability to increase taxation. From the Nine Years' War to the American War, the annual tax revenue increased more than three times. Taking a longer view, from the reign of Charles II to the Treaty of Paris, it increased six times. There was a growing concern that the nation would not be able to bear much higher taxes, or at least that the increase in taxation would fail to keep pace with the increasing costs of debt servicing. Hume warned about this in his essay on public credit, written in the middle of the century. This warning became standard fare in all works on public affairs for the rest of the eighteenth century, and after the Seven Years' War it increasingly became a worry also for the persons involved in running the government.[28]

It is tempting to poke fun at the failure of eighteenth-century men and women to take into account the growth of the economy and the extent to which the wealth of a nation could be tapped by the government. What is of interest for present purposes, however, is the crucial role that was ascribed to public credit in underpinning government strength. Hume's claim that eventually either the nation would destroy credit, or credit would destroy the nation, is well known. But although his discussion captures the problem of the funded debt well enough, the idea that the British nation had any real choice of action is false. If the nation destroyed credit, this would put an end to borrowing, but putting an end to borrowing was Hume's definition of how credit destroyed the nation. Hence, both alternatives came to the same thing: The government would be rendered impotent by its inability to raise money through loans. To Hume, this was a matter of considerable importance. At stake was nothing less than the future of liberty in Britain. "We have always found," he wrote, "where a government has mortgaged all its revenues, that it necessarily sinks into a state of languor, inactivity and impotence." The rights of Englishmen depended on an active foreign policy that could contain the enemies on the Continent. Without recourse to loans, Britain would have to watch in idleness while France grew stronger and devoured her neighbors one by one. Finally, the time would come when Britain herself was conquered and English liberties would come to an end.[29]

III

As the analysis of the conflict over the Constitution's military clauses noted, Federalists and Antifederalists agreed that responsibility for the defense of the nation fell on the union and not the states. But the experience from the War of Independence, no less than the Antifederalist response to the Constitution, had demonstrated that there was far less agreement on how to raise the money required to pay for war and defense. To the Federalists, the issue was simple enough. "Where we demand an object," said Christopher Gore, "we must afford the means necessary for its attainment." In other words, if the national government was responsible for defense, it had to possess the funds necessary to see this responsibility through. Ultimately, then, the Federalists based their demand for unlimited federal taxation on the cost to wage war. It was a reasonable thing to do, considering that making war and levying taxes were the primary activities of early modern states. Nor is it surprising that, just like the Antifederalists, they identified the ability to extract money from society as the very foundation of military power. This had been a truism at least since the sixteenth century. In the modern age, wars were "as much (and more) carried on by the length of purse, as by that of the sword. They cannot be carried out without money."[30]

But no more than in other nations could the military power of Congress be based on tax revenue. Instead, it had to depend on public credit. Just as in Britain, the federal government would have to mortgage future tax returns to raise the money needed to avert future crises. "In the modern system of war," Alexander Hamilton wrote, "nations the most wealthy are obliged to have recourse to large loans."[31] But even though it was the established "practice of all nations to anticipate their resources by loans,"[32] this was not an option open to Congress. Its dismal record of maltreating creditors of every hue and kind had made American public credit all but extinct. Public credit, said Edmund Randolph, was "depressed, and irretrievably gone, without a change of that system which has caused its depression."[33] To the Federalists, however, the lengths to which their opponents were willing to go to change the American system of taxation were not enough to restore public credit.

As we have seen, the Antifederalists raised no objections against granting Congress the impost. But the income from the impost would not save public credit. Federalists believed that it would meet most of the expenses for servicing the foreign and public debt, running the civil administration and providing for a small military establishment, that is, it would cover the peacetime costs of government.[34] By no means, however, could it be expected to yield enough to serve as security for future loans. As the impost would be mortgaged to the holders of the present debt, a Congress restricted to customs duties as its sole source of income would find itself cornered whenever it had to raise money beyond the impost. Indeed, its situation would be similar to that which Hume predicted for Britain. All income would be used for interest charges, and in a crisis the government would face the grim choice of inaction or defaulting on its creditors, by diverting its income from interest payments to defense spending. If it chose the latter, Congress would ruin its credit at the time when it was most needed. Because hostilities would interrupt trade, the scanty resources of the national government would be reduced even further. The combination of a decreasing income and a failure to honor the claims of public creditors would mean the end of the government's ability to secure new loans. As Hamilton asked, "who would lend to a government that prefaced its overtures for borrowing, by an act which demonstrated that no reliance could be placed on the steadiness of its measures for paying?" The loans offered to such a government would be similar to the contract between the usurer and the bankrupt, money lent "with a sparing hand, and at enormous premiums."[35]

A "suspended" power to lay and collect direct taxes only after requisitions had failed would be of no help in this respect. As we have seen, Federalists believed requisitions to be the cause of Congress's low credit rating. As Whitmill Hill asked, "is it not to them that we must impute the loss of our credit and respectability?" The idea of "suspended" taxation would not change this. It would not make the states more able, or more willing, to pay what the national government asked for. Hence, the only means to raise money would be through violent coercion. This would be both costly and time consuming and hardly the sort of guarantee that would endear the union to potential lenders. "Foreigners," said James Iredell, "who would view our situation narrowly before they lent their money, would certainly be less willing to risk it on such contingencies as these, than if they knew that there was a direct fund for their payment, from which no ill consequences could be apprehended."[36]

To the Federalists, there was only one way to restore the credit of the United States: All limits to Congress's power to tax had to be removed. The federal fiscal power could not be limited to certain types of taxes, that is, external or indirect taxes. Nor was it possible to restrict the power to lay taxes directly on, and to collect from, the citizens without the interposition of the states. In a telling comparison, Madison asked if Britain's credit would not "have been ruined, if it was known that her power to raise money was limited?" In fact, he said, "no Government can exist, unless its powers extend to make provisions for every contingency." To be able to secure loans, the national government had to have the authority to raise direct taxes without limit. "What hopes have we of borrowing, unless we have something to pledge for payment?" Robert Livingston asked his opponents in the New York convention. Given that the impost was already mortgaged to pay for the existing debt, "the avails of direct taxes are the only positive fund which can be pledged." Soon after, Hamilton picked up this thread. "Limiting the powers of government to certain resources, is rendering the fund precarious," he said, "and obliging the government to ask, instead of empowering them to command, is to destroy all confidence and credit."[37] The precondition for the restoration of the credit of the national government was therefore that Congress was given "full command over the resources of the Union," by being invested with an unlimited power over taxation. As Edmund Randolph noted, "the credit of a nation will be found to be co-extensive with its ability."[38]

Even though they regarded the Articles of Confederation to be seriously flawed, the Federalists were hopeful about the future. The nation did not lack resources. Its problems lay in the structure of government, which did not allow Congress to honor its obligations. Given this, the solution was obvious. What had to be done was simply to "establish a power which can discharge its engagement, and you insure the confidence and friendship of the world," Thomas Hartley promised.[39] Once it was known among foreign nations that the finances of the union were "upon a respectable footing," there would be no difficulty to secure beneficial loans, for the lender now knew that his claims would be honored.[40] Similarly, if the moneyed men in America knew that the national government commanded resources that "were competent and well established, and that no doubt remained of them" they would "cheerfully" lend their property "for the general defence." "There will be always credit given, where there is good security," Samuel Johnston said. "Mankind wish to make their money productive; they will therefore lend it where there is a security and certainty of recovering it, and no longer keep it hoarded in strong boxes." Summing up the Federalist view, Hamilton wrote that the "power of creating new funds upon new objects of taxation by its own authority, would enable the national government to borrow, as far as its necessities might require. Foreigners as well as the citizens of America, could then reasonably repose confidence in its engagements."[41]

As was the case with the creation of standing armies, so augmentation of government income through loans was an established practice of early modern statecraft. For this reason, the United States faced little choice whether or not to conform to European practice. A strong credit was an exceptionally important advantage in any power struggle, as the case of Britain demonstrated. If the Constitution willfully undermined Congress's credit by forcing it to rely on the states for money, this was building a dangerous weakness into the structure of the federal government. In the modern age, "operations of war are sudden, and call for large sums of money." Under such circumstances, the inability to raise that money and to prepare for defense would amount to "courting our enemies to make war upon us." Oliver Ellsworth best expressed this concern. As wars had become "rather wars of the purse, than of the sword," it was vital that Congress possessed full command over society's resources, because a "government, which can command but half its resources, is like a man with but one arm to defend himself." Such a crippled government could easily find itself outspent by an enemy. A hostile nation, said Ellsworth, "may look into our constitution, see what resources are in the power of Government, and calculate to go a little beyond us; then they may obtain a decided superiority over us, and reduce us to the utmost distress."[42]

IV

The Federalists rejected all restrictions on the federal power to tax except those already written into the Constitution. They did so because they believed that public credit could only be restored if the national government had complete command over all the resources of the union. In the eighteenth century, governments financed extraordinary expenses, primarily war, by borrowing money. By doing so, they increased their spending power far beyond what their revenue would have allowed. In the case of Britain, the ability to borrow money for long terms and at low interest underpinned the military power of the Hanoverian state. But the credit rating of the British government depended on a religious attention to debt servicing. Interest payments were made punctually in hard cash and the bonds were freely alienable. The Federalists wished to create a similar asset by restoring the credit of Congress. This would allow the national government to mobilize the wealth of society far beyond what the revenue allowed, if ever the need arose. In itself, this ability would act as a deterrent to the ambitions of other nations.

Although loans rather than taxes paid for war, loans could not be had without taxes. Hence, the more efficient the revenue administration, the better the credit rating of the nation. A federation of sovereign states was at an obvious disadvantage in this respect, because the federal government that contracted for the loans depended on the member-states for their payment.[43] Federalists believed that this system had been tried without success in America. It was necessary to vest the power to borrow, and the power to service the public debt, in the same government. For this reason, they rejected any suggestion that the fiscal power of the national government be restricted in any way. It would not do to limit it to certain objects of taxation or to certain critical situations. Nor would it do to let the states have anything to do with raising the federal revenue. Any restriction on Congress's power to tax would reflect on its ability to procure loans and ultimately, therefore, on its strength against foreign and domestic adversaries.

12

THE COSTS OF GOVERNMENT

Only rarely did the Antifederalists raise any objections to Congress's right to borrow money. The New Yorker "Brutus" was one of the few to do so, and the New York convention the only convention to propose as an amendment to the Constitution that "no money be borrowed on the credit of the United States, without the assent of two-thirds of the Senators and Representatives present in each House."[1] But even though "Brutus" could "scarcely contemplate a greater calamity that could befall this country" than to be laden with a perpetual debt, he still accepted that public borrowing could sometimes be legitimate. "It may possibly happen that the safety and welfare of the country may require, that money be borrowed, and it is proper when such a necessity arises that the power should be exercised by the general government." He then went on to suggest the amendment that eventually turned up in the New York ratifying convention.[2]

The fact that the Antifederalists seemed to accept that public borrowing might sometimes be necessary did not mean that they accepted the need for an unlimited federal power over taxation. In their opposition to the Constitution's tax clauses, the Antifederalists continued an Anglo-American political tradition of opposition against state growth, which in turn is but an instant of a universal resistance to the centralization of power, characteristic of early modern Europe. The Antifederalist opposition centered on the future role of the state legislatures. In Antifederalist thought, the state assembly had come to take on the function filled by the House of Commons in English Country thought. It was regarded as a crucial barrier against government abuse and as the only institution that made possible taxation with the consent of the governed.

I

A crucial aspect of European state expansion was the increased ability of the government to extract money from society by means of taxation. Building strong royal power meant coopting, subordinating, or destroying local deliberative assemblies that had had influence over taxation. This changed the nature of taxes from an extraordinary grant for a special purpose to a command issued by the monarch. It was a change that was also followed by a great increase in taxation. Americans experienced this development through the growth of the British state. Although Britain differed significantly from continental powers in that the House of Commons successfully retained the power over taxation, the government's numerous critics claimed that Britain was well on its way to follow the example of other European nations.

British taxation both increased dramatically and changed in composition from the end of the seventeenth century onward. The tax revenue grew far beyond what can be accounted for by the growth of either the population or the economy. Instead, the rise in revenues must be ascribed to successful political and administrative management, which allowed existing taxes to be raised and new ones to be imposed. The structure of British taxation also changed markedly away from direct taxes, of which the land tax was the most important, to indirect taxes in the form of customs duties and excises. While the customs revenue did increase, it was the excise that made the real difference. From a low level in the late seventeenth century, it grew to generate between 40 and 55 percent of government income after the War of the Spanish Succession.[3] The significance of this change was that fiscal administration increasingly fell into the hands of the central government rather than local institutions. The excise administration was a hierarchical, centralized, and professional administrative department. Its officers had no personal links to the district they taxed and they were strictly controlled by a chain of command leading to London. The administration was further removed from local influence by making offences against the excise subject to trial not in the local courts by a jury of the vicinage but in a special court that disregarded important common law elements. These characteristics of the excise administration made it the very symbol of state power grown beyond popular control. In the shape of the excise, and the excisemen, the state came to interfere in the lives of ordinary people to an extent, and in a way, it had not done before. It was not a generally welcomed development. Significantly, the excise was often described as a "monster." Like the frequent stories of the sexual promiscuity of excisemen, this was intended to bring home the point that the excise, and therefore the growing state, was something that threatened the traditional way of life of the English people.[4]

The land tax differed so much from the excise that it has been described as the "antithesis" of the excise.[5] There was no uniformity in its administration, its agents were not professionals, nor were they alien to the tax-payers. The land tax administration remained in the hands of the local elite. A benevolent reading therefore makes the land tax a case of "self-taxation," the ultimate form of taxation by consent. The flip side to such "self-rule" was inefficiency. Land values were underassessed, remittances slow, and the tax often in arrears, none of which would have happened had the administration been bureaucratically organized. Yet the Crown tolerated inefficiency because local administration ensured political stability. Local administration may have meant a lower tax return but it also removed the need for government coercion, which would have risked alienating the gentry, that is, the land-owning class that ran the counties. "In administering the land tax," one historian writes, "the political nation was attached to the apparatus of the state, and not alienated from it."[6]

"The political nation" was of course the class of men that made up the majority of the House of Commons. Although much of the critique against the excise emanated from the Commons, it was this body that opposed increasing the tax on land. Because Parliament would not grant the Crown other sources of income, indirect taxation had to be increased. By increasing the tax on consumption, and increasingly on objects of mass consumption, such as beer, malt liquor, and sugar, the tax burden was shifted on to a wider part of the population than the gentry. Considering the behavior of the Commons, it is easy to agree with the assessment that the parliamentary contentions over the excise were merely "shadow boxing" and not a serious attempt to change the policy of taxation.[7]

The process of state formation and growing central power characteristic of the early modern era did not pass unnoticed to contemporaries. Eighteenth-century historians described this increase of power as a general trend affecting all Europe and everywhere threatening the liberty of the subjects. In their account, they took full notice of the great increase in taxation and they realized that tax base and public credit were decisive in determining the power of a nation. According to these writers, kings increased their revenue and established their right to tax the people at will and pleasure all over the Continent. With this money, they bought the service of mercenaries and made themselves independent of the military assistance provided by the nobility.[8] In Britain, the case seemed different because the House of Commons retained control over taxation. Yet to contemporaries, the independent power of Parliament was more apparent than real. First of all, there was the obvious problem of "corruption," that is, that many members of Parliament had an interest in serving the king's wishes for different, but mostly material, reasons. The influence of the executive over the legislative branch of government undermined the Commons' control over fiscal policy. But the need to maintain credit, coupled with the policy of funding wars with borrowed money, also restricted the options open to Parliament. There were many and strong interests inside and outside the House of Commons that wished to maintain an active and aggressive foreign policy. But, with each war, the debt and the interest charges grew. As public credit was the basis for Britain's military capacity, the Commons had little choice but to vote ever more taxes to service the debt. In short, in Britain, the popular assembly had not been destroyed but neither had it retained its independence toward the monarch. Rather, it had been coopted to become part of the government itself. This development of the British government was condemned by Tories such as William Blackstone no less than by radicals such as Richard Price and James Burgh. These political commentators all professed to prefer liberty to national power, greatness and wealth. And they all shared the same understanding of what had gone wrong in England. The moment that the legislature had let go of the power over taxation was the moment that liberty began to give in to power.[9] As Montesquieu wrote:

> If the executive power enacts on the raising of public funds without the consent of the legislature, there will no longer be liberty, because the executive power will become the legislator on the most important point of legislation. If the legislative power enacts, not from year to year, but forever, on the raising of public funds, it runs the risk of losing its liberty, because the executive power will no longer depend upon it; and when one holds such a right forever, it is unimportant whether that right comes from oneself or from another.[10]

But Montesquieu was in no way unique. Reflecting on the revolutionary settlement, Blackstone claimed that the funded debt and the mortgaged revenue had "thrown such a weight of power in the executive scale of government, as we cannot think was intended by our patriot ancestors."[11]

It was this understanding that the Americans took over and brought to bear on Parliament's attempt to extend its power over taxation to the colonies after the Seven Years' War. Significantly, they argued that what they were up against was not a modest tax rise but an attempt to crush the local assemblies, which alone made possible taxation by the consent of the governed. To the colonists, Parliament's final goal was nothing other than to establish an arbitrary power over taxation in America. "If the Parliament succeeds in this attempt," John Dickinson wrote in his famous attack against the Stamp Act, "other statutes will impose other duties and thus the Parliament will levy upon us such money as they choose to take, *without any other* LIMITATION *than their* PLEASURE."[12]

As I noted in chapter 11, the Articles of Confederation lodged the power over taxation squarely in the state legislatures. The Constitution changed this by giving Congress a power to tax independent of the states. To the Antifederalists, this was an attempt to increase the power of the central government by undermining or abolishing the state assembly. Contrary to their opponents, the Antifederalists did not see in Congress an assembly representing the American people. They believed that the representation provided by the Constitution was too narrow to adequately represent the people and that Congress usurped rights properly belonging to the states. The taxation clauses of the Constitution, therefore, seemed similar to Parliament's attempt to tax the colonies without representation—yet another attempt of power to overcome liberty. They tailored their response accordingly. As subjects of the British Crown, Americans had refused to be taxed by virtual representatives. Now, as citizens of independent states, they should do no less. In 1765, Patrick Henry had argued in favor of five resolutions against the Stamp Act in Virginia's House of Burgesses, the third of which declared that

> the Taxation of the People by themselves, or by Persons chosen by themselves to represent them, who can only know what Taxes the People are able to bear, or the easiest Method of raising them, and must themselves be affected by every Tax laid on the People, is the only Security against a burthensome Taxation, and the distinguishing Characteristick of *British* Freedom, without which the ancient Constitution cannot exist.[13]

Two decades later, Henry's opinion had not changed. "We fought then, for what we are contending now: To prevent an arbitrary deprivation of our property, contrary to our consent and inclination."[14] The struggle against Britain, others noted, had not been about "a threepenny duty on tea" but about the right of Parliament "to tax us and bind us in all cases whatever." Was this not precisely the right that the Constitution gave Congress? "Does it not take away all that we have—all our property?" In the same way, "Centinel" recalled how the American people had combined vigilance with the will to defend their freedom both during the Stamp Act controversy and the Tea Crisis. In neither case was it the actual taxes that led the people to protest but the fact that the government's policies "were considered as signals of approaching despotism, as precedents whereon the superstructure of arbitrary sway was to be reared."[15]

Antifederalists believed that the Constitution betrayed the American ideal of simple and cheap government. To them, it seemed that the Federalists wanted to introduce an expensive and powerful state, because they wished America *"to be like other nations."*[16] In the Virginia convention, Henry complained that the Federalist plan for a new government was incompatible with the "American spirit" and would be a threat to the nation's character.

> The American spirit has fled from hence: It has gone to regions, where it has never been expected: it has gone to the people of France in search of a splendid Government—a strong energetic Government. Shall we imitate the example of those nations who have gone from a simple to a splendid Government? Are those nations more worthy of our imitation? What can make an adequate satisfaction to them for the loss they suf-

fered in attaining such a Government for the loss of their liberty? If we admit this Consolidated Government it will be because we like a great splendid one. Some way or other we must be a great and mighty empire; we must have an army, and a navy, and a number of things: When the American spirit was in its youth, the language of America was different: Liberty . . . was then the primary object.[17]

The remainder of this chapter will be devoted to a closer look at the Antifederalist opposition to Congress's power to tax.

II

The point of much Antifederalist criticism against Congress's fiscal power aimed to demonstrate that, under the new government, the states would be deprived of all sources of income. The Constitution would make the national government supreme over the states and the insatiable demands of Congress would monopolize all taxable objects. Left without an income, the state governments would soon dwindle out of existence.

The argument that the national government would be superior to the states took as its starting point the "necessary and proper" and the "supremacy" clauses of the Constitution.[18] According to the Antifederalist interpretation, the second of these gave Congress the right to repeal state tax laws, "for the power of enacting laws necessarily implies the power of repealing laws."[19] The Constitution's declaration that Congress had the right to levy taxes to provide for the "general welfare" of the union generated a similar response. It gave the national government the right to interfere with the taxation policies of the states to "abrogate and repeal the laws whereby they are imposed, upon the allegation that they interfere with the due collection of their taxes, duties or excises."[20] Congress's reason to interfere in state taxation, the Antifederalists claimed, was that the people would not be able to bear a double taxation. The national government would therefore make sure that its own taxes were collected first and it would then relieve the people of state taxation. Obviously, this would mean the end to the states because a government without money could not exist.[21]

This argument was easy enough for the Federalists to meet. The Constitution, they said, granted Congress only a concurrent—not exclusive—power to tax. Nothing in the Constitution supported an attempt to deprive the states of their right to tax their citizens. Nor could the Federalists see that federal taxation would exhaust suitable objects of state taxation. There would be enough for both governments.[22] Such arguments might have reassured those who feared for the future existence of state revenues. They did not, however, answer what was arguably the far more serious objection the Antifederalists raised against Congress's right to levy taxes directly on the American people. This power, they claimed, meant that the state legislatures could no longer act as a check on the national government. To understand this argument, we have to look closer at the function that Antifederalists ascribed to the state legislatures in the federal system of government.

Antifederalists believed that the Constitution made Congress's power over taxation unlimited. At the heart of this claim lay their refusal to recognize Congress as an assembly representing the American people, together with their understanding—in accordance with the prevalent Anglo-American understanding of the division of power—that the legislature controlled the executive through its control over taxation. To the Antifederalists, this was a function that could only be carried out by the state legislatures. What the Constitution lacked, according to them, was the institutional check provided by a legislature controlling taxation and thereby offering protection from executive abuse of power. True, the Constitution did contain some formal rather than institutional limits to Congress's power as well. Although it may seem feeble, the Philadelphia Convention intended the charge that Congress could tax the people of America "to pay the Debts and provide for the common Defence and general Welfare of the United States" to be a restriction on Congress's power. To the Antifederalists this made little sense, as "those very men who raise and appropriate the taxes are the only judges of what shall be deemed the general welfare and common defence of the national government."[23] Federalists might as well claim that government was limited by the charge that it "should have power to lay taxes, &c. at will and pleasure."[24] The high-pitched rhetoric of the ratification debate expressed nothing less than the fear that Americans, like the peoples of continental Europe—and, many would add, the British, too—would come to be governed by a government possessing an "uncontrolled jurisdiction over the purses of the people" and a corollary position of strength toward them.[25]

Because the power over taxation and the power to raise armies were the most fundamental government powers, they could be lodged safely only "where the strength and guardians of the people are collected." As the Constitution demonstrated beyond doubt, it was not possible to create a national government that contained "a secure, full, and equal representation of the people."[26] In Britain, it was reasonable to place the powers of government with the king and Parliament jointly, but in a federal republic a different principle applied. This form of government had grown out of the circumstance that while the weakness of the states necessitated their combination under a "federal head" for "general," that is, interstate and international, reasons, the extensive territory prohibited the collection of the people in one assembly. "It is the essential characteristic of a confederated republic," a prominent Antifederalist pamphlet claimed, "that this head be dependant on, and kept within limited bounds by, the local governments; and it is because, in these alone, in fact, the people can be substantially assembled or represented." Congressional powers ought therefore to be "limited, and specifically enumerated," whereas the state legislatures ought to be "strong and well guarded."[27]

This of course was precisely what the Antifederalist amendment proposals aimed at. The national government could be granted the impost and an excise on spirits, because these were specified taxes the effect of which, as well as the income from, could both be assessed in advance. Direct taxes, by contrast, because they had no obvious inherent limit and could with ease become oppressive, ought to remain the instrument of the states. It was obviously the case, too, that the American economy ensured that direct taxes were much more important than indirect taxes, and hence that the states would be financially more powerful than the national government.

To the Antifederalists, state legislatures were important as only they could claim to be popular assemblies. It followed that only they could carry out the function that the Anglo-American theory of the division of powers ascribed to the popular assembly, that is, to control the executive by controlling the power over taxation.[28] Just as the state-controlled militia was regarded by Antifederalists as an institution allowing the people to defend their rights against the national government, so the state legislatures had a similar function. With the Constitution's adoption, however, this would be a function that they would no longer be able to fulfill. As one Antifederalist said, "the State which gives up the power of taxation has nothing more to give."[29] It would no longer be in a position to offer resistance to the demands of the executive. To "Federal Farmer," the various powers, primarily the right to levy taxes and raise armies, which the Constitution lodged in the national government, appeared "to comprehend all the essential powers in the community," whereas "those which will be left to the states will be of no great importance."[30] In short, the removal of the need for consent to federal requisitions from the state legislature meant that there would be no popular check on the national government's attempts to extract money from society.

Interestingly, the Antifederalists did not believe that the people would offer any resistance to the destruction of the states, despite the fact that they were deemed crucial to the protection of popular liberties. Neither state patriotism nor long-term political self-preservation would be enough to overcome the citizens' immediate personal interests. As we have seen, taxes pressed hard on the people in the 1780s and Antifederalists believed that they would press them even harder if the Constitution was adopted. First taxed by the federal government and then by the state governments, the people would be "like sheep twice shorne; the skin must follow the fleece."[31] Although it may appear a trivial detail, the fact that Congress would levy taxes before the states was of great importance. Once the federal collector had received his due, the national government had no interest in supporting further levies on the people, something that could only threaten to erode its tax base. As long as national taxes were "sufficiently heavy," and there was no reason to doubt that they would be so, the state tax levied on top of them would be "considered as a tyrannical act" by the people. Consequently, they would "lose their respect and affection for a government which cannot support itself without the most grievous impositions upon them."[32]

An equally important factor that the Antifederalists believed worked against the state legislatures was that they would become politically insignificant institutions. As the national government assumed responsibility for foreign policy, trade regulation, and defense, together with the levying of the taxes needed to carry out these functions, there were not many meaningful things left for the states to do. When developing this argument, the Antifederalists referred to the opposition against Parliamentary taxation before the Revolution, using the prominent Federalist John Dickinson's well-known attack on Parliament's attempt to levy direct taxes in America for this purpose. Should such a right be given to Parliament, Dickinson had then said, the colonial legislatures would first face contempt, and then fall into disuse. Nothing "would be left for them to do, higher than to frame bye-laws for empounding of cattle or the yoking of hogs."[33] Now the state legislatures faced the same future. They would become "but forms and shadows" and it would even be difficult to find men willing to serve in them. "After this constitution is once established," one critic wrote, "it is too evident that we shall be obliged to fill up the offices of assemblymen and councillors, as we do those of constables, by appointing men to serve whether they will or not, and fining them if they refuse."[34] The citizens could not be expected to support such a government. No less than their opponents, the Antifederalists thought that the "attachment of citizens to their government and its laws is founded upon the benefits which they derive from them, and it will last no longer than the duration of the power to confer those benefits."[35] Reasoning from such premises, the conclusion was evident. Would not the people "by and by, be saying, Here, we are paying a great number of men for doing nothing: we had better give up all the civil business of our state, with its powers, to Congress, who are sitting all the year round: we had better get rid of the useless burden."[36] As a final tragedy, then, the American people would themselves remove their greatest protection against arbitrary power. And they would do so from the most paltry of motives, allured by the prospect of a tax cut.

III

With the state legislatures gone, there was nothing to stop the national government from levying oppressive taxes. The Antifederalists had little doubt that the new government would be expensive. Most obviously there would be the costs of debt servicing, something the people had already protested against in most states, forcing their governments to suspend payments on federal requisitions. But debt payment was not generally a question that the opponents of the Constitution chose to complain about, as it was in their eyes—no less than in the eyes of the Federalists—a necessary and legitimate expense. Instead, Antifederalists focused on the costs of a standing army and a navy, which together with debt servicing were the biggest budget items in all European states. They also pointed to the costs for a "multiplicity of officers hitherto unknown" in the legislative, executive, and judiciary departments. Of course, most of these posts would be sinecures, rather than real offices. The policy of the new government, promised "Centinel," "will lead it to institute numerous and lucrative civil offices, to extend its influence and provide for the swarms of expectants." "The new government will be EXPENSIVE beyond any we have ever experienced," wrote "An Officer of the Late Continental Army," "the *judicial* department alone, with its concomitant train of *judges, justices, chancellors, clerks, sheriffs, coroners, escheators, state attornies and solicitors, constables, etc.* in every state and in every county in each state, will be a burden beyond the utmost abilities of the people to bear." On top of this there would also be the expense of "a superb presidential court" and of "the federal town."[37]

Although the Federalists claimed that taxes would become less oppressive after adoption, this failed to convince their opponents. Considering the expected new expenses, it was clear that a "plain understanding cannot conceive how the taxes can be diminished, when our expences are augmented, and the means of paying them not increased."[38] According to one estimate, albeit by all signs not a very serious one, the people of America could expect a fivefold increase in taxes to follow close on the heels of ratification.[39] Taxes, then, could be expected to be oppressive and the Antifederalists engaged in some very high-charged rhetoric to drive home this point. Amos Singletary said that Congress would levy a land tax and "take all we have got," while another Antifederalist claimed that "the whole produce of our farms" would not be enough to support the new government. Indeed, "the whole produce of the lands cultivated by three millions and an half of people, could not satiate the desires of such a government." To Mercy Otis Warren, there was little doubt that the farmer's lot would be hard under the new government. While the people of the Eastern states would be reduced to make a living "*only* on the gleanings of their fields," their impoverished brethren in the South would have their harvests expropriated because the "*exigencies* of government require that the collectors of the revenue should transmit it to the *Federal City*."[40]

When Antifederalists speculated about fiscal developments under the new government, they sometimes pointed to Europe and Britain as warning examples of expanding taxation. "In England," it was said, "the people are not only oppressed by a variety of other heavy taxes, but, if my information is right, absolutely pay taxes for births, marriages, and deaths, for the light of heaven, and even for paying their debts. What reason have we to suppose that our rulers will be more sympathetic, and heap lighter burdens upon their constituents than the rulers of other countries?"[41] More than anything else, it was Congress's power to levy an excise that suggested to the Antifederalists that American taxation would develop along lines established in Europe. Federalists might claim that there was no danger that the new government would exercise its powers to levy an extensive excise and that the Antifederalists were mere scaremongers. "To this I would only say," "Brutus" replied, "that these kinds of taxes exist in Great Britain, and are severely felt."[42] Other Antifederalists described the excise as "one of the greatest grievances, under which the English nation has labored for almost a century and a half."[43] It was a power extending "to every thing we eat, drink, or wear, and in Europe it is thus extensively put in practice."[44]

Although Antifederalists returned repeatedly to the claim that the Constitution would mean heavy taxes, it was in fact not so much the *amount* of money extracted from the people that bothered them as the *way* that this money was extracted. They denounced every imaginable federal tax as oppressive. This was true of the land tax, stamp duties, the excise, and— most especially—the poll tax.[45] "With respect to excises, I can never endure them," Henry told the Virginia convention. "They have been productive of the most intolerable oppressions every where."[46] The poll tax, others said, "is a most unjust, unequal, and ruinous tax" because it meant "heaping the support of the government on the poor; it is making them beasts of burden to the rich." "Cato" described poll taxes as "slavish" and as "the offspring of despotic governments," and the dissenting minority of the Pennsylvania convention claimed that poll taxes were "so congenial to the nature of despotism, that it has ever been a favorite under such governments."[47]

But there was one exception to Antifederalist complaints. One tax was always regarded as legitimate for the federal government to raise. This, of course, was the impost. The Antifederalists approved of the impost for precisely the same reasons that their opponents did so. The impost was collected on the waterfront by comparatively few officers; therefore, its administration interfered hardly at all with the internal matters of the states. As "Brutus" wrote, "the objects from which the general government should have authority to raise a revenue, should be of such a nature, that the tax should be raised by simple laws, with few officers, with certainty and expedition, and with the least interference with the internal police of the states." The impost fitted this ideal precisely. But it was also the case that the impost by its very nature could never be an oppressive tax. When duties were raised beyond the level that trade could bear, smuggling would increase. As a consequence, the government would find that higher duties did not raise the revenue and consequently duties would be lowered. Thus, the impost had an inherent check against abuse.[48]

Granting the impost to Congress was uncontroversial. For this reason, it became an important issue if the Federalists were correct in claiming, as they did, that the national government could be run almost exclusively on the proceeds from customs duties. The debate over ratification is weak on detailed accounts of the expectations of government incomes and expenditures. This makes it difficult to appreciate on what the debaters based their claims about the way that the new national government would work. There are some exceptions, however. In his fifth paper, "Cincinnatus" challenged James Wilson's assertion, made in a printed and widely circulated public speech, that the impost would suffice to cover peacetime government expenditure. According to "Cincinnatus," the total income from the impost was $800,000 per year. By contrast, he calculated, on the basis of figures published by the Confederation Congress, the expenses at $3 million. Interestingly, "Cincinnatus" added the costs to the federal government of assuming the state debts to this sum. As far as I have been able to establish, "Cincinnatus" was the only person in the debate to predict federal assumption. Together this brought the annual expenditures to a staggering $4.8 million, all of which had to be paid in hard cash, as the Constitution prohibited paying the debt in paper money. At present, "Cincinnatus" commented, "there is not one half of this sum in specie raised in all the states; and yet the complaints of intolerable taxes has produced one rebellion."[49] In the next paper, he further undermined Wilson's claim by quoting a report written by Robert Morris five years earlier about the expected incomes from the 1781 impost proposal. Morris had then believed that the impost would produce no more than $500,000 and that it had to be complemented by a land tax, a poll tax, and an excise on distilled spirituous liquors, each yielding a further $500,000. Now the Federalists expected customs duties to yield ten times as much as in 1782. It was hardly a credible claim.[50]

What was at stake in the objections to federal taxation can be most clearly discerned in the Antifederalists' response to the prospect of a federal excise. Admittedly, to most of them an excise on distilled spirits would not be a problem, but they all agreed that an uncontrolled power to levy excises was a serious threat to liberty.[51] It should be made clear that Antifederalists did not object to the excise because it was a tax on consumption. After all, so was the impost. Rather, like opponents to the excise in Britain, they focused on excise *administration*. Tactically, the Antifederalist concentration on the excise had both a weakness and a strength. Its weakness lay in the fact that the structure of the American economy made sure that the excise would never be the milch cow it was in England. Its strength, by contrast, lay in the symbolic value of the excise as the embodiment of state expansion, which had been a persistent theme in eighteenth-century British tracts. Enemies to excise legislation in Massachusetts had tapped this source of opposition arguments some twenty years before the Constitution was written.[52] Now Antifederalists did so again, realizing that the connotations of a general excise were well understood by the American people. Hence, the opposition against the excise was not about taxing consumables but about opposition to the introduction of a centrally controlled fiscal bureaucracy that would allow the national government to interfere in the daily lives of the citizens. Adopt the Constitution, Luther Martin wrote, and Congress "may impose *duties* on every *article* of *use* or *consumption*, on the *food* that we *eat*—on the *liquors* we *drink*—on the *cloathes* that we *wear*—the *glass* which *enlighten* our *houses*—or the *hearths* necessary for our *warmth* and *comfort*."[53] But the clearest statement about what was involved in excise legislation was made in the sixth essay of "Brutus."

> This power, exercised without limitation, will introduce itself into every corner of the city, and country—It will wait upon the ladies at their toilett, and will not leave them in any of their domestic concerns; it will accompany them to the ball, the play, and the assembly; it will go with them when they visit, and will, on all occasions, sit beside them in their carriages, nor will it desert them even at church; it will enter the house of every gentleman, watch over his cellar, wait upon his cook in the kitchen, follow the servants into the parlour, preside over the table, and note down all that he eats or drinks; it will attend him to his bed-chamber, and watch him while he sleeps; it will take cognizance of the professional man in his office, or his study; it will watch the merchant in the counting-house, or in his store; it will follow the mechanic to his shop, and in his work, and will haunt him in his family, and in his bed; it will be a constant companion to the industrious farmer in all his labour, it will be with him in the house, and in the field, observe the toil of his hands, and the sweat of his brow; it will penetrate into the most obscure cottage; and finally, it will light upon the head of every person in the United States. To all these different classes of people, and in all these circumstances, in which it will attend them, the language in which it will address them, will be GIVE! GIVE![54]

When "Federal Farmer" set about to describe the difference between a federal and a "consolidated" government, he noted that the former "makes the existence of the state governments indispensable, and throws all the detailed business of levying and collecting the taxes, &c. into the hands ... of many thousand of officers solely created by, and dependent on the state." The consolidated government, by contrast, employed federal officers dependent only on the national government, making "the existence of the state government of no consequence in the case."[55] Antifederalists further stressed the independence of the tax collector toward the tax payers by pointing out that the Constitution did not ensure "that those revenue officers and excisemen, against whom free governments have, always, justly entertained a jealousy, should be citizens of the state." In the future, this Virginian continued, New England would no longer export apples and onions to the South, but revenue officers.[56] But New Englanders were just as unhappy with out-of-state collectors as Southerners. The federal power to tax, one of them said, was a power "to burden us with a standing army of ravenous collectors,—harpies, perhaps from another state, but who, however, were never known to have bowels for any purpose, but to fatten on the life-blood of the people."[57] Collectors who were not residents of the community in which they administered taxes were problematical for a very basic reason. It was believed that "a Continental collector will not be so likely to do us justice in collecting the taxes, as collectors of our own."[58]

Excise officers, Antifederalists warned their readers, would be authorized to "go into your *houses*, your *kitchens*, your *cellars*, and to examine into your *private concerns*."[59] Quite literally, Antifederalists wished to be able to close the door on government in order to preserve the private sphere inviolate from the demands of the public. An unrestricted excise made this impossible. Now doors would fly open "before the magic wand of the exciseman," so that, in the words of "A Son of Liberty," "our bed chambers will be subjected to be searched by brutal tools of power, under pretence, that they contain contraband or smuggled merchandize, and the most delicate part of our families, liable to every species of rude and indecent treatment, without the least prospect, or shadow of redress, from those by whom they are commissioned."[60] This suggestion of excisemen insulting, sexually and otherwise, the female members of the household—"the daring brutality of the *publican*, perhaps offered to the wife of thy bosom" as another Antifederalist put it[61]—aptly symbolized the citizen's impotence against the powers of the new government.

IV

It was important to keep the administration of taxes in the hands of the states because, as Henry said, "oppression arising from taxation, is not from the amount but, from the mode." Hence, the wish to retain the power over federal taxes in the state legislatures did not stem from a "wish to have strength to refuse to pay them, but to possess the power of raising the taxes in the most easy mode for the people."[62] This belief was grounded in the idea that the "weight" of a tax depended on the *type* of tax. It was for this reason that Antifederalists did not care for federal taxes other than the impost. In addition to being easily administered and by the nature of things not oppressive, the federal impost was accepted because it was a tax on imported goods collected in the ports. In other words, it was levied on "luxury" items and collected from men possessing hard cash. It was therefore a light tax regardless of the amount it yielded. A direct tax, by contrast, might be levied on persons or land. It affected the necessities of life and the farmer who was asked to pay the tax typically had very limited liquid assets and often possessed no specie at all. Even if the tax yielded little, it was a heavy tax to those who had no cash to pay it. Clearly, then, George Mason had a point when he noted that "the same sum raised one way with convenience and ease, could be very oppressive if raised another way."[63]

To tax a people so as to create as little hardship as possible demanded that the men who passed fiscal laws possessed an adequate knowledge of the habits and situation of the people they taxed. Legislators had to know what the people produced and what they consumed, and consequently the extent and nature of their incomes and expenditures. In this respect, the state legislatures "were much *better judges* of the circumstances of their citizens, and what sum of money could be collected from them by *direct taxation*, and of the manner in which it could be raised, with the *greatest ease* and *convenience* to their citizens, than the *general government* could be."[64] Under the Constitution, however, the convenience of the people would no longer be the guiding principle of tax policy. This was simply because the representation in Congress would be too narrow to allow the legislators to possess an intimate knowledge of the people they represented.[65] Instead, Congress would levy such taxes as would be the most productive and easiest to collect, "without consulting the real circumstances of convenience of a country, with which, in fact, they cannot be sufficiently acquainted."[66]

According to the Antifederalists, only the state legislatures knew the limits of the people's ability to pay taxes. Furthermore, only they would be willing to offer relief when the pressure from the taxmen became too hard to bear. As I showed in chapter 10, relief legislation had been common in almost all the states in the 1780s. One of the most important forms of relief was postponement of tax payment, which gave the citizens time to scrape together the money demanded by the taxman. Postponement of this sort could not be expected from the federal government. When the "hard-hearted federal officer" came to collect, the cash starved farmer would plead in vain for abatement of taxes. His property would be auctioned away for a pittance and the farmer and his family would fall from the height of freeholder to become "servants and slaves" to the rich.[67] The Antifederalists never doubted that the American people had failed to pay taxes because they lacked the means, not the will, to do so. Public and private creditors pressed them hard and what they needed was for taxes to be postponed so that they could extricate themselves from their difficult situation through industry and frugality. What they would get from the Constitution, however, was a government intending to "*squeeze* from them the little money they may acquire, the hard earnings of their industry, as you would squeeze the juice from an orange, till not a drop more can be extracted, and then let *loose* upon them, their *private creditors*, to whose *mercy* it *consigns* them."[68] The Antifederalists feared that the days of heavy taxation, which had ended in a wave of relief legislation all over the continent, would now return with a vengeance. Although they had their doubts that such policies would restore public credit, one thing was certain—it would "grind the poor to dust."[69]

If the government was unresponsive to popular demands for relief legislation, the only means available to the people were tax boycotts and physical resistance to tax collections. But, according to Antifederalist charges, this would be to no avail. If needed, taxes would be collected by soldiers, who "by the magnetism of that most powerful of all attractives, the *bayonet*" would extract the money demanded by Congress.[70] The standing army, said the Constitution's opponents, was "the mean by which you will be made to pay taxes."[71] Faced with such superiority of force, any resistance would be in vain and the taxpayers had "either to pay the tax, or let their property be taken."[72]

There was, however, a possibility that the Federalist extreme strategy of extracting money from society at any political and social cost would backfire. As I showed in chapter 11, the Federalists held the primary purpose of federal taxation to be to restore public credit. To their opponents, however, it was clear that the people had demanded relief legislation because they had no money with which to pay taxes. It followed that heavy taxes would not save national credit because they would not produce a significantly higher income. "Perhaps it will be found, that the supposed want of power in Congress to levy taxes, is at present a veil happily thrown over the inability of the people; and that the large powers given to the new government, will to every eye, expose the nakedness of our land." If the new government failed to deliver on the Federalist promises, the United States would be in a worse position than ever. Public credit would then be "irretrievably ruined."[73]

13

A GOVERNMENT FOR FREE

In 1790, the first secretary of the treasury of the United States presented his plan how to handle the public debt, an issue that had plagued the states and the union since the end of the war against Britain. The federal government assumed the remains of the state debts and added them to the federal debt. The total debt was then transformed into a "funded debt" on the British model, that is, into long-term interest bearing government bonds. By this move, the cost of servicing the debt was significantly lowered, as the government now only had to pay the interest charges, and no installments, on the debt. A cut in the interest rate further contributed to reduce the cost of debt servicing. But the success of the Federalist administration did not end here. It secured the greatest part of the money needed for funding the debt by a more efficient collection of the impost. In this way, the government managed to reduce the tax pressure under which the American people had suffered in the postwar years. The assumption of the state debts led to a dramatic cut in state expenses and, consequently, in state taxation. Despite the fact that federal taxes increased at the same pace as state taxes decreased, the overall result was a reduction of the burden of taxation. This was because the states levied mostly direct taxes on land and polls, which were regressive in nature, whereas the national government levied progressive indirect taxes on articles of consumption.[1]

In the debate over ratification there was little discussion about the exact way in which the Federalists intended to organize the revenue administration. Very rarely did they mention the amount of money the impost would produce or, apart from distilled spirits, on which items there would be a duty and how much that duty would be. Nevertheless, it is the argument of this chapter that with the important exception of the assumption of the state debts, the general outline of Hamiltonian public finance was in place in 1787 and widely shared by the Constitution's supporters. Thus, the idea that the least oppressive tax was also the most productive;

the claim that adoption of the Constitution would mean a change in the structure of taxation from direct to indirect taxes and a reliance on the impost; the ideal of the federal government as a "waterfront state" hardly noticed by the people, were all among the most important points made in Federalist rhetoric.

The national government had to raise enough money from society to service the public debt, to form and maintain a small military establishment, and to support the civil administration. The costs may not have come to much in comparison with what European governments charged their subjects for similar "services," but experience had demonstrated that Americans were a lot less willing than Europeans to regard impositions on society by the central government as legitimate. The Antifederalist critique confirmed this further. As there is no suggestion that they ever contemplated to govern by force, the situation facing the Federalists was therefore daunting. The Federalists wished to govern with the consent of the governed, but the people they set out to govern were not fond of government. Hence, if the national government were to restrict its actions to what the people regarded as legitimate, and which therefore received popular consent, the freedom of action it possessed was much more limited than the freedom of action possessed by contemporary European governments.

In the ratifying debate, the Federalists presented a solution to the equation of how to create a sufficiently powerful government without making unacceptable demands on society. The government they created was potentially very strong. There were very few constitutional limits on Congress's power to tax and the institutional impediment made up by the state legislatures was removed. As a result, this was a government that had the right to mobilize the full resources of society at will and, therefore, a government that promised to be powerful whenever it had to be. In peacetime, however, the federal government would keep a very low profile. But this low profile did not mean that the national government would be unimportant. On the contrary, it would assume the payment of the union's debts and the cost of defense, the two main items in the budgets of all European states, and it would raise the money needed for this by means of taxation. The federal assumption of expenses that had earlier been carried by the states, and the mode of raising the taxes to pay for this, however, ensured that overall taxation would not increase, as the Antifederalists claimed, but that taxes would in fact become less burdensome to the majority of the people.

I

It has recently been argued that the Federalists created the Constitution with the intention to extract money from society at any cost. According to this view, strikingly reminiscent of Antifederalist accusations, the Federalists were aware of no limits to the pressure that the federal government could exert on the taxpayers. They believed that the state governments had failed to collect the taxes they had levied because the people were lazy and the governments lax. A stronger federal government would have no problem to raise the money needed for the well-being of the union, because it would not hesitate to exert the force needed to bring forth necessary resources. As far as individual taxpayers were concerned, heavy taxation would be a way to boost degenerating morals. When the people knew that the demands of the government were unconditional, they would have to become industrious and frugal.[2]

There is, however, very little in the debate over ratification to support this portrayal of the Federalists' ideas about the tax policy proper for the national government. Patricians may well have regarded the average taxpayer as a lazy spendthrift, but, if they did so, they never suggested that force was the solution to the problem. The Federalists were well aware that they were up against a nation unwilling, or unable, to support government if the price was heavy taxes. Republican government and economic depression created limits to what the government could achieve through pressure. "The popular system of administration," Alexander Hamilton succinctly summed up the postwar history of taxation, "inherent in the nature of popular government, coinciding with the real scarcity of money, incident to a languid and mutilated state of trade, has hitherto defeated every experiment for extensive collections, and has at length taught the different Legislatures the folly of attempting them."[3] Although they did not discuss human nature extensively during the ratifying struggle, the glimpses we get do not confirm the idea that Federalists believed that heavy taxes would improve the mores of the people. Instead, they show a willingness to work with what was at hand, regardless of whether they liked it or not. To raise money by means of direct taxes, Federalists said, "people must be provident; they must be constantly laying up money to answer the demands of the collector. But you cannot make people thus provident; if you would do any thing to purpose, you must come in when they are spending, and take a part with them."[4]

To "come in when they are spending" meant levying indirect taxes on consumption rather than direct taxes on polls and land. Federalists accepted that there were certain parameters to what the federal government could legitimately do. Far from challenging the Antifederalist understanding of what these parameters were, Federalists agreed that they ran along the direct-indirect taxes divide, with the impost being unproblematical and the excise a borderline case. They also agreed with their opponents in seeing oppression from taxation as arising from the *mode* of taxation rather than the *amount* levied. In America, it was "evident from the state of the country, from the habits of the people, from the experience we have had on the point itself, that it is impracticable to raise any very considerable sums by direct taxation."[5]

What they suggested instead was to raise the money needed for the exigencies of government by means of the impost. Their reasons for finding this the best tax policy reveal much about their perception of the relationship between the national government and society. Their ideal was a government whose impositions were felt as little as possible by the people. The great advantage of the impost was that the tax was "blended" with the price of the commodity taxed, which made the taxpayer "often not sensible of the payment."[6] Money could not "be raised in a more judicious manner, than by imposts," George Nicholas said. "It is not felt by the people."[7] This argument was common among eighteenth-century political economists and political theorists. "Duties on commodities are the ones the least felt by the people, because no formal request is made for them," wrote Montesquieu. "They can be so wisely managed that the people will be almost unaware that they pay them. To do this, it is of great consequence that it be the one who sells the commodity who pays the duty. He well knows that he is not paying for himself; and the buyer, who ultimately pays it, confounds it with the price."[8] David Hume agreed.

> The best taxes are such as are levied upon consumptions, especially those of luxury; because such taxes are least felt by the people. They seem, in some measure, voluntary; since a man may chuse how far he will use the commodity which is taxed: They are paid gradually and insensibly: They naturally produce sobriety and frugality, if judiciously imposed: And being confounded with the natural price of the commodity, they are scarcely perceived by the consumers.[9]

Thinkers as diverse as William Blackstone and Adam Smith made very similar statements.[10]

James Wilson went further than most other commentators in claiming that the impression of not paying for government was more than mere illusion. A great part of the income from customs duties might "be so contrived as not to be taken from the citizens of this country," he said. It was not necessarily the case that the consumer paid the tax through a higher price on the item purchased. Sometimes the importing merchant paid the tax and sometimes the foreign exporter did. "Had a duty of this nature been laid at the time of the peace," Wilson continued, "the greatest part of it would have been the contribution of foreigners."[11] Quite clearly, the ideas expressed here are diametrically opposed to the idea that heavy taxes should be collected by means of force. Although it is true that the Constitution placed few limits on Congress's power to tax, the Federalists did not therefore intend to laden the people with heavy taxes.

It was not the case, then, that there was disagreement between Federalists and Antifederalists about the kind of tax pressure that the American people were willing to endure from the federal government. Just like their opponents, the Federalists settled on the impost, perhaps with the addition of an excise on spirituous liquors and the sale of the western lands, as its proper source of income. There was one difference, however. Federalists believed that this revenue would be able to yield enough money to cover the expenses of the national government in peacetime.[12] Certainly, they had a different idea about government expenses than the Antifederalists, but they also believed that the impost could be made much more productive if it was levied at the national level rather than in individual states. As Hamilton said, "the capital resource of commercial imposts, which is the most convenient branch of revenue, can be prudently improved to a much greater extent under fœderal than under State regulation."[13] Discussions of exact figures were not common on either side in the debate, despite the fact that so much hinged on the extent to which customs duties would suffice to support the national government. The two exceptions to this rule, however, presented rather different conclusions than those of "Cincinnatus," when he claimed that the impost would never come close to generate the income needed by the federal government. Oliver Ellsworth believed that a general impost of 5 percent would produce some £225,000. This sum would almost cover government expenses, although he tactfully forgot to include the cost of servicing the domestic debt. Hamilton believed that overall customs duties could well be closer to 10 than 5 percent and, like Ellsworth, he argued that some articles could bear a higher duty than others. Thus, "ardent spirits" alone could be made to yield £200,000 annually to the federal treasury.[14]

But the exact figures are not as important as the Federalist insistence that the impost would prove sufficient to cover most government expenses in times of peace. This last qualification, however, cannot be emphasized enough. Federalists repeatedly made clear that these incomes would not be adequate in the event of a war or similar crisis. Should this happen, the government had to be able to bring forth all the resources of the nation, even to the extent of levying a tax on polls.[15] As Robert Livingston pointed out, "there are no governments which have not, in certain emergencies, been compelled to call for all the capital resources of the country."[16] This was especially true if the nation became involved in a war, because trade would then slump and with it the incomes from customs duties.[17] Suppose, said Wilson, that indirect taxes proved insufficient; "ought the public debts to remain unpaid or the exigencies of government be left unprovided for? Should our tranquility be exposed to the assaults of foreign enemies, or violence among ourselves, because the objects of commerce may not furnish a sufficient revenue to secure them all?"[18]

Like their opponents, the Federalists believed that sending forth agents from the national government among the people to collect taxes was likely to generate friction. This was the reason why they had objections to the excise, which they otherwise regarded as both a just and a light tax. In

America, said Hamilton, the excise had to be "confined within a narrow compass," that is, restricted to only a few carefully selected items. "The genius of the people will ill brook the inquisitive and peremptory spirit of excise laws." Here the impost had an advantage over the excise, because "the collection of it will interfere less with the internal police of the States, than any other species of taxation. It does not fill the country with revenue officers, but is confined to the sea coast and is chiefly a water operation."[19] The similarity to words used by the Antifederalists is striking.

Federalists anticipated resistance, or at least hostility, to federal tax collectors if they were to be centrally controlled and lack any attachment to the people they taxed. Because of this, they suggested that in the event, admittedly unlikely, that the federal government would have to levy internal taxes, these could be collected by state officers and according to state regulations. Such a mode of collection would be both "economical, and agreeable to the people."[20] In *Federalist* 36 Hamilton wrote about federal tax collectors that

> there are two cases, in which there can be no room for double sets of officers; one where the right of imposing the tax is exclusively vested in the Union, which applies to the duties on imports; and the other, where the object has not fallen under any State regulation or provision, which may be applicable to a variety of objects. In other cases, the probability is, that the United States will either wholly abstain from the objects pre-occupied for local purposes, or will make use of the State officers and State regulations, for collecting the additional imposition. This will best answer the views of revenue, because it will save expence in the collection, and will best avoid any occasion of disgust to the State governments and to the people.[21]

The Federalist concern for a frictionless government can also be seen in their reply to the Antifederalist charge that federal taxes would be oppressive because they would be universal. They accepted that a tax hardly felt by New Englanders might well be oppressive in the South, and vice versa. The first strategy therefore, would be for the national government to restrict itself, if possible, to "certain extensive and uniform *objects of revenue* which the United States will improve," whereas those "objects which are more limited, and in respect to which the circumstances of the states differ, will be reserved for their use."[22] Should this not be possible, however, it was "in the power of Congress to lay taxes in each State, according to its particular practice." "The national Legislature can make use of *the system of each State within that State*. The method of laying and collecting this species of taxes in each State, can, in all its parts, be adopted and employed by the Fœderal Government."[23] Hence, Congress could make the demands of the federal government less disagreeable to the population by levying different taxes in different states. There was no need to levy taxes in precisely the same way, and on precisely the same objects, throughout the nation. Why could not "Congress make thirteen distinct laws, and impose the taxes on the general objects of taxation in each State, so as that all persons of the society shall pay equally as they ought?"[24]

II

The Federalists never accepted the accusation, levied against them by their opponents, that ratification of the Constitution would result in heavy taxation. Instead, they consistently argued that the tax pressure on the American people would diminish. One reason for this was that the national government would assume the most expensive tasks of government. As the discussion about Britain showed, the costs of the military establishment and debt servicing dwarfed all other government expenditures in this period. In Britain, Hamilton said, the expense of the army and the navy was fifteen times as great as the expense of "domestic police." There was no ground to believe that things would be different in America.[25] Because "domestic police" would be the concern of the states and the military establishment the concern of the national government, it followed that the latter had to have a greater budget than the former.[26]

Commenting on this passage in *Federalist* 34, Jack Rakove has taken Hamilton to task for believing that "the revenue needs of the states would verge on insignificance!" This, Rakove continues, was the result of "a harsh but typically Hamiltonian view of world politics in which the great sources of public expence arose from the imperatives of national security—'wars and rebellions' were 'the chief sources of expence in every government'—and the burden of debt they engendered." But considering the nature of eighteenth-century public finance, Hamilton's conclusion was only natural. When Hamilton said that the union ought to be in charge of the defense of the nation and that military expenses far surpassed civil expenses this was hardly a controversial claim, nor was his view in any way idiosyncratic but rather representative of the Federalist position in general. As Rakove perceptively notes, the insistence on "*unlimited* national powers" shows "that Hamilton still believed that the great conceptual problem of federalism was not to explain how the states would retain sufficient sovereignty but to make Americans realize that a vigorous national government was essential to their security and welfare."[27]

Other Federalists believed so, too. "It should be considered," Robert Livingston said, "that the burdens of government will be supported by the United States. They are to pay the interest of loans; they are to maintain the army and navy, and the most expensive civil establishment."[28] The states' need for tax money, therefore, could be expected to decline rather than increase. In the future, once they had paid off their debts from the war, the state governments would be able to survive on a "small land tax."[29] This decline in tax pressure, however, would be accompanied by a transfer of most of the levying, collecting, and spending of taxes from the states to the national government, and it could be expected that this discrepancy in the importance of the two levels of government would continue to increase. Whereas the costs of "domestic police" were stable, the costs of the military establishment were prone to considerable fluctuations and "could be susceptible of no limits, even in imagination."[30] Furthermore, and contrary to the national government, the states would never again have reason to borrow money to pay for war, and therefore would never again have to take responsibility for debt servicing.[31]

But more important than a decrease in the taxes levied by the state governments before and after the adoption of the Constitution was that the structure of taxation was likely to change for the better with adoption. For the structure of taxation would then change from direct taxes on land and polls levied by the states to indirect taxes, chiefly the impost, raised by the national government. Direct taxes were regressive because they affected the poor and the middling sort more than the rich. As Hugh Williamson said, they were "taxes that cannot fail to grind the face of the poor." "We have strained the point of dry taxation to its highest pitch," wrote one Federalist. "The farmer, who has a moderate decent farm just sufficient comfortably to support himself and family, finds it exceedingly hard to save enough out of his yearly earnings to pay the frequent demands of collectors." "By impost and excise," by contrast, Nathaniel Gorham noted, "the man of luxury will pay; and the middling and the poor parts of the community, who live by their industry, will go clear." Once the "poor and industrious" had been thus "eased of their present burthensome taxes," America promised to become "the best *poor man's* country upon earth."[32]

Another important advantage with indirect taxes was that, as long as they were levied on "luxuries" rather than "necessities," they were voluntary. "No man is obliged to consume more than he pleases, and each buys in proportion only to his consumption," Wilson noted. In *Federalist* 21, Hamilton praised the impost and excise duties partly because "the amount to be contributed by each citizen will in a degree be at his own option, and can be regulated by an attention to his resources. The rich may be extravagant, the poor can be frugal. And private oppression may always be avoided by a judicious selection of objects proper for such impositions."[33] Was it not easier, wondered one Federalist addressing "the People of Connecticut,"

> for you to give a little dearer for the goods you buy when you can pay in your own way, and if they are higher, can buy a little the less; is it not easier than it is to have a collector come and dun you for a round sum of money, and pay it you must or your cattle and land must be sold

at public vendue? Everyone must see that this way of indirect taxation is by far the easiest for the people.[34]

The power to finance wars by taking up loans can be regarded as a further way to ease the pressure of the national government on society. After all, with a 5 percent interest charge, they provided a means, albeit only in the short run, to multiply incomes twenty times, allowing taxes to be kept down. Extraordinary expenses could be paid for by a tax "sufficiently productive to pay the interest" on a loan but nothing more. The alternative was to raise the money through heavy taxes, a strategy that had already been tried but had not worked. "Upon a critical emergency," James Iredell said, "it may be impossible to raise the full sum wanted immediately upon the people. In this case, if the public credit is good, they may borrow a certain sum, and raise for the present only enough to pay the interest, deferring the payment of the principal till the public is more able to bear it." This argument was also applicable to the existing debt. America's population and economy were growing fast and it would surely benefit the further growth of both if payment on the principal of the debt could be postponed "till such time as the country be rich and populous." By then the per capita debt would have diminished significantly while the people had grown richer. Hence, the debt could then "be paid with great facility."[35]

Contrary to their opponents, the supporters of the Constitution believed that it would be a good thing if American fiscal policy and public finance came to resemble policies and public finance in the nations of Europe. According to George Nicholas, the part of the British revenue made up of indirect taxes was nine tenths of the total. "Connecticutensis" put it at "more than three-fourths," whereas Ellsworth believed the figure to be two thirds.[36] Despite their differences in detail, they all pointed out that the United States differed significantly from most European powers in relying on direct, rather than indirect, taxes as their chief source of revenue. They were also aware that this reliance on direct taxes created a heavy pressure on the people. Had Great Britain and France tried to raise their revenues "by direct taxes, they would be exceedingly oppressive," Nicholas said, while according to Ellsworth not even the entire British army could enforce the collection of the nation's vast revenue had Britain relied on direct taxes.[37]

European monarchs relied on indirect taxation because it was more productive than direct taxation. The Federalists shared with the Antifederalists the idea that oppression from taxation arose from the mode rather than the sums involved. They differed from the enemies of the Constitution, however, in arguing that the tax that was the *least oppressive* was also the *most productive*. Hence, it would also be the natural choice of government. What, Nicholas asked, "will be the consequence of laying taxes on improper objects? Will the funds be increased by it? By no means: I may venture to say, the amount of the taxes will diminish in proportion to the difficulty and impropriety of the mode of levying them."[38]

III

The Antifederalists were certain that the new government was destined to end in despotism because the representation in Congress was too narrow to allow the legislators to know the needs and sentiments of the people they taxed. The Federalists did not accept this argument and they countered it in two ways. First, they challenged the idea that a good administration of government was a function of a broad representation in the legislature. Second, they argued that even a government that cared not at all for the feelings and situation of the people would still try to raise taxes in a way that the people found the least objectionable.

James Madison's *Federalist* 10 is generally believed to epitomize Federalist ideas about representative government.[39] According to the argument Madison set out there, the new national government would be precisely as unresponsive to popular pressure as the Antifederalists feared it would be. The size of the country meant that majority factions would have a hard time trying to secure the kind of relief legislation that had prevailed in the states during the mid-1780s. It was hardly an argument likely to reassure those with an Antifederalist inclination that their fear of the new government was exaggerated. In other words, it was hardly the right answer to the accusations made by the Antifederalists and this seems a likely reason why the tenth *Federalist* failed to make much of an impression on contemporaries.

The most typical Federalist response to criticism about the composition of Congress was instead to ensure the people that, because the representatives were chosen from their ranks, they could "have no separate interests from ourselves."[40] Thus, Noah Webster rejected the Antifederalist "false principle" that Congress would be independent of the people. Congress would have "the *same interest* as the people—they are a *part* of the people—their interest is *inseparable* from that of the people; and this union of interest will eternally remain, while the right of election shall continue in the people." The idea that popular election would ensure that the representatives would be "able and upright rulers" was standard fare in Federalist rhetoric. Sometimes it was expressed in terms of "virtue" and "corruption,"[41] but it was more straightforwardly put by North Carolina's governor, when faced by obstinate backcountry Antifederalists in the ratifying convention of his state:

> It is said . . . that our representatives [to Congress] will be taken from the seacoast, and will not know in what manner to lay the tax to suit

the citizens of the western part of the country. I know not whence that idea arose. The gentlemen from the westward are not precluded from voting for representatives. They have it, therefore, in their power to send them from the westward or the middle part of the state. They are more numerous, and can send them, or the greater part of them. I do not doubt but they will send the most proper, and men in whom they can put confidence, and will give them, from time to time, instructions to enlighten their minds.[42]

But if it was a straightforward answer, it was an answer that skirted around the issue of the need not only for popularly elected representatives but also for a numerous representative assembly. Hamilton and Madison, however, addressed this issue directly. The principle that a representative ought to possess knowledge of the situation and interests of his constituents seemed sound enough to them. The knowledge that senators and representatives needed was of a general kind, however, because they would typically legislate only on general matters. Hence, "in determining the extent of information required in the exercise of a particular authority, recourse then must be had to the objects within the purview of that authority." The kind of knowledge needed by the representative had not necessarily to be acquired through personal experience. Therefore, even a small number of representatives, if sufficiently enlightened, could easily possess enough knowledge to levy a prudent internal tax. If the largest state of the union were to be divided into ten or twelve districts, it would "be found that there will be no peculiar local interest in either, which will not be within the knowledge of the representative of the district." Furthermore, there were other sources of information available to the representative than local knowledge and personal experience. Published state laws were one such source. Often enough, there would be little more to do for Congress than to "review the different laws, and reduce them into one general act. A skilful individual in his closet, with all the local codes before him, might compile a law on some subjects of taxation for the whole union, without any aid from oral information."[43]

There was no area of government business, Hamilton said, that demanded a greater knowledge of a country and its inhabitants than revenue administration. But, he asked, is

the knowledge of local circumstances, as applied to taxation, a minute topographical acquaintance with all the mountains, rivers, streams, high-ways and bye-paths in each State, or is it a general acquaintance with its situation and resources—with the state of its agriculture, commerce, manufactures—with the nature of its products and consumptions—with the different degrees and kinds of its wealth, property and industry?[44]

The answer was obvious. Indeed, in most nations it was not the legislatures but boards, or even individual men, in charge of public finance who prepared plans for taxation, which were then accepted or rejected by the legislature. "Inquisitive and enlightened statesmen," Hamilton wrote, "are deemed every where best qualified to make a judicious selection of the objects proper for revenue; which is a clear indication, as far as the sense of mankind can have weight in the question, of the species of knowledge of local circumstances requisite for the purposes of taxation."[45] In the Virginia convention, Madison responded to Antifederalist objections in a similar way.

It has been said, that ten men deputed from this State, and others in proportion from other States, will not be able to adjust direct taxes so as to accommodate the various citizens in thirteen States.

I confess I do not see the force of this observation. Could not ten intelligent men, chosen from ten districts from this State, lay direct taxes on a few objects in the most judicious manner? It is to be conceived, that they would be acquainted with the situation of the different citizens of this country. Can any one divide this State into any ten districts so as not to contain men of sufficient information? Could not one man of knowledge be found in a district? When thus selected, will they not be able to carry their knowledge into the General Council? I may say with great propriety, that the experience of our own Legislature demonstrates the competency of Congress to lay taxes wisely. Our Assembly consists of considerably more than a hundred, yet from the nature of the business, it devolves on a much smaller number. . . . It will be found that there are seldom more than ten men who rise to high information on this subject.[46]

The feasibility of a revenue law was demonstrated by how well it worked in practice. The Antifederalist John Smilie had claimed that the "attachment of citizens to their government and its laws is founded upon the benefits which they derive from them, and it will last no longer than the duration of the power to confer those benefits."[47] All Federalists could have seconded this view and none could have expressed it better. As Hamilton pointed out, the people's "confidence in and obedience to a government, will commonly be proportioned to the goodness or badness of its administration."[48] Because the national government would rely on indirect taxes on consumption, the test of how good, or how proper, a tax law was would be shown in the people's willingness to buy the item on which the tax was levied. "Imposts, excises and in general all duties upon articles of consumption may be compared to a fluid," Hamilton wrote, "which will in time find its level with the means of paying them." There was obviously no need to use force in order to raise a revenue in this way. No government would be absurd enough to try to coerce the people into buying an item they found too expensive. Instead, the tax was self-regulating. If it was too heavy, the returns from it diminished and the government would have to adjust the tax level. Hence, there was "a signal advantage of taxes on articles of consumption, that they contain in their own nature a security against excess."[49]

The claim that indirect taxes on consumption could not by definition be oppressive leads on to the second argument made by the Federalists in response to the Antifederalist charge that the adoption of the Constitution would lead to heavy taxes. This was the claim that even if the government cared not at all for the needs of the people, it would still try to levy taxes in a way that made them as lenient as possible. For this reason, Congress would simply have to rely on indirect rather than direct taxes. Because indirect taxation was "at once less obnoxious, and more productive, the interest of the government will be best promoted by the accommodation of the people," the Federalists claimed.[50] In other words, the American people were protected from heavy taxation and harsh enforcement of tax laws by a barrier stronger than any institutional check or formal rule: the self-interest of the government.

"Even ambitious and unprincipled men will form their systems so as to draw forth the resources of the country in the most favorable and gentle methods," Hamilton said in the New York convention, "because such will be ever the most productive. They never can hope for success by adopting those arbitrary modes which have been used in some of the states." Because an oppressive tax would yield a smaller return than a light one, what advantage "would it be to the members of Congress, to render the collection of taxes oppressive to the people? They would be certainly out of their senses to oppress the people, without any prospect of emolument to themselves."[51] On the contrary, Congress would "necessarily" rely on the mode of taxation "which was easiest to the people." The first choice would be the impost, the second the excise, and only as a last resort would Congress levy direct taxes. Drawing "money from the people, by direct taxes, being difficult and uncertain, it would be the last source of revenue applied to by a wise legislature." It was because the national government could be counted on to discern its self-interest, not because it was fully representative of the citizens of the United States, that the people could be "assured that the delegation of a power to levy them [i.e., taxes] would not be abused."[52] As Hamilton put it, "happy it is when the interest which the government has in the preservation of its own power, coincides with a proper distribution of the public burthens, and tends to guard the least wealthy part of the community from oppression!"[53]

Thus, the Federalists answered the accusation that the new national government would levy oppressive taxes because it was not representative of the people it taxed. But they did so in a way that can have done little to mitigate the Antifederalists' concern about the future status of the state governments in the union. Although the states would perhaps not be overrun by the blunt power of Congress, they would be made redundant by Congress's assumption and efficient management of all the central government functions. According to the Federalists, the national government would pay the costs for the military establishment and debt servicing, which the states had repeatedly failed to do. Furthermore, the national government would raise the money it needed in ways that were not oppressive to the people, while even the unsuccessful attempt of the states to raise money had resulted in severe pressure on the people.

It would therefore seem that the question of the future relevance of the state governments was as valid as ever. The Federalist claim that the national government would not be oppressive created a problem for the Antifederalists, however, as it challenged the primary reason they had provided for the existence of the state legislatures within the federal structure of government. In a nation inhabited by a people who had a limited love for government, there was no possibility to defend the existence of the state governments in the eyes of the people in other than instrumental terms. Any other attempt would have opened the Antifederalists to the charge that they were first and foremost interested in maintaining lucrative state offices, an accusation frequently made by the Federalists. Antifederalists had made the value of the state governments hinge on their function as protectors of the people against Congress. As "Centinel" said, the primary purpose of government was "to check and controul the ambitious and designing."[54] But if the national government could manage to provide essential government functions without being oppressive, the states would in fact have very little to do save passing by-laws on matters of little significance. Furthermore, they ran the risk of alienating the people because they provided so little in return for their tax bills.

IV

Although the details of the Federalist program of taxation were not worked out, or at least were not presented in public, during the ratification struggle, its general outlines were there. Its most important aspect was the awareness, which the Antifederalists shared with the Federalists and also reminded them of, that the demands that the national government could make on the people of America with any hope of success, was limited. Federalists and Antifederalists were in agreement on what constituted a proper tax policy in America. Both sides accepted that the oppression from taxation arose from the mode of taxation rather than the amount taxed. Both sides regarded the impost as the easiest and the most productive tax that could be levied, and they did so for the same reasons. The impost restricted the federal government to becoming a "waterfront state," a state that would not make itself felt in the daily lives of the vast majority of Americans. The impost would not give rise to federal tax assessors and collectors or, even worse, to federal sheriffs and constables, roaming the countryside to extract money from the people. Ideally, the people would not even notice when they paid their taxes. Furthermore, should they notice the taxes imposed on them and should they object to them, the people could choose not to consume items taxed. By definition, there would be no need for warrants and tax auctions if the revenue was raised on consumption. There would be no families evicted from their land because of nonpayment of taxes. Surely no form of taxation could be either lighter or more just than this.

14

THE FEDERALISTS AND THE
USES OF FISCAL POWERS

On 1 December 1794, having just returned from the expedition to suppress the Whiskey Rebellion, Alexander Hamilton informed the president of his decision to resign as secretary of the treasury. A week later, Hamilton wrote to his sister-in-law telling her about his resignation and assuring her that all was now "well with the public." The suppression of the insurrection in Pennsylvania had strengthened the government, and the public finances, Hamilton said, "are in a most flourishing condition. *Having contributed to place those of the Nation on a good footing, I go to take a little care of my own; which need my care not a little.*"[1] As his words reveal, Hamilton was proud over his achievement as the nation's first secretary of the treasury. But he also felt that these achievements had been misrepresented by his numerous and virulent critics. After his resignation, Hamilton began to draft an essay known as the "Defense of the Funding System," intended as an explanation and vindication of his actions. Hamilton never completed the essay and it would take more than a century before it was first published. Nevertheless, the "Defense of the Funding System" provides important insights into the reasons behind Federalist policies of taxation and public finance in the first half of the 1790s.

In the modern age, Hamilton noted, the high costs of warfare forced governments to finance war either through credit or by imposing heavy burdens on their subject populations. The great advantage of sound credit was that it enabled the nation "in great and dangerous emergencies to obtain readily and copiously the supplies of money of which it stands in need for its defence[,] safety and the preservation or advancement of its interests."

> They enable it to do this too without crushing the people beneath the weight of intolerable taxes, without taking from industry the resources necessary for its vigorous prosecution, without emptying all the property

of individuals into the public lap, without subverting the foundations of social order.

Indeed Wars in the modern system of it offers only two options— Credit or the devastation of private property. Tis impossible merely with that portion of the income of the community which can be spared from the wants conveniences & industrious pursuits of individuals to force the expences of a serious War during its progress. There must be antic-ipation by Credit, or there must be violent usurpation of private property. The State must trench upon the Capital instead of the Revenue of the People and thus every war would involve a temporary ruin.[2]

Even if it was conceded that funding systems and the credit they gave rise to were inherently evil, they gave governments great strength. Much like standing armies, public debts were an invention that no nation could afford to be without. "It is so immense a power in the affairs of war that a nation without credit would be in great danger of falling a victim in the first war with a power possessing a vigorous and flourishing credit." The recent crisis with England as well as the Whiskey Rebellion demonstrated that the promise held out by certain "Dreamers or Impostors" that the American republic was destined to enjoy "a perpetual exemption from war" was false. These crises also demonstrated how important it was that the government was able to raise money through loans in order to address them with vigor. From Hamilton's perspective, therefore, every attack on the funding system amounted to an attempt to weaken the nation. The destruction of public credit threatened "a mean surrender of our rights and interests to every enterprising invader." Conversely, a sound credit put the nation "in a condition to exercise the greatest portion of strength to which it is capable," thereby having "its destiny most completely in its own hands."[3]

A sound public credit demanded adequate government revenue. Yet, as Hamilton well knew, the American people did not tolerate high taxes. The costs of the War of Independence had forced some of the states to impose taxes that were almost unbearable to the citizens. Thus, in Connecticut taxation "embraced every object and was carried as far [as] it could be done without absolutely oppressing individuals," while in neighboring Massachusetts, "taxation was carried still farther even to a degree too burthernsome for the comfortable condition of the Citizens." Indeed, Shays's Rebellion, which was to "a great degree the offspring of this pres-sure," showed that taxation had reached the point where it threatened public order. The federal assumption of state debts engineered by Hamilton necessitated an extension of federal taxation beyond the impost and thereby risked exposing the new government to "clamour and unpopular-ity." Nevertheless, Hamilton claimed that one of his principal aims as sec-retary of the treasury was "lightening the burthens absolutely of all the citizens of the United States."[4]

Despite increased federal taxation, by 1794 this had been achieved. "It

is a curious fact which has not made its due impression," Hamilton remarked, "that in every state the people have found relief from assumption
while an incomparably better provision than before existed has been made
for the state debts." Challenging the men who had now appeared as his
principal opponents, Thomas Jefferson and his former ally James Madison,
Hamilton wrote:

> Let the citizens of Virginia be appealed to whether they have not in
> consequence of being exonerated from the necessity of providing for
> their debt been relieved in degree or kind from burthens which before
> pressed heavily upon them. They must answer [in] the affirmitave [sic].
> The same inquiry will find the same answers in every state. Men wonder
> at the lightness of their burthens and yet at the capacity of the Govern-
> ment to pay the interest of its debt[,] to absorb a portion of the principal
> and to find extensive resources for defence against Indian Ravages.[5]

This book cannot attempt a full investigation of Hamilton's and his
successor Oliver Wolcott's terms as secretaries of the treasury. Neither the
details of "Hamiltonian finance," nor the controversies the Federalist's policies gave rise to can be covered here. Nevertheless, it is possible to briefly
outline the Federalists' fiscal and financial policy, thereby assessing Hamilton's claim to have restored public credit while reducing the tax pressure
on the citizens, and also to say something about the fate of their program
after the Federalists had lost power to the Jeffersonian Republicans.

I

There is no question that, in restoring public credit, Hamilton's term in
office was a great success. As he wrote in "Defence of the Funding System," the federal government assumed the state debts and merged them
with the federal debt. The total public debt was then transformed into a
long-term "funded" debt on the British model. This meant that the debt
was turned into interest bearing bonds on which the government pledged
to pay interest in hard money. The government did not pledge to redeem
the principal but, because the bonds were freely alienable, they could pass
as large denomination money. As long as the bonds held their nominal
value, creditors had no reason to demand payment of the principal. Public
credit returned with the government's ability to pay the interest charge in
hard cash. Government securities rose rapidly in value, reaching par early
in 1792.[6]

The federal government made use of its renewed ability to borrow
money almost from its inception. From 1791 to 1795 the public debt increased by $6.6 million. This was not a large increase in terms of the total
debt of around $80 million, but in relation to the annual tax revenue of

$4 to $6 million it was certainly substantial. Loans were authorized repeatedly to deal with recurrent deficits as well as with crises. Thus, the volunteer force sent to put down the Whiskey Rebellion was paid for by a $1 million loan from the Bank of the United States. Similarly, the arms buildup during the Quasi-War with France was also financed largely by borrowing. But it was the Republicans who made the greatest use of the improved credit rating of the United States. Given their ideological aversion to public debts as well as the Jefferson administration's phenomenal record of debt redemption this is obviously ironic. Nevertheless, Jefferson's Louisiana Purchase was made possible by a loan of $11.5 million raised mainly from foreign investors, while Mr. Madison's War made the debt leap from $45.2 million in 1811 to $127.3 million in 1815.[7] No matter how one views these actions, it cannot be denied that the ability to borrow money had important consequences for the ability of the federal government to act and that it allowed it to pursue policies that would have been unthinkable in the 1780s.

The prerequisite for the restoration of public credit was the punctual payment of interest in specie. Even if Hamilton's measures had reduced the cost of debt servicing, it was still a substantial expense, amounting to approximately $3 million annually. During Hamilton's tenure, debt charges made up between 50 and 62 percent of total expenditure. His second great achievement as secretary of the treasury was to secure a federal tax income that was almost, if not quite, enough to cover these charges in addition to the costs of the military establishment and the civil list. Tax revenue rose rapidly throughout the 1790s. In the two-year period 1790–1791, the revenue amounted to $4.4 million. By 1793, the annual income was $4.6 million and, by 1795, $5.9 million. Apart from the last two years of the decade, tax income continued to grow. The growth of tax income then picked up again and in 1801 the federal government raised $12.3 million in taxes.[8]

This rapid growth in income is in itself remarkable. The revenue of the United States may appear tiny compared to the amounts raised by states such as Britain at this time. The records of the Washington and Adams administrations should not, however, be compared to the record of the English government but to the requisitions of the Confederation Congress in the early 1780s. Against the performance of the Confederation Congress, that of the new federal government is impressive. The tax receipts for 1792 alone superceded the total amount paid by the states to the federal treasury in the period 30 October 1781 to 31 March 1787. Although there remained a deficit until 1796, the tax income now went a long way to meet the expenses of the federal government.[9]

But it is also important to notice that the federal revenue was made up almost exclusively of the proceeds from customs duties. When Hamilton was secretary of the treasury, the impost generated about 93 to 94 percent of total tax income. The introduction of new forms of taxation during the crisis with France reduced the share of total tax revenue contributed by the impost to roughly 87 percent. During the War of 1812, it would fall as low as 50 percent. But these figures are atypical. In times of peace, under both Federalists and Republicans, customs duties were by far the greatest source of federal income.[10] In creating a fiscal system based almost exclusively on the impost, the Federalists fulfilled a promise made during the ratification debate. This was a system in which the tax incidence fell almost entirely on a small and well-defined group while sparing the population at large. Although the consumers may ultimately have paid the duties, they were collected from the merchants.

In order for the Federalists' fiscal system to work, it was necessary that the merchants were made to comply with revenue legislation. Even if they were the persons who perhaps stood to gain the most from the creation of an energetic federal government, the long tradition of customs evasion meant that it was not self-evident that they would comply with the government's policies. The strategies followed by Hamilton reveal that the Federalists did not believe in coercing the merchants to pay their duties. When the first Congress created the Customs Service, they gave the Customs only limited means of control and coercion. Instead, the Federalists relied on the active cooperation of the merchants. To ensure this, the administration took pains to nurture their relations with the merchant class and strove hard not to alienate them. The Treasury Department demonstrated a willingness to listen to the complaints of the mercantile community and to accommodate their wishes as far as possible without endangering the revenue.[11]

Thus, after traders in Providence had complained about the "rigorous and severe execution of the Revenue Laws; contrary as they Apprehend to the True Intent, & meaning of them," Hamilton wrote to the collector of the port that

> I have considered it as possible that your ideas of precise conformity to the laws, may have kept you from venturing upon relaxations in cases in which, from *very special* circumstances, they may have been proper. The good will of the Merchants is very important in many senses, and if it can be secured without any improper sacrafice [sic] or introducing a looseness of practice it is desirable to do it.

Measures to secure the goodwill of the merchants ranged from decisions by local collectors to accept short-term postponements of the payment of duties, to Hamilton's instruction that collectors should accept notes issued by local banks in addition to specie. This last decision helped the merchants as well as the banks—where merchants often had an interest—to prosper. If the merchants were to continue to pay the impost despite the fact that the government lacked the coercive powers to force them to do so, it was simply necessary that the mercantile community thought that it benefited from the government. For, as the Providence merchant John Brown told the local collector, "the Merchants will support the Government as long as the Government will support them but the Dutys are Resipprocal and both parteys must have Accommodations or the Whole Fabrick will fall to the Ground."[12]

II

In the fields of public finance and taxation, the Federalists fulfilled the promises both to restore the public debt and to finance the federal government on the proceeds from the impost. But they had also promised that the pressure on the taxpayers would be reduced as the states reduced their taxes. According to the Federalists, the state governments would be able to cut taxes considerably when the federal government took over responsibility for the costs of debt servicing and defense. Federal assumption of state debts obviously made it possible to reduce taxes even further.

Fiscal developments in the states after the adoption of the Constitution has not attracted a great deal of interest from historians. The evidence, however, suggests that state taxes were reduced very substantially. During the period following the War of Independence, Massachusetts pursued the most ambitious tax policy of all the states. Between 1781 and 1786, Massachusetts levied poll taxes of £1 5s per poll (local currency) on three occasions, on two occasions a poll tax of 16s 8d and once a tax of 11s 8d per poll. In 1786 the tax was £1 5s, but in the late 1780s and early 1790s the poll tax levied fell to merely a tenth of this level. Already in 1788 the poll tax had been reduced to 5s 5d; in 1789 it was 2s 3d; and both in 1790 and 1791 the tax was 1s 9d. The poll tax fell to a mere 10d in 1793 before rising to 1s 8d in 1794. From 1789 and onward, the poll tax was actually lower than the taxes levied in the years immediately preceding the Revolution. By 1794, for the first time since the inception of the struggle against Britain, the governor of Massachusetts could report in his annual message that the fiscal affairs of the state prospered.[13]

Developments in North Carolina were similar to those in Massachusetts. In the period 1785 to 1787 the state annually levied a land tax of 6s per 100 acres, a poll tax of 18s per poll and a tax on town lots of 18s per £100 worth, all in local currency. The adoption of the Constitution led to a sharp reduction of all these taxes. The land tax had been reduced to 8d and the poll tax and the tax on town lots to 2s each by 1790. State taxes remained at this level for the rest of the 1790s.[14] As was the case in Massachusetts, this represents a tax cut of roughly 90 percent of the poll tax and the tax on town lots, whereas the reduction of the land tax was slightly less than 80 percent.

The only attempt to measure the effect of the Federalists' fiscal policies on state taxation nationwide confirms the experience of Massachusetts and North Carolina. This investigation of direct taxation levied by eleven states between 1785 and 1795 shows a clear trend of rapidly falling state taxes after the adoption of the Constitution.[15] Calculated on a per capita basis, direct state taxes fell by 75 to 90 percent. But, whereas direct taxes fell rapidly, the federal impost increased with the same speed, and the combined state and federal taxes therefore remained fairly constant before and after the Constitution was ratified. The really significant change was that the direct taxes levied by the states were now completely dwarfed by the federal tax revenue. Wolcott was certainly right when in 1796 he casually remarked in a report to the House of Representatives that "it is well known that the State taxes have generally been very insignificant."[16]

It seems, therefore that the Federalists fulfilled their promise not only to finance the federal government by means of customs duties but also to introduce a fiscal regime that would allow for a sharp reduction of direct state taxes. This was immensely important, because it was direct taxes that had caused the taxpayers hardship and that had given rise to such strong protests in the years after the war against Britain. As Roger Brown points out, by the early 1790s, taxation was no longer the inflamed issue it had been in the 1780s. "Thus, the Constitution brought tax relief to rural America."[17]

III

To many historians writing about the early republic, Brown's conclusions may appear controversial. All too often, the Federalists' fiscal policies have been associated more with the Whiskey Rebellion and Fries's Rebellion than with the reforms described here. The Whiskey Rebellion seems to belie the claim that Federalists wished to raise taxes only in ways that caused the taxpayers no hardship. Thus, despite the conclusion he reached, Brown argues that the Federalists designed the Constitution with the aim to build a strong state that could collect heavy taxes no matter what the people said or did. The introduction of the excise and the response to the protests against them seem to confirm this interpretation.

In the early stages of the Washington administration, there were occasional arguments by Federalists in favor of direct taxes. John Trumbull, for instance, asked John Adams if Hamilton was "ignorant that direct Taxation to a moderate amount is the strongest link in the chain of Government, and the only measure, which will make every man feel that there is a power above him in this world?"[18] But such sentiments were typical of neither Federalist policies nor Federalist ideas. As secretary of the treasury, Hamilton was no less aware of the difficulty of taxing a republican people than he had been when writing *The Federalist*. When he took up his position in September 1789, Hamilton believed that the assumption of the state debts would require a greater income than the impost alone could produce. In October, he asked the advice of Madison on the best way to expand federal taxation beyond the impost, noting that the difficulty "lay not so much in the want of [taxable] objects as in the prejudice which may be feared in regard to almost every object. The question is very much What further taxes will be *least* unpopular?"[19]

In light of the later break between Madison and the administration and Madison's later struggle to restrict the sphere of the federal government, his answer is noteworthy. "The supplemental funds which at present occur to me as on the whole most eligible," Madison replied, "are 1. an excise on home distilleries. If the tax can be regulated by the size of the Still it will shun every objection that renders excises unpopular or vexatious." Madison's second proposition was to increase the duties on imported liquors, his third a federal land tax, and his fourth a stamp tax on legal transactions in federal courts. Of the land tax, he wrote that it "seems to be recommended by its simplicity, its certainty, its equity, and the cheapness of collecting it. It may be well also for the General Govt. to espouse this object before a preoccupancy by the States become an impediment."[20]

Madison's suggestion to levy a federal land tax was as bold as it was idiosyncratic. Within a week after he had written to Hamilton, Henry Lee told Madison to

> never adventure direct taxation for years. This event now would be attended with serious consequences. Can you not make your W[estern] lands equal to the support of your domestic debt & its redemption? This being done will the revenue arising from commerce be sufficient for the support of govt. & the payment of the interest on the foreign debt. I hope so, for indeed if it is not I am at a loss to see what you will or can do.[21]

Madison's proposal for an excise on spirits and increased duties on imported alcohol was more in line with Federalist thinking. Even the Antifederalists had agreed that this was the second-best choice after the impost. Thomas Slaughter has claimed that, during the ratification debate, Antifederalists were universally opposed to federal excise duties and that the Federalists promised that "a direct [*sic*] excise would only be a tax of last resort."[22] But, as this study has shown, the Federalists repeatedly said that even if the impost would contribute by far the largest share of the federal government's income, it would be complemented with land sales and perhaps an excise on domestically produced alcohol. Despite the general dislike of excises, this had not given rise to substantial protests. Antifederalist proposals for amendments aimed to restrict the federal government's right to levy *direct* taxes, such as a federal land or poll tax. Of the eight ratifying conventions that proposed amendments, only three limited Congress's power to introduce excises, and none forbade it outright. Significantly, one of them proposed a limitation on federal excises on "any article (except ardent spirits)."[23]

When Hamilton followed Madison's advice and proposed that Congress both levy an excise on domestically produced spirits and increase the duties on imported wines and spirits, this was not a break with Federalist ideals about light taxation. Hamilton's explanation for his choice shows that he was still very much concerned with limiting the hardship caused by federal taxation. The objects taxed, he said, were "all of them, in reality—luxuries—the greatest part of them foreign luxuries; some of them, in the excess in which they are used, pernicious luxuries." Taxing these objects would "lessen the necessity, both of having recourse to direct taxation, and of accumulating duties where they would be more inconvenient to trade, and upon objects which are more to be regarded as necessaries of life." Even so, the resistance to the whiskey excise is important. But it is so less for what it reveals about Federalist intentions than for what it reveals about the impediments to federal taxation. During the rest of Hamilton's term, there would be no more attempts to raise taxes on domestically produced articles of mass consumption. Further taxes were instead laid on articles that could more properly be described as "luxuries," such as the excises on snuff and carriages and the stamp duty on legal documents. Rather than press the attempt to raise taxes from a people reluctant to pay them, Hamilton chose to finance the budget deficit by means of borrowing.[24]

The fiscal regime introduced by the Federalists proved to be long-lived. Under the administrations of George Washington and John Adams, internal taxation was substantial only during the conflict with France and even then it made up less than 13 percent of total tax revenue. Internal taxation reached much higher levels during the War of 1812, but this was not representative of the fiscal policies of the Republicans or of later administrations. Apart from the years of war against Britain, the federal government raised no or only negligible internal taxes between 1804 and 1862. Even after the Civil War, duties on imports formed the greatest share of federal revenue up until the entry of the United States in World War I.[25]

IV

Based—as it was—almost solely on the income from customs duties, the fiscal system created by the Federalists was very sensitive to disruptions of trade. Although the wars of the French Revolution benefited American trade, and thereby the treasury, it also demonstrated the fragility of the tax system. British depredations of American trade in the mid-1790s led to the negotiation of the Jay Treaty, which averted war with Britain for the rest of the decade. But the rapprochement with Britain angered France and led to sustained French attacks on American trade, eventually leading to the Quasi-War. Both British and French disruptions of American trade made Congress consider the prudence of relying exclusively on income from customs duties. This concern was further underlined by the fact that war in Europe made it more difficult for the United States to raise loans abroad. By the mid-1790s, there appeared to be a genuine risk that the republic was to be drawn into the European war. The full limitations of the fiscal system would then be felt, as the war effort would require additional income at the same time as the war would reduce income from the impost. Although the conflict with France never developed into full-scale war, its fiscal history reveals precisely this trend. Government expenses rose from $6.0 million in 1797 to $9.2 million in 1799, whereas the income from the impost fell from $7.6 million to $6.6 million in the same period. To close the deficit, the government borrowed money from domestic creditors, but it also levied new taxes.[26]

In addition to the excises and stamp duties introduced by Hamilton, the Federalists now also came to levy direct taxes for the first time. They did so hesitantly, fully aware that it meant a radical reformulation of the relationship between the federal government and the citizens. As Frederic Dalzell writes, direct taxes "would involve the government in an unprecedented extension of federal authority into the countryside. In other words, direct taxation implied a distinct and qualitative reformulation of the federal presence in local communities, one that the impost had, theretofore, prevented."[27] But, even as they levied direct taxes, the Federalists tried to limit the impact on the ordinary taxpayer. Both the stamp tax and the tax on houses levied by the Adams administration were deliberately designed to let the incidence fall disproportionally on the urban mercantile elite. In the same way, the direct tax on land and slaves aimed to tax the rich rather than ordinary farmers. Only after the tax on slaves and houses had been assessed would the land tax be levied. The rate would then be set so that the combined yield from the various taxes would add up to the quota Congress had decided for each state, and it was hoped that this procedure would result in a very modest tax on land. According to the calculation made, the land tax would make up less than a fourth of the total income of $2 million that the government aimed to raise from direct taxes.[28]

A direct tax levied in peacetime was a clear break with the fiscal policy that the Federalists had sketched during the ratification struggle. As I have shown in this book, Federalists defended Congress's unlimited fiscal power by saying that the federal government could only safeguard the interests of the republic if it could command the full resources of American society in times of crisis. Much will therefore depend on whether the fiscal measures adopted in 1798 and 1799 are interpreted as the fulfillment of a Federalist plan to burden the American people with heavy taxes in order to establish "big government," or if they are seen as a response to crisis. The latter appears the more reasonable interpretation. One should note that Congress debated the extension of the fiscal system well before the Quasi-War, but at that time Congress did not feel that the situation was critical enough to excuse further taxes. Only when the XYZ Affair conjured up a broad and strong francophobia did Congress feel that the people were ready to accept that new taxes were absolutely necessary.[29]

The Federalists' worry that the American people would not accept the new imposition was well founded. Throughout the nation, it proved difficult to collect the new taxes and in Pennsylvania they sparked another tax rebellion. By levying direct taxes, the Federalists had expanded the sphere of the federal government. Had the conflict with France escalated into full-blown war, the popular response would perhaps have been different. With the French affair in limbo, it was inevitable that the policies of the Federalists handed the opposition a formidable weapon in the upcoming presidential election. Thomas Jefferson himself sensed this from the very beginning. Commenting on the war fever that had gripped the nation in the wake of the XYZ Affair, he confidently remarked that "the Doctor is now on his way to cure it, in the guise of a tax gatherer."[30]

The Federalists' fall from power in the elections of 1800 cannot be explained as a direct effect of the arms buildup and the imposition of direct taxes. The superior organization and adept political maneuvering of the Republicans as well as the split in the Federalist party between the followers of Hamilton and Adams are important reasons for the Republican victory that have nothing to do with differences over policies and principles. But it appears reasonable to assume that the introduction of direct taxes and plans to greatly expand the army made it possible for the Republicans to mobilize support by playing on popular aversion to standing armies and oppressive taxation. Such aversion had informed political action both during the struggle against Britain and during the ratification debate, and, more recently, during the Whiskey Rebellion. Once again, political leaders and the press made use of the conceptual scheme provided by the Country ideology to argue that the true Federalist aim was the creation of a standing army and the oppression of the people under heavy taxes as a necessary preliminary to the establishment of tyranny.[31]

V

Jefferson described his election to the presidency as "the revolution of 1800"—"as real a revolution in the principles of our government as that of 1776 was in its form."[32] Although historians have often accepted his words, the relationship between the Republican administration and its predecessor is characterized more by continuity than by change. In Congress, Republicans had sometimes criticized the Federalist principle of light and inconspicuous taxation. Pursuing an argument with origins in their principled anti-statism and their ideal of transparent government, they argued that customs duties ought to be replaced, or at least supplemented, by direct taxes. In doing so, they provided the elements for a principle of taxation radically different from that of the Federalists. The actions of the federal government in the fiscal sphere, these Republicans said, ought always to be noticed and felt by the citizens. Only then could they uphold the jealous supervision of government that was a prerequisite for the preservation of liberty. Thus, the Virginia Republican John Page wrote to his constituents that "an equalized land tax has been thought by many to be more equal, and better adapted to a free people, than only imposts, and excise, which have been found to pick the peoples pockets without their missing their money, till they were beggared or enslaved." According to their critics, by devious means the Federalists made it possible for the government to spend more than the nation could afford or republican citizens would accept. Furthermore, this was done by relying on a source of income that was permanently exposed to the caprice of corrupt European nations. Yet nothing became of the Republican critique. It was clearly incompatible with their strong aversion to federal taxation in general and to the presence of a federal fiscal bureaucracy in the states in particular. It is significant that the Republicans retreated once direct federal taxes were proposed in Congress. Instead, the administrations of the Virginia dynasty continued to rely on both Federalist principles and policies of taxation.[33]

On the eve of the American Revolution, Adam Smith remarked of the American colonists that they

> have never yet contributed anything towards the defence of the mother country, or towards the support of its civil government. They themselves, on the contrary, have hitherto been defended almost entirely at the expence of the mother country. But the expence of fleets and armies is out of all proportion greater than the necessary expence of civil government. The expence of their own civil government has always been very moderate.[34]

The attempt to make the colonists contribute to the costs of empire through parliamentary taxation was not successful. As an independent nation, however, the United States had to assume the cost of the War of Independence as well as the cost of preserving the nation's independence in a hostile world. A return to the prewar state of no or negligible contributions to state and central government was therefore not possible. Instead, it had become necessary to raise taxes to a much higher level than before independence. But this necessity still left several options when it came to raising taxes. The Federalists opted for customs duties, because they imposed the least possible hardship on the people and required a minimum interference by the federal government in the internal affairs of the states. The Antifederalists shared the view that this was the most beneficial strategy. By making sure that government demands on the property of the citizens were no longer visible to, nor much felt by, the taxpayers, the Constitution and the Federalists took the American people some way back toward prewar conditions, when they could enjoy the benefits of government without paying for its costs.[35]

With the "Revolution of 1800," this peculiarly American system of taxation was perfected; the Republicans abolished internal taxation and made the federal government rely solely on the impost for its tax revenue. With evident self-satisfaction, Jefferson could declare in his second inaugural address that his prudent policies had made it possible to discontinue internal taxation.

> The remaining revenue on the consumption of foreign articles, is paid cheerfully by those who can afford to add foreign luxuries to domestic comforts, being collected on our seaboards and frontiers only, and incorporated with the transactions of our mercantile citizens, it may be the pleasure and pride of an American to ask, what farmer, what mechanic, what laborer, ever sees a tax-gatherer of the United States?[36]

CONCLUSION:
THE CONSTITUTION,
THE FEDERALISTS, AND
THE AMERICAN STATE

W ith the adoption of the Constitution by ratifying conventions in Virginia and New York in the summer of 1788,
the Federalists emerged victorious from the great struggle over ratification.
In orations, poems, toasts, and songs, the friends of the Constitution celebrated America's entry into "An Era new."[1] But, while the Federalists
enjoyed their success, Antifederalists refused to accept defeat. Instead, they
began the campaign for a second constitutional convention. Although that
campaign came to nothing, many of the men who had voted against the
Constitution soon became virulent critics of the first Federalist administrations. Thus, ratification did not mean the end of politics, nor did it mean
that debate about the future course of the American republic ended. Nevertheless, the votes in Richmond and Poughkeepsie were certainly important. Now the Federalists faced the next step of state building, creating the
institutions of government that would realize their ideas about a national
state in America.

The mainstream interpretation of the Federalist argument presents it
as a call for limited government and protection of minority rights. This
study has offered a different interpretation. It sees the Federalist argument
as an attempt to convince the American public about the need to build a
powerful state and to explain how this state would work. The idea of an
American national state that they developed during the ratification debate
was the result of creative thinking in the face of serious challenges. Although the rest of this conclusion is devoted to an explication of both the
challenge the Federalists faced and the concept of the state they developed,
it is possible to sum up the basic issue here: What the Federalists had to
do, and what they did, in the debate over ratification, was to develop a
conceptual framework that made it possible to accommodate the creation
of a powerful national government to the strong anti-statist current in the
American political tradition.

I

The Federalists argued that the national government had to be reformed because independence demanded a more powerful central authority than the Articles of Confederation could provide. No longer part of the British Empire, the erstwhile colonies now had to fend for themselves. Their most pressing problem was the inability of Congress to protect either the union's territorial integrity or its commercial interests. In the eighteenth century, no less than today, territory and national interest were defended by state power. Although modern states have taken on a number of new responsibilities, the "fiscal-military state" of the eighteenth century and early modern period was an institution designed for war, whether aggressive or defensive. The need for a stronger state in America emanated from the ambitions of such powerful and efficient "fiscal-military states" in Europe. In the late eighteenth century, professional armies, navies, public debts, and large revenues were standard features of all major European powers. A state that did not possess these institutions was exposed to the states that did. In this way, the choice facing the American people was whether to risk independence by remaining weak, or accept the need for a strong national state in America. Even if the people were free to choose between them, the alternatives were framed by the way the international system of states—of which the United States was now a member, albeit a peripheral one—worked. It may be an exaggeration to claim that America in 1787 was a stateless nation, but it is not a great one. The necessary powers to create a strong national state were certainly there, but they rested with the state governments, and the recent history of the union had demonstrated the difficulty of coordinating the actions of thirteen sovereign states. As long as the Articles of Confederation governed the relationship between the state governments and the union, it would not be possible for the national government to fully and efficiently mobilize the resources of the American nation in a way that was open to the governments of Europe.

If the American Revolution is regarded as a revolt against the extension of the British "fiscal-military state" to the colonies, it is of course ironic that the Revolution's very success should create the demand for an American "fiscal-military state." But, however ironic it may be, the Federalist conclusion was not very controversial. At times, individual Antifederalists did express doubt that the situation of the United States was really as bleak as the Federalists made it out to be, but the vast majority of them agreed with their opponents about the need to strengthen Congress's power. Furthermore, Antifederalists also agreed with their opponents about the specific points where the union's weakness was most critical: Congress had to become more powerful financially and militarily if the union was to protect American commercial and territorial interests with any hope of success.

Among historical sociologists, one of the most common explanations for the process of state building is the pressures of war and the competitive environment of the international system of states. The response made by both Federalists and Antifederalists to American independence may seem to confirm the validity of such explanations. Yet further reflection on state building suggests that external pressure did not determine the development of states in any absolute sense. Even though the creation of a "fiscal-military state" may have been a prerequisite for a nation's political survival and economic well-being, the historical record demonstrates that this type of state could be formed by different trajectories. Thus, although both France and Britain developed "fiscal-military states" that provided the same basic functions, they did so by radically different paths: France through absolutism and Britain through a parliamentarian system.

In the debate over ratification, the conflict between the Federalists and the Antifederalists did not concern the need for stronger government or the nature of this strength. Rather, their disagreement turned on the questions of how this strong government would be created and what the consequences of it would be. The crucial issues to the Antifederalists were the likely effect strong government would have on popular rights and liberties and the need for limits to the state's extractive capacity. These questions may appear distinctly separate but were, in fact, closely intertwined. A strong government would affect traditional Anglo-American rights to property and person primarily through its extractive capacity. It would do so not only by making claims on the citizen's property by means of taxation but also, to a lesser extent, on his person through demands for military service. For this reason, the disagreement between the Federalists and the Antifederalists can be reduced to the single question about the acceptable extent of the new government's extractive powers.

Federalists and Antifederalists approached this question differently. The latter fell back on a tradition of anti-statism that was well established in America, resorting to arguments employed in the struggle against the expansion of British power during the 1760s and 1770s. Before the Peace of Paris in 1763, the colonists had lived happily under the protective wing of the British Empire. It was only when the British state tried to extend its powers of extraction that the colonists turned against the Empire and in the process developed a reasoned argument why it was legitimate to do so.

Like the ideologues of the Revolution, the Antifederalists based their critique of the Constitution on the importance of maintaining the state governments' monopoly on extractive powers. The power over direct taxation and the command over the militia had to remain in the states, or else the state governments would dwindle away and the people be exposed to the insatiable demands of a distant and expensive government. By their choice of rhetoric, the Antifederalists became the bearers of the Country tradition, which had informed the Revolution and which would soon inform the opposition politics of the Democratic-Republicans. This choice bestowed a certain degree of legitimacy on the Antifederalist position on the Constitution, but it was also a move that made them ill equipped to address the question about the necessary reformation of the national government in a constructive way. By adopting a Country stance, the Antifederalists were largely left to a negative critique of the Constitution. Nowhere in their writings or speeches will one find a fully explicated alternative plan for a national government, and an attempt to reconstruct their position would result in little more than a defense of the status quo.

Nevertheless, it would be wrong to conclude that the Antifederalist rhetorical choice stopped them from contributing to the founding of the American republic. Rather, they did so precisely by being nothing more than the bearers of the anti-statist arguments of the Country tradition. By repeating the familiar fear of government abuse, they reminded the Federalists that any government created in America would have to pay respect to the fact that "the habits of the people"[2] were incompatible with big and expensive government. This led Federalists to work out an understanding of the structure and functioning of the national state that would allow the state to be powerful yet respect the widespread fear of government abuse of extractive powers.

Such popular fear of, or aversion to, government was probably universal in early modern Europe. What made it especially trenchant in America, however, was that the socioeconomic structure and the political system— among the most important factors were the equal distribution of property and the absence of legal privileges, the widespread suffrage, and the short terms of government office—allowed this aversion to be translated into action. Furthermore, the government's administrative weakness coupled with dominant political ideals made it possible to govern only with the cooperation of the governed. If the new government introduced by the Constitution was to be made to work, therefore, the Federalists had to convince the citizens of the United States that, on balance, this government was to their advantage. By bringing up the traditional objections to strong central government, the Antifederalists forced the Federalists to overcome these objections and to develop an idea of the state that respected them. Regardless of their intention, in the end, the Antifederalist critique made the new government more, not less, legitimate, because it made it accord better with popular sentiment.

II

Before proceeding to a discussion of the Federalists' idea of a national American state, it may be useful to briefly recapitulate the argument so far. The Federalist understanding of their national state developed from the awareness that the national government was too weak to defend the territorial and commercial interests of the United States. That weakness was caused by a structural deficiency of the union. The Articles of Confederation gave Congress certain responsibilities but failed to provide the means to attain them. Such a parsimonious grant of power from the states to the union conformed to the widespread aversion to distant and costly government among the people. This was where the Federalists faced a challenge. They wished to create a powerful national state, but they would only be able to secure popular acceptance of such a state if they could demonstrate that in exercising its extractive capacity, it would not threaten the persons, liberty or well-being of the citizens. The Federalists solved this dilemma by developing a blueprint for a state that would be powerful yet respectful of the people's aversion to government. The key to this understanding was *federalism*.

The creation of a "fiscal-military state" demanded the centralization of authority. Britain and continental Europe had achieved this by strengthening the position of Parliament and the monarch respectively. Even if the Federalists had been inclined to either of these alternatives, and there is nothing to suggest that they were, these alternatives were hardly feasible in America. A federal system of government, by contrast, provided a partial centralization of authority, that is, a centralization only of certain specified powers. Federalism, therefore, promised the creation of a limited and "focused" yet strong national government. The idea that the Constitution was a transfer of specified powers—made by the American people—from the states to the national government appeared soon after the Constitution had been made public. The national and the state governments, the Federalists argued, were fundamentally different institutions. Whereas the states were established by a grant of every power and right that the people had not explicitly reserved, the national government was established through a grant of specified powers. Everything that was not granted was reserved by the people or vested in the states.

The federalist principle confined the national government to a sphere in which it was generally recognized that the union had to act as one nation: essentially, the areas of defense, commercial regulations, and foreign relations. Ensuring that it would not stray into other government activities was one important way to increase the legitimacy of the new national government. Nevertheless, the most significant problem remained: How would the Federalists' state raise the means that would allow it to act vigorously within its sphere of government, without putting so much pressure on the citizens that they would find it oppressive? Here the road to legitimate government went through good statesmanship, or good administration. It was sometimes held that, in the long run, the people would gradually develop loyalty to the new government when they found that it governed well. In the short run, however, Federalists hoped that the new government would acquire legitimacy by reducing the overall pressure of government on the people. Although the long- and the short-term strategies of the Federalists converge to some extent, there is also a tension between them. While the former aimed at winning the hearts and minds of the American people, the latter aimed to reduce contact between the national government and the citizens to a minimum. I will confine discussion to the short-term strategy, which was more important to the argument the Federalists presented during the ratification struggle.

Contact between the government and the people could be reduced by making the right choices about the state's resource mobilization. If administered correctly, the national government could be both powerful, on the one hand, and *light* and *inconspicuous*, on the other. It could be argued that this equation was easier to solve because a fortunate geopolitical situation and modest foreign policy goals meant that the United States could manage with only a small national state. Yet this argument is open to doubt, because geopolitics and foreign policy aims can with equal validity be regarded as, respectively, a principal cause and a principal consequence of the powerful anti-statist tradition that served as the foremost barrier to American state-building. But, regardless of how we view these matters, there is nothing in the debate over ratification that suggests that the Federalists contemplated the creation of a big and expensive government. A few thousand soldiers and a small civil administration, mainly made up of customs men and a handful of law officers, would prove sufficient.

Even though the Federalist national state was intended to be small, it would still need resources and it could still raise these in ways that were more or less conducive to the sentiment of the people. In general, the Federalists planned to reduce the "friction" that was likely to arise from resource mobilization, by making the national government as independent of the people as possible. Their aim was to create a government that was *light*, in the sense that its demands did not press too heavily on the people. Thus, there would be no demand on the citizens to provide for the defense of their country. Instead, this would be taken care of by professional soldiers, thereby freeing the citizens for the pursuit of private happiness. There would be no direct taxes on polls and land and, consequently, no more tax auctions or evicted families. Direct taxes would be replaced by a national impost and, possibly, an excise on spirits. In this way, the overall tax burden would actually decrease and the pressure on the people be eased. By their very nature, indirect taxes on consumer items were unoppressive. If the tax became too heavy, consumption would decrease and tax evasion increase, thereby leading to a reduced revenue. Self-interest would therefore force the government to avoid levying too heavy taxes. Yet another way to reduce the pressure on the citizens was by restoring public credit. If the union's credit rating was good, the national government could raise money enough to pay only the interest charges on the debt and postpone payment on the principal. In future crises, sound public credit would allow the mobilization of resources without a dramatic increase in tax pressure, thereby ensuring a minimum of state interference in the lives of the citizens.

Aiming to reduce contact between the national government and the people, the Federalists also tried to make the new government as *inconspicuous* as possible. Thus, the actual physical presence, the very visibility, of the national government would be limited. The small peacetime army would be garrisoned in posts along the western and northern borders. There would be no soldiers quartered among the civilian population, as the case was in Britain and in major American ports in the years preceding independence. The concentration of the troops to a distant and thinly populated border area also ensured that American regulars would not be used to enforce law and order, a further difference from British and European conditions. The revenue service, which in all "fiscal-military states" made up by far the greatest part of the civil administration, would essentially be a waterfront operation. It would come into direct contact only with merchants involved in overseas trade. Like the settlers on the frontier, such merchants—and, indeed, the rest of the population in the port cities—were likely to support the new government because they very obviously stood to gain from it.

Federalists even argued that *if* direct taxes ever had to be levied by Congress, they would not be administered by a separate department of federal tax collectors and surveyors. Instead, the national government would employ state officers in a federal capacity, thereby investing the federal taxman with the legitimacy of the state government. This idea also appeared in discussions of the federal judiciary. Thus, according to some Federalists, there would be no construction of federal courthouses, nor would a distinct corps of federal judges be created. As with the internal revenue, Congress would use state courthouses and employ state judges to hear federal cases. In short, as soon as the national government entered the American interior, it would try to merge as fully as possible with the already existing government apparatus of the states.

Once the Constitution was adopted and the Federalists were in power, they came to pursue policies and create institutions consistent with the principles they had expressed in the ratification debate. The state they made was financed almost exclusively by the proceeds from customs duties. Federal assumption of state debts and of the union's expenses for its defense and common debt allowed the states to reduce taxation dramatically, thereby easing the burdens of the people. The Federalist peace establishment came to exist of a small regular army, which served as a border constabulary securing western expansion by overcoming the Indian tribes that stood in the republic's way. Together with Congress's unwillingness to reform the militia, all this made sure that the demands made by the national government on the citizens in the fiscal and military sphere were next to nonexistent.

Despite their success in creating a state that was inconspicuous and light, the Federalists fell from power in the election of 1800. Yet the shift in power was not accompanied by any radical reform of government policies and institutions. In the fiscal and military sphere, the Federalists had created institutions that outlived them. In fact, they laid the groundwork for what would serve as the American national state throughout the nineteenth century.

Even though the principle of federalism would limit the national government to a few specified functions, and even though it would strive to reduce contact with the citizenry by imposing as little pressure as possible and by becoming almost invisible, it would be wrong to conclude that the Federalist state would be a weak state. As the Antifederalist opposition suggests, the Constitution created a government possessing all the important powers of the European "fiscal-military state." If we return momentarily to the structure of the Hanoverian state, we can better appreciate the Antifederalists' objections to the Constitution and their claim that the state governments would wither away as a result of its adoption. In Britain, as much as 90 percent of government expenses went to pay for activities relating to the "fiscal-military sphere," that is, armies, navies, and debt servicing. If the Constitution was adopted, all the functions pertaining to the "fiscal-military state" would belong to the national government, and it would become vastly more important than the state governments. Furthermore, considering that state growth in the eighteenth century consisted of growing armies and fleets, as well as growing revenues and public debts, there was every reason to believe that the state governments would be completely dwarfed by the national government in the future.

The Antifederalists also made another objection that helps us see the strength rather than the weakness of the new national state. In important respects, this government was not a limited government, as the conventional interpretation of the Constitution holds, but an *unlimited* government. True, the national government would be limited to specified functions but, within its sphere, there would be no limits to its power. It would act directly on the citizens with no intermediate function left to the state governments, and there would be no serious limits to its extractive capacity. As long as a majority could be secured in Congress, the national government could raise as many men and as much money as it thought the nation could provide. There were to be no limits on the size or kind of troops that Congress could establish, nor any restrictions on when they could be raised. Similarly, Congress could raise revenue by means of any kind of tax and there were to be no restrictions on its right to borrow money.

The Constitution gave the national government the means to completely mobilize the resources of the American nation. To the Federalists this was a necessary consequence of the functions that the union had been created to provide. There was simply no way to determine in advance what sort of resources would prove sufficient to defend the United States against the ambitions of other nations. Because the needs of the union were potentially endless, there could be no restrictions on the national government's right to extract the resources necessary to meet these needs. Although in peacetime the national government could be counted on to be small, light, and inconspicuous, it was a government that held the full powers of the "fiscal-military state" in reserve.

III

The Madisonian interpretation of the Federalist persuasion presents the adoption of the Constitution as a history of frustrated intentions. James Madison did not leave Philadelphia feeling like the proud "father of the Constitution," as he is routinely portrayed. Madison left disappointed, because the Convention had not heeded his proposal for a congressional veto, or negative, on state legislation. Contrary to what he intended with the Virginia plan, the Constitution would therefore find it difficult to influence the way that the state legislatures acted against minorities. Religious and economic life, the two areas in which abuse against minorities were most likely to occur, would remain within the jurisdiction of the state governments, and the national government would have no power to prevent or correct wrongs that originated in state laws or state administration. Considering this, it is not surprising that the Madisonian interpretation sees the fulfillment of the Constitution in the adoption of the fourteenth amendment.[3]

The interpretation offered in this work may seem to present a similar argument of intentions never realized. Thus, while the Federalists may have won the battle over the Constitution, they lost the war over the political development of the United States. No powerful centralized state developed in America after the ratification of the Constitution. In the 1790s, the Federalist administrations used their fiscal and military powers sparingly. Toward the end of the decade, when they did make plans to raise a substantial army and when they embarked on an ambitious program of taxation, they suffered defeat at the polls and lost power to the Jeffersonian Republicans. When the Antifederalists expressed their fear that the national government would supplant the states, they had assumed that state growth would continue to take place only within the fiscal-military sphere, as the case had been throughout the eighteenth century. Because of the appeasement following on the defeat of Napoleonic France, however, the nineteenth-century state, both in America and Europe, came to develop differently. The military sphere contracted in absolute terms, but there was also a shift in the priorities of the state that further eroded the "fiscal-military state." Increasingly, government spending shifted from military to civilian expenses. In 1760, civilian expenses in European states amounted to about 25 percent. In 1910, the figure was 75 percent. The fastest growing areas of spending were infrastructure and education. American government spending conformed to this pattern. The European "fiscal-military states" of the eighteenth century had spent their revenue on the army, the navy and debt servicing. In the 1790s and the early nineteenth century, the federal government outspent the state governments by far; almost all the money it spent went to meet the costs of debt servicing and defense. In contrast, the biggest items in the budget of American government—at state *and* national level—in the last quarter of the nineteenth-century, was education, highways, and postal services. To the greatest part, these functions belonged with the states and not the national government.[4]

If the purpose of the Constitution was to create a powerful national government, then the development of the American republic may be read as one of the great ironies of history. There is much truth in such a reading. The Constitution created an Old Regime state adapted to American conditions and prejudices and the Federalists did not foresee the great shift in government priorities that took place in the nineteenth century. Contrary to what Federalists and Antifederalists alike had predicted, the states continued to be the most important element in the federal structure. Left with powers and tasks that the Antifederalists had considered insignificant, the states in fact expanded the sphere of legitimate government activity beyond anything that the participants in the ratification debate had expected. Meanwhile, the era of free trade and free security reduced the importance of the national government and, for well over a century, it remained "a midget institution in a giant land."[5]

Nevertheless, it would not be altogether true to say that the actual trajectory of the American republic ran counter to the Federalists' plan for a national government. The Federalists had intended their national state to be light and almost invisible in periods of peace and tranquillity. Thus, in comparison to European governments that added on functions to their core of fiscal-military concerns, the American national government remained focused on the concerns for which it was first created.[6] Only when the republic faced insurrections and international crises would it employ all its considerable powers.

The creation of a state that was focused on the fiscal-military sphere and that was geared toward wartime exigencies but intended to keep a low profile in peacetime had important consequences for the political development of the United States. This was a government ill equipped to address the nation's growing internal contradictions. The compromise reached by the Philadelphia Convention on the question of slavery is the most important example of the Federalists' inability to find a national solution to a crucial domestic issue. During the long period of peace following Napoleon's defeat, the federal government had no need to assert its superiority over the state governments. Peace also allowed the national government to be both inconspicuous and light, "continually at a distance and out of sight" of the citizens, as Hamilton put it in *The Federalist*. But, as he had also noted, such a government could "hardly be expected to interest the sensations of the people."[7] In the antebellum decades, the federal government never captured the hearts and minds of its citizens. Popular identification with the nation never challenged loyalty to state and sectional identity. In the absence of a strong national government in the internal political life of the nation, sectionalism was allowed to grow unabated until it reached the point where it tore the union apart in civil war.

The Federalists' state performed better in crisis. During the Quasi-War, the War of 1812, and the Mexican War, the American national state showed that it could expand when the need arose. Nevertheless, these were minor engagements, and it is fair to say that the "fiscal-military state" remained a potentiality, rather than a reality, throughout the seventy years that followed on the Constitution's adoption. Although the Civil War marked the failure of the founders' attempt to create a lasting union, it also demonstrated that they had created a national state well adapted to mobilize resources in response to crises. As the war showed, the North could mobilize social resources to an extent never before attempted by any other nation, within the institutional framework provided by the Constitution. A century later, a constitution that is universally regarded as the paragon of limited government allowed for the creation of what today remains the world's only superpower.

NOTES

Annals of Congress	*The Debates and Proceedings in the Congress of the United States* (Washington, D.C., 1834–1849).
AHR	*American Historical Review*
Doc. Hist.	*The Documentary History of the Ratification of the Constitution*, ed. Merrill Jensen, John P. Kaminski, and Gaspare J. Saladino, 16 vols. to date (Madison: State Historical Society of Wisconsin, 1976–).
Elliot, *Debates*	*The Debates in the Several State Conventions, on the Adoption of the Federal Constitution*, ed. Jonathan Elliot, 5 vols. (Philadelphia, 1907).
JAH	*Journal of American History*
PAH	*The Papers of Alexander Hamilton*, ed. Harold C. Syrett, 27 vols. (New York: Columbia University Press, 1961–1987).
WMQ	*The William and Mary Quarterly*

Introduction

1. Thanks to *The Documentary History of the Ratification of the Constitution*, ed. Merill Jensen, John P. Kaminski and Gaspare J. Saladino, 16 vols. to date (Madison: State Historical Society of Wisconsin, 1976–).

2. Although the account of the dominant interpretation of the Federalist argument and intellectual achievement offered here is brief, I believe it captures its important elements. For authoritative expressions and discussions of the dominant interpretation of the Federalists, see, in addition to the works cited here, Gordon S. Wood, *The Creation of the American Republic, 1776–1787* (Chapel Hill: University of North Carolina Press, 1969), 409–13, 499–518; Jack N. Ra-

kove, "The Great Compromise: Ideas, Interests, and the Politics of Constitution Making," *WMQ*, 3d ser., 44 (1987), 424–57; Rakove, *Original Meanings: Politics and Ideas in the Making of the Constitution* (New York: Knopf, 1996), 35–56, and *passim*; Lance Banning, *The Sacred Fire of Liberty: James Madison and the Founding of the Federal Republic* (Ithaca, N.Y.: Cornell University Press, 1995).

3. Jack N. Rakove, "From One Agenda to Another: The Condition of American Federalism, 1783–1787," in *The American Revolution: Its Character and Limits*, ed. Jack P. Greene (New York: New York University Press, 1987), 95.

4. Lance Banning, "The Practical Sphere of a Republic: James Madison, the Constitutional Convention and the Emergence of Revolutionary Federalism," in *Beyond Confederation: Origins of the Constitution and American National Identity*, ed. Richard Beeman, Stephen Botein, and Edward C. Carter II (Chapel Hill: University of North Carolina Press, 1987), 162–87, quotation at 185.

5. Lance Banning, "Some Second Thoughts on Virtue and the Course of Revolutionary Thinking," in *Conceptual Change and the Constitution*, ed. Terence Ball and John Pocock (Lawrence: University Press of Kansas, 1988), 194–207, quotation at 207.

6. Rakove, "From One Agenda to Another," 84–98, quotation at 98.

7. Banning, "Practical Sphere of a Republic," 181–7. In his later work, however, Banning downplays the significance of *The Federalist*, arguing that Madison's contributions to the *Federalist* can only be fully understood by paying attention to the context in which Madison wrote and by making careful use of his later writings.

8. Ibid., 181; Banning, *Sacred Fire of Liberty*, 402. See also 206, 208, 212, 228, 294–8, and 396–402 for more on Madison's disagreements with Hamilton.

9. Banning, "Practical Sphere of a Republic," 180.

10. As a companion project to his edition of Antifederalist writings, *The Complete Anti-Federalist*, 7 vols. (Chicago: University of Chicago Press, 1981), Herbert Storing identified and analyzed 105 Federalist essays in "The 'Other' Federalist Papers: A Preliminary Sketch," *The Political Science Reviewer*, 6 (1976), 215–47. This remains one of the few attempts to analyze non-Madisonian Federalism. A quantitative content analysis of a broad sample of Federalist rhetoric has been carried out by William E. Riker in "Why Negative Campaigning is Rational: The Rhetoric of the Ratification Campaign of 1787–1788," *Studies in American Political Development*, 5 (1991), 224–50.

11. Thus, it certainly can no longer be claimed that the Antifederalists "have found only a cramped place in the shadow of the great constitutional accomplishment of 1787," Herbert J. Storing, *What the Anti-Federalists Were For* (Chicago: University of Chicago Press, 1981), 3. Storing's book is one of several excellent works that have been written about the Antifederalists. Other important works are Cecelia M. Kenyon, "Men of Little Faith: The Anti-Federalists on the Nature of Representative Government," *WMQ*, 3d ser., 12 (1955), 3–43; Kenyon, "Introduction" to *The Antifederalists*, ed. Kenyon (Indianapolis: Bobbs-Merrill, 1966); Jackson Turner Main, *The Antifederalists: Critics of the Constitution* (Chapel Hill: University of North Carolina Press, 1961); Saul Cornell, "Aristocracy Assailed: The Ideology of Back-Country Anti-Federalism," *JAH* 76 (1990), 1148–70; Cornell, *The Other Founders: Anti-Federalism and the Dissenting Tradition in America, 1788–1828* (Chapel Hill: University of North Carolina Press, 1999).

12. See note 1.

13. The most important influence on my understanding of the issues that made up the ratification debate has been the reinterpretation of the British eighteenth-century state undertaken over the last fifteen years. See in particular John Brewer, *The Sinews of Power: War, Money and the English State, 1688–1783* (London: Unwin Hyman, 1989); Patrick K. O'Brien, "The Political Economy of British Taxation, 1680–1810," *Economic History Review*, 2d ser., 41 (1988), 1–32; *An Imperial State at War: Britain from 1689 to 1815*, ed. Lawrence Stone (London: Routledge, 1994).

14. See for instance Charles Tilly, *Capital, Coercion and European States, AD 990–1990* (Oxford: Blackwell, 1990), 28; Tilly, "Reflections on the History of European State-Making," *The Formation of National States in Western Europe*, ed. Tilly (Princeton, N.J.: Princeton University Press, 1975), 42. For a recent statement of this view applied to the twentieth century, see Michael C. Desch, "War and Strong States, Peace and Weak States?" *International Organization*, 50 (1996), 237–68.

15. Cathy D. Matson and Peter S. Onuf, *A Union of Interests: Political and Economic Thought in Revolutionary America* (Lawrence: University Press of Kansas, 1990), 82–123; Banning, *Sacred Fire of Liberty*, 210–31.

16. Kramnick, "The 'Great National Discussion': The Discourse of Politics in 1787," *WMQ*, 3d ser., 45 (1988), 23.

17. Some of the most important works are Richard F. Bensel, *Yankee Leviathan: The Origins of Central State Authority in America, 1859–1877* (Cambridge, U.K.: Cambridge University Press, 1990); Stephen Skowronek, *Building a New American State: The Expansion of National Administrative Capacities, 1877–1920* (Cambridge, U.K.: Cambridge University Press, 1982); Theda Skocpol, *Protecting Soldiers and Mothers: Political Origins of Social Policy in the United States* (Cambridge, Mass.: Harvard University Press, 1992). But see also *Shaped by War and Trade: International Influences on American Political Development*, ed. Ira Katznelson and Martin Shefter (Princeton, N.J.: Princeton University Press, 2002), especially the contributions by Katznelson and Aristide R. Zolberg, which address some of the the issues I raise in this book. For two works by historians dealing with the early republic, see Richard R. John, *Spreading the News: The American Postal System from Franklin to Morse* (Cambridge, Mass.: Harvard University Press, 1995); Andrew R. L. Cayton, " 'Separate Interests' and the Nation-State: The Washington Administration and the Origins of Regionalism in the Trans-Appalachian West," *JAH*, 79 (1992), 347–80.

18. The modern classic is of course *Formation of National States in Western Europe*, ed. Tilly. Principal recent works include *The Origins of the Modern State in Europe, Thirteenth- to Eighteenth Centuries*, ed. Wim Blockmans and Jean-Philippe Genet, 7 vols. (Oxford: Oxford University Press, 1995–); Brian M. Downing, *The Military Revolution and Political Change: Origins of Democracy and Autocracy in Early Modern Europe* (Princeton, N.J.: Princeton University Press, 1992); Thomas Ertman, *Birth of the Leviathan: Building States and Regimes in Medieval and Early Modern Europe* (Cambridge, U.K.: Cambridge University Press, 1997); *Fiscal Crises, Liberty, and Representative Government, 1450–1789*, ed. Philip T. Hoffman and Kathryn Norberg (Stanford: Stanford University Press, 1994). The important exception to the predominant Euro-centrism is Michael Mann, *The Sources of Social Power 2: The Rise of Classes and Nation-States, 1760–1914* (Cambridge, U.K: Cambridge University Press, 1993).

1: Legitimacy and Meaning

1. I have of course been influenced by the thesis Jürgen Habermas presented in *The Structural Transformation of the Public Sphere: An Inquiry Into a Category of Bourgeois Society* (Cambridge, Mass.: MIT Press, 1989 [1962]) and in the short article "The Public Sphere," in *New German Critique*, 3 (1974), 49–55 (originally published in 1964). Habermas has lately had considerable influence on American historians. This began with work on the French enlightenment and Revolution but has now reached Early American history. For a discussion of Habermas's thesis and its influence on French and European historiography, see Deena Goodman, "Public Sphere and Private Life: Toward a Synthesis of Current Historiographical Approaches to the Old Regime," *History and Theory*, 31 (1992), 1–20; Anthony J. LaVopa, "Conceiving a Public: Ideas and Society in Eighteenth-Century Europe," *Journal of Modern History*, 61 (1992), 79–116. Three examples of works on early America inspired by Habermas, though that inspiration has led to very different results, are Michael Warner, *The Letters of the Republic: Publication and the Public Sphere in Eighteenth-Century America* (Cambridge, Mass.: Harvard University Press, 1990); David Waldstreicher, *In the Midst of Perpetual Fetes: The Making of American Nationalism, 1776–1820* (Chapel Hill: University of North Carolina Press, 1997) and Saul Cornell, *The Other Founders: Anti-Federalism and the Dissenting Tradition in America, 1788–1828* (Chapel Hill: University of North Carolina Press, 1999).

2. "Centinel" 1, *Doc. Hist.* v. 13, 331; Wilson, Pennsylvania Ratifying Convention, *Doc. Hist.* v. 2, 483–4.

3. For the American system of government see the references cited in ch. 2, note 43.

4. William E. Nelson, "Reason and Compromise in the Adoption of the Constitution," *WMQ*, 3d ser., 44 (1987), 459.

5. Art. 13.

6. "Confederation Congress Calls the Constitutional Convention," 21 February 1787, *Doc. Hist.* v. 1, 187.

7. "Resolutions of the Convention Recommending the Procedures for Ratification and for the Establishment of Government under the Constitution by the Confederation Congress," 17 September 1787, ibid., 318.

8. Jack N. Rakove, *Original Meanings: Politics and Ideas in the Making of the Constitution* (New York: Knopf, 1996), 96–108.

9. Ibid., 106–8.

10. See Willie Paul Adams, *The First American Constitutions: Republican Ideology and the Making of the State Constitutions in the Revolutionary Era* (Chapel Hill: University of North Carolina Press, 1980), 91–3, 96–7.

11. Before the Massachusetts constitution of 1780, state constitutions had been adopted in a procedure similar to ordinary legislation. For ratification procedure in the states, see ibid., 63–98. Massachusetts is discussed at 86–93 and 96–7.

12. Charles Thomson, "Circular Letter to the Executives of the States," *Doc. Hist.* v. 13, 241; Patrick T. Conley, "First in War, Last in Peace: Rhode Island and the Constitution 1786–1790," in *The Constitution and the States: The Role of the Original Thirteen in the Framing and Adoption of the Federal Constitution*, eds. Conley and John P. Kaminski (Madison: University of Wisconsin Press, 1988), 274.

13. Willie Jones and Thomas Person, North Carolina ratifying convention, Elliot, *Debates* 4, 4.

14. Albert Furtwangler, *The Authority of Publius: A Reading of the Federalist Papers* (Ithaca, N.Y.: Cornell University Press, 1984), 87, 90–3, quotation at 87.

15. This point is also made by Nelson, "Reason and Compromise," 475.

16. "Publicola," "An Address to the Freemen of North Carolina," *Doc. Hist.* v. 16, 438–9, emphasis in the original. The North Carolina assembly resolutions of 6 December 1787 called for the election of delegates "for deliberating and determining on the said Constitution" see the editors' note 2, 441.

17. Elliot, *Debates* 4, 4–5.

18. Ibid., 13–14.

19. Ibid., 102.

20. William Shepherd and Archibald Maclaine, ibid., 29–30.

21. North Carolina ratifying convention, ibid. 4, 30.

22. Cornell, *Other Founders*; Furtwangler, *Authority of Publius*, 98–111. The quotation is from the title of Furtwangler's fourth chapter.

23. These are the words of Amos Singletarry, Massachusetts ratifying convention, Elliot, *Debates* 2, 102. Furtwangler argues that Singletarry is representative of the Antifederalist position in *Authority of Publius*, 99.

24. Elliot, *Debates* 2, 159 and 161.

25. Ibid., 159–61, quotation at 161.

26. Bloodworth and Rutherford, North Carolina ratifying convention, Elliot, *Debates* 4, 30.

27. "Franklin's Speech," *Doc. Hist.* v. 13, 213–14.

28. Virginia ratifying convention, *Doc. Hist.* v. 10, 1366.

29. For the role of "impartiality" in Habermas's theory of the public sphere, see *Structural Transformation*, 35–6 and his "Further Reflections on the Public Sphere," in *Habermas and the Public Sphere*, ed. Craigh Calhoun (Cambridge, Mass.: MIT Press, 1992), 449.

30. Innes, Virginia ratifying convention, *Doc. Hist.* v. 10, 1520; Jay, New York ratifying convention, Elliot, *Debates* 2, 285. For a few other examples from the ratification campaign, see West, Massachusetts ratifying convention, ibid., 33; Tweed, South Carolina ratifying convention, Elliot, *Debates* 4, 332; Dawson, Virginia ratifying convention, *Doc. Hist.* v. 10, 1489–90; Johnston, ibid., 1530.

31. "Philadelphiensis" 1, *Doc. Hist.* v. 14, 577.

32. [Tobias Lear] "Brutus," *Doc. Hist.* v. 14, 152; "Valerius," *Doc. Hist.* v. 13, 314. See also the discussion of "Brutus" and "Valerius" in Cornell, *Other Founders*, 74–6.

33. Bailyn, "The Ideological Fulfilment of the American Revolution," in *Faces of Revolution: Personalities and Themes in the Struggle for American Independence* (New York: Knopf, 1990), 233–4; "Philadelphiensis" 4, *Doc. Hist.* v. 14, 418; "Philadelphiensis" 10, *Doc. Hist.* v. 16, 158, emphasis in the original.

34. "Centinel" 1, *Doc. Hist.* v. 13, 329; "Centinel" 12, *Doc. Hist.* v. 15, 448; "Dissent of the Minority of the Pennsylvania Convention," *Doc. Hist.* v. 15, 15–16.

35. Luther Martin, "Genuine Information" 1, *Doc. Hist.* v. 15, 151; "Centinel" 4, *Doc. Hist.* v. 14, 322–3. See also "An Officer of the Late Continental Army," *Doc. Hist.* v. 2, 215; "Federal Republican," *Doc. Hist.* v. 14, 259; Luther Martin, "Report to the Maryland Assembly," ibid, 288; "Centinel" 14, *Doc. Hist.*

v. 16, 32, 37–8; [Workman] "Philadelphiensis" 10, ibid., 158–60; [Warren] "A Columbian Patriot," ibid., 285–6.

36. "A Native of Virginia," *Doc. Hist.* v. 9, 657–8.

37. *Massachusetts Centinel,* 9 January, *Doc Hist.* 15, 294.

38. *Federalist* 1, *Doc. Hist.* v. 13, 494; Robert A. Rutland, "The Great Newspaper Debate: The Constitutional Crisis of 1787–1788," *Proceedings of the American Antiquarian Society,* 97 (1987), 47; *Pennsylvania Packet, Doc. Hist.* v. 13, 222; "Extract of a Letter from Salem County," *Doc. Hist.* v. 3, 140.

39. Ames, Massachusetts ratifying convention, Elliot, *Debates* 2, 10–11; [Oliver Ellsworth] "Landholder" 1, *Doc. Hist.* v. 13, 562; Simeon Baldwin, "Fourth of July Oration 1788," *Doc. Hist.* v. 18, 237. As Ralph Lerner points out, the Federalists' faith in reason was not altogether elitist as they believed in the common people's ability to see reason; see "The Constitution of the Thinking Revolutionary," in *Beyond Confederation: Origins of the Constitution and American National Identity,* ed. Richard Beeman, Stephen Botein, and Edward C. Carter II (Chapel Hill: University of North Carolina Press, 1987), 67–8.

40. [Hamilton] *The Federalist* 15, *Doc. Hist.* v. 15, 324–5. Bernard Bailyn points out that much of the Federalist contribution to the debate over ratification consisted of attempts to refute Antifederalist interpretations; see "Ideological Fulfilment of the American Revolution," 246–54. It can be said, therefore, that to the Federalists, deliberation aimed at arriving at the truth about the meaning and consequences of the Constitution *negatively,* by proving the Antifederalists wrong. In the Virginia convention Madison at one point thought that there was no point in continuing a discussion with persons who refused to follow rules of logic. What is the object of our discussion, Madison asked. "Truth, Sir. To draw a true and just conclusion.—Can this be done without rational premises, and syllogistic reasoning?" Virginia ratifying convention, *Doc. Hist.* v. 10, 1265.

41. "Centinel" 1, *Doc. Hist.* v. 13, 329; "Centinel" 8, *Doc. Hist.* v. 15, 233. For further charges that Federalists relied on "the magic of names," see "Centinel" 9, ibid., 309; "Centinel" 11, ibid., 446–7; "Cato Uticensis," *Doc. Hist.* v. 8, 71–2.

42. This point is also made by Nelson, who claims that both Federalists and Antifederalists tried "to persuade the public by reason" and even goes as far as suggesting that both groups can be perceived as "disinterested statesmen working together in pursuit of the public good"; see "Reason and Compromise," 475 and 482. Saul Cornell has argued that there were varieties of Antifederalism that differed in their conception of the value of public discussion in the press. However, according to Cornell, only "plebeian" Antifederalists denied that deliberation was important. While this may have been the most numerous part of the Antifederalists, they were true to their convictions and, consequently, were not well represented in the ratification debate. For the views of "elite," "middling," and "plebeian" Antifederalists on the public sphere, the press, and public deliberation, see Cornell, *Other Founders,* 74–80, 103–6, 115–16.

43. *Pennsylvania Mercury, Doc. Hist.* v. 18, 209–10; Hitchcock, "Oration," ibid., 234.

44. However, it has been argued that the late eighteenth century was a transition period to interest-group politics; see Gordon Wood, "Interests and Disinterestedness in the Making of the Constitution," in *Beyond Confederation,* ed. Beeman, Botein, and Carter, 93–103; Wood, *The Radicalism of the American*

Revolution (New York: Knopf, 1992), 258–9. A contrary view is offered by Nelson in "Reason and Compromise," 458–84.

45. Here I am indebted to the methodological writings of Quentin Skinner. See in particular, Skinner "Bolingbroke versus Walpole: The Principle and Practice of Opposition," in *Historical Perspectives: Studies in English Thought and Society in Honour of J. H. Plumb*, ed. Neil McKendrick (London: Europa, 1974), 93–128; Skinner, "Some Problems in the Analysis of Political Thought and Action," in *Meaning and Context: Quentin Skinner and His Critics*, ed. James Tully (Cambridge, U.K.: Polity Press, 1988), 97–118; Skinner, *The Foundations of Modern Political Thought I: The Renaissance* (Cambridge, U.K.: Cambridge University Press, 1978), ix–xv.

46. The best known statement of this point is a speech by James Wilson. See his "Speech at a Public Meeting in Philadelphia," *Doc. Hist.* v. 13, 339–40. For a few further examples see Iredell, North Carolina ratifying convention, Elliot, *Debates* 4, 172; Pinckney, South Carolina assembly debates, ibid., 259–60; Nicholas, Virginia ratifying convention, *Doc. Hist.* v. 10, 1333; Randolph, ibid., 1456.

47. Cornell, *Other Founders*, 147–73; Richard E. Ellis, "The Persistence of Antifederalism after 1789," in *Beyond Confederation*, ed. Beeman, Botein, and Carter, 295–314.

48. Cornell, *Other Founders*, 157–71, 221–45; Rakove, *Original Meanings*, 337–65; Lance Banning, "Republican Ideology and the Triumph of the Constitution, 1789 to 1793," *WMQ*, 3d ser., 31 (1974), 167–88. For Antifederalists' views of the Bill of Rights, see especially Kenneth R. Bowling, " 'A Tub to the Whale': The Founding Fathers and Adoption of the Bill of Rights," *Journal of the Early Republic*, 8 (1988), 223–51.

2: The Elusive Meaning of the Debate over Ratification

1. Herbert J. Storing, *What the Antifederalists Were For* (Chicago: University of Chicago Press, 1981), 5. Storing was not alone in making this claim. See the similar conclusions reached by other historians: "The Federalists . . . acted to secure individual rights. The Antifederalists . . . fought to secure individual rights." The disagreement between them, "while serious, was not fundamental. . . . While they disagreed over the means, . . . the Americans of 1787 agreed on the end of government. They agreed with the Americans of 1776 that government exists to secure the rights of the governed," Gary J. Schmitt and Robert H. Webking, "Revolutionaries, Antifederalists, and Federalists: Comments on Gordon Wood's Understanding of the American Founding," *The Political Science Reviewer* 9 (1979), 228–9; "Federalists did not differ from Anti-Federalists in seeing protection of private rights as the fundamental purpose of government; but they doubted that Anti-Federalists understood what most threatened those rights and what was necessary to protect them," David F. Epstein, "The Case for Ratification: Federalist Constitutional Thought," in *The Framing and Ratification of the Constitution*, ed. Leonard W. Levy and Denis J. Mahoney (New York: Macmillan 1987), 298.

2. James H. Hutson, "Country, Court and the Constitution: Antifederalists and the Historians," *WMQ*, 3d ser., 38 (1981), 356.

3. William E. Riker, "Why Negative Campaigning Is Rational: The Rhetoric of the Ratification Campaign of 1787–1788," *Studies in American Political Development*, 5 (1991), 235, 241.

4. Herbert J. Storing, "The 'Other' Federalist Papers: A Preliminary Sketch," *The Political Science Reviewer*, 6 (1976), 215; Riker, "Negative Campaigning," 245 and table 4.

5. In his recent work on the ratification debate Jack N. Rakove was puzzled to discover "how much emphasis I have given to *The Federalist*. The reason for this is the obvious one: Nothing equals it in analytical breadth and conceptual power," see *Original Meanings: Politics and Ideas in the Making of the Constitution* (New York: Knopf, 1996), xv. In the same way Storing notes how "the 'other' Federalist writings stand in the shadow cast by the towering *Federalist* papers." The reason is that "there is nothing in the Federalist writings comparable to the range and depth of *The Federalist*"; see Storing, " 'Other' Federalist papers," 215. As Bernard Bailyn remarks, the "endless outpouring of scholarly writing on [*The Federalist*] inundates everything written on the history of the Constitution and on American political thought. A complete bibliography would include hundreds, perhaps thousands, of items"; see "The Ideological Fulfillment of the American Revolution: A Commentary on the Constitution," in *Faces of the Revolution: Personalities and Themes in the Struggle for American Independence* (New York: Knopf 1990), n12.

6. Storing, " 'Other' Federalist Papers," 215. Similarly, Riker notes that while the major part of the content of the Federalist campaign was negative, most of the remaining "positive features derived from the Federalist position that, as reformers, they were obliged to justify their proposed reform against Antifederal attacks. Consequently, the main part of the positive Federalist argument is not a balanced rationale for their reforms, but rather and simply an answer to the particular Antifederal criticisms"; see "Negative Campaigning," 245.

7. *The Federalist* 1, *Doc. Hist.* v. 13, 496. For a discussion of *The Federalist* as a reply to Antifederalist criticism, see Albert Furtwangler, *The Authority of Publius: A Reading of the Federalist Papers* (Ithaca, N.Y.: Cornell University Press, 1984), 52–3, 74–9, and Bernard Bailyn, "The Federalist Papers," in *To Begin the World Anew: The Genius and Ambiguities of the American Founders* (New York: Knopf, 2003), 100–25.

8. It is perhaps more common to say that the importance of the progressive perspective in American history declined already in the 1950s. But at least as far as the struggle over ratification is concerned, historians such as Jackson Turner Main and Gordon Wood published important books on the Constitution in the 1960s that were firmly rooted in this tradition, even though the authors would perhaps not style themselves progressives.

9. Charles A. Beard, *An Economic Interpretation of the Constitution of the United States* (New York: Free Press, 1954 [1913]), 258. Here Beard is commenting on Samuel Harding's *The Contest over Ratification of the Federal Constitution in the State of Massachusetts* (New York: Longmans, Green & Co, 1896). Harding had identified a conflict of interest between the agricultural and the commercial sections of Massachusetts underlying which was the "pronounced antagonism" between the aristocratic and democratic elements of society, and he also claimed that the experience of Massachusetts was representative of other states. "Of course," Beard commented, "this second element of opposition—aristocracy *versus* democracy—introduced by Harding is really nothing but the first under another guise; for the aristocratic party was the party of wealth with its professional dependents; and the democratic was the agrarian

element, which, by the nature of economic circumstances, could have no large body of professional adherents."

10. Merill Jensen, *The Articles of Confederation: An Interpretation of the Social-Constitutional History of the American Revolution 1774–1781* (Madison: University of Wisconsin Press 1976 [1940]), xiii–xxix, 7–15, 109–10, 239–45; Jensen, *The New Nation: A History of the United States During the Confederation 1781–1789* (New York: Knopf, 1950), 3–5, 21–3, 42–53, 125–8, 399–400, 422–8. Quotations from *New Nation*, 128, and *Articles of Confederation*, 245 and xv.

11. Cecelia M. Kenyon, "Men of Little Faith: The Anti-Federalists and the Nature of Representative Government," *WMQ*, 3d ser., 12 (1955), 21–43, quotation at 42–3.

12. Jackson Turner Main, *The Antifederalists: Critics of the Constitution 1781–1788* (Chapel Hill: University of North Carolina Press, 1961), 280–1, see also 249–81 *passim*.

13. Saul A. Cornell, "Aristocracy Assailed: The Ideology,of Back-Country Anti-Federalism," *JAH*, 76 (1990), 1148–50, 1156–70; Cornell, *The Other Founders: Anti-Federalism and the Dissenting Tradition in America, 1788–1828* (Chapel Hill: University of North Carolina Press, 1999), 51–143. In his later work, as noted earlier, Cornell divides Antifederalist thought and the Antifederalist opposition into "elite," "plebeian," and "middling" variants.

14. For both the importance and the varied readings of Wood's work, see the comments by twelve leading historians and Wood's answer in "Forum: *The Creation of the American Republic, 1776–1787*. A Symposium of Views and Reviews," *WMQ*, 3d ser., 44 (1987), 549–640. Wood tried to synthesize two conflicting approaches to the political history of the founding era. The first was that of Jensen and his students, whereas the second approach focused on political ideas. This latter approach was first developed by Wood's teacher, Bernard Bailyn. Wood's attempt is most explicit in his "Rhetoric and Reality in the American Revolution," *WMQ*, 3d ser., 23 (1966), 3–32. On the occasion of its republication in *In Search of Early America*, ed. Michael McGiffert (Williamsburg: Institute of Early American History and Culture, 1994), 77, Wood notes in a postscript that "I wanted to acknowledge the importance both of ideas and underlying psychological determinants in shaping human behavior and yet avoid returning to the crude Beardian polarities of the past. In parts of *Creation of the American Republic* I tried to do just that, which is probably why so many historians could not decide what camp that book put me in."

15. Gordon S. Wood, *The Creation of the American Republic, 1776–1789* (Chapel Hill: University of North Carolina Press, 1969), 476, 478, 481–5, 488–92, 495, 497, 507, 510–11, 513, 516. Quotation from Wood, "Interests and Disinterestedness in the Making of the Constitution," in *Beyond Confederation: The Origins of the Constitution and American National Identity*, ed. Richard Beeman, Stephen Botein, and Edward C. Carter II (Chapel Hill: University of North Carolina Press, 1987), 93.

16. Wood, *Creation of the American Republic*, 485, emphasis added. Wood repeats this position in his recent *The Radicalism of the American Revolution* (New York: Knopf, 1992), 258.

17. Wood, *Radicalism of the American Revolution*, 258–8. See Wood, "Interests and Disinterestedness," 93–103 for a fuller statement.

18. Wood, "Interests and Disinterestedness," 96–100. It is the speeches by William Findley, who later became one of the Antifederalist leaders in Penn-

sylvania, which are identified as expressions of "real" Antifederalism. In all significant respects, Wood's account has recently been supported by Gary J. Kornblith and John M. Murrin, "The Making and Unmaking of an American Ruling Class," in *Beyond the American Revolution: Explorations in the History of American Radicalism*, ed. Alfred F. Young (DeKalb: Northern Illinois University Press, 1993), 54–8.

19. Beard's argument was refuted by Robert E. Brown, *Charles Beard and the Constitution: A Critical Analysis of "An Economic Interpretation of the Constitution"* (Princeton, N.J.: Princeton University Press, 1956) and Forrest McDonald, *We the People: The Economic Origins of the Constitution* (Chicago: University of Chicago Press, 1958). Works later than Beard's have been much more sophisticated and also much more difficult to disprove.

20. See, for instance, Main's review of *Creation of the American Republic* in *WMQ*, 3d ser., 26 (1969), 604–9.

21. Wood, *Creation of the American Republic*, viii, 606.

22. Bernard Bailyn, *The Ideological Origins of the American Revolution* (Cambridge, Mass.: Harvard University Press, 1967), vi–x, quotation at viii. This work was an expansion of Bailyn's "The Transforming Radicalism of the American Revolution," the introduction to *Pamphlets of the American Revolution* I, ed. Bailyn (Cambridge, Mass.: Harvard University Press, 1965).

23. Bailyn, *Ideological Origins of the American Revolution*, ix–xii; Wood, *Creation of the American Republic*, 13–17.

24. J. G. A. Pocock, "Virtue and Commerce in the Eighteenth Century," *The Journal of Interdisciplinary History*, 3 (1972), 120.

25. Ibid., 134.

26. Pocock, "Machiavelli, Harrington and English Political Ideologies in the Eighteenth-Century," *WMQ*, 3d ser., 22 (1965), 555–7, 566–7.

27. Pocock, *The Machiavellian Moment: Florentine Political Thought and the Atlantic Republican Tradition* (Princeton, N.J.: Princeton University Press, 1975), 486.

28. Robert E. Shalhope, "Republicanism and Early American Historiography," *WMQ*, 3d ser., 39 (1982), 335. For a review of the rapid development of early American intellectual history in the 1960s, see idem, "Toward a Republican Synthesis: The Emergence of an Understanding of Republicanism in American Historiography," *WMQ*, 3d ser., 29 (1972), 49–80.

29. Pocock, *Machiavellian Moment*, 526–52; Lance Banning, *The Jeffersonian Persuasion: Evolution of a Party Ideology* (Ithaca, N.Y.: Cornell University Press, 1978), 273–302.

30. Schmitt and Webking, "Revolutionaries, Antifederalists, and Federalists," 195–229.

31. Joyce O. Appleby, "The Social Origins of American Revolutionary Ideology," *JAH*, 64 (1978), 940–58; Isaac Kramnick, "Republican Revisionism Revisited," *AHR*, 87 (1982), 629–64.

32. Bailyn, *Ideological Origins of the American Revolution*, xi–xii. Similarly, Wood writes that the revolution seemed to the colonists "a peculiar moment in history when all knowledge coincided, when classical antiquity, Christian theology, English empiricism, and European rationalism could all be linked. Thus Josiah Quincy, like other Americans, could without any sense of incongruity cite Rousseau, Plutarch, Blackstone, and a seventeenth-century Puritan all on the same page," *Creation of the American Republic*, 7.

33. Bernard Bailyn, "The Central Themes of the American Revolution," in

Faces of Revolution, 206. The original article, which does not contain the passage quoted, was published in *Essays on the American Revolution*, ed. Stephen G. Kurtz and James H. Hutson (Chapel Hill: University of North Carolina Press, 1973). Wood, "Ideology and the Origins of Liberal America," *WMQ*, 3d ser., 64 (1987), 634.

34. Knud Haakonsson, "Republicanism," in *A Companion to Contemporary Political Philosophy*, ed. Robert E. Goodin and Philip Pettit (Oxford: Blackwell, 1993), 571. Even Lance Banning now concedes that "major difficulties will arise if we suppose that the analytical distinctions we detect were evident to those we study," Banning, "Jeffersonian Ideology Revisited: Liberal and Classical Ideas in the New American Republic," *WMQ*, 3d ser., 43 (1986), 12.

35. Banning writes that "logically, it may be inconsistent to be simultaneously liberal and classical. Historically, it was not: Eighteenth-century opposition thought was always a complex blend of liberal and classical ideas. So was the thought of America's revolutionary generation," Banning, "Jeffersonian Ideology Revisited," 12. See also his "Some Second Thoughts on Virtue and the Course of Revolutionary Thinking," in *Conceptual Change and the Constitution*, ed. Terence Ball and J. G. A. Pocock (Lawrence: University Press of Kansas, 1988), 194–212, especially 204–6. Kramnick writes about the struggle over ratification that several ideologies "coexisted in the discourse of politics in 1787–1788. None dominated the field, and the use of one was compatible with the use of another by the same writer or speaker." He also notes that no "one paradigm cleared the field in 1788 and obtained exclusive dominance in the American political discourse. There was no watershed victory of liberalism over republicanism," Kramnick, "The 'Great National Discussion': The Discourse of Politics in 1787," *WMQ*, 3d ser., 45 (1988), 4, 32. See also Shalhope, "Republicanism and Early American Historiography," 350; Joyce O. Appleby, "Republicanism in New and Old Contexts," *WMQ*, 3d ser., 43 (1986), 20–34. It should be noted, however, that the major battleground of the historians' disagreement has not been the ratification debate but Jeffersonian republicanism in the 1790s.

36. Kramnick, " 'Great National Discussion,' " 3–32, quotation at 4; Kramnick, "Ideological Background," in *The Blackwell Encyclopedia of the American Revolution*, ed. Jack P. Greene and Jack R. Pole (Oxford: Blackwell, 1991), 84–91.

37. Kramnick, " 'Great National Discussion,' " 32. Kramnick writes that a "persuasive case can be made for the Federalists as liberal modernists and the Antifederalists as nostalgic communitarians seeking desperately to hold on to a virtuous moral order threatened by commerce and market society" (5). On the other hand, an "equally strong case can be made for the Federalists as republican theorists, and here we see full-blown the confusion of idioms, the overlapping of the political languages, in 1787" (12).

38. *JAH*, 74 (1987), 661. For a good review article on the state of the art at the time of the bicentennial, see Peter S. Onuf, "Reflections on the Founding: Constitutional Historiography in Bicentennial Perspective," *WMQ*, 3d ser., 46 (1989), 341–75. For references to the bicentennial as an "intellectual bust," see 341 and n1.

39. In the most recent major work on the ratification debate, Jack Rakove seems to have abandoned the attempt to identify ideological categories in the cacophonous and multifaceted ratification debate, merely noting that from "such a body of writings, many an interpretation can be plausibly sustained, few conclusively verified or falsified," *Original Meanings*, 133.

40. Merrill Jensen, *The American Revolution Within America* (New York: New York University Press, 1974), 137, quoted in Hutson, "Country, Court, and the Constitution," 365; Bailyn, "Ideological Fulfillment of the American Revolution," 231–2. For similar conclusions see Main, *The Antifederalists*, 8–20; Forrest McDonald, *E Pluribus Unum: The Formation of the American Republic* (Indiana: Liberty Press, 1979, 2d ed.), preface to the second edition, 13–14; Wood, *Creation of the American Republic*, 520–1, 523. For the claim that the Revolution's rhetoric survived into the 1790s, see Cornell, "Aristocracy Assailed," and Thomas P. Slaughter, *The Whiskey Rebellion: Frontier Epilogue to the American Revolution* (New York: Oxford University Press, 1986) for popular political rhetoric and Lance Banning, "Republican Ideology and the Triumph of the Constitution, 1789 to 1793," *WMQ*, 3d ser., 31 (1974), 167–88; Pocock, *Machiavellian Moment*, 506–52 and Banning, *Jeffersonian Persuasion* for the elite.

41. Bailyn, *Ideological Origins of the American Revolution*, 56–8, 60, 65, 100–1; Banning, "Some Second Thoughts," 196–207. For the concept of "jealousy," see James H. Hutson, "The Origin of 'the Paranoid Style in American Politics': Public Jealousy from the Age of Walpole to the Age of Jackson," in *Saints and Revolutionaries: Essays on Early American History*, ed. David D. Hall, John M. Murrin and Thad W. Tate (New York: Norton, 1984), 332–72 and Gordon S. Wood, "Conspiracy and the Paranoid Style: Causality and Deceit in the Eighteenth Century," *WMQ*, 3d ser., 29, 401–44.

42. For descriptions of the jury trial in these terms, see for instance "Impartial Examiner" 1, *Doc. Hist.* v. 8, 423; Luther Martin, "Genuine Information" 10, *Doc. Hist.* v. 16, 9. For the militia and the assembly, see chapters 7 and 12 respectively.

43. On the courts and the jury, see Jack P. Greene, "From the Perspective of Law: Context and Legitimacy in the Origins of the American Revolution," *The South Atlantic Quarterly*, 85 (1986), 56–75; Douglas Greenberg, *Crime and Law Enforcement in the Colony of New York, 1692–1776* (Ithaca, N.Y.: Cornell University Press, 1976); Hendrig Hartog, "The Public Law of a County Court: Judicial Government in Eighteenth-Century Massachusetts," *The American Journal of Legal History*, 20 (1976), 282–329; Hartog, "Losing the World of the Massachusetts Whig," in *Law in the American Revolution and the Revolution in Law: A Collection of Review Essays on American Legal History*, ed. Hartog (New York: New York University Press, 1981), 143–66; Peter C. Hoffer, "Introduction" to *Criminal Proceedings in Virginia*, ed. Hoffer and William B. Scott (Athens: Georgia University Press, 1984), xvi–xliv; Catherine Menand, "Juries, Judges, and the Politics of Justice in pre-Revolutionary Boston," in *The Law in America, 1607–1861*, ed. William Pencak and Wythe W. Holt, Jr. (New York: New-York Historical Society, 1989), 155–79; William E. Nelson, *The Americanization of the Common Law: The Impact of Legal Change on Massachusetts Society, 1760–1830* (Cambridge, Mass.: Harvard University Press, 1975); Nelson, "The Eighteenth-Century Background to John Marshall's Constitutional Jurisprudence," *Michigan Law Review*, 76 (1977–78), 893–960; John Philip Reid, *In a Defiant Stance: The Conditions of Law in Massachusetts Bay, the Irish Comparison, and the Coming of the American Revolution* (University Park: Pennsylvania State University Press, 1977); Donna Spindel, *Crime and Society in North Carolina, 1673–1776* (Baton Rouge: Louisiana State University Press, 1989); L. Kinvin Wroth and Hiller B. Zobel, "Introduction" to *The Legal Papers of John Adams* 1, ed. Wroth and Zobel (Cambridge, Mass.: Harvard University Press, 1975), xxxviii–lii.

For the ability of the militia to determine the effectiveness of government decisions, with regard both to the maintenance of law and order and to the ability to stage military operations, see Van Beck Hall, *Politics Without Parties: Massachusetts, 1780–1791* (Pittsburgh: University of Pittsburgh Press, 1972), 212; Pauline Maier, "Popular Uprisings and Civil Authority in Eighteenth-Century America," *WMQ*, 3d ser., 27 (1970), 3–35; Maier, *From Resistance to Revolution* (New York: Knopf, 1972); John Philip Reid, *In Defiance of the Law: The Standing-Army Controversy, the Two Constitutions, and the Coming of the American Revolution* (Chapel Hill: University of North Carolina Press, 1981), 103–10; John Shy, *Toward Lexington: The Role of the British Army in the Coming of the American Revolution* (Princeton, N.J.: Princeton University Press, 1965), 40; Albert H. Tillson, Jr., "The Militia and Popular Culture in the Upper Valley of Virginia, 1740–1755," *The Virginia Magazine of History and Biography*, 94 (1986), 285–306; Gordon S. Wood, "A Note on Mobs in the American Revolution," *WMQ*, 3d ser., 23 (1966), 635–42.

The importance of the state assemblies lay primarily in their control over taxation. For a discussion of the assemblies in this respect see chapter 10.

44. See chapters 7 and 12. As has often been pointed out, the Antifederalists refused to accept the concept of shared sovereignty. There had to be one supreme power in any state. The Antifederalists' ideas about state sovereignty and their fears of a "consolidated" government are reviewed in Peter S. Onuf, *The Origins of the Federal Republic: Jurisdictional Controversies in the United States 1775–1787* (Philadelphia: University of Pennsylvania Press, 1983), 186–9, 201; Rakove, *Original Meanings*, 181–4; and Storing, *What the Anti-Federalists Were For*, 9–11, 32–7.

45. Antifederalist ideas about representation are reviewed in Edmund S. Morgan, *Inventing the People: The Rise of Popular Sovereignty in England and America* (New York: Norton, 1988), 277–9; Rakove, *Original Meanings*, 228–34 and Storing, *What the Antifederalists Were For*, 17–18, 43–5.

46. See chapters 7 and 12. No one who has studied the Country tradition has failed to notice the anti-army argument as well as criticism of the public debt. Much less has been made of the aversion to taxes, which to my mind appears the more interesting argument. Edmund Morgan describes the Antifederalist objection to Congress's power to tax as "probably the most pervasive Antifederalist objection to the Constitution," *Inventing the People*, 280, n46. On Antifederalist objections to Congress's right to raise armies, Bernard Bailyn writes that "nothing excited antifederalist passions more than Congress's power, under Article 1, Section 8, 'to raise and support armies.' . . . There is simply no way to measure the volume and fervor of the antifederalists' denunciation of this provision, which revived for them not simply a general fear of military power but the specific danger of 'standing armies,' a peculiar and distinctive threat to liberty that had been formulated for all time, they believed, in England in the 1690s, and had been carried forward intact to the colonies," Bailyn, "Ideological Fulfillment of the American Revolution," 237.

47. Ibid., 228.

48. Jack P. Greene, *The Intellectual Construction of America: Exceptionalism and Identity from 1492 to 1800* (Chapel Hill: University of North Carolina Press, 1993), 72–3, 100. Quotations from Gabriel Thomas, "An Historical and Geographical Account of Pensilvania and of West-New-Jersey" (1698) and John Norris, *Profitable Advice for Rich and Poor* (London, 1712). See also Adam Smith, *An Inquiry Into the Nature and Causes of the Wealth of Nations*, ed. R. H. Camp-

bell, Andrew S. Skinner and W. B. Todd (Oxford: Oxford University Press, 1976), vol. 2, bk. 4, ch. 4, part 2, 573–4.

49. In *Cato's Letters*, a series of essays published early in the eighteenth century and generally agreed to have been very influential in the colonies, John Trenchard and Thomas Gordon wrote that "most of the princes of Europe have been long introducing the Turkish government into Europe; and have succeeded so well, that I would rather live under the Turk than under many of them. They practice the cruelties and oppressions of the Turks, and want the tolerating spirit of the Turk; and if some unforeseen check be not thrown in their way, the whole polity of savage Turkey will be established by them in all its parts and barbarity; as if the depopulation which is already so quick, and taking such dreadful strides, were still too slow. It is not enough for tyrants to have consumed mankind so fast, that out of twenty parts, they have within these two thousand years destroyed perhaps nineteen (for so much at least I take to be the disproportion), but fresh machines of cruelty are still sought after, besides never laying aside any of the old, till the destruction be fully completed. They seem to think, that they shall have enemies so long as any men remain; which indeed is a reasonable apprehension: But it is astonishing at first view, that mankind should have so long borne these unrelenting slaughterers of mankind. But, alas! who knows not the force of corruption, delusion, and standing armies!," Letter no. 73, "A Display of Tyranny, Its Destructive Nature, and Tendency to Dispeople the Earth," in *Cato's Letters: Or Essays on Liberty, Civil and Religious, and Other Important Subjects*, ed. Ronald Hamowy (Indianapolis: Liberty Press, 1995), 2, 542–3.

50. Bailyn, *Intellectual Origins of the American Revolution*, 64–5; Pauline Maier, *American Scripture: Making the Declaration of Independence* (New York: Knopf, 1997), 69–90. Late eighteenth-century Americans, no less than other peoples at the time, inhabited an intellectual world where history was regarded as the best guide to the present and the future. What had come to pass in other nations, even if in the distant past, was likely to happen in America as well. As James Burgh wrote in the preface to his *Political Disquisitions* (London, 1774), I, vi, "I considered, that history is the inexhaustible mine, out of which political knowledge is to be brought up." For the role of history in the reasoning of the revolutionary generation, see Douglass Adair, " 'Experience Must Be Our Only Guide': History, Democratic Theory, and the United States Constitution," in *Fame and the Founding Fathers: Essays by Douglass Adair*, ed. H. Trevor Colbourn (New York: Norton, 1974), 108–13; H. Trevor Colbourn, *The Lamp of Experience: Whig History and the Intellectual Origins of the American Revolution* (Chapel Hill: University of North Carolina Press, 1965), 185–93 and *passim*.

51. One may say that armies and taxes received their symbolic significance from their place in a narrative of the republic. Primarily for the role of the army, see Bailyn, "Ideological Fulfillment of the American Revolution," 234–9; Bailyn, *Ideological Origins of the American Revolution*, 61–3, 112–19; Quentin Skinner, "The Principle and Practice of Opposition: The Case of Bolingbroke versus Walpole," in *Historical Perspectives: Studies in English Thought and Society in Honour of J. H. Plumb*, ed. Neil McKendrick (London: Europa, 1974), 93–128.

52. British policy is described as a failed attempt to expand the British "fiscal-military state" to the American colonies in John Brewer, *The Sinews of Power: War, Money and the English State, 1688–1783* (London: Unwin Hyman, 1989), 176, 132; Patrick K. O'Brien, "Inseparable Connections: Trade, Econ-

omy, Fiscal State, and the Expansion of Empire, 1688–1815," in *The Oxford History of the British Empire*, ed. Wm. Roger Louis (Oxford: Oxford University Press, 1998), 2, 68. As Mark D. Kaplanoff writes about the colonists' response, since 1689 "Britain had experimented with fiscal and economic reforms which ultimately created the machinery of a modern nation state and which promoted new capital markets, industrial development, and rapid economic growth. But it had been precisely this nexus of administrative and fiscal reform—when applied to the colonies—which had sparked the American Revolution. Most Revolutionaries had contrasted American simplicity with the degeneration and corruption which they saw developing in Britain; they sought to preserve a simpler, freer way of life, freed from the encroachments of a developing nation state or advanced fiscal and credit systems." See "Confederation: Movement for a Stronger Union," in *The Blackwell Encyclopedia of the American Revolution*, ed. Greene and Pole, 444–5. For accounts of the changes in British imperial policy and the resistance which they met, see for instance Ian K. Steele, "The Anointed, the Appointed, and the Elected: Governance of the British empire, 1689–1784," in *The Oxford History of the British empire*, ed. Louis, 2, 105–26 and Jack P. Greene, *Peripheries and Center: Constitutional Development in the Extended Polities of the British Empire and the United States, 1607–1788* (Athens: Georgia University Press, 1986), 79–150.

The historiography on the American Revolution is enormous and the event is very contested. What I have said should not be interpreted to mean that the expansion of the British state in the colonies explains the Revolution. Clearly, the Revolution is a very complex event, something that is mirrored in the fact that historians hardly agree on what the term means. Nevertheless, I doubt that anyone would disagree with the claim that British policy worked as a catalyst for revolution. The conditions for, and consequences of, revolution, however, are a different story.

53. "A Columbian Patriot," *Doc. Hist.* v. 16, 284.

54. "A Citizen of the State of Maryland," "Remarks on a Standing Army," *Doc. Hist.* v. 17, 89; "Centinel" 7, *Doc. Hist.* v. 15, 178. "On the New Constitution," *State Gazette of South Carolina*, 28 January, *Doc. Hist.* v. 15, 486. See also Luther Martin, "Address No. IV," *Doc. Hist.* v. 17, 20 and "Philadelphiensis" 2, *Doc. Hist.* v. 14, 254: "Before we confirm this new constitution, let us ask ourselves this question—For what did we withdraw our allegiance from Great Britain; was it because the yoke of George the third was not sufficiently galling, that we cast it off, at the expence of so much blood and treasure, in order to accommodate ourselves with one of our own construction more intolerable? or, was it because the tyrant was three thousand miles off, that we revolted, in order to appoint one at home, who should correct us with scorpions instead of whips?"

55. "Brutus" 1, *Doc. Hist.* v. 13, 419; "Brutus" 9, *Doc. Hist.* v. 15, 394. "A Columbian Patriot" [Mercy Otis Warren], "Observations on the Constitution," *Doc. Hist.* v. 16, 280; "A Son of Liberty," *Doc. Hist.* v. 13, 481.

56. "Philadelphiensis" 5, *Doc. Hist.* v. 15, 46.

57. For the view, common in both Europe and America, that America was a social experiment, see Greene, *Intellectual Construction of America*, 131–61.

58. "Brutus" 7, *Doc. Hist.* v. 15, 236. In *The Rights of Man*, Thomas Paine compared the new systems of government established in America and France with the old systems of government: "Government on the old system is an assumption of power for the aggrandizement of itself; on the new a delegation

of power for the common benefit of society. The former supports itself by keeping up a system of war; the latter promotes a system of peace as the true means of enriching a nation. The one encourages national prejudices; the other promotes universal society as the means of universal commerce. The one measures its prosperity by the quantity of revenue it extorts; the other provides its excellence by the small quantity of taxes it requires," *Political Writings*, ed. Bruce Kuklick (Cambridge, U.K.: Cambridge University Press, 1989), pt. 2, ch. 3, 161. Obviously, to the extent that the social experiment really was emancipatory, such emancipation affected only part of the American population.

59. Michael Mann, "The Autonomous Power of the State: Its Origins, Mechanisms and Results," in *States in History*, ed. John A. Hall (Oxford: Blackwell, 1986), 112. See also Max Weber, "Politik som yrke" ("Politik als Beruf"), in *Tre klassiska texter* (Göteborg: Korpen, 1991 [1919]), 40–3.

60. Charles Tilly, *Capital, Coercion and European States, AD 990–1990* (Oxford: Blackwell, 1990), 96; Tilly, "War-Making and State-Making as Organized Crime," in *Bringing the State Back In*, ed. Peter B. Evans, Dietrich Rueschemeyer, and Theda Skocpol (Cambridge, U.K.: Cambridge University Press, 1985), 181–3.

3: European States, American Contexts

1. Principal recent works of a comparative nature include *Economic Systems and State Finance*, ed. Richard Bonney (Oxford: Oxford University Press, 1995); Brian M. Downing, *The Military Revolution and Political Change: Origins of Democracy and Autocracy in Early Modern Europe* (Princeton, N.J.: Princeton University Press, 1992); Thomas Ertman, *Birth of the Leviathan: Building States and Regimes in Medieval and Early Modern Europe* (Cambridge, U.K.: Cambridge University Press, 1997); Jack A. Goldstone, *Revolution and Rebellion in the Early Modern World* (Berkeley: University of California Press, 1991); *Fiscal Crises, Liberty and Representative Government*, ed. Philip T. Hoffman and Kathryn Norberg (Stanford: Stanford University Press, 1994); Michael Mann, *The Sources of Social Power 2: The Rise of Classes and Nation-States, 1760–1914* (Cambridge, U.K.: Cambridge University Press, 1993); Charles Tilly, *Coercion, Capital and European States, AD 990–1990* (Oxford: Blackwell, 1990).

2. Tilly, *Coercion, Capital and European States*, 28. "The building of an effective military machine imposed a heavy burden on the population involved: taxes, conscription, requisitions, and more. The very act of building it—when it worked—produced arrangements which could deliver resources to the government for other purposes. (Thus almost all the major European taxes began as 'extraordinary levies' earmarked for particular wars, and became routine sources of governmental revenue.) It produced the means of enforcing the government's will over stiff resistance: the army. It tended, indeed, to promote territorial consolidation, centralization, differentiation of the instruments of government and monopolization of the means of coercion, all the fundamental state-making processes. War made the state, and the state made war," Charles Tilly, "Reflections on the History of European State-Making," in *The Formation of National States in Western Europe*, ed. Tilly (Princeton, N.J.: Princeton University Press, 1975), 42.

3. Thomas Ertman, "*The Sinews of Power* and European State-Building Theory," in *An Imperial State at War: Britain from 1689 to 1815*, ed. Lawrence S.

Stone (London: Routledge, 1994), 34. Thus, in an article first published in 1902, Hintze wrote about the early modern period that "war became the great flywheel for the whole political enterprise of the modern state. This is how the standing armies with all their consequences, the battle fleets, the war industries, the new tax-systems (the backbone of which were war taxes), the new bureaucratic administration of finances, the amassing of a war chest and the system of state debt came into being. It was precisely the constant rivalry among the [great] powers . . . which produced an unheard-of exertion of energy, especially military and financial energy." Perhaps better known is Weber's similar statement in *Wirtschaft und Gesellschaft* (*Economy and Society*), that "it was most often needs arising from the creation of standing armies called forth by power politics, and the development of financial systems connected with them, that more than anything else has furthered the trend towards bureaucratization." Both quoted in Ertman.

4. The term "fiscal-military state" originated in John Brewer, *The Sinews of Power: War, Money and the English State, 1688–1783* (London: Unwin Hyman, 1989). It may be argued that the term is inappropriate as a description of the early modern state as war and taxation have always been basic features of the state. What distinguishes the modern from the medieval state is rather that it expanded into the areas of economic- and commercial policy as well as public welfare. However, because state expansion before the nineteenth century was restricted to growth in the size of troops and navies, in higher taxes and increased indebtedness, the term can be defended; see Lawrence S. Stone, "Introduction," to *Imperial State at War*, 9. Brewer employs the term in a polemic with the traditional view that the British state differed from the states in Continental Europe.

5. Although it may suggest otherwise, rather than a sharp break with earlier modes of warfare, the "military revolution" was in fact a process evolving throughout the sixteenth and seventeenth centuries. On the one hand the term refers to a change in military technology—such as more effective fire arms, mobile artillery and new fortification designs—and in strategy, tactics and organization—such as maneuvers, troop composition and training. On the other hand it refers to the dramatic increase of the size of the armed forces and to the increasing impact of armies and wars on society and the state. The term "military revolution" was coined by Michael Roberts in *The Military Revolution 1560–1660: An Inaugural Lecture Delivered Before the Queen's University of Belfast* (Belfast: M. Boyd, 1956). Although generally supportive of Robert's thesis, Geoffrey Parker has extended its dates to 1530–1710 and developed it further in other respects in "The 'Military Revolution,' 1560–1660—a Myth?" *Journal of Modern History*, 48 (1976), 195–214; Parker, "Warfare," in *The New Cambridge Modern History* 13, ed. Peter Burke (Cambridge, U.K.: Cambridge University Press, 1979); Parker, *The Military Revolution: Military Innovation and the Rise of the West, 1500–1800* (Cambridge, U.K.: Cambridge University Press, 1996, 2d ed.). In an afterword to this last volume Parker discusses some of the criticism directed against the thesis, 155–75. The concept is also discussed in the introduction to *The Military Revolution and the State 1500–1800*, ed. Michael Duffy (Exeter: Exeter University Press 1980), 1–9.

6. The development of the "tax state" in early modern Europe is traced in Marjolein t'Hart, "The Emergence and Consolidation of the 'Tax State.' 2: The Seventeenth Century," 286; Winfried Schulze, "The Emergence and Consolidation of the 'Tax State.' 1: The Sixteenth Century," 271; Richard Bonney, "The

Eighteenth Century. 2: The Struggle for Great Power Status," 319, 336–8, 344–5; Richard Bonney, "Early Modern Theories of State Finance," 181–2, all in *Economic Systems and State Finance*, ed. Bonney.

7. Michael Mann, "The Autonomous Power of the State: Its Origins, Mechanisms and Results," in *States in History*, ed. John A. Hall (Oxford: Blackwell, 1986), 113.

8. Thus there were clear limits to a ruler's right to levy taxes without the consent of the subjects. Even Jean Bodin claimed that "it is not in the power of any prince in the world, at his pleasure to raise taxes upon the people, no more than to take another man's goods from him," Bonney, "Early Modern Theories of State Finance," 165, 167–9. Practitioners of absolutism recognized these limits as well, if only for pragmatic reasons. Cardinal Richelieu believed in taxation by consent because fair taxes ensured efficient collection, and the surest way to guarantee fairness was by securing the consent of the tax payer, J. Gelabert, "The Fiscal Burden," in *Economic Systems and State Finance*, ed. Bonney, 543. But see the remark in Jean Nicolas, Julio Valdeón Baruque, and Sergij Vilfan, "The Monarchic State and Resistance in Spain, France, and the Old Provinces of the Habsburgs, 1400–1800," in *Resistance, Representation, and Community*, ed. Peter Blickle (Oxford: Oxford University Press, 1997), 113, that Bodin "had given monarchic authority its most 'absolute' definition, and the heads of our great monarchies [France, Spain and Austria] simply had to put it in practice. In the words of Bodin, the sovereign is answerable to no one but himself, and he has 'legislative powers over the community as a whole as well as over every single individual . . . without the consent of his betters, his peers or his subjects.' There is no *jus resistendi* or right to resist to justify opposition to his unique and sovereign will."

9. Tilly, *Coercion, Capital and European States*, 101–3; Nicolas, Valdeón Baruque and Vilfan, "The Monarchic State and Resistance," 103, 106–7, 112–13; Peter Blickle, Steven Ellis, and Eva Österberg, "The Commons and the State: Representation, Influence, and the Legislative Process," in *Resistance, Representation and Community*, ed. Blickle, 153.

10. Tilly, *Coercion, Capital and European States*, 103–4. Tilly defines direct rule as "unmediated intervention in the lives of local communities, households, and productive enterprises." It is often noted that a consequence of direct rule was that the category of the "subject" or "citizens" gained in importance in political theory and law. Blickle et al. note that the "rise of the modern state is inextricably linked with the creation of the subject. Throughout Europe, the state consolidated its control over its territory, vindicating its sovereignty by overcoming the various internal and external challenges to its authority and in the process turning the inhabitants of that territory into subjects. Thus, the general development of Europe until the end of the *ancien régime* was characterized by a growing state monopoly of political power. This was achieved in various ways[:] through the development of an administration which answered only to the king[,] by the gradual establishment of a system of state taxation (which no longer distinguished between estates, but, instead, was increasingly based on the rational criteria of property and income) and, finally, also by the political theory which used traditional concepts and divine grace to emphasize the pre-eminent position of the king or territorial prince. The members of a society who had been politically strongly differentiated in their relationships toward the state became a uniform body of subjects. This was

truer of burghers and peasants, than of the lower nobility, whose position varied considerably from country to country, although, on the whole, it became more and more tenuous," Blickle, Ellis, and Österberg, "The Commons and the State," 115.

11. André Corvisier, *Armies and Societies in Europe* (Bloomington: Indiana University Press, 1979) 41–60, 63–4, 73–7; Parker, "The 'Military Revolution,' 1560–1660—a Myth?" 208–10; Parker, "Warfare," 205–8; Parker, *Military Revolution*, 12, 39, 45–81; Roberts, *Military Revolution*, 15–16. Indeed, what administration there was in the early modern European state was predominantly created to serve the needs of war. Gerald E. Aylmer writes that "by far and away the biggest preoccupation of all states was with the preparations for and the effective waging of war," Aylmer, "Bureaucracy," in *The New Cambridge Modern History* 13, ed. Burke, 173–4.

12. Richard Bonney, "Revenues," in *Economic Systems and State Finance*, ed. Bonney, 423–63; t'Hart, "Emergence and Consolidation of the 'Tax State,' 2," 281–93. Bonney notes that "by the mid-eighteenth century there was a strong tendency away from farming and towards direct administration (regié), both in theory (most notably in the works of Montesquieu) and practice" (440).

13. Schulze, "Emergence and Consolidation of the 'Tax State,' 1," 273–9; · t'Hart, "Emergence and Consolidation of the 'Tax State,' 2," 288–93; Nicolas, Valdeón Baruque, and Vilfan, " 'The Monarchic State and Resistance," 82–3, 86–8, 91–2, 96–7, 98–9, 103. The latter note (103) regarding France that from "the 1710s in particular, we can . . . observe a gradual reduction in the number of violent rebellions of the traditional kind. However, this decrease was neither the result of a complete disappearance of social resistance, nor of a simple transfer of conflicts onto a legal or political level. Rather, there was now a combination of factors . . . which helped to restrict the potential for violent confrontation. The eighteenth century still saw thousands of disputes to the very eve of 1789, but they were certainly less vigorous than in earlier times."

14. Ertman, "*Sinews of Power* and European State-Building Theory," 35–6.

15. Brewer, *The Sinews of Power*; Patrick K. O'Brien, "The Political Economy of British Taxation, 1680–1810," *Economic History Review*, 2d ser., 41 (1988), 1–32; Patrick K. O'Brien and P. A. Hunt, "The Rise of the Fiscal Military State in England, 1485–1815," *Historical Research*, 66 (1993), 129–76; P. Harling and P. Mandler, "From Fiscal Military to Laissez-Faire State, 1760–1850," *Journal of British Studies*, 32 (1993), 44–70.

16. Brewer, *Sinews of Power*, 7–8, 31–3, 41–2, and fig. 2.1, p. 30; Corvisier, *Armies and Societies*, table 1, 113.

17. O'Brien, "Political Economy of British Taxation," table 2. Population figures from Edward A. Wrigley and Roger S. Scholfield, *The Population History of England 1541–1871* (London, 1981), table 7.8.

18. Peter Mathias and Patrick O'Brien, "Taxation in England and France, 1715–1810: A Comparison of the Social and Economic Incidence of Taxes Collected for the Central Governments," *Journal of European Economic History*, 5 (1976), 610 and tables 7 and 8.

19. Brian R. Mitchell, *British Historical Statistics* (Cambridge, U.K.: Cambridge University Press, 1988), 600–601; O'Brien, "Political Economy of British Taxation," table 2.

20. Paul Langford, *A Polite and Commercial People: England 1727–1783* (Oxford: Oxford University Press, 1989), 692.

21. Körner, "Expenditure," fig. 63. For a general discussion of the structure of expenditure in European states, cities and republics in the seventeenth and eighteenth centuries, see 409–22.

22. Brewer, *Sinews of Power*, 38–40, 114–116, figures 2.1 and 4.7.

23. See for instance, Richard F. Bensel, *Yankee Leviathan: The Origins of Central State Authority in America, 1859–1877* (Cambridge, U.K.: Cambridge University Press, 1990), 106–10. Of course, the existence of autonomy has largely been denied by both marxist and pluralist theories of the state. For a discussion of state autonomy and state strength, see Peter B. Evans, Dietrich Rueschemeyer, and Theda Skocpol, "On the Road Toward a More Adequate Understanding of the State," in *Bringing the State Back In*, ed. Evans, Rueschemeyer, and Skocpol (Cambridge, U.K.: Cambridge University Press, 1985), 350–7.

24. Brewer, *Sinews of Power*, 130–2; Downing, *Military Revolution and Political Change*, 181–3; Ertman, *Birth of Leviathan*, 221; Mann, *Sources of Social Power* 2, 115–116; Kathryn Norberg, "The French Fiscal Crisis and the Revolution of 1789," in *Fiscal Crises*, eds. Hoffman and Norberg, 296–7; Philip T. Hoffman and Kathryn Norberg, "Conclusion," ibid, 299–310.

25. Mann, *Sources of Social Power* 2, 108–9, 170–97, quotation at 109, emphasis added. Norberg, "French Fiscal Crisis," 291–9. The role of the British parliament in helping the government to mobilize social resources was noted in France, where the king's ministers worked to create a French counterpart to the Commons.

26. Mann, *Sources of Social Power* 2, 107–20. For a general discussion of the way state-society relations have been organized in different political systems, see 54–75.

27. Ibid., 110–20.

28. O'Brien, "Political Economy of British Taxation," 14–26 and tables 4 and 5, quotation at 18. For more on the development of British taxation, see J. V. Beckett, "Land Tax or Excise: The Levying of Taxation in Seventeenth-and Eighteenth-Century England," *English Historial Review*, 100 (1985), 305–6 and table 2; J. V. Beckett and M. Turner, "Taxation and Economic Growth in Eighteenth-Centruy England," *Economic History Review*, 2d ser., 43 (1990) 383–8, figures 1 and 3a-3d, and table 1; Brewer, *Sinews of Power*, 95, 99, 116–23 and figures 4.2 and 4.3; Brewer, "The Eighteenth-Century British State: Contexts and Issues," in *Imperial State at War*, ed. Stone, 63–4; Paul Langford, *The Excise Crisis: Society and Politics in the Age of Walpole* (Oxford: Oxford University Press, 1975), 31–5, 39–40. On the House of Commons see also Wilfred Prest, *Albion Ascendant: English History, 1660–1815* (Oxford: Oxford University Press, 1998), 65, 132–3, 156, 311, 314–15 and 318.

29. John Brewer, "English Radicalism in the Age of George III," in *Three British Revolutions: 1640, 1688, 1776*, ed. J.G.A. Pocock (Princeton, N.J.: Princeton University Press, 1980), 323–67; Eliga H. Gould, *The Persistence of Empire: British Political Culture in the Age of the American Revolution* (Chapel Hill: University of North Carolina Press, 2000), 172.

30. Joseph Priestley, *Political Writings*, ed. Peter N. Miller (Cambridge, U.K.: Cambridge University Press, 1993), 17.

31. James Burgh, *Political Disquisitions* 1 (London, 1774), 51.

32. Brewer, *Sinews of Power*, 132–3; Brewer, "Eighteenth-Century British State," 61–2, 66–7; Langford, *Excise Crisis*, 166; Mann, *Sources of Social Power* 2, 108–15. Hoffman and Norberg, "Conclusion," 304. For Ireland, see Prest, *Albion Ascendant*, 216–18; Langford, *Polite and Commercial People*, 544–6.

33. Beckett, "Land Tax or Excise," 295 and 301; Becket and Turner, "Taxation and Economic Growth," 391; Brewer, *Sinews of Power*, 101–10; O'Brien, "Political Economy of British Taxation," 12–13, 19, 28. See also Collin Brooks, "Public Finance and Political Stability: The Administration of the Land Tax 1688–1720," *The Historical Journal*, 17 (1974), 281–300.

34. Linda Colley, *Britons: Forging the Nation 1707–1837* (New Haven, Conn.: Yale University Press, 1992), 287–8; Gould, *Persistence of Empire*, 14–30, 72–105, quotation at 74; Langford, *Polite and Commercial People*, 334–5; John R. Western, *The English Militia in the Eighteenth Century: The Story of a Political Issue, 1600–1802* (London: Routledge, 1965), 127–61, 245–64. The Militia Act allowed men picked for service the choice of hiring a substitute or paying a fine. In effect, therefore, the Militia Act became another tax rather than a system of conscription.

35. But see the discussion of popular support in Britain for an aggressive and expansive foreign policy, and consequently for state growth, in Colley, *Britons*, 52–4, 322, 364–72; Kathleen Wilson, "Empire, Trade and Popular Politics in Mid-Hanoverian Britain: The Case of Admiral Vernon," *Past and Present*, 121 (1988), 74–109; Wilson, "Empire of Virtue: The Imperial Project and Hanoverian Culture c.1720–1785," *Imperial State at War*, ed. Stone, 128–64.

36. For a discussion of the American economy, see John J. McCusker and Russell R. Menard, *The Economy of British America, 1607–1789* (Chapel Hill: University of North Carolina Press, 1985). For taxation, see Mark D. Kaplanoff, "The Hamiltonian moment," paper presented at the 1998 meeting of the Society for Historians of the Early American Republic (SHEAR), Harpers Ferry, West Virginia. New York managed to cover almost half its expenses by taxing foreign imports. Much of what was imported through New York City was "re-exported" to other states, which meant that consumers in these states contributed to the public revenue of New York. For New York's incomes from customs duties, see Roger H. Brown, *Redeeming the Republic: Federalism, Taxation, and the Origins of the Constitution* (Baltimore: Johns Hopkins University Press, 1993), 135; John P. Kaminski, "Adjusting to Circumstances: New York's Relationship with the Federal Government 1776–1787," in *The Constitution and the States: The Role of the Original Thirteen in the Framing and Adoption of the Federal Constitution*, ed. Paul T. Conley and Kaminski (Madison: Madison House, 1988), 227–30.

37. Robert J. Dinkin, *Voting in Provincial America: A Study of Elections in the Thirteen Colonies, 1689–1776* (Westport, Conn.: Free Press, 1977), 28–49; Robert J. Dinkin, *Voting in Revolutionary America: A Study of Elections in the Original Thirteen States* (Westport, Conn.: Free Press, 1982); Jackson T. Main, "Government by the People: The American Revolution and the Democratization of the Legislatures," *WMQ*, 3d ser., 23 (1966), 391–407; Mann, *Sources of Social Power* 2, 142, 153–4; Jack N. Rakove, *Original Meanings: Politics and Ideas in the Making of the Constitution* (New York: Knopf, 1996), 212; Gordon S. Wood, *The Radicalism of the American Revolution* (New York: Knopf, 1992), 244–51.

38. Robert A. Becker, *Revolution, Reform, and the Politics of American Taxation, 1763–1783* (Baton Rouge: Louisiana State University Press, 1980), 6–7, 17–27, 42, 76–7, 82, 121, quotation at 17. Becker writes that "throughout the American colonies, tax laws overburdened the politically impotent in general and the poor in particular and favored the politically powerful and wealthy, particularly the landed wealthy," 6. However, he notes that tax reforms follow-

ing on independence made taxation more equitable, as a consequence of the change in the composition of the assemblies noted earlier, 154–60, 189, 192–3, 196–8, 200, 209–10, 213–14, 224–5. See also H. James Henderson, "Taxation and Political Culture: Massachusetts and Virginia, 1760–1800," *WMQ*, 3d ser., 47 (1990), 103–5, 109–10.

39. "The apportionment of taxes on the various descriptions of property, is an act which seems to require the most exact impartiality; yet there is perhaps no legislative act in which greater opportunity and temptation are given to a predominant party, to trample on the rules of justice," *The Federalist* 10, *Doc. Hist.* v. 14, 178.

4: The Ideological Response to State Expansion

1. Quentin Skinner, *The Foundations of Modern Political Thought* 1: *The Renaissance* (Cambridge, U.K.: Cambridge University Press, 1978), xi.

2. Geoffrey Parker, *The Military Revolution: Military Innovation and the Rise of the West, 1500–1800* (Cambridge, U.K.: Cambridge University Press, 1996, 2d ed.), 9.

3. Quentin Skinner, *Machiavelli* (Oxford: Oxford University Press, 1981), 6–8, 31–4, 75–6. See also the discussion in *The Prince*, chs. 12, 13, and 26, where the recruitment, organization and tactics of the armed forces are singled out as the keys to Italian political independence, *Fursten* (Stockholm: Natur och Kultur, 1958), 62–72, 128–32.

4. See the discussion of Robertson's *History of the Reign of Charles V* (1769) in Herbert G. Sloan, *Principles and Interests: Thomas Jefferson and the Problem of Debt* (New York: Oxford University Press, 1995), 89–90.

5. *Spirit of the Laws*, ed. Anne Cohler, Basia Miller, and Harold Stone (Cambridge, U.K.: Cambridge University Press, 1989), pt. 2, bk. 13, ch. 17, 224–5. There is a similar account in Andrew Fletcher, *A Discourse of Government with Relation to Militias*, in *Political Works*, ed. John Robertson (Cambridge, U.K.: Cambridge University Press, 1997), 6–7. The growth of the state was also interrelated with the rise of new fields of knowledge, such as political arithmetic, statistics, cameralism, police science and political economy that spilled over into, and influenced, political discussions. See for instance Richard Bonney, "Early Modern Theories of State Finance," in *Economic Systems and State Finance*, ed. Bonney (Oxford: Oxford University Press, 1995), 163–229.

6. *The Federalist* 41, *Doc. Hist.* v. 15, 420. Madison may have had this information directly from Robertson, who wrote that Charles "not only established that formidable body of regular troops" but was also "the first monarch of France who, by his royal edict, without the concurrence of the States-general of the kingdom, levied an extraordinary subsidy on his people." Furthermore, he rendered "several taxes perpetual, which had formerly been imposed occasionally," quoted in Sloan, *Principle and Interest*, 89. Another possible source is William Blackstone's *Commentaries on the Laws of England*. At least later editions contain the remark that "the fashion of keeping standing armies (which was first introduced by Charles VII in France, A. D. 1445) has of late universally prevailed over Europe." In a footnote Blackstone cites Robertson's *History* as his source. See *Commentaries* 1 (Oxford, 1775, 7th ed.), 413–14.

7. *The Federalist* 17, *Doc. Hist.* v. 14, 354–5. According to Isaac Kramnick this essay makes "evident" Hamilton's "sense that the pattern of European development, with the triumph of coercive centralized nation-states, should be

reproduced in America under the Constitution," Kramnick, "The 'Great National Discussion': The Discourse of Politics in 1787," *WMQ*, 3d ser., 45 (1988), 26. Although the central claim of my study is indeed that the Federalists sought to create a national state with powers similar to those of contemporary European states, this cannot be inferred from *Federalist* 17. While it is true that Hamilton claims that the United States under the Articles of Confederation "may be aptly compared with the feudal baronies," the whole point of the essay is to argue that the states will remain powerful entities upheld by the support of their population and so "able effectually to oppose all incroachments of the national power" also under the Constitution (355).

8. *The Federalist* 45, *Doc. Hist.* v. 15, 478.

9. "Editors' Note: Publication of Volume II of the Book Edition of *The Federalist*, 28 May," *Doc. Hist.* v. 18, 83–4.

10. Richard Price, *Two Tracts*, in *Political Writings*, ed. David O. Thomas (Cambridge, U.K.: Cambridge University Press 1992), 89–90.

11. Jean-Jacques Rousseau, *The Social Contract* and *A Discourse on Political Economy*, in *The Social Contract and Discourses*, ed. J. H. Brumfit and John C. Hall (London: Everyman's Library, 1973), 231, 144–5. Compare Rousseau to the quotations in chapter 2 from *Cato's Letters* (note 49) and to "Brutus" (text accompanying note 58).

12. Bernard Bailyn, *The Ideological Origins of the American Revolution* (Cambridge, Mass.: Harvard University Press, 1967), 66–80; John Brewer, *Party Ideology and Popular Politics at the Accession of George III* (Cambridge, U.K.: Cambridge University Press, 1976), 241–5; Jack P. Greene, "Empire and Identity from the Glorious Revolution to the American Revolution," in *The Oxford History of the British Empire*, ed. Wm. Roger Louis (Oxford: Oxford University Press, 1998), 2, 208–30; Eliga H. Gould, *The Persistence of Empire: British Political Culture in the Age of the American Revolution* (Chapel Hill: University of North Carolina Press, 2000), 14–34.

13. Montesquieu, *Spirit of the Laws*, pt. 2, bk. 11, ch. 5, 156.

14. In addition to the references cited in note 12, see Linda Colley, *Britons: Forging the Nation 1707–1837* (New Haven, Conn.: Yale University Press, 1992), 11–54; John Philip Reid, "The Rule of Law," in *The Blackwell Encyclopedia of the American Revolution*, ed. Jack P. Greene and Jack R. Pole (Oxford: Blackwell, 1991), 629–32.

15. Blackstone, *Commentaries* 1, 127–45, quotation on 127. The rights of Englishmen—"which, taken in a political and extensive sense, are usually called their liberties"—were declared in a number of statutes beginning with Magna Carta and leading up to the petition of rights assented to by Charles I, the Habeas Corpus Act under Charles II, the Bill of Rights of 1689, and the Act of Settlement of 1701. "The rights themselves, thus defined by these several statutes, consists in a number of private immunities; which will appear, from what has been premised, to be indeed no other; than either that *residuum* of natural liberty, which is not required by the laws of society to be sacrificed to public convenience; or else those civil privileges, which society hath engaged to provide, in lieu of the natural liberties so given up by individuals" (129).

16. See ibid., 1, ch 2, "Of the Parliament," 146–153, quotation at 147. Blackstone wrote that in "all tyrannical governments the supreme magistracy, or the right both of *making* and *enforcing* the laws, is vested in one and the same man, or one and the same body of men; and wherever these two powers are united together, there can be no public liberty. The magistrate may erect

tyrannical laws, and execute them in a tyrannical manner, since he is possessed in quality of dispenser of justice, with all the power which he as legislator thinks proper to give himself. But where the legislative and executive authority are in distinct hands, the former will take care not to entrust the latter with so large a power, as may lend to the subversion of its own independence, and therewith of the liberty of the subject" (146).

Montesquieu made a similar point but distinguished between three "sorts of power": legislative power and two forms of executive power. The first of the latter were the power to execute defense and foreign policy, which Montesquieu called "the executive power of the state." The second was the power to punish crimes and to adjudicate disputes between the subjects, which he called the power of judging. "When legislative power is united with executive power in a single person or in a single body of the magistracy, there is no liberty, because one can fear that the same monarch or senate that makes tyrannical laws will execute them tyrannically. Nor is there liberty if the power of judging is not separate from legislative power and from executive power. If it were joined to legislative power, the power over the life and liberty of the citizens would be arbitrary, for the judge would be the legislator. If it were joined to executive power, the judge could have the force of an oppressor. All would be lost if the same man or the same body of principal men, either of nobles, or of the people, exercised these three powers: that of making the laws, that of executing public resolutions, and that of judging the crimes or the disputes of individuals. In most kingdoms in Europe, the government is moderate because the prince who has the first two powers, leaves the exercise of the third to his subjects. Among the Turks, where the three powers are united in the person of the sultan, an atrocious despotism reigns," *Spirit of the Laws*, pt. 2, bk. 11, ch. 6, 156–7.

17. Blackstone, *Commentaries* I, 154–5, 169–70; Montesquieu, *Spirit of the Laws*, 162, 164–5. In the Bill of Rights it was stated that "the raising and keeping a standing Army within the Kingdom in time of Peace unlesse it be with the Consent of Parlyament is against Law" and that "levying Money for the Use of the Crowne by pretence of Prerogative without Grant of Parlyament for longer time or in other manner then the same is or shall be granted is Illegal." These and other restrictions on royal power corresponded to the acts by which James II "by the Assistance of diverse evill Councellors Judges and Ministers imployed by him did endeavour to subvert and extirpate the Protestant Religion and the Lawes and Liberties of this Kingdome." See *The Law and Working of the Constitution: Documents 1660–1914* I, ed. W. C. Costin and J. Steven Watson (London: Adam & Charles Black, 1952), 68–9. Blackstone commented on the demand for the consent of the commons to taxation that this right stemmed not from the right to property as the lords, too, had property but only possessed a negative on taxation laws. The power instead stemmed from the need for the commons to be able to defend liberty against executive abuse. "The true reason, arising from the spirit of our constitution, seems to be this. The lords being a permanent hereditary body, created at pleasure by the king, are supposed more liable to be influenced by the crown, and when once influenced to continue so, than the commons who are a temporary body, freely nominated by the people. It would therefore be extremely dangerous, to give the lords any power of framing new taxes for the subject," *Commentaries* I, 169–70.

In his speech "On Conciliation with the Colonies," Edmund Burke singled out taxation by consent as the single most important "object" of liberty in

England and the colonies. "Abstract liberty," he said, "like other mere abstractions, is not to be found. Liberty inheres in some sensible object; and every nation has formed to itself some favourite point, which by way of eminence becomes the criterion of their happiness. It happened you know . . . that the great contests for freedom in this country were from the earliest times chiefly upon the question of taxing. Most of the contests in the ancient commonwealths turned primarily on the election of magistrates, or on the balance of the several orders of the state. The question of money was with them not so immediate," Edmund Burke, *Speeches and Letters on American Affairs by Edmund Burke*, ed. Hugh Law (London: Dent & Sons, 1908), 91.

18. Price, *Two Tracts*, 26.

19. Blackstone, *Commentaries* 1, 233, 235–6. For a similar argument, see Montesquieu, *Spirit of the Laws*, 161. In the coronation oath as prescribed by the Act. I Will. & Mar., ch. 6, the monarch made three promises: To "Governe the People of this Kingdome of England and the Dominions thereto belonging according to the statutes in Parlyament Agreed on and the same Laws and Customs of the same"; to "cause Law and Justice in Mercy to be Executed in all Your Judgements"; and to "Maintaine the Laws of God the true Profession of the Gospell and the Protestant Reformed Religion Established by Law" and to "Preserve unto the Bishops and Clergy of this Realme and the Churches committed to their Charge all such Rights and Priviledges as by Law doe or shall appertaine unto them or any of them," in *Law and Working of the Constitution* 1, 58–9.

20. Quotation from Joseph Priestley, *An Essay on the First Principles of Government*, in *Political Writings*, ed. Peter N. Miller (Cambridge, U.K.: Cambridge University Press, 1993), 22. See also David Hume, *The History of England from the Invasion of Julius Caesar to the Revolution of 1688* (London, 1802) 8, 216–41.

21. Price, *A Discourse on the Love of Our Country*, in *Political Writings*, 189.

22. Fletcher, *Discourse of Government*, 18.

23. Blackstone, *Commentaries* 1, 413–14, 326; Tobias Smollet, *The History of England from the Revolution to the Death of George the Second* (London, 1804) 1, 443. Blackstone's discussion shows most clearly the degree to which contemporaries possessed detailed knowledge about the affairs of the British state in the late eighteenth century, a result, of course, of the openness about government affairs that was a unique feature of British politics at the time: "In order to make a clear and comprehensive view of the nature of this national debt, it must first be premised, that after the revolution, when our new connections with Europe introduced a new system of foreign politics, the expences of the nation, not only in settling the new establishment, but in maintaining long wars, as principals on the continent, for the security of the Dutch barrier, reducing the French monarchy, settling the Spanish succession, supporting the house of Austria, maintaining the liberties of the Germanic body, and other purposes, increased to an unusual degree: insomuch that it was not thought to be advisable to raise all the expences of any one year by taxes to be levied within that year, lest the unaccustomed weight of them should create murmurs among the people. It was therefore the policy of the times to anticipate the revenues of their posterity, by borrowing immense sums for the current service of the state, and to lay no more taxes upon the subject than would suffice to pay the annual interest of the sums so borrowed: by this means converting the principal debt into a new species of property, transferable from

one man to another at any time and in any quantity. . . . This laid the foundation to what is called the national debt: for a few long annuities created in the reign of Charles II. will hardly deserve that name. And the example then set has been so closely followed during the long wars in the reign of queen Anne, and since, that the capital of the national debt (funded and unfunded) amounted in January 1771 to above 140,000,000 *l.* to pay the interest of which, and the charges of management, amounting to upwards of four millions and a half, the extraordinary revenues just now enumerated (excepting only the land-tax and the annual malt-tax) are in the first place mortgaged, and made perpetual by parliament" (326–7).

24. James Burgh, *Political Disquisitions* (London, 1774) 1, 273–4.

25. Blackstone, *Commentaries* 1, 335–6; Burgh, *Political Disquisitions* 1, 272.

26. Smollet, *History of England* 2, 524–5.

27. For eighteenth-century British political thought, see Harry T. Dickinson, *Liberty and Property: Political Ideology in Eighteenth-Century Britain* (London: Methuen, 1977); Isaac Kramnick, *Bolingbroke and His Circle: The Politics of Nostalgia in the Age of Walpole* (Cambridge, Mass.: Harvard University Press, 1968); J. G. A. Pocock, "Machiavelli, Harrington and English Political Ideologies in the Eighteenth Century," *WMQ*, 3d ser., 22 (1965), 549–83; Pocock, "Virtue and Commerce in the Eighteenth Century," *Journal of Interdisciplinary History*, 3 (1972), 119–34; Pocock, *The Machiavellian Moment: Florentine Political Thought and the Atlantic Republican Tradition* (Princeton, N.J.: Princeton University Press, 1975); Pocock, "The Varieties of Whiggism from Exclusion to Reform: A History of Ideology and Discourse," in *Virtue, Commerce and History: Essays on Political Thought and History, Chiefly in the Eighteenth Century* (Cambridge, U.K.: Cambridge University Press, 1985), 215–310; Caroline Robbins, *The Eighteenth-Century Commonwealthman: Studies in the Transmission, Development and Circumstance of English Liberal Thought from the Restoration of Charles II until the War with the Thirteen Colonies* (Cambridge, Mass.: Harvard University Press, 1959); Quentin Skinner, "The Principle and Practice of Opposition: The Case of Bolingbroke versus Walpole," in *Historical Perspectives: Studies in English Thought and Society in Honour of J. H. Plumb*, ed. Neil McKendrick (London: Europa, 1974), 93–128.

28. Burgh, *Political Disquisitions* 1, 6–21, quotation on 21.

29. Blackstone, *Commentaries* 1, 127–45, quotations on 127 and 129.

30. *Spirit of the Laws*, pt. 2, bk. 11, ch. 6, 166.

31. Thomas Paine, *Common Sense*, in *Political Writings*, ed. Bruce Kuklick (Cambridge, U.K.: Cambridge University Press, 1989), 15.

32. David Hume, "Whether the British Government Inclines More to Absolute Monarchy or to a Republic," in *Political Essays*, ed. Knud Haakonsen (Cambridge, U.K.: Cambridge University Press, 1993), 31, 32.

33. Paine, *Common Sense*, 15. Hume had a different opinion of the consequences to the constitution of executive influence in the House of Commons. In "Of the Independency of Parliament," he argued that the "share of power, allotted by our constitution to the house of commons, is so great, that it absolutely commands all the other parts of the government. The king's legislative power is plainly no proper check to it. For though the king has a negative in framing laws; yet this, in fact, is esteemed of so little moment, that whatever is voted by the two houses, always is sure to pass into a law, and the royal assent is little better than a form. The principle weight of the crown lies in the executive power. But besides that the executive power in every government is

altogether subordinate to the legislative; besides this, I say, the exercise of this power requires an immense expence; and the commons have assumed to themselves the sole right of granting money. How easy, therefore, would it be for that house to wrest from the crown all these powers, one after another; by making every grant conditional, and choosing their time so well, that their refusal of subsidies should only distress the government, without giving foreign powers any advantage over us? Did the house of commons depend in the same manner on the king, and had none of the members any property but from his gift, would not he command all their resolutions, and be from that moment absolute?" The solution was to allow the Crown some influence in the Commons. To Hume this was what the practice, if not the letter, of the British constitution demonstrated. "The crown has so many offices at its disposal, that, when assisted by the honest and disinterested part of the house, it will always command the resolutions of the whole; so far, at least, as to preserve the ancient constitution from danger. We may, therefore, give to this influence what name we please; we may call it by the invidious appellations of *corruption* and *dependence;* but some degree and some kind of it are inseparable from the very nature of the constitution, and necessary to the preservation of our mixed government," *Political Essays,* 25–6.

34. At the start of the eighteenth century the Court and Country distinction co-existed with the division between Tories and Whigs. The importance of the latter division soon declined. By the time of the accession of George III, there also existed a body of radical political writers who were less complacent about the basic soundness of the British constitution than Country adherents and who pressed for electoral reforms. In much of their criticism of the state, however, the radicals repeated the Country argument. For Tories and Whigs, see Dickinson, *Liberty and Property,* 13–90. For the radicals, see ibid., 195–269; Brewer, *Party Ideology,* 256–64; Brewer, "English Radicalism in the Age of George III," in *Three British Revolutions: 1641, 1688, 1776,* ed. J.G.A. Pocock (Princeton, N.J.: Princeton University Press, 1980), 323–67.

35. See the references cited in note 27.

36. For the historical argument of the Country perspective, in addition to the works cited in note 27, see H. Trevor Colbourn, *The Lamp of Experience: Whig History and the Intellectual Origins of the American Revolution* (Chapel Hill: University of North Carolina Press, 1965), 40–56. For the American response, see Bailyn, *Ideological Origins,* 55–159; Pauline Maier, *American Scripture: Making the Declaration of Independence* (New York: Knopf, 1997), 69–96.

37. Brewer, *Sinews of Power,* 157–8. For a discussion of how eighteenth-century men and women analyzed social and political events, see Gordon Wood, "Conspiracy and the Paranoid Style: Causality and Deceit in the Eighteenth Century," *WMQ,* 3d ser., 39 (1982), 401–41.

38. In addition to the references cited in notes 40 and 41 of chapter 2, see Bernard Bailyn, *The Origins of American Politics* (New York: Knopf, 1968), 3–58; Bailyn, "Political Experience and Radical Ideas in Eighteenth-Century America," in *Faces of Revolution: Personalities and Themes in the Struggle for American Independence* (New York: Knopf, 1990), 185–99; Bailyn, *Ideological Origins,* 22–54; Colbourn, *Lamp of Experience;* J.G.A. Pocock, "Civic Humanism and Its Role in Anglo-American Thought," in *Politics, Language and Time: Essays on Political Thought and History* (London: Methuen, 1972), 80–103; Pocock, "Virtue and Commerce"; Pocock, *Machiavellian Moment,* 506–52; Pocock, "Varieties of Whiggism," 264–74.

39. The link between the Antifederalists and the Country interest in Britain has been explicitly made in John H. Hutson, "Country, Court and the Constitution: Antifederalists and the Historians," *WMQ* 3d ser., 38 (1981), 363–8, and in John M. Murrin, "The Great Inversion, or Court versus Country: A Comparison of the Revolutionary Settlements in England (1688–1721) and America (1776–1816)," in *Three British Revolutions*, ed. Pocock, 403–4.

40. Leonard Levy, *Original Intent and the Framers' Constitution* (New York: Macmillan, 1988), 4, quoted in Jack N. Rakove, *Original Meanings: Politics and Ideas in the Making of the Constitution* (New York: Knopf, 1996), 373, note 19. For a general discussion of "the paranoid style" in early American political rhetoric, see John H. Hutson, "The Origins of 'the Paranoid Style in American Politics.' Public Jealousy from the Age of Walpole to the Age of Jackson," in *Saints and Revolutionaries: Essays in Early American History*, ed. David D. Hall, John M. Murrin, and Thad W. Tate (New York: Norton, 1984), 332–72.

41. This has been suggested by Hutson in "Country, Court, and Constitution," 367, and by Murrin in "Great Inversion," 363–4. See also the discussion in E. James Ferguson, "Political Economy, Public Liberty, and the Formation of the Constitution," *WMQ*, 3d ser., 40 (1983), 387–412. Neither of the cited works, however, has analyzed Federalist rhetoric during the ratification campaign. In his discussion of the Federalist view on military establishment expressed in the debate over ratification, Lawrence Cress concludes that they relied on arguments drawn from Court Whigs; see *Citizens in Arms: The Army and the Militia in American Society to the War of 1812* (Chapel Hill: University of North Carolina Press, 1982), 108–9.

42. Dickinson, *Liberty and Property*, 148–9, 154–5, 157–8; Kramnick, *Bolingbroke*, 122–3. See also Hume, "Of the Independency of Parliament" and "Of the parties of Great Britain," both in *Political Essays*, 26 and 40. Court thinkers have attracted much less interest from historians than their Country opponents. Accounts of Court ideas tend invariably to collapse into accounts of the development of the British post-Revolutionary state, i.e., from Court principles to Court practice. In part this is because of the amorphous nature of Court ideology. Richard Browning, *Political and Constitutional Ideas of the Court Whigs* (Baton Rouge: State University of North Carolina Press, 1982) is the only work dedicated solely to the ideas of the Court.

43. Art. I, sect. 6 states that "No Senator or Representative shall, during the Time for which he was elected, be appointed to any civil Office under the Authority of the United States which shall have been created, or the Emoluments whereof shall have been encreased during such time; and no Person holding any Office under the United States, shall be a member of either House during his Continuance in Office."

44. Kramnick, *Bolingbroke*, 52 (quotation); Cress, *Citizens in Arms*, 25–6; Brewer, *Sinews of Power*, 142.

45. [Tench Coxe] "An American Citizen" 1, *Doc. Hist.* v. 13, 248.

46. "Curtius," ibid., 269. Nevertheless, both "Curtius" and Coxe found the Constitution superior to the British system of government.

47. "Fabius" 9, *Doc. Hist.* v. 17, 261.

48. [Alexander Hamilton] *The Federalist* 34, Doc. Hist. v. 15, 260–1.

49. Wilson Nicholas, quoted in Herbert J. Storing, *What the Anti-Federalists Were For* (Chicago: University of Chicago Press, 1981), 27.

50. John Brooks, "Fourth of July oration," *Doc. Hist.* v. 13, 160.

5: An Impotent Congress

1. Articles of Confederation, Art. VI-IX, XIII.

2. For an account of the Convention's deliberations on the proposal of the committee of style, see Max Farrand, *The Framing of the Constitution* (New Haven, Conn.: Yale University Press, 1913), 140–54.

3. Max Farrand, *Records of the Constitutional Convention,* 3 vols. (New Haven, Conn.: Yale University Press, 1911), I, 18–19, 242–3.

4. The preceding two paragraphs draw on the analysis of the Constitutional Convention's debate on taxation and public finance presented in Donald R. Stabile, *The Origins of American Public Finance: Debates over Money, Debt, and Taxes in the Constitutional Era, 1776–1836* (Westport: Greenwood Press, 1998), 53–65 and in Cathy D. Matson and Peter S. Onuf, *A Union of Interests: Political and Economic Thought in Revolutionary America* (Lawrence: University Press of Kansas, 1990), 113–20.

5. Farrand, *Records* 2, 329, 385, 329–30.

6. Charleston *Columbian Herald,* 26 July 1787, *Doc. Hist.* v. 13, 179–80.

7. See for instance "Richard Price: On the American Government," *Doc. Hist.* v. 13, 101; *Pennsylvania Herald,* 19 May, ibid., 104–5; "Connecticut Legislature Debates the Appointment of Delegates to the Constitutional Convention," ibid., 107; Baltimore *Maryland Gazette,* 22 May 1787, ibid., 112–13; "Harrington" [Benjamin Rush], "To the Freemen of the United States," ibid., 117–19; "Alexander Hamilton Attacks Governor George Clinton," ibid., 137; Philadelphia *Independent Gazeteer,* 26 June, ibid., 146–7; *Pennsylvania Gazette,* 1 August, ibid., 183; Philadelphia *Independent Gazeteer,* 22 August, ibid., 189; *Pennsylvania Gazette,* 12 September, ibid., 193–5.

8. Philadelphia *Independent Gazeteer,* 8, 11, 12, 17, 18 September, *Doc. Hist.* v. 2, microform supplement, 316–17, 319, 321, 354–6, 362, quotation on 321, 356.

9. Frederick W. Marks III, *Independence On Trial: Foreign Affairs and the Making of the Constitution* (Baton Rouge: Louisiana State University Press, 1973), 152; Curtis P. Nettels, *The Emergence of a National Economy, 1775–1815* (New York: Knopf, 1962), 101–2.

10. Accounts of the early stages of the military conflict of the Revolution and the origins of the Continental Army can be found in Donald Higginbotham, *The War of American Independence: Military Attitudes, Policies, and Practice, 1763–1789* (New York: Macmillan, 1971), 57–121, and Robert Middlekauff, *The Glorious Cause: The American Revolution 1763–1789* (New York: Oxford University Press, 1982), 250–311. The classic study of the role of the militia and the volunteer force in colonial conflicts and society is John Shy, "A New Look at the Colonial Militia," *WMQ,* 3d ser., 20 (1963), 175–85. Pauline Maier, *American Scripture: Making the Declaration of Independence* (New York: Knopf, 1997), 58.

11. For brief accounts of the military presence in the colonies prior to the Revolution and the role of the colonies in the Seven Years War, see John Shy, "The American Colonies in War and Revolution, 1748–1783," in *The Oxford History of the British Empire* 2, ed. Wm. Roger Louis (Oxford: Oxford University Press, 1998), 300–10; Douglas Edward Leach, "The British Army in America, Before 1775," in *The Blackwell Encyclopedia of the American Revolution,* ed. Jack P. Greene and Jack R. Pole (Oxford: Blackwell, 1991), 146–52. For the forces

serving in the Seven Years' War, see Frederic W. Anderson, "A People's Army: Provincial Military Service in Massachusetts During the Seven Years War," *WMQ* 3d ser., 40 (1983), 521–5; John Ferling, "Soldiers for Virginia: Who Served in the French and Indian War?" *The Virginia Magazine of History and Biography*, 94 (1986), 307–28. See also the discussion of the prevalent view among New England volunteers that enlistment meant entering into a mutually binding contract, in Frederic W. Anderson, "Why Did Colonial New Englanders Make Bad Soldiers? Contractual Principles and Military Conduct During the Seven Years War," *WMQ* 3d ser., 38 (1981), 394–414. Quotation from John R. Van Atta, "Conscription in Revolutionary Virginia: The Case of Culpeper County, 1780–1781," *The Virginia Magazine of History and Biography*, 92 (1984), 279.

12. Higginbotham, *War of American Independence*, 104–5; Stephen Conway, *The War of American Independence, 1775–1783* (London: Edward Arnold, 1995), 55.

13. Middlekauff, *Glorious Cause*, 355. Richard Montgomery and Benedict Arnold similarly decided to assault Quebec on 30 December 1775 because the New England contingent would leave the next day, ibid., 307–8.

14. Conway, *War of American Independence*, 30. Higginbotham's estimate is slightly lower, around forty percent; see his *War of American Independence*, 389.

15. Charles A. Royster, *A Revolutionary People at War: The Continental Army and American Character, 1775–1783* (Chapel Hill: University of North Carolina Press, 1979), 268. Significantly, all studies of the compositions of American forces, from the Seven Years War through to the post-war Confederation regulars shows men with no or limited property, recent immigrants, unskilled laborers and city-dwellers to be over-represented in the ranks. See Ferling, "Soldiers for Virginia," 307–28; Van Atta, "Conscription," 263–81; Eric C. Papenfuse and Gregory A. Stiverson, "General Smallwood's Recruits: The Peacetime Career of a Revolutionary War Private," *WMQ*, 3d ser., 20 (1973), 117–32; William B. Skelton, "The Confederation's Regulars: A Social Profile of Enlisted Service in America's First Standing Army," *WMQ*, 3d ser., 46 (1989), 770–85.

16. Recruitment is discussed in Arthur J. Alexander, "How Maryland Tried to Raise Her Continental Quotas," *Maryland Historical Magazine*, 42 (1942), 184–96; Richard Buel, Jr., *Dear Liberty: Connecticut's Mobilization for the Revolutionary War* (Middletown, Conn.: Wesleyan University Press, 1980); Higginbotham, *War of American Independence*, 389–98; Middlekauff, *Glorious Cause*, 510–12; Papenfuse and Stiverson, "General Smallwood's Recruits," 117–27; Royster, *Revolutionary People*, 48–9, 64–9, 131–8, 267–8; Van Atta, "Conscription," 263–81. Jefferson is quoted in ibid., 256.

17. Royster, *Revolutionary People*, 329–30, 333, 358–60, quotation at 68.

18. Russell F. Weigley, *Towards an American Army: Military Thought from Washington to Marshall* (New York: Columbia University Press, 1962), 4, 5, and 7; Weigley, *History of the United States Army* (New York: Macmillan, 1967), 73.

19. The major engagements are treated in Higginbotham, *War of American Independence*, 68–77, 152–62, 165–71, 185–98, 246–7, 359–60, 369–70, 376–83, and in Middlekauff, *Glorious Cause*, 281–92, 340–6, 357–62, 380–4, 386–9, 392–5, 423–8, 454–7, 481–7, 559–70. Accounts of the development of the Continental army into a professional army resembling its European counterparts can be found in Royster, *Revolutionary People at War*, 213–47; Robert K.

Wright, Jr., " 'Nor Is Their Standing Army to Be Despised': The Emergence of the Continental Army as a Military Institution," *Arms and Independence: The Military Character of the American Revolution*, ed. Ronald Hoffman and Peter J. Albert (Charlottesville: University Press of Virginia, 1984), 50–74. The role of the militia outside the major army campaigns is discussed in John Shy, "The American Revolution: The Military Conflict Considered as a Revolutionary War," in *Essays on the American Revolution*, ed. Stephen G. Kurtz and James H. Hutson (Chapel Hill: University of North Carolina Press, 1973), 124–56; Donald Higginbotham, "The American Militia: A Traditional Institution with Revolutionary Responsibilities," in *Reconsiderations on the Revolutionary War* (Westport, Conn.: Greenwood, 1978), 83–103.

20. Quotations from Paul David Nelson, "Citizen Soldiers or Regulars: The Views of American General Officers on the Military Establishment, 1775–1781," *Military Affairs*, 43 (1979), 129 and Weigley, *History of the United States Army*, 42. Other officers believed that "the militia are not to be depended on" (Philip Shuyler); that it was "vain to trust to a Militia" (William Heath); and that "means must be devised to raise your regular battalions, for as to your Militia, they are grown the more detestable than ever" (Charles Lee). When Washington sought the opinion of his generals about using the militia in an attack on British positions outside Philadelphia in December 1777, they were overwhelmingly negative. Nathanael Greene spoke of "the uncertain success of the [militia's] most Spirited exertions, the impatience they discover to be gone, and the trouble of managing them when here." Others claimed that there was no possibility that the "Militia can be brought to stand in line of Battle" (William Woodford), that using the militia went against "reason, or common Military knowledge" (Henry Knox), and that even if Washington was "Aided by all the Militia the States on this Continent Can furnish, they would only Serve to make the Carnage, or the Route, the greater" (Lord Sterling). All quotations in Nelson, "Citizen Soldiers," 129–30.

21. Richard H. Kohn, *Eagle and Sword: The Federalists and the Creation of the Military Establishment in America, 1783–1802* (New York: Free Press 1975), 9–13.

22. E. Wayne Carp, "The Problem of National Defence in the Early American Republic," in *The American Revolution: Its Character and Limits*, ed. Jack P. Greene (New York: New York University Press, 1987), 20–3; Lawrence D. Cress, "Radical Whiggery and the Role of the Military: Ideological Roots of the American Revolutionary Militia," *Journal of the History of Ideas* 40 (1979), 43; Cress, *Citizens in Arms: The Army and the Militia in American Society to the War of 1812* (Chapel Hill: University of North Carolina Press, 1982), 12–13, 51, 53; Cress, "An Armed Community: The Origins and Meaning of the Right to Bear Arms," *The Journal of American History*, 71 (1984), 22–42; Cress and Robert E. Shalope, "The Second Amendment and the Right to Bear Arms: An Exchange," ibid., 587–93; Royster, *Revolutionary People at War*, 38–9. But see the discussion in Donald Higginbotham, "The Early American Way of War: Reconnaissance and Appraisal," *WMQ*, 3d ser., 44 (1987), 245–53; and Higginbotham, "The Military Institutions of Colonial America: The Rhetoric and the Reality," in *War and Society in Revolutionary America: The Wider Dimensions of Conflict* (Columbia: University of South Carolina Press, 1988), 23–4.

23. J.G.A. Pocock, "Machiavelli, Harrington and English Political Ideologies in the Eighteenth Century," *WMQ*, 3d ser., 22 (1965), 553–7, 566–7, quotation

at 566; Pocock, *The Machiavellian Moment: Florentine Political Thought and the Atlantic Republican Tradition* (Princeton, N.J.: Princeton University Press, 1965), 56–66, 156–218, 383–400.

24. Shy, "New Look at the Colonial Militia," 181–4. For similar accounts drawing on Shy, see Cress, *Citizens in Arms*, 5–11 and Higginbotham, "Military Institutions," 23–34. The development of the Continental army into a professional force made up of men who possessed neither property nor the right to vote is described in Cress, *Citizens in Arms*, 58–60, 71; Royster, *Revolutionary People at War*, 42–3, 48–51, 268. The Continental army contained not only men with little or no property but also British deserters, prisoners of war, indentured servants and slaves; see Van Atta, "Conscription in Revolutionary Virginia," 263–4, 267–8, 271–3, 276–9; Alexander, "How Maryland Tried to Raise Her Continental Quotas," 191–3; Higginbotham, *War of American Independence*, 394–6; Benjamin Quarles, "The Colonial Militia and Negro Manpower," *The Mississippi Valley Historical Review*, 45 (1959), 551–2; Royster, *Revolutionary People at War*, 326.

25. Shy, "New Look," 182–3; Cress, *Citizens in Arms*, 7–8. Charles Royster admits that the social composition of the Continental army does make it look like a contemporary European standing army, but claims that a crucial difference lay in the soldiers' motivation. Continentals served because of their political ideals, European regulars did not; see Royster, *Revolutionary People at War*, appendix: "A Note on Statistics and Continental Soldiers' Motivation," 373–8.

26. Lois G. Schwoerer, *"No Standing Armies!" The Antiarmy Ideology in Seventeenth-Century England* (Baltimore: Johns Hopkins University Press, 1974), 1. John Philip Reid, *In Defiance of the Law: The Standing-Army Controversy, the Two Constitutions, and the Coming of the American Revolution* (Chapel Hill: University of North Carolina Press, 1981), *passim* but especially 3–13, 79–100, makes it clear that it was the permanence and peacetime existence of the British army that was of primary importance to eighteenth-century antiarmy writers in England. According to Pocock, this represents a break within the republican tradition with an older view on the source of the threat to popular liberty: "In Harringtonian thought . . . the commonwealth and the militia were one and the same; but where Harrington contrasted the republic of armed proprietors with the feudal combination of monarchy and aristocracy, the neo-Harringtonians contrasted it with the professional army maintained by the executive power. . . . But whether in 1656, 1675, or later, the ideal of citizenship is the same," Pocock, "Machiavelli, Harrington and English Political Ideologies," 567.

27. See Sylvia R. Frey, "The Common British soldier," *Societas: A Review of Social History*, 5 (1975), 118, 120, 122–6; Frey, "Courts and Cats: British Military Justice in the Eighteenth Century," *Military Affairs*, 43 (1979), 5–11; John Brewer, *The Sinews of Power: War, Money and the English State, 1688–1783* (London: Unwin Hyman, 1989), 31–2, 49–50; Nelson, "Citizen Soldiers," 128; Royster, *Revolutionary People*, 214–15; John Shy, *Toward Lexington: The Role of the British Army in the Coming of the American Revolution* (Princeton, N.J.: Princeton University Press, 1965), 118. Martial law, wrote the protesters against the Mutiny Act of 1718, was "a Law unknown to our Constitution, destructive of our Liberties, not endured by our Ancestors, and never mentioned in any of our Statutes but in order to condemn it." Subjected to martial law the officers and soldiers were "divested of all those Rights and Privileges which render the

People of this Realm the Envy of other Nations, and become liable to such Hardships and Punishments as the Lenity and Mercy of our known Laws utterly disallow: And we cannot but think those Persons best prepared, and most easily tempted, to strip others of their Rights, who have already lost their own." See "Protest Against the Mutiny Act, 1718," in *The Law and Working of the Constitution: Documents, 1660–1914*, ed. W. C. Costin and J. Steven Watson (London: Adam and Charles Black, 1952), I, 211.

28. Schwoerer, *"No Standing Armies!"* 162, 180–1; Schwoerer, "The Literature of the Standing Army Controversy, 1697–1699," *The Huntington Library Quarterly*, 28 (1965), 197–9; E. Arnold Miller, "Some Arguments Used by English Pamphleteers, 1697–1700, Concerning a Standing Army," *The Journal of Modern History*, 18 (1946), 307–8.

29. John Shy, "The American Military Experience: History and Learning," *The Journal of Interdisciplinary History*, I (1971), 213, 215–16.

30. Kohn, *Eagle and Sword*, 40–72; Skelton, "Confederation's Regulars," 770–85.

31. Ibid., 770–85.

32. Kohn, *Eagle and Sword*, 87–8, 277–9.

33. But Richard Kohn's extensive study of Federalist military policy has found no support for the claim that the Federalists wished to govern by force at any time during the Federalist administrations of Washington and John Adams, with the possible exception of Alexander Hamilton. See ibid., 279–86.

34. Petersburgh, Va., town meeting, *Doc. Hist.* v. 8, 97.

35. "A Native of Virginia," *Doc. Hist.* v. 9, 692. For a discussion of national pride as a motive for the framing and ratification of the Constitution, see Marks *Independence on Trial*, 96–141; Marks, "American Pride, European Prejudice and the Constitution," *The Historian*, 34 (1972), 579–97.

36. [Oliver Ellsworth] "Landholder" 2, *Doc. Hist.* v. 25, 92.

37. "A True Friend," *Doc. Hist.* v. 8, 159–60.

38. John J. McCusker and Russel R. Menard, *The Economy of British America, 1607–1789* (Chapel Hill: University of North Carolina Press, 1985), 358–67; James F. Shepherd, "British American and the Atlantic Economy," in *The Economy of Early America: The Revolutionary Period, 1763–1790*, ed. Ronald Hoffman (Charlottesville: University Press of Virginia, 1988), 24.

39. McCusker and Menard, *Economy of British America*, 373–7. Jacob Price supports this claim in "Reflections on the Economy of Revolutionary America," in *Economy of Early America*, ed. Hoffman, 321–2. Merill Jensen is alone in describing the Confederation era as "one of extraordinary economic growth"; see Jensen, *The New Nation: A History of the United States During the Confederation* (New York: Knopf, 1950), 423.

40. To some extent this is also true of their opponents. For a few Federalist examples, see Benjamin Rush, Pennsylvania ratifying convention, *Doc. Hist.* v. 2, 457; "A Jerseyman," "To the Citizens of New Jersey," *Doc. Hist.* v. 3, 147; Petersburg, Va., town meeting, *Doc. Hist.* v. 8, 97; "A Freeholder," *Doc. Hist.* v. 9, 726, 729; "A Delegate Who Has Catched Cold," *Doc. Hist.* v. 10, 1641; North Carolina *Wilmington Centinel*, 9 July, ibid., 1751; "P.R.," ibid., 1754; *New Hampshire Spy*, 3 April, *Doc. Hist.* v. 13, 76; "Z," ibid., 100; [Benjamin Rush] "Harrington," "To the Freemen of the United States," ibid., 120; "A True American," ibid., 267; "One of the People," ibid., 394–5; "A Slave," ibid., 480–1; [Oliver Ellsworth] "A Landholder" 2, *Doc. Hist.* v. 14, 93; [Roger Sherman] "A Citizen of New Haven," "Observation on the New Federal Constitution," *Doc. Hist.* v.

15, 283; *Massachusetts Gazette,* 8 January, ibid., 293; Hugh Williamson, "Speech at Edenton, N.C.," *Doc. Hist.* v. 16, 208; Jonathan Williams, Jr., "The Fabrick of Freedom," ibid., 360–1; [John Dickinson] "Fabius" 8, *Doc. Hist.* v. 17, 250; *Pennsylvania Mercury,* 28 June, *Doc. Hist.* v. 18, 210; Francis Hopkinson, "An Ode," ibid., 247; William Pitt Smith, "Ode on the Adoption of the Constitution," ibid., 292; *Massachusetts Gazette,* 8 July 1788, ibid., Appendix I, 391. See also the lists of toasts at reported celebrations of the adoption of the Constitution: *Virginia Journal,* 3 July, *Doc. Hist.* v. 10, 1717; *Maryland Journal,* 1 July, ibid., 1719; *Norfolk and Portsmouth Journal,* 9 July, ibid., 1735; *Virginia Independent Chronicle,* 9 July, ibid., 1744; "An Old Man," *Doc. Hist.* v. 15, 228.

41. Stanley L. Engerman, "Mercantilism and Overseas Trade, 1700–1800," in *The Economic History of Britain Since 1700,* 3 vols., ed. Roderick Floud and Donald McCloskey (Cambridge, U.K.: Cambridge University Press, 1994, 2d ed.), 1, 169–9; McCusker and Menard, *Economy of British America,* 46–7; Richard C. Simmons, "Trade Legislation and Its Enforcement, 1748–1776," in *The Blackwell Encyclopedia of the American Revolution,* ed. Greene and Pole, 161–9. Quotation from James H. Hutson, "Early American Diplomacy: A Reappraisal," in *The American Revolution and "A Candid World,"* ed. Lawrence S. Kaplan (Kent, Ohio: Kent State University Press, 1977), 44–5.

42. Engerman, "Mercantilism and Overseas Trade," 197–8.

43. McCusker and Menard, *Economy of British America,* chs. 5–6 and 8–9, especially tables 5.2, 6.1, 8.2, 9.3, and 124 and 179.

44. For discussion about the early American economy stressing market integration, see Joyce O. Appleby, "Commercial Farming and the 'Agrarian Myth' in the Early Republic," *JAH* 68 (1982), 838–42; Timothy H. Breen, "The Meanings of Things: Interpreting the Consumer Economy in the Eighteenth Century," in *Consumption and the World of Goods,* ed. John Brewer and Roy Porter (London: Routledge, 1993), 251–4; Thomas M. Doerflinger, "Farmers and Dry Goods in the Philadelphia Market Area, 1750–1800," *Economy of Early America,* ed. Hoffman, 173–83; James A. Henretta, "The War for Independence and American Economic Development," in ibid., 53–5; Adrienne D. Hood, "The Material World of Cloth: Production and Use in Eighteenth-Century Rural Pennsylvania," *WMQ,* 3d ser., 53 (1996), 43–66; Carole Shammas, "How Self-Sufficient was Early America?" *Journal of Interdisciplinary History,* 13 (1982), 254–68; Laurel Thatcher Ulrich, "Wheels, Looms, and the Gender Division of Labor in Eighteenth-Century New England," *WMQ,* 3d ser., 55 (1998), 3–35; Daniel Vickers, "Competency and Competition: Economic Culture in Early America," *WMQ,* 3d ser., 47 (1990), 4–12.

For a general discussion of the transformation of the early modern household toward market dependence, see Jan deVries, "Between Purchasing Power and the World of Goods: Understanding the Household Economy in Early Modern Europe," in *Consumption and the World of Goods,* ed. Brewer and Porter, 108–17.

45. McCusker and Menard, *Economy of British America,* 80–6 and table 4.1; Jacob M. Price, "The Transatlantic Economy," in *Colonial British America: Essays in the New History of the Early Modern Era,* ed. Jack P. Greene and Jack R. Pole (Baltimore: Johns Hopkins University Press, 1984), 27–9 and tables 2.1 and 2.2; Shepherd, "British America and the Atlantic Economy," 4–19; Russell R. Menard, "Slavery, Economic Growth and Revolutionary Ideology in the South Carolina Low Country," in *Economy of Early America,* ed. Hoffman, 256–8; Engerman, "Mercantilism and Overseas Trade," 193.

46. Doerflinger, "Farmers and Dry Goods," 182–3; Nettels, *Emergence of a National Economy*, 46–8.

47. McCusker and Menard, *Economy of British America*, 72–6, 80–6, 92, 100, 109–11 and tables 4.1 and 5.2; Price, "Transatlantic Economy," 35–6, quotation on 36; Shepherd, "British America and the Atlantic Economy," 4, 9–11; Marks, *Independence on Trial*, 52–3.

48. Marks, *Independence on Trial*, 56, 59, 63; Drew McCoy, *The Elusive Republic: Political Economy in Jeffersonian America* (Chapel Hill: University of North Carolina Press, 1980), 91–2; McCusker and Menard, *Economy of British America*, 370; Nettels, *Emergence of a National Economy*, 47, 65–6; Price, "Reflections on the Economy of Revolutionary America," 319.

49. Lawrence S. Kaplan, "Towards Isolationism: The Rise and Fall of the Franco-American Alliance, 1775–1801," in *American Revolution*, ed. Kaplan, 146; Marks, *Independence on Trial*, 23–45, 105–13; Nettels, *Emergence of a National Economy*, 67–9. In 1786, New York's Chamber of Commerce lamented that all Europe "did indeed desire to see us independent, but now that we are become so, each power is desirous of rendering our interests subservient to their commercial policy," quoted in Marks, *Independence on Trial*, 113.

50. Daniel A. Baugh, "Great Britain's 'Blue Water' Policy, 1689–1815," *International History Review* 10 (1988), 33–58; Baugh, "Maritime Strength and Atlantic Commerce: The Uses of 'a Grand Marine Empire,' " in *An Imperial State at War: Britain From 1689 to 1815*, ed. Lawrence S. Stone (London: Routledge 1994), 185–223; Michael Duffy, "The Foundations of British Naval Power," *The Military Revolution and the State, 1500–1800*, ed. Duffy (Exeter, U.K.: Exeter University Press, 1980), 56–79; Patrick Crowhurst, *The Defence of British Trade, 1689–1815* (Folkestone, U.K.: Dawson, 1977), ch. 1–2.

51. Andrew R. L. Cayton, " 'Separate Interests' and the Nation-State: The Washington Administration and the Origins of Regionalism in the Trans-Appalachian West," *JAH*, 89 (1992), 39–67; Marks, *Independence on Trial*, 3–36; Peter S. Onuf, "Settlers, Settlements, and New States," in *The American Revolution*, ed. Greene, 171–96; Onuf, *The Origins of the Federal Republic: Jurisdictional Controversies in the United States, 1775–1787* (Philadelphia: University of Pennsylvania Press, 1983), ch. 7–8; Samuel Flagg Bemis, *Pinckney's Treaty: America's Advantage from Europe's Distress, 1783–1800* (New Haven, Conn.: Yale University Press, 1960, rev. ed.); Arthur P. Whitaker, *The Spanish-American Frontier, 1783–1795; The Western Movement and the Spanish Retreat in the Mississippi Valley* (Boston: Houghton Mifflin, 1927).

52. "A True Friend," *Doc. Hist.* v. 8, 162.

53. Art. VI; Art. III, sect. 1–2. As Edmund Randolph pointed out, if "the general government will be responsible to foreign nations, it ought to be able to annul any offensive measure" taken by the states or their citizens in their dealing with foreign powers, and to "inforce any public right" even against their will. Edmund Randolph, "Letter on the Federal Constitution," *Doc. Hist.* v. 15, 127. "It was necessary to institute some federal authority, sufficient to punish any individual or State, who shall violate our treaties with foreign nations, insult their dignity, or abuse their citizens, and compel due reparation in all such cases," "Citizen of Philadelphia" [Pelatiah Webster], "The Weakness of Brutus Exposed," *Doc. Hist.* v. 14, 66. Perhaps it was Hamilton who summed it up best in *Federalist* 22: "The treaties of the United States, under the present constitution [i. e. the Articles of Confederation], are liable to the infractions of thirteen different Legislatures, and as many different courts of final jurisdic-

tion, acting under the authority of those Legislatures. The faith, the reputation, the peace of the whole union, are there continually at the mercy of the prejudices, the passions and the interests of every member of which it is composed. Is it possible that foreign nations can either respect or confide in such a government? Is it possible that the People of America will longer consent to trust their honor, their happiness, their safety, on so precarious a foundation?" *Doc. Hist.* v. 14, 442–3.

54. James Madison, Virginia ratifying convention, *Doc. Hist.* v. 9, 1034. See also the discussion about the Constitution in Nettels, *Emergence of a National Economy*, 101–2. For a discussion of attitudes to and problems with treaty-making in this period, see Peter Onuf and Nicholas Onuf, *Federal Union, Modern World: The Law of Nations in an Age of Revolutions 1776–1814* (Madison: Madison House, 1993), 97–129.

55. Davie, North Carolina convention, Elliot, *Debates* 4, 18; "Social Compact," *Doc. Hist.* v. 3, 356.

56. A navy was regarded as a necessity if Americans meant "to be a commercial people," [Hamilton] *The Federalist* 24, *Doc. Hist.* v. 15, 43. See also [Hamilton] *The Federalist* 34, ibid., 260. The belief in the importance of a navy to ensure commercial success is perhaps best revealed by the fact that several Antifederalists supported the idea that the United States should possess a navy. According to one of the Constitution's more vitriolic critics, it was obvious that if America was "to be a commercial neutral power, she ought to have some naval strength to intitle her to the appellation," "Philadelphiensis" 7, ibid., 338. Another Antifederalist believed that the "great advantages to be derived from [a navy],—the strength,—the consequence, which it adds to a nation, are such, that every well-wisher to this country would rejoice to see as large a navy established, as the circumstances of the state can at any time admit of." The problem to this commentator was rather that the proposed government would squander away the nation's wealth and so make it impossible to build a navy. "An Impartial Examiner," *Doc. Hist.* v. 8, 463. Not all Antifederalists believed that it would be beneficial for America to possess a navy, however. For a skeptical view, see William Grayson, Virginia ratifying convention, *Doc. Hist.* v. 10, 1188–9, 1315–16.

57. *Albany Gazette*, *Doc. Hist.* v. 13, 523.

58. "A Citizen of Philadelphia" [Pelatiah Webster], "Remarks on the Address of the Seceding Assemblymen," ibid., 305.

59. George Nicholas, Virginia ratifying convention, *Doc. Hist.* v. 9, 1129–30. In the same way Ellsworth asked if "our weakness [will] induce Spain to relinquish the exclusive navigation of the Mississippi, or the territory which she claims on the east side of that river?" "Speeches in the Connecticut Convention," *Doc. Hist.* v. 15, 247. The Spanish, wrote Tench Coxe, "will never listen to our demands *for the navigation of the Missis[s]ippi*, while we remain in *our present unconnected situation*. We are not an object *even of respect* to them, much less of *apprehension;* . . . Our Minister at that Court expects to effect *no arrangements there*, without an efficient government being *first adopted here*," "An American," *Doc. Hist.* v. 9, 836. See also James Marshall, *Doc. Hist.* v. 9, 1117, 1123; George Nicholas, Virginia ratifying convention, ibid., 1152; Edmund Pendleton, *Doc. Hist.* v. 10, 1200; James Madison, ibid., 1225; Virginia *Independent Chronicle*, 18 June 1788, ibid., 1634–4.

60. Thus Madison said that it "has been considered for some time past,

that the flames of war, already kindled, would spread, and that France and England were likely to draw those swords which were so recently put up. This is judged probable. We should not be surprised in a short time, to consider ourselves as a neutral nation—France on one side, and Great-Britain on the other," Virginia ratifying convention, *Doc. Hist.* v. 9, 1143-4. See also [Hamilton] *The Federalist* 34, *Doc. Hist.* v. 15, 260-1.

61. Ramsay, Oration, 5 June 1788, *Doc. Hist.* v. 18, 162. Ramsay also said that the "wealth and colonies of the most powerful nations of Europe are near our borders. In case of their future contentions, these states will stand on high ground; that scale into which they throw their weight, must, in the ordinary course of events, infallibly preponderate."

62. [Jay] *The Federalist* 4, *Doc. Hist.* v. 13, 571.

63. The passage from which these words of Hamilton are taken is worth quoting at length: "There can be no doubt, that the continuance of the Union, under an efficient government, would put it in our power, at a period not very distant, to create a navy, which, if it could not vie with those of the great maritime powers, would at least be of respectable weight, if thrown into the scale of either of two contending parties. This would be more peculiarly the case in relation to operations in the West-Indies. A few ships of the line sent opportunely to the reinforcement of either side, would often be sufficient to decide the fate of a campaign, on the event of which interests of the greatest magnitude were suspended. Our position is in this respect a very commanding one. And if to this consideration we add that of the usefulness of supplies from this country, in the prosecution of military operations in the West-Indies, it will readily be perceived that . . . a situation so favourable would enable us to bargain with great advantage for commercial privileges. A price would be set not only upon our friendship, but upon our neutrality. By a steady adherance to the Union, we may hope ere long to become the Arbiter of Europe in America; and to be able to incline the ballance [*sic*] of European competitions in this part of the world as our interest may dictate," *The Federalist* 11, *Doc. Hist.* v. 14, 211-12.

64. "Civis" [David Ramsay], *Doc. Hist.* v. 16, 26. "Let us be under one vigorous government, established on liberal principles; possessed of coercion and energy sufficient to pervade and invigorate the whole—we will then rise immediately into the highest consideration—our friendship and trade will be courted by all the powers of Europe, and in a few years, the Algerines themselves will stand in awe of the brave and enterprising American," Philadephia *Independent Gazeteer*, 27 June, *Doc. Hist.* v. 13, 146.

65. "Landholder" 2, *Doc. Hist.* v. 14, 92. Because the federal government was so weak, the Federalists argued, Britain still dictated the terms of American trade, despite a nominal independence, saying "with effect, to our flag, in such seas shall your *stripes* unfurl—and on such coasts shall your *stars* twinkle—and in no others," *New Jersey Journal*, *Doc. Hist.* v. 18, 185. In the Virginia convention Adam Stephens provided an allegorical description of the "American genius" that linked strong government to defense of both territory and trade: "Yonder she is in a mournful attire, her hair disheveled—distressed with grief and sorrow—supplicating our assistance, against gorgons, fiends and hydras, which are ready to devour her, and carry desolation throughout her country. She bewails the decay of trade and neglect of agriculture—her farmers discouraged—her ship-carpenters, blacksmiths and other tradesmen un-

employed. She casts her eyes on these, and deplores her inability to relieve them. She sees and laments that the profit of her commerce goes to foreign States," *Doc. Hist.* v. 10, 1529.

66. Social Compact, *Doc. Hist.* v. 3, 356.

6: Independence, Commerce, and Military Strength

1. Art. IX of the Articles of Confederation stated that "The united states in congress assembled shall have authority . . . to agree on the number of land forces, and to make requisitions from each state for its quota, in proportion to the number of white inhabitants in such state; which requisitions shall be binding and thereupon the legislature of each state shall appoint the regimental officers, raise the men and cloath, arm and equip them in a soldier like manner, at the expence of the united states, and the officers and men so cloathed, armed and equipped shall march to the place appointed, and within the time agreed on by the united states in congress assembled." The article also contained a further limit to Congress's power by prohibiting it from engaging in war or raising either men or money "unless nine states assent to the same."

Art. I, sect. 8 of the Constitution gave Congress the power to "raise and support Armies, but no Appropriation of Money to that Use shall be for a longer Term than two years." Congress was also granted the power to declare war.

2. Art. I, sect. 8. The states would retain the right to appoint militia officers and "the Authority of training the Militia according to the discipline prescribed by Congress." The Articles of Confederation, art. VI, demanded that "every state shall always keep a well regulated and disciplined militia, sufficiently armed and accoutred, and shall provide and constantly have ready for use, in public stores, a due number of field pieces and tents, and a proper quantity of arms, ammunition and camp equipage."

3. Art. VI of the Articles of Confederation stated that "No vessels of war shall be kept up in time of peace by any state, except such number only as shall be deemed necessary by the united states in congress assembled, for the defence of such state, or its trade; nor shall any body of forces be kept up by any state, in time of peace, except such numbers only, as in the judgement of the united states in congress assembled, shall be deemed requisite to garrison the forts necessary for the defence of such state."

Art. I, sect. 10 of the Constitution says that "No State shall, without the Consent of Congress, . . . keep Troops, or Ships of War in time of Peace . . ."

4. "Federal Farmer," "An Additional Number of Letters to the Republican," *Doc. Hist.* v. 17, 364. In the first series of "Letters to the Republican," "Federal Farmer" proposed that the power of the national government "extend exclusively to all foreign concerns, causes arising on the seas, to commerce, imports, armies, navies, Indian affairs, peace and war, and to a few internal concerns of the community," but leaving "the internal police of the community, in other respects, exclusively to the state governments," *Doc. Hist.* v. 14, 24. Similarly, "A Farmer" believed that in addition to the powers of making peace and war Congress ought also "to have all powers which cannot be exercised by one state, without endangering the other states, such as the power of raising troops, treating with foreign nations, &c." "A Farmer," *Doc. Hist.* v. 17, 138.

5. "Brutus" 10, New York Journal, 24 January 1788, *Doc. Hist.* v. 15, 465. In a public speech held in Philadelphia soon after the publication of the Con-

stitution James Wilson had argued that the right of Congress to raise armies in time of peace was not a new power but one exercised by the confederation congress in posting troops along the Ohio. "Speech at a Public Meeting in Philadelphia, 6 October 1787, *Doc. Hist.* v. 13, 341. Antifederalists soon responded by denying the validity of Wilson's argument because the "few troops that are on the banks of the Ohio, were sent for the express purpose of repelling the invasion of the savages, and protecting the inhabitants of the frontiers.—It is our misfortune that we are never at peace with those inhuman butchers of their species, and while they remain in our neighbourhood, we are always, with respect to them, in a state of war," "A Democratic Federalist," ibid., 390. See also "Centinel" 2, ibid., 463; Virginia *Independent Chronicle*, 31 October 1787, *Doc. Hist.* v. 8, 138.

6. "Brutus" 9, *Doc. Hist.* v. 15, 394.

7. Max Farrand, *Records of the Constitutional Convention*, 3 vols. (New Haven, Conn.: Yale University Press, 1911), 2, 329.

8. Because some conventions did and some did not propose a bill of rights, and because there was sometimes flexibility as to whether the proposals ought to "be taken collectively as a bill of rights, or separately as amendments to the general form of government proposed" (Robert Whitehill, Pennsylvania ratifying convention, 12 December, *Doc. Hist.* v. 2, 597), similar proposals could end up either as amendments or as part of a proposed bill of rights. Not all Antifederalists were certain about the efficacy of the recommendatory declarations typical of bills of rights, as they were perhaps "too general to be of much service." Nevertheless, they might serve to remind the people and their governors of basic political principles. See "Federal Farmer," "An Additional Number of Letters to the Republican," *Doc. Hist.* v. 17, 362.

9. Virginia Convention Amendments, *Doc. Hist.* v. 18, 202–3. "That the people have a right to keep and bear arms" was an addition to the Virginia declaration of rights, which was otherwise almost identical to the convention's declaration, "The Virginia Declaration of Rights," *Doc. Hist.* v. 8, appendix 1, 531. North Carolina's declaration was identical to Virginia's while New York's differed only slightly. See North Carolina Convention Amendments, *Doc. Hist.* v. 18, 316; New York Convention Declaration of Rights and Form of Ratification, ibid., 298. Robert Whitehill moved in the Pennsylvania convention "that the people have a right to bear arms for the defense of themselves and their own state, or the United States, or for the purpose of killing game; and no law shall be passed for disarming the people or any of them, unless for crimes committed, or real danger of public injury from individuals; and as standing armies in the time of peace are dangerous to liberty, they ought not to be kept up; and that the military shall be kept under strict subordination to and be governed by the civil power," Pennsylvania ratifying convention, 12 December 1787, *Doc. Hist.* v. 2, 597–8. This amendment proposal was also printed in the "Dissent of the Minority of the Pennsylvania Convention," *Doc. Hist.* v. 15, 18–20.

10. "Federal Farmer," "An Additional Number of Letters to the Republican," *Doc. Hist.* v. 17, 364. "Federal Farmer" suggested a limit of 2,000 troops in peacetime and 12,000 in time of war. If more troops were needed they could be raised through requisition in the "normal" manner. When states failed to comply with requisitions, Congress should have the right "by its own laws and officers, to raise the states quota that may neglect, and to charge it with the expence." Luther Martin described in his "Genuine Information" essays how

in the Constitutional convention he "took the sense of the convention on a proposition, by which the Congress should not have power, *in time of peace*, to keep embodied more than a certain number of regular troops—*that number* to be ascertained by what should be considered a *respectable peace establishment.*— This proposition was rejected by a majority, it being their determination that the *power* of Congress to keep up a *standing army*, even *in peace* should *only* be restrained by *their will* and *pleasure*," Luther Martin, "Genuine Information" 7, *Doc. Hist.* v. 15, 410. For this proposal, which originated with Elbridge Gerry but was supported by Martin, and its response in the Convention, see Farrand, *Records* 2, 329–30.

11. "Brutus" 10, *Doc. Hist.* v. 15, 465.

12. The tenth amendment proposal of the Virginia convention stated that "no soldier shall be inlisted for any longer term than four years, except in time of war, and then for no longer term than the continuance of the war." This was in contrast to British practice where soldiers enlisted for life. See Virginia convention amendments, *Doc. Hist.* v. 18, 204. North Carolina copied its neighboring state, while Maryland Antifederalists offered a proposal which was very similar, also suggesting a limit of four years. North Carolina Convention Amendments, ibid., 317–18; "Address of the Minority of the Maryland Convention," *Doc. Hist.* v. 17, 244.

13. This demand was more often placed in the proposed declarations of rights, however. New Hampshire tagged it on to its tenth amendment, and the Maryland committee also suggested it as an amendment. New Hampshire Convention Amendments, *Doc. Hist.* v. 18, 188; "Address of the Minority of the Maryland Convention," *Doc. Hist.* v. 17, 245. Virginia, North Carolina and New York placed it in their declarations of rights. Virginia Convention Amendments, *Doc. Hist.* v. 18, 203; New York Convention Declaration of Rights and Form of Ratification, ibid., 298. In the latter case it had the weaker "ought" form, in the former the absolute "shall" form (but in Maryland's case the somewhat quaint formulation "soldiers be not").

14. Virginia Convention Amendments, ibid., 204. North Carolina's proposal was identical to Virginia's but the convention also added, as a twenty-sixth amendment, "That Congress shall not introduce foreign troops into the United States without the consent of two-thirds of the members present of both houses." North Carolina Convention Amendments, ibid., 317, 320. The New York convention and the Antifederalist minority in Maryland also demanded a two-thirds majority of both houses to raise and keep up armies in peacetime, but in the case of Maryland this was refused by the Federalist majority in the committee appointed to consider amendments. The convention in New Hampshire demanded the consent of three-quarters of the members of both houses, New York Recommendatory Amendments, ibid., 302; "Address of the Minority of the Maryland Convention," *Doc. Hist.* v. 17, 245; New Hampshire Convention Amendments, *Doc. Hist.* v. 18, 188. There were also demands from individual Antifederalists that a qualified majority of two-thirds, occasionally three-fourths, of the delegates to Congress be necessary to raise peacetime troops. See "Richard Henry Lee's Amendments, The Confederation Congress and the Constitution, 26–28 September 1787," *Doc. Hist.* v. 13, 239, later printed in Richard Henry Lee to Governor Randolph, Petersburgh *Virginia Gazette*, 6 December 1787, *Doc. Hist.* v. 14, 371; "Centinel" 2, *Doc. Hist.* v. 13, 463; "Federal Farmer," "Letters to the Republican," *Doc. Hist.* v. 14, 39; "Brutus" 10, *Doc. Hist.* v. 15, 465; Amendments Proposed by William Paca, *Doc. Hist.* v.

17, 241; "Federal Farmer," "An Additional Number of Letters to the Republican," ibid., 364.

15. See note 1.

16. For instance, when Antifederalists criticized the treaty making power of the president, which demanded the consent of two-thirds of present senators, they put little stock in the value of a qualified majority in the Senate. Art. II, sect. 2 of the Constitution states that the president "shall have Power, by and with the Advice and Consent of the Senate, to make Treaties, provided two thirds of the Senators present concur." The issue came up in the Virginia convention in relation to the Jay-Gardoqui treaty. Two-thirds of the senate's quorum of fourteen made ten senators. Thus, it would be possible for the representatives of five states to pass a treaty detrimental to the common interest of the union while advantageous to some sectional interest. In the case of the Jay-Gardoqui treaty, seven states had been in favor of the treaty but because the Articles of Confederation (art. IX) demanded the concurrence of nine states, the southern states could stop the treaty. See Patrick Henry, Virginia ratifying convention, *Doc. Hist.* v. 9, 1039, 1041; William Grayson, *Doc. Hist.* v. 10, 1192.

17. "Federal Farmer," "Letters to the Republican," *Doc. Hist.* v. 14, 38–9.

18. "Federal Farmer," "An Additional Number of Letters to the Republican," *Doc. Hist.* v. 17, 362. For further discussion, see chapter 7.

19. Thus, the New York convention proposed the amendment that "the militia of any State shall not be compelled to serve without the limits of the State for a longer term than six weeks, without the consent of the Legislature thereof," New York Convention Recommendatory Amendments, *Doc. Hist.* v. 18, 305. In Maryland, similarly, the Antifederalist majority tried in vain to make their opponents agree to the amendment that "the militia, unless selected by lot or voluntarily enlisted, shall not be marched beyond the limits of an adjoining state, without the consent of their legislature or executive," "Address of the Minority of the Maryland Convention," *Doc. Hist.* v. 17, 244. The New York convention felt that the demand was of sufficient weight to also be included in its form of ratification, *Doc. Hist.* v. 18, 300, while the Maryland minority believed it to be "essential" and singled it out as one of the most important amendments rejected by their opponents. In the Pennsylvania convention the second part of Robert Whitehill's suggested eleventh amendment declared that "Congress shall not have authority to call or march any of the militia out of their own state, without the consent of such state and for such length of time only as such state shall agree," see Pennsylvania Ratifying Convention, *Doc. Hist.* v. 2, 598, also printed in the "Dissent of the Minority of the Pennsylvania Convention," *Doc. Hist.* v. 15, 19. Antifederalists in the South Carolina convention failed to secure backing for an amendment to limit Congress's use of state militias, "Editors' Note," South Carolina Convention Amendments, *Doc. Hist.* v. 18, 71. Luther Martin also suggested amendments to this effect in his writings, see "Genuine Information" 7, *Doc. Hist.* v. 15, 410; "Address, no. I," *Doc. Hist.* v. 16, 419.

20. The second part of the eleventh amendment proposed by the Virginia convention declares that "the militia shall not be subject to martial law, except when in actual service in time of war, invasion or rebellion, and when not in the actual service of the United States, shall be subject only to such fines, penalties and punishments as shall be directed or inflicted by the laws of its own state." See Virginia Convention Amendments, *Doc. Hist.* v. 18, 204. North

Carolina used the Virginia proposal and the Maryland committee proposal was similar to it. New York placed this qualification in its proposal for a declaration of rights, stating that "the militia should not be subject to martial law, except in time of war, rebellion or insurrection." See North Carolina Convention Amendments, ibid., 318; "Address of the Minority of the Maryland Convention," *Doc. Hist.* v. 17, 244; New York Convention Declaration of Rights and Form of Amendment, *Doc. Hist.* v. 18, 298.

21. The normal stipulation was that such a person should be given the opportunity to pay for a replacement. This was placed in the proposed declaration of rights in Virginia and North Carolina, whereas the Maryland committee placed it among the amendments. See Virginia Convention Amendments, *Doc. Hist.* v. 18, 203; North Carolina Convention Amendments, ibid., 316; "Address of the Minority of the Maryland Convention," *Doc. Hist.* v. 17, 244.

22. This was the meaning of "the right to bear arms" that was stipulated by many proposed declarations of rights, although in some states it formed part of the amendment proposals. New Hampshire was the most explicit in declaring that "Congress shall never disarm any citizen, unless such as are or have been in actual rebellion," New Hampshire Convention Amendments, *Doc. Hist.* v. 18, 188. Pennsylvania, Virginia, New York, and North Carolina spoke about "the right to bear arms." See references cited in note 9.

23. In Pennsylvania, which held the first convention where Antifederalists proposed amendments, the opposition wished to exclude Congress from any power over the militia whatsoever. Thus, Pennsylvania Antifederalists demanded that "the power of organizing, arming, and disciplining the militia (the manner of disciplining the militia to be prescribed by Congress) remain with the individual states," Pennsylvania ratifying convention, *Doc. Hist.* v. 2, 598; "Dissent of the Minority of the Pennsylvania Convention," *Doc. Hist.* v. 15, 19. In later conventions, this demand was softened. In Virginia and North Carolina the proposal was instead that "each state respectively shall have the power to provide for organizing, arming and disciplining its own militia, whensoever Congress shall omit or neglect to provide for the same." Virginia Convention Amendments, *Doc. Hist.* v. 18, 204; North Carolina Convention Amendments, ibid., 318.

24. On 2 October 1787 the seceding Pennsylvania assemblymen published their address in which they told Pennsylvanians that they would, among other things, have "to determine, whether in a free government there ought or ought not to be any provision against a standing army in time of peace?" See "The Address of the Seceding Members of the Pennsylvania Assembly," *Doc. Hist.* v. 13, 296. See also "Cato" 1, ibid., 257; "Centinel" 1, ibid., 332–3; "George Mason's Objections," ibid., 350; "Brutus" 1, ibid., 419; "Brutus" 2, ibid., 527–8. Mason's "Objections" were not printed until 22 November after which they were reprinted in twenty-five papers in six weeks. Before being printed they circulated widely in manuscript. In early Antifederalist writings, the suggestion for a qualified majority can be found in "Centinel" 2, ibid., 463.

25. [Hamilton], *The Federalist* 23 *Doc. Hist.* v. 15, 4–5; [Hamilton], *The Federalist* 25, ibid, 59; [Madison], *The Federalist* 41, ibid., 419; "A Freeman" [Tench Coxe], ibid., 456; Alexander White, Winchester *Virginia Gazette*, 29 February 1788, *Doc. Hist.* v. 8, 438–9; Gore, Massachusetts ratifying convention, Elliot, *Debates* 2, 66; Dawes, ibid., 98; Davie, North Carolina ratifying convention, Elliot, *Debates* 4, 17.

26. Speeches in the Connecticut Convention, *Doc. Hist.* v. 15, 277–8. Alexander Hamilton also noted that "as a national sentiment" the aversion to standing armies in time of peace "must be traced to those habits of thinking, which we derive from the nation from whom the inhabitants of these States have in general sprung." But like Ellsworth he thought that the idea was misunderstood in America, because in England "no security against the danger of standing armies was thought requisite, beyond a prohibition of their being raised or kept up by the mere authority of the executive magistrate," *The Federalist* 26, ibid., 66. See also Dawes, Massachusetts ratifying convention, Elliot, *Debates* 2, 97–8; [Hamilton] *The Federalist* 25, *Doc. Hist.* v. 15, 62; "Aristides" [Alexander Contee Hanson], ibid., 532; "Marcus" 4, *Doc. Hist.* v. 16, 384. To Thomas McKean it was clear that the power to raise and maintain armies could be vested in no other body than Congress. "To whose judgement, indeed, could be so properly referred the determination of what is necessary to accomplish those important objects, as the judgement of a Congress elected, either directly or indirectly, by all the Citizens of the United States? For if the people discharge their duty to themselves, the persons that compose that body will be the wisest and best amongst us; the wisest to discover the means of common defense and general welfare, and the best to carry those means into execution without guile, injustice, or oppression." Pennsylvania ratifying convention, *Doc. Hist.* v. 2, 414.

27. [Madison] *The Federalist* 41, *Doc. Hist.* v. 15, 419.

28. Edmund Randolph, "Letter on the Federal Constitution," *Doc. Hist.* v. 15, 123 (quotation); Oliver Ellsworth, "Speech in the Connecticut Convention," ibid., 246–7; "A Freeman" [Tench Coxe], ibid., 456.

29. [Hamilton] *The Federalist* 22, *Doc. Hist.* v. 14, 438; Robert Livingston, New York ratifying convention, Elliot, *Debates* 2, 214; Hamilton, ibid., 231–2; Madison, Virginia ratifying convention, *Doc. Hist.* v. 9, 1145.

30. [Hamilton], *The Federalist* 22, *Doc. Hist.* v. 14, 438.

31. James Marshall, Virginia ratifying convention, *Doc. Hist.* v. 9, 1120. Had it not been for the French minister's readiness to draw the bills that financed the Yorktown expedition, Davie said, the war would have been lost. In 1781 Congress was bankrupt; see Davie, North Carolina ratifying convention, Elliot, *Debates* 4, 17. For the financing of the Yorktown expedition and the crucial role of Robert Morris, see E. Wayne Carp, *To Starve the Army at Pleasure: Continental Army Administration and American Political Culture, 1775–1783* (Chapel Hill: University of North Carolina Press, 1984), 212–13.

32. [Hamilton], *The Federalist* 23, *Doc. Hist.* v. 15, 5.

33. Ibid., 6.

34. [Hamilton] *The Federalist* 15, *Doc. Hist.* v. 14, 327. Faced with the Antifederalist assertion that this was actually nothing more than a proper check against abuses of the federal government, Parsons responded by saying: "But it may be said, as the ways and means are reserved to the several states, they have a check upon Congress, by refusing a compliance with the requisitions. Sir, is this the boasted check?—a check that can never be exercised but by perfidy and a breach of public faith; by a violation of the most solemn stipulations? It is this check that has embarrassed at home, and made us contemptible abroad; and will any honest man plume himself upon a check which an honest man would blush to exercise?" Massachusetts ratifying convention, Elliot, *Debates* 2, 89–90.

35. "An Impartial Citizen" 4, *Doc. Hist.* v. 8, 498–9.

36. James Marshall, Virginia ratifying convention, *Doc. Hist.* v. 9, 1120.

37. Edmund Randolph, "Letter on the Federal Constitution," *Doc. Hist.* v. 15, 124.

38. [Hamilton] *The Federalist* 15, *Doc. Hist.* v. 14, 327–9, quotation at 328; [Hamilton] *The Federalist* 23, *Doc. Hist.* v. 15, 5.

39. [Madison] *The Federalist* 45, ibid., 480.

40. Linda Colley, *Britons: Forging the Nation 1707–1837* (New Haven, Conn.: Yale University Press, 1992), 11–54; Wilfred Prest, *Albion Ascendant: English History, 1660–1815* (Oxford: Oxford University Press, 1998), 52, 49–80, 120–1; J.-F. Boucher, "The Franco-Catholic Danger, 1660–1715," *History*, 79 (1994), 5–30. In *Britain's Happiness*, to take but one example, Richard Price claimed that should Britain lose to France, Britons would become "ignoble and miserable slaves" as the consequence of the reintroduction of Catholicism, "that religion which would crush all our liberties and privileges," in *Political Writings*, ed. David O. Thomas (Cambridge, U.K.: Cambridge University Press, 1992), 11.

41. Boucher, "Franco-Catholic Danger," 21–4; Colley, *Britons*, 71–85, Paul Langford, *A Polite and Commercial People: England 1727–1783* (Oxford: Oxford University Press, 1989), 197–203; Prest, *Albion Ascendant*, 130–1.

42. Quoted in Lawrence D. Cress, *Citizens in Arms: The Army and the Militia in American Society to the War of 1812* (Chapel Hill: University of North Carolina Press, 1982), 26.

43. Quoted in John Brewer, *The Sinews of Power: War, Money and the English State 1688–1783* (London: Unwin Hyman, 1989), 142.

44. Lawrence Cress dates the end to widespread fear of the army to 1738 when the Walpole ministry won a major parliamentary debate about the legitimacy of the peacetime standing army, *Citizens in Arms*, 28. Paul Langford notes that what had been both a strongly felt and widely held fear of the standing army seemed to have all but vanished by the reign of George III. By that time experience had demonstrated that the constitution could survive the existence of the army. It was also increasingly felt among men of property and the political elite that the threat to the constitution came from the weakness rather than the strength of executive power. Another factor was that the Seven Years' War had established the army as a patriotic force in the eyes of many Englishmen who took great pride in its victories; see *Polite and Commercial People*; 688–9; Price, *Britain's Happiness*, 6–7.

45. For Walpole and Pitt, see Langford, *Polite and Commercial People*, 11–57, 333–47. For the increase in indebtedness, see Brewer, *Sinews of Power*, table 2.1.

46. Colley, *Britons*, 52–4, 322, 364–72; Kathleen Wilson, "Empire, Trade and Popular Politics in Mid-Hanoverian Britain: The Case of Admiral Vernon," *Past and Present*, 121 (1988), 74–109; Wilson, "Empire of Virtue: The Imperial Project and Hanoverian Culture c.1720–1785," in *An Imperial State at War: Britain from 1689–1815*, ed. Lawrence S. Stone (London: Routledge, 1994), 128–64.

47. James Wilson, Pennsylvania ratifying convention, 11 December 1787, *Doc. Hist.* v. 2, 577, 576. "Which of all the European powers is destitute of an army? Which of them, if they were free, could be secure of remaining so, without a standing force? I might go further, and demand whether any of them have lost their liberties, by means of a *standing* army?" "Aristides" [Alexander Contee Hanson], *Doc. Hist.* v. 15, 532.

48. *The Federalist* 41, ibid., 420.

49. James Wilson, Speech at a public meeting in Philadelphia, 6 October 1787, *Doc. Hist.* v. 13, 341.

50. [Hamilton] *The Federalist* 25, *Doc. Hist.* v. 15, 62. But it should be noted that often Federalists preceded denouncements of the militia by praising its feats during the War of Independence, no doubt a policy dictated by political prudence. See for example ibid.; Henry Lee, Virginia ratifying convention, 9 June, *Doc. Hist.* v. 9, 1073. It was Edmund Randolph who put it best: "I will pay the last tribute of gratitude to the militia of my country: They performed some of the most gallant feats during the last war, and acted as nobly as men enured to other avocations could be expected to do," Randolph, Virginia ratifying convention, 6 June, ibid., 981.

51. George Nicholas, Virginia ratifying convention, 14 June, *Doc. Hist.* v. 10, 1278–9. See also Edmund Randolph, Letter on the Federal Constitution, *Doc. Hist.* v. 15, 124–5; Randolph, Virginia ratifying convention, 6 June, *Doc. Hist.* v. 9, 981; James Madison, ibid., 6 June, 993.

52. Henry Lee, Virginia ratifying convention, ibid., 1073–4. See also the account by Archibald Maclaine of how a British force occupying Wilmington had held off a militia force three times their number and of how that same force could plunder Newbern without challenge from the militia, "Publicola" [Archibald Maclaine], *Doc. Hist.* v. 16, 439.

53. [Hamilton], *The Federalist* 25, *Doc. Hist.* v. 15, 62.

54. [Madison] *The Federalist* 41, ibid., 420.

55. James Madison, Virginia ratifying convention, *Doc. Hist.* v. 9, 1031; Oliver Ellsworth, Speeches in the Connecticut convention, *Doc. Hist.* v. 15, 247. "A Freeholder" also said that by partitioning the republic, "they would not only acquire an additional territory; and increase their naval resources; but they would cut off at a single stroke the head of their formidable rival—of a rival which the tyrants of Europe look upon as about to eclipse their glory, diminish the number of their subjects in that quarter of the globe, and rob them totally of them in this, annihilating their sovereignty in America," "A Freeholder," *Doc. Hist.* v. 9, 728.

56. [Hamilton], *The Federalist* 24, *Doc. Hist.* v. 15, 41–3; [Jay] *The Federalist* 4, *Doc. Hist.* v. 13, 569; James Wilson, Pennsylvania ratifying convention, *Doc. Hist.* v. 2, 577; Edmund Randolph, Virginia ratifying convention, 6 June, *Doc. Hist.* v. 9, 977; "Americanus," *Doc. Hist.* v. 13, 72; "Harrington" [Benjamin Rush], ibid., 119; *Pennsylvania Gazette*, 29 August 1787, ibid., 191; *Pittsburgh Gazette*, 17 November, *Doc. Hist.* v. 14, 136; *Virginia Independent Chronicle*, 28 November 1787, ibid., 245; Harrison Gray Otis, Oration 4 July 1788, *Doc. Hist.* v. 18, 228; *Pittsburgh Gazette*, *Doc. Hist.* v. 14, 136.

57. James Wilson, Pennsylvania ratifying convention, 11 December 1787, *Doc. Hist.* v. 2, 576. "What are the objects of the national Government? To protect the United States, and to promote the general welfare. Protection in time of war is one of its principal objects. Until mankind shall cease to have ambition and avarice, wars will arise. The prosperity and happiness of the people depend on the performance of these great and important duties of the General Government," James Marshall, Virginia ratifying convention, 10 June, *Doc. Hist.* v. 9, 1119.

58. [Hamilton] *The Federalist* 25, *Doc. Hist.* v. 15, 62. In the Virginia convention James Marshall responded to Patrick Henry's claim "that we need not be afraid of war" in a similar way. "Look at history, which has been so often quoted. Look at the great volume of human nature. They will foretell you, that

a defenceless country cannot be secure. The nature of man forbids us to conclude, that we are in no danger from war. The passions of men stimulate them to avail themselves of the weakness of others. The powers of Europe are jealous of us. It is our interest to watch their conduct, and guard against them. They must be pleased with our disunion. If we invite them by our weakness to attack us, will they not do it? If we add debility to our present situation, a partition of America may take place. It is then necessary to give the Government that power in time of peace, which the necessities of war will render indispensable, or else we shall be attacked unprepared," Virginia ratifying convention, 10 June, *Doc. Hist.* v. 9, 1119–20.

59. Francis Hopkinson, "The New Roof," *Doc. Hist.* v. 15, 184; "Ship news," *Doc. Hist.* v. 13, 523.

60. James Bowdoin, Massachusetts ratifying convention, Elliot, *Debates* 2, 84–5.

61. Oliver Ellsworth, Speeches in the Connecticut convention, *Doc. Hist.* v. 15, 247. See also the reference to partition in Marshall's speech quoted in note 58. Another reference to partitioning can be found in "A Freeholder," who discussed the claims of the creditor nations, France, Spain, Holland and England. "May not these nations," he asked, "provoked by our unworthy treatment of them, and at the same time invited, and tempted by our distracted and defenceless situation, resolved to divide the states amongst them, make such a partition as they are well acquainted with in Europe?" "A Freeholder," *Doc. Hist.* v. 9, 728.

62. See for instance "An Impartial Citizen" 6, *Doc. Hist.* v. 8, 498; "A Citizen of Philadelphia" [Pelatiah Webster], "Remarks on the Address of Sixteen Members," *Doc. Hist.* v. 13, 302; "Cassius" 3, *Doc. Hist.* v. 9, 749; John Marshall, Virginia ratifying convention, *Doc. Hist.* v. ibid., 1120; James Iredell, North Carolina ratifying convention, 26 July, Elliot, *Debates* 4, 96.

63. [Hamilton], *The Federalist* 25, *Doc. Hist.* v. 15, 62.

64. *The Federalist* 41, ibid., 420.

65. As Hamilton wrote: "The authorities essential to the care of the common defence are these—to raise armies—to build and equip fleets—to prescribe rules for the government of both—to direct their operations—to provide for their support. These powers ought to exist without limitation: *Because it is impossible to foresee or define the extent and variety of national exigencies, or the correspondent extent & variety of the means which may be necessary to satisfy them. . . .* The *means* ought to be proportioned to the *end;* the persons, from whose agency the attainment of any *end* is expected, ought to possess the *means* by which it is to be attained," *The Federalist* 23, ibid., 4. "Let the federal head be constituted as it may, there can be no perfect security, without both a land force and a naval armament. It is impossible to say how much will, at all times of peace, be sufficient," "Aristides" [Alexander Contee Hanson], ibid., 532.

66. [Oliver Ellsworth] "Landholder" 5, *Doc. Hist.* v. 14, 336.

67. Dawes, Massachusetts convention, Elliot, *Debates* 2, 58.

68. [Oliver Ellsworth] "Landholder" 3, *Doc. Hist.* v. 15, 140.

69. Rutledge, South Carolina assembly debates, Elliot, *Debates* 4, 275.

70. [Oliver Ellsworth] "Landholder" 3, *Doc. Hist.* v. 14, 140. In another place he laid down that "A people cannot long retain their freedom, whose government is incapable of protecting them," "Landholder" 5, ibid., 336.

7: A Government of Force

1. "You may sleep in safety forever [from] them," Patrick Henry ensured the Virginia convention with reference to the powers of Europe, Virginia ratifying convention, *Doc. Hist.* v. 9, 955. Antifederalists saw in the Federalist depiction of the union's critical situation a chimera designed to intimidate the people into adopting the Constitution; see John Tyler, Virginia ratifying convention, *Doc. Hist.* v. 10, 1525. Thus for instance, William Grayson responded with ridicule to Edmund Randolph's description of the dangers that faced Virginia should she reject the Constitution: "We are told by the Honorable Gentleman (Governor *Randolph*) that we shall have wars and rumours of wars; that every calamity is to attend us, and that we shall be ruined and disunited forever, unless we adopt this Constitution. Pennsylvania and Maryland are to fall upon us from the North, like the Goths and Vandals of old—the Algerines, whose flat sided vessels never came further than Madeira, are to fill the Chesapeake with mighty fleets, and to attack us on our front. The Indians are to invade us with numerous armies on our rear, in order to convert our cleared lands into hunting grounds—And the Carolinians from the South, mounted on alligators, I presume, are to come and destroy our corn fields and eat up our little children! These, Sir, are the mighty dangers which await us if we reject," Virginia ratifying convention, *Doc. Hist* 9, 1167. See also Norman A. Graebner, "Isolationism and Antifederalism: The Ratification Debates," *Diplomatic History* 11 (1987), 340, 352–3.

2. "A Son of Liberty," *Doc. Hist.* v. 13, 481. See also "Petition Against Confirmation of the Ratification of the Constitution," January 1788, *Doc. Hist.* v. 2, 711; "The Impartial Examiner" 1, *Doc. Hist.* v. 8, 422; "Brutus," *Doc. Hist.* v. 13, 415, 419; "Centinel" 2, ibid., 463; Martin, "Genuine Information" 7, *Doc. Hist.* v. 15, 410; Nason, Massachusetts ratifying convention, Elliot, *Debates* 2, 136.

3. To make this point, the New York Antifederalist "Brutus" quoted at length from a famous and often reprinted speech that William Pulteney had delivered before the House of Commons more than five decades previously. In this speech Pulteney noted that "the nations around us . . . are already enslaved . . . by means of their standing armies they have every one lost their liberties; it is indeed impossible that the liberties of the people in any country can be preserved where a numerous standing army is kept up. Shall we then take our measures from the example of our neighbours? No, . . . on the contrary, from their misfortunes we ought to learn to avoid those rocks upon which they have split," "Brutus" 8, *Doc. Hist.* v. 15, 337. For the claim that the speech was well-known, see Bernard Bailyn, "The Ideological Fulfillment of the American Revolution," in *Faces of Revolution: Personalities and Themes in the Struggle for American Independence* (New York: Knopf, 1990), 238.

"Brutus" 's extended quotation of Pulteney illustrates the way in which political arguments retained their validity, or usefulness, both in time and space. Although more than fifty years old the speech retained all its relevance, being "so full to the point, and so much better than any thing I can say." Nor, obviously, was there any problem with applying to America a point made in the context of British politics.

4. "Philadelphiensis" 4, *Doc. Hist.* v. 14, 420.

5. Lois G. Schwoerer, *"No Standing Armies!" The Antiarmy Ideology in*

Seventeenth-Century England (Baltimore: Johns Hopkins University Press, 1974), 1, 155.

6. John Brewer, *Party Ideology and Popular Politics at the Accession of George III* (Cambridge, U.K.: Cambridge University Press, 1976), 251–2.

7. Richard H. Kohn, *Eagle and Sword: The Federalists and the Creation of the Military Establishment in America, 1783–1802* (New York: Free Press, 1975), 2. See also Pulteney's speech quoted in "Brutus" 8, *Doc. Hist.* v. 15, 337.

8. E. Arnold Miller, "Some Arguments Used by English Pamphleteers, 1697–1700, Concerning a Standing Army," *The Journal of Modern History* 18 (1946), 307–11; Lois G. Schwoerer, "The Literature of the Standing Army Controversy, 1697–1699," *The Huntington Library Quarterly* 28 (1965), 197–9, 201–2; Schwoerer, *"No Standing Armies!"* 162, 180–3.

9. William Blackstone, *Commentaries on the Laws of England*, 4 vols. (Oxford, 1775, 7th ed.), 1, 336; David Hume, "Idea of a Perfect Commonwealth" in *Political Essays*, ed. Knud Haakonssen (Cambridge, U.K.: Cambridge University Press, 1994), 232 and n10, 330.

10. John A. Houlding, *The Training of the British Army, 1715–1795* (Oxford: Oxford University Press, 1981), 3; John Brewer, *The Sinews of Power: War, Money and the English State, 1688–1783* (London: Unwin Hyman, 1989), 51–4. By becoming a law enforcement body the army took on tasks that had earlier belonged only to other institutions for the preservation of law and order, although it far from entirely replaced them. Traditionally, the law was enforced within a community by the members of the community themselves. It was the "hue and cry," the *posse comitatus* and the militia—all institutions made up of local men and law enforcement amateurs—who apprehended felons and maintained the law, not the army—an alien institution controlled by the central government.

11. Tony Hayter, *The Army and the Crowd in Mid-Georgian England* (London: Macmillan, 1978), 34; Houlding, *Training*, 57–74; Brewer, *Sinews of Power*, 51–4.

12. John Philip Reid, *In Defiance of the Law: The Standing-Army Controversy, the Two Constitutions, and the Coming of the American Revolution* (Chapel Hill: North Carolina University Press, 1981), 112–29, quotation at 121. See also Hayter, *Army and the Crowd*, 1–43.

13. Gordon S. Wood, "A Note on Mobs in the American Revolution," *WMQ*, 3d ser. 23 (1966), 639.

14. Reid, *Defiance*, 177–88, 202–3; According to a leading military historian, the British army successfully performed police duties in the colonies only once, see John Shy, *Toward Lexington: The Role of the British Army in the Coming of the American Revolution* (Princeton, N.J.: Princeton University Press, 1965), 400–1.

15. Bernard Bailyn, *The Ideological Origins of the American Revolution* (Cambridge, Mass.: Harvard University Press, 1967), 115–17; Pauline Maier, *From Resistance to Revolution: Colonial Radicals and the Development of American Opposition to Britain 1765–1776* (London: Routledge, 1973), 194–5. For an account of the events at St. George's Fields, see George Rudé, *Wilkes and Liberty: A Social Study of 1763 to 1774* (Oxford: Clarendon, 1962), 49–52 and Rudé, *The Crowd in History: A Study of Popular Disturbances in France and England 1730–1848* (New York: Wiley, 1964), 57.

16. Shy, *Toward Lexington*, 376.

17. There had been a few independent companies stationed in New York

and South Carolina earlier. At this time a company consisted of officers, NCOs and forty soldiers, hence the numbers involved were very small. These forces tended to be neglected by the imperial government.

18. Douglas Edward Leach, "The British Army in America, Before 1775," in *The Blackwell Encyclopedia of the American Revolution*, ed. Jack P. Greene and Jack R. Pole (Oxford: Blackwell, 1991), 146–52; Shy, *Toward Lexington*, 290–320, 376–98.

19. Reid, *In Defiance of the Law*, 103–10, 124–8; Peter D. G. Thomas, "The Stamp Act Crisis and Its Repercussions, Including the Quartering Act Controversy," *Blackwell Encyclopedia of the American Revolution*, ed. Greene and Pole, 113–16.

20. Reid, *In Defiance of the Law*, 71–9, quotation at 79. See also the discussion in Bailyn, *Ideological Origins of the American Revolution*, 112–21.

21. Declaration of Independence, in *Doc. Hist.* v. 1, 73–5. See also Pauline Maier, *American Scripture: Making the Declaration of Independence* (New York: Knopf, 1997), 47–90.

22. For examples of bills of rights, see the "Massachusetts Constitution, Preamble and Declaration of the Rights," section XVII, *Doc. Hist.* v. 4, 444, and the Virginia Declaration of Rights, section 13, *Doc. Hist.* v. 8, 531.

23. "The Federalist Political Creed," *Doc. Hist.* v. 18, 5.

24. See Jack N. Rakove, *Original Meanings: Politics and Ideas in the Making of the Constitution* (New York: Knopf, 1996), 181–4.

25. Patrick Henry, Virginia ratifying convention, *Doc. Hist.* v. 9, 1068.

26. Melanchton Smith, New York ratifying convention, Elliot, *Debates* 2, 313.

27. "A Farmer," *Doc. Hist.* v. 17, 142.

28. Wilson concluded from the method of appointment that "it is evidently absurd to suppose, that the annihilation of the separate governments will result from their union; or, that having that intention, the authors of the new system would have bound their connection with such indissoluble ties." "Speech at a Public Meeting in Philadelphia," 6 October 1787, *Doc. Hist.* v. 13, 342. He did not use the term "sovereignty" in this context, however. Wilson's use of the concept of popular sovereignty as a theoretical solution to the question where sovereignty resided in a federal system of government was presented in the Pennsylvania ratifying convention, *Doc. Hist.* v. 2, 361–2. Accounts of the Federalist concept of popular sovereignty can be found in Edmund S. Morgan, *Inventing the People: The Rise of Popular Sovereignty in England and America* (New York: Norton, 1988), 280–2; Peter S. Onuf, *The Origins of the Federal Republic: Jurisdictional Controversies in the United States 1775–1787* (Philadelphia: University of Philadelphia Press, 1983), 199–200, 207; Rakove, *Original Meanings*, 189–90; Gordon S. Wood, *The Creation of the American Republic, 1776–1787* (Chapel Hill: University of North Carolina Press, 1969), 527–35; Wood, "The Political Ideology of the Founders," in *Toward a More Perfect Union: Six Essays on the Constitution*, ed. Neil L. York (Provo, Utah: Brigham Young University, 1988), 20–4.

29. "Cincinnatus" 5, *Doc. Hist.* v. 14, 307.

30. "A Farmer," *Doc. Hist.* v. 17, 142–3; Robert Whitehill, Pennsylvania ratifying convention, *Doc. Hist.* v. 2, 396.

31. "Federal Farmer," "An Additional Number of Letters to the Republican," *Doc. Hist.* v. 17, 297.

32. Patrick Henry, Virginia ratifying convention, *Doc. Hist.* v. 9, 1068.

33. Melanchton Smith, New York ratifying convention, Elliot, *Debates* 2, 312–13.

34. Benjamin Gale, "Speech," *Doc. Hist.* v. 3, 428. "By organizing the Militia Congress have taken the whole power from the State Governments," Luther Martin, "Speech in the Maryland State House of Delegates," *Doc. Hist.* v. 14, 290–1.

35. See the "Report on a Military Peace Establishment," 18 June 1783, *PAH* 3, 387–97.

36. "Federal Farmer," "Letters to the Republican," *Doc. Hist.* v. 14, 39. It was especially troublesome that the select militia would be recruited from "the young and ardent part of the community, possessed of but little or no property." "When a select militia is formed," John Smilie said, "the people in general may be disarmed," Pennsylvania ratifying convention, *Doc. Hist.* v. 2, 509.

37. Luther Martin, "Address no I," *Doc. Hist.* v. 16, 419. See also George Mason, Virginia ratifying convention, *Doc. Hist.* v. 10, 1270; William Grayson, ibid, 1306.

38. Luther Martin, "Genuine Information" 7, *Doc. Hist.* v. 15, 412.

39. James Wilson's notes in the Pennsylvania convention shows that John Smilie opposed the Constitution because the "Senate and President may dismiss the Representatives, when once a standing army is established with funds; and there this government will terminate," *Doc. Hist.* v. 2, 509. In a satirical Antifederalist item, purported to be a letter from James Bowdoin to "James de Caledonia," i.e., James Wilson, the former writes that "as you say, what need we care for the sentiments of the people, if we can only get the army a-foot." In another passage it is noted that once the Constitution was ratified "we shall never again be troubled with the people, never dread the event of elections; we shall enjoy our places, honors, and preferments, and leave them to our children after us," "James Bowdoin to James de Caledonia," *Doc. Hist.* v. 16, 239–40. A writer in the *Freeman's Journal* pointed to the French people's struggle against a recent imposition of a heavy land tax as a warning example to Americans. "The people complain of it loudly, but what does this avail? their complaints are treated with contempt, as that government has a large *standing army* at their command, and we find those who dare to complain are banished, or sent to the *Bastile!*" Philadelphia *Freeman's Journal*, 5 March 1788, ibid., 320.

40. Pennsylvania *Independent Gazetteer*, 5 May 1788, *Doc. Hist.* v. 17, 386.

41. "A Ploughman," *Doc. Hist.* v. 8, 508.

42. Patrick Henry, Virginia ratifying convention, *Doc. Hist.* v. 10, 1299. Henry is reported to have said "existing power." I have assumed that he has been misrepresented, or else his words seem to make little sense. The full passage reads: "Mr. *Henry* thought it necessary and proper that they should take a collective view of this whole section, and revert again to the first clause. He adverted to the clause which gives Congress the power of raising armies, and proceeded as follows. To me this appear a very alarming power, when unlimited. They are not only to raise, but to support armies; and this support is to go to the utmost abilities of the United States. If Congress shall say, that the general welfare requires it, they may keep armies continually on foot. There is no controul on Congress in raising or stationing them. They may billet them on the people at pleasure. This unlimited authority is a most dangerous power: Its principles are despotic. If it be unbounded, it must lead to despotism. For

the power of the people in a free Government, is supposed to be paramount to the existing power."

43. "A Ploughman," *Doc. Hist.* v. 8, 508. And he added that it was "eternally true, that a free government and a standing army are absolutely incompatible."

44. See for instance Patrick Henry, Virginia ratifying convention, *Doc. Hist.* v. 10, 1275–6; Edmund Randolph, ibid., 1288; Nason, Massachusetts ratifying convention, Elliot, *Debates* 2, 137.

45. John Smilie, Pennsylvania ratifying convention, *Doc. Hist.* v. 2, 508.

46. Lenoir, North Carolina convention, Elliot, *Debates* 4, 203. As the English radical Richard Price had put it, "no wise people will trust their defence out of their own hands, or consent to hold their rights at the mercy of armed slaves." Price's *Observations on the Importance of the American Revolution* (1784) was quoted in "Tamony," *Doc. Hist.* v. 15, 323. See also Henry's warning to his countrymen that when "you have given up your militia, and Congress shall refuse to arm them, you have lost everything. Your existence will be precarious, because you depend on others, whose interests are not affected by your infe-licity," *Doc. Hist.* v. 10, 1278. The role of popular violence to protect liberty was demonstrated even during the ratification struggle. A correspondent to the *Independent Gazetteer* claimed that the people in western Pennsylvania were arming themselves to force the calling of a second constitutional convention, Philadelphia *Independent Gazetteer*, 30 April 1788, *Doc. Hist.* v. 17, 251–2.

47. George Mason, Virginia ratifying convention, *Doc. Hist.* v. 10, 1271. Antifederalists placed little value in their opponents' claim that if wronged by Congress the people could assemble in convention to recall delegated powers and punish the offences of their representatives. It would be "fine times in-deed," mocked Henry, "if to punish tyrants, it were only sufficient to assemble the people." Without arms this would affect nothing. "Did you ever read of any revolution in any nation, brought about by the punishment of those in power, inflicted by those who had no power at all?" Patrick Henry, Virginia ratifying convention, *Doc. Hist.* v. 9, 957.

48. Patrick Henry, Virginia ratifying convention, ibid., 954.

49. "A standing army in the hands of a government placed so independent of the people, may be made a fatal instrument to overturn the public liberties; it may be employed to enforce the collection of the most oppressive taxes, and to carry into execution the most arbitrary measures," "The Dissent of the Minority of the Pennsylvania Convention," *Doc. Hist.* v. 15, 32.

50. Standing armies, the Antifederalists told the people, would be "the mean by which you will be made to pay taxes!" Nason, Massachusetts ratifying convention, Elliot, *Debates* 2, 136. Taxes and soldiers were intimately con-nected. "Money can purchase soldiers;—soldiers can produce money; and both together can do any thing," "The Impartial Examiner" 1, *Doc. Hist.* v. 8, 465.

51. "Address of the Seceding Assemblymen"; "Centinel" 1, *Doc. Hist.* v. 13, 296, 333.

52. "Dissent of the Minority of the Pennsylvania Convention," *Doc. Hist.* v. 15, 31. According to "A Son of Liberty," the citizens would be "constantly subjected to the insults of *military* collectors, who will, by the magnetism of that most powerful of all attractives, the *bayonet*, extract from their pockets (without their consent) the exorbitant taxes imposed on them by their haughty lords and masters, for the purpose of keeping them under, and breaking their spirits, to prevent revolt," *Doc. Hist.* v. 13, 482.

53. For the American system of government, see references cited in note 43, chapter 2.

54. "Dissent of the Minority of the Pennsylvania Convention," *Doc. Hist.* v. 15, 32.

55. "Centinel" 2, *Doc. Hist.* v. 13, 465; "Philadelphiensis" 4, *Doc. Hist.* v. 14, 420; "Cincinnatus" 4, *Doc. Hist.* v. 14, 187; "A Ploughman," *Doc. Hist.* v. 8, 508. In the Pennsylvania convention Smilie remarked that the Constitutional "Convention, in framing this government, knew it was not a free one; otherwise they would not have asked [for] the power of the purse and the sword," *Doc. Hist.* v. 2, 508. According to "Brutus," the Federalists were of the opinion that "no people can be kept in order, unless the government have an army to awe them into obedience," "Brutus" 9, *Doc. Hist.* v. 15, 396.

56. "Report of New York's Delegates to the Constitutional Convention," *Doc. Hist.* v. 15, 370.

57. "Brutus" 1, *Doc. Hist.* v. 13, 419–20. See also "A Citizen of Maryland," *Doc. Hist.* v. 17, 90, who believed that a standing army would be created as a result of domestic commotion and then be used to oppress the people.

58. "Federal Farmer," "Letters to the Republican," *Doc. Hist.* v. 14, 29; Patrick Dollard, South Carolina ratifying convention, Elliot, *Debates* 4, 338.

59. "A Federal Republican," *Doc. Hist.* v. 14, 265.

60. "Brutus" 1, *Doc. Hist.* v. 13, 419.

61. The power of Congress to "provide for calling forth the Militia to execute the Laws of the Union" (art. I, sect. 8) again drew protests that the Federalists wished to establish a "military Government" (Greene Clay, Virginia ratifying convention, *Doc. Hist.* v. 10, 1274) or a "Government of force" (Patrick Henry, Virginia ratifying convention, ibid., 1300). It was a right regarded as "unprecedented" (Henry, ibid., 1301), as "a novel one, in free governments" ("Brutus" 4, *Doc. Hist.* v. 14, 301) and a breach against "the old established custom of executing the laws" (Greene Clay, Virginia ratifying convention, *Doc. Hist.* v. 10, 1274). The old established custom was for the local officers of the peace to call out the *posse comitatus* or the militia under civil command. The Constitution made no mention of these officers and the Antifederalist conclusion was that "the militia in general, or any select part of it, may be called out under military officers, instead of the sheriff to enforce an execution of federal laws, in the first instance and thereby introduce an entire military execution of the laws," "Federal Farmer," "Letters to the Republican," *Doc. Hist.* v. 14, 39. See also "Brutus" 4, ibid., 301. This of course went against the important rule that "the military power ought not to interpose till the civil power refused," Patrick Henry, Virginia ratifying convention, *Doc. Hist.* v. 10, 1277.

62. "Dissent of the Minority of the Pennsylvania Convention," *Doc. Hist.* v. 15, 32; John Smilie, Pennsylvania ratifying convention, *Doc. Hist.* v. 2, 508. There are several other examples of similar statements. Governments "ought not to depend on an army for their support, but ought to be so formed as to have the confidence, respect and affection of the citizens," John Dawson, Virginia ratifying convention, *Doc. Hist.* v. 10, 1494. "Will this consolidated republic, if established, in its exercise beget such confidence and compliance, among the citizens of these states, as to do without the aid of a standing army—I deny that it will," "Cato" 3, *Doc. Hist.* v. 13, 475–6.

63. "Brutus" 1, *Doc. Hist.* v. 13, 419. In this context it might be interesting to compare "Brutus" 's words with William Blackstone's about the "military and maritime states" in England. "In a land of liberty it is extremely dangerous

to make a distinct order of the profession of arms. In absolute monarchies this is necessary for the safety of the prince, and arises from the main principle of their constitution, which is that of governing by fear: but in free states the profession of a soldier, taken singly and merely as a profession, is justly an object of jealousy," *Commentaries* I, 408.

See also the speech by Benjamin Gale: "Mankind, vile as they be, see the necessity of civil government and will submit to all reasonable laws and all reasonable demands of taxes to support that government, and whenever there are any stubborn refractory individuals that will not submit to civil government there are always men enough, when properly called upon, to support the civil magistrate in the execution of laws. But if the laws are oppressive and arbitrary, the public demands above the ability of the people to pay, they will eternally kick. You may depend upon it in a country where the people have anything they call their own, and they must be governed by a standing army who carry with them the instruments of death if they are governed at all," *Doc. Hist.* v. 3, 427.

64. "Letter from Massachusetts," *Doc. Hist.* v. 3, 378.

65. "Landholder" 10, *Doc. Hist.* v. 16, 267. In the Virginia convention, George Nicholas noted that some of his opponents praised the select militia of England while others voiced strong oppositions to select militias, Virginia ratifying convention, *Doc. Hist.* v. 10, 1314 (Nicholas), 1306 (William Grayson), 1312 (George Mason).

66. André Corvisier, *Armies and Societies in Europe, 1494–1789* (Bloomington: Indiana University Press, 1979), 51–60.

67. John R. Western, *The English Militia in the Eighteenth Century: The Story of a Political Issue, 1600–1802* (London: Routledge, 1965), 127–61, 245–64; Eliga H. Gould, *The Persistence of Empire: British Political Culture in the Age of the American Revolution* (Chapel Hill: University of North Carolina Press, 2000), 72–105; Paul Langford, *A Polite and Commercial People: England 1727–1783* (Oxford: Oxford University Press, 1989), 334–5.

68. "Blessings of the new government," *Doc. Hist.* v. 13, 345.

69. "Brutus" 8, *Doc. Hist.* v. 15, 336.

70. George Mason, Virginia ratifying convention, *Doc. Hist.* v. 10, 1289. See also Mason, ibid. 1304.

71. Luther Martin, "Genuine Information" 7, *Doc. Hist.* v. 15, 410. See also Luther Martin, "Address no. I," *Doc. Hist.* v. 16, 419; John Smilie, Pennsylvania ratifying convention, *Doc. Hist.* v. 2, 509; "An Old Whig" 5, *Doc. Hist.* v. 13, 540; "Centinel" 3, *Doc. Hist.* v. 14, 60; "Dissent of the Minority of the Pennsylvania Convention," *Doc. Hist.* v. 15, 32. This Antifederalist objection may appear a strained construction of the Constitution's militia clauses, but it was regarded as serious enough to be corrected by the fifth amendment.

72. "Address of the Minority of the Maryland Convention," *Doc. Hist.* v. 17, 244.

73. The dominance of Philadelphia Antifederalists among those raising this objection reveals the Quaker presence in that state. For the charge that conscientious objectors would be made to serve in the militia, see "Dissent of the Minority of the Pennsylvania Convention," *Doc. Hist.* v. 15, 32–3; "An Officer of the Late Continental Army," *Doc. Hist.* v. 2, 212; William Findley, Pennsylvania ratifying convention, ibid., 509; "An Old Whig" 5, *Doc. Hist.* v. 13, 540; "Philadelphiensis" 2, *Doc. Hist.* v. 14, 252–3; "Timothy Meanwell," ibid., appendix 3, 513; Luther Martin, "Address no. I," *Doc. Hist.* v. 16, 419.

For the more general claim that militiamen would be forced to act contrary to their moral standards, see "A Son of Liberty," *Doc. Hist.* v. 13, 482; "Centinel" 3; "Philadelphiensis" 2, *Doc. Hist.* v. 14, 60, 253. To take but one example, the dissenting members of the Pennsylvania convention claimed that the "militia of Pennsylvania may be marched to New England or Virginia to quell an insurrection occasioned by the most galling oppression, and aided by the standing army, they will no doubt be successful in subduing their liberty and independency; but in so doing, although the magnanimity of their minds will be extinguished, yet the meaner passions of resentment and revenge will be increased, and these in turn will be the ready and obedient instruments of despotism to enslave the others; and that with an irritated vengeance. Thus may the militia be made the instruments of crushing the last efforts of expiring liberty, of riveting the chains of despotism on their fellow citizens, and on one another. This power can be exercised not only without violating the constitution, but in strict conformity with it; it is calculated for this express purpose, and will doubtless be executed accordingly," "Dissent of the Minority of the Pennsylvania Convention," *Doc. Hist.* v. 15, 33.

74. Blackstone wrote of the militia that "the general scheme of which is to discipline a certain number of the inhabitants of every county, chosen by lot for three years, and officered by the lord lieutenant, the deputy lieutenants, and other principal landholders, under a commission from the crown. They are not compellable to march out of their counties, unless in case of invasion or actual rebellion, nor in any case compellable to march out of the kingdom," *Commentaries* 1, 412.

75. "Centinel" 3, *Doc. Hist.* v. 14, 60. For similar statements see William Findley and John Smilie, Pennsylvania ratifying convention, *Doc. Hist.* v. 2, 509–10; Greene Clay, Virginia ratifying convention, *Doc. Hist.* v. 10, 1274; "An Old Whig" 5, *Doc. Hist.* v. 13, 540; Luther Martin, "Genuine Information" 7, *Doc. Hist.* v. 15, 410; Luther Martin, "Address no. I," *Doc. Hist.* v. 16, 419; "Philadelphiensis" 9, ibid., 58. One of the more fantastic claims was that Congress would order the militia to the ten mile square, where Congress would have "exclusive legislation," to be kept there for life, William Lenoir, North Carolina ratifying convention, Elliot, *Debates* 4, 203.

76. In fact, service in the militia both in colonial times and during the war against Britain was notoriously unpopular as is demonstrated by frequent refusals to serve and widespread desertion, Arthur J. Alexander, "Pennsylvania's Revolutionary Militia," *The Pennsylvania Magazine of History and Biography* 69 (1945), 23; Don Higginbotham, "The Military Institutions of Colonial America: The Rhetoric and the Reality," in *War and Society in Revolutionary America: The Wider Dimensions of Conflict* (Columbia: University of South Carolina Press, 1988), 23–4; Douglas Edward Leach, *Arms for Empire: A Military History of the British Colonies in North America, 1607–1763* (New York: Macmillan, 1973), 20; Albert H. Tillson, Jr., "The Militia and Popular Culture in the Upper Valley of Virginia, 1740–1755," *The Virginia Magazine of History and Biography*, 94 (1986), 291, 293–5.

77. "Address of the Minority of the Maryland Convention," *Doc. Hist.* v. 17, 246.

78. George Mason, Virginia ratifying convention, *Doc. Hist.* v. 10, 1272. "Such severities might be exercised on the militia as would make them wish the use of the militia to be utterly abolished; and ascent to the establishment of a standing army," Mason, ibid., 1289; "The government might improperly

oppress and harrass [*sic*] the militia, the better to reconcile them to the idea of regular troops, who might relieve them from the burthen, and to render them less opposed to the measures it might be disposed to adopt for the purpose of reducing them to that state of insignificancy and uselessness," Luther Martin, "Address no. I," *Doc. Hist.* v. 16, 419.

79. Luther Martin, "Speech in the Maryland State House of Assembly," *Doc. Hist.* v. 14, 291.

80. Luther Martin, "Genuine Information" 7, *Doc. Hist.* v. 15, 412. This remark, however, was made with reference to the likelihood that the people would not complain about neglect and disarmament, rather than the oppressiveness, of militia duty. However, this obviously does not challenge the claim that the Antifederalist believed that most citizens found militia service annoying, but rather strengthens it. "In *this* system," Martin wrote, "we give the general government every provision it could wish for, and even *invite* it to *subvert* the *liberties* of the *States* and *their citizens*, since we give them the right to encrease and keep up a standing army as numerous as *it* would wish, and by placing the militia under *its* power, enable it to leave the militia *totally unorganized, undisciplined,* and *even to disarm them;* while the *citizens,* so far from complaining of this *neglect,* might even esteem it a favour in the general government, as thereby they would be freed from the burthen of militia duties, and left to their own private occupations or pleasures."

8: Government by Consent

1. Patrick Henry and James Madison, Virginia ratifying convention, *Doc. Hist.* v. 10, 1300, 1302.

2. South Carolina assembly debates, Elliot, *Debates* 4, 260–1.

3. *Albany Gazette,* 21 June 1787, *Doc. Hist.* v. 13, 143–4: "Let no one suppose that I am an enemy to freedom—I am a friend to liberty, and to secure it inviolate to the people, would wish to banish licentiousness.—But let them know, that without a sacred regard to the laws—a reverential submission to authority—an impartial and sometimes a severe administration of justice—this invaluable jewel, this boasted liberty will be inevitably lost—For when the laws are vague—when the administration of justice becomes feeble and irregular—when political empirics, ever courting popularity, give to a distempered multitude whatever their depraved appetites might crave—when the people are wallowing in the superfluity of liberty—then, unless their eyes were darkened, would they see tyranny in his horrid form, brandishing the bloody scourge and entering the door—then, unless they were deafer than adders, would they hear the chain of slavery clanging in their ears."

4. William Phillips, Massachusetts ratifying convention, Elliot, *Debates* 2, 67. Federalists liked to present their opponents not as enemies to the Constitution as much as enemies to government in general. In a satirical essay, allegedly written by the prolific Pennsylvania Antifederalist "Centinel," the Antifederalists are made to ask "of what service is a man's liberty to him, unless he can do as he pleases? And what man can do as he pleases, who lives under a government?-The very end of government is to bind men down to certain rules and duties; therefore 'tis only fit for slaves and vassals.-Every freeman ought to govern himself, and then he will be governed most to his own mind," "Spurious Centinel" 15, *Doc. Hist.* v. 16, 134.

5. Simeon Baldwin, "4 July Oration," *Doc. Hist.* v. 18, 237.

6. "A Citizen of Philadelphia" [Pelatiah Webster], "Remarks on the Sixteen Members," *Doc. Hist.* v. 13, 304.

7. Thus William Pierce declared himself to be "at a loss to know whether any government can have sufficient energy to effect its own ends without the aid of military power," *Gazette of the State of Georgia,* 20 March 1788, *Doc. Hist.* v. 16, 445.

8. "Letter from New York," *Doc. Hist.* v. 3, 389.

9. [Hamilton] *The Federalist* 27, *Doc. Hist.* v. 15, 97.

10. [Hamilton] *The Federalist* 16, *Doc. Hist.* v. 14, 342–3. Art. VI of the Constitution declares that "this Constitution, and the Laws of the United States which shall be made in Pursuance thereof; and all Treaties made, or which shall be made, under the Authority of the United States, shall be the supreme Law of the Land; and all the Judges in every State shall be bound thereby, any Thing in the Constitution or Laws of any State to the Contrary notwithstanding." Furthermore it states that "all executive and judicial Officers; both of the United States and of the several States, shall be bound by Oath or Affirmation, to support this Constitution."

11. [Hamilton] *The Federalist* 27, *Doc. Hist.* v. 15, 97.

12. [Hamilton] *The Federalist* 16, *Doc. Hist.* v. 14, 342–3.

13. *The Federalist* 27, *Doc. Hist.* v. 15, 97.

14. James Wilson, "Speech at a Public Meeting in Philadelphia," *Doc. Hist.* v. 13, 343. "The good sense of the citizens of the United States is not to be alarmed by the picture of taxes collected at the point of the bayonet. There is no more reason to suppose, that the delegates and representatives in Congress, any more than the legislature of Pennsylvania, or any other state, will act in this manner. Insinuations of this kind, made against one body of men, and not against another, though both the representatives of the people, are not made with propriety, nor will they have the weight of argument," Wilson, Pennsylvania ratifying convention, *Doc. Hist.* v. 2, 558. See also "One of the People," *Doc. Hist.* v. 2, 190; "Publicola" [Archibald Maclaine], "An Address to the Freemen of North Carolina," *Doc. Hist.* v. 16, 440; Virginia *Independent Chronicle,* 28 November 1787, *Doc. Hist.* v. 14, 244.

15. [Hamilton] *The Federalist* 27, *Doc. Hist.* v. 15, 95–6.

16. Art. IV, sect. 4 stated that "The United States shall guarantee to every State in this Union a Republican Form of Government, and shall protect each of them against Invasion; and on Application of the Legislature, or of the Executive (when the Legislature cannot be convened) against domestic Violence." There are numerous statements where Federalists declare that protection against internal violence was one of the primary functions of the union. See for instance Thomas McKean and James Wilson, Pennsylvania ratifying convention, *Doc. Hist.* v. 2, 415, 577; "An Impartial Citizen," *Doc. Hist.* v. 8, 498; "Cassius" 3, *Doc. Hist.* v. 9, 754; [Hamilton] *The Federalist* 23, *Doc. Hist.* v. 15, 4; Edmund Randolph, "Letter on the Federal Constitution," ibid., 123.

17. [Hamilton] *The Federalist* 25, *Doc. Hist.* v. 15, 62–3; "Brutus" 10, ibid., 466.

18. Or, as Hamilton put it, "a force constituted different from the militia," [Hamilton] *The Federalist* 28, ibid., 103–4.

19. Virginia ratifying convention, *Doc. Hist.* v. 10, 1269.

20. *The Federalist* 43, *Doc. Hist.* v. 15, 443.

21. "Landholder" 5 [Oliver Ellsworth], *Doc. Hist.* v. 14, 336. In the South

Carolina assembly. Edward Rutledge said that "if a spirit of resistance should appear, surely it ought to be in the power of government to compel a coercion in the people," South Carolina assembly debates, Elliot, *Debates* 4, 299.

22. *The Federalist* 43, *Doc. Hist.* v. 15, 443. "I take no notice of an unhappy species of population abounding in some of the States, who during the calm of regular government are sunk below the level of men; but who in the tempestuous scenes of civil violence may emerge into the human character, and give a superiority of strength to any party with which they may associate themselves."

23. Ibid., 442–3.

24. Edmund Randolph, "Letter on the Federal Constitution," *Doc. Hist.* v. 15, 125.

25. *The Federalist* 28, *Doc. Hist.* v. 15, 102–3.

26. Ibid., 104.

27. "Plain Truth," "Reply to an Officer of the Late Continental Army," *Doc. Hist.* v. 2, 220; James Wilson, Pennsylvania ratifying convention, *Doc. Hist.* v. 2, 478; Alexander White, Winchester *Virginia Gazette*, 22 February, *Doc. Hist.* v. 8, 406; "An American Citizen" 4 [Tench Coxe], *Doc. Hist.* v. 13, 435; [Hamilton] *The Federalist* 8, *Doc. Hist.* v. 14, 145; [Hamilton] *The Federalist* 28, *Doc. Hist.* v. 15, 102–3; [Madison] *The Federalist* 46, ibid., 492–3; "Aristides" [Alexander Contee Hanson], ibid., 533.

28. "Cincinnatus" 4, *Doc. Hist.* v. 14, 186 (quotation); Providence *United States Chronicle*, 5 June 1788, *Doc. Hist.* v. 18, appendix 1, 376 (100,000); "Dissent of the Minority of the Pennsylvania Convention," *Doc. Hist.* v. 15, 33; "Brutus" 9, ibid., 396.

29. "Centinel" 2, *Doc. Hist.* v. 13, 465; "Philadelphiensis" 4, *Doc. Hist.* v. 14, 420.

30. *The Federalist* 46, *Doc. Hist.* v. 15, 492; "Aristides" [Alexander Contee Hanson], ibid., 551 (note [m]).

31. Richard H. Kohn, *Eagle and Sword: The Federalists and the Creation of the Military Establishment in America, 1783–1802* (New York: Free Press, 1975), 48.

32. "Report on a Military Peace Establishment," 18 June 1783, in *PAH* 3, 378–97.

33. "A Citizen of Philadelphia" [Pelatiah Webster], "Remarks on the Address of Sixteen Members," *Doc. Hist.* v. 13, 302; [Hamilton] *The Federalist* 28, *Doc. Hist.* v. 15, 105.

34. The possession of these military posts would "include the command of large districts of territory and facilitate future invasions of the remainder," *The Federalist* 24, *Doc. Hist.* v. 15, 42–3; James Wilson, Pennsylvania ratifying convention, *Doc. Hist.* v. 2, 577.

35. Hugh Williamson, "Public Speech in Edenton," *Doc. Hist.* v. 16, 206.

36. Harrison Gray Otis, "4 July Oration," *Doc. Hist.* v. 18, 228; "Americanus," *Doc. Hist.* v. 13, 72; *Pittsburgh Gazette*, *Doc. Hist.* v. 14, 136. A correspondent to the Virginia *Independent Chronicle* believed that a standing army was needed to protect the exposed frontier "from indiscriminating cruelties and horrid devastations of the savages." "Let a man reflect a moment on the promiscuous scenes of carnage committed by Indians in their midnight excursions, and he must have a heart callous indeed, if he would object to an army supported for the benevolent purpose of preventing them," Virginia *Independent Chronicle*, 28 November 1787, *Doc. Hist.* v. 14, 245. Only a strong government

could keep the Indians at bay. "Let the citizens of America who inhabit the western counties of our states fly to a fœderal power for protection," wrote Benjamin Rush. "The Indians know too well the dreadful consequences of confederacy in arms, ever to disturb the peaceful husbandman, who is under the cover of the arsenals of thirteen states," Harrington, *Doc. Hist.* v. 13, 119. While the Philadelphia Convention was drawing to its close the *Pennsylvania Gazette* wrote that all economic activities had ground to a halt while the entire nation was holding its breath in anticipation of the result. "The embarrassed farmer and the oppressed tenant, who wish to become free and independent, by emigrating to a frontier county, wait to see whether they shall be protected by a national force from the Indians" *Pennsylvania Gazette*, 29 August 1787, ibid., 191.

37. But Hamilton also argued that in addition to guarding the western frontier "moderate garrisons" would also be necessary in the seaports to guard dock-yards, arsenals and the navy and merchant ships. These troops "will in all likelihood be found an indispensable security against descents for the destruction of the arsenals and dock-yards and sometimes of the fleet itself," *The Federalist* 24, *Doc. Hist.* v. 15, 42–3.

38. Figures are taken from Brewer, *The Sinews of Power: War, Money and the English State, 1688–1783* (London: Unwin Hyman, 1989), 32 (British army); Roger Schofield, "British Population Change, 1700–1871," in *The Economic History of Britain since 1700*, ed. Roderick Floud and Donald McCloskey, 3 vols. (Cambridge, U.K.: Cambridge University Press, 1994, 2d ed.), I, tables 4.1 and 4.7; U.S. Bureau of the Census, *Historical Statistics of the United States, Colonial Times to 1970, Bicentennial Edition* (Washington, D.C., 1975), 8; André Corvisier, *Armies and Societies in Europe, 1494–1789* (Bloomington: Indiana University Press, 1979), table 1, 113 (ratio of soldiers to civilians, Prussia). Note that the figures for Irish and Scottish population are from 1800 which may mean that the ratio of soldiers to civilians was somewhat higher in 1790 than my computations suggests.

39. According to this view, British freedom was in fact the result of geography: "If . . . Britain had been situated on the continent, and had been compelled, as she would have been, by that situation, to make her military establishments at home co-extensive with those of the other great powers of Europe, she, like them, would in all probability, be at this day a victim to the absolute power of a single man. 'Tis possible, though not easy, that the people of that island may be enslaved from other causes, but it cannot be by the powers of an army so inconsiderable as that which has been usually kept up in that kingdom," [Hamilton] *The Federalist* 8, *Doc. Hist.* v. 14, 146.

40. [Madison] *The Federalist* 41, *Doc. Hist.* v. 15, 421; [Hamilton] *The Federalist* 8, *Doc. Hist.* v. 14, 146. Similarly, Tench Coxe wrote that "our *detached* situation will seldom give occasion to raise an army, though *a few scattered companies* may often be necessary," "An American Citizen" 4, *Doc. Hist.* v. 13, 435.

41. [Madison] *The Federalist* 41, *Doc. Hist.* v. 15, 421. Here Madison is echoing Hamilton's words in *Federalist* 8. "If we are wise enough to preserve the Union, we may for ages enjoy an advantage similar to that of an insulated situation. . . . But if we should be disunited, and the integral parts should either remain separated, or which is the most probable, should be thrown together into two or three confederacies, we should be in a short course of time, in the

predicament of the continental powers of Europe—our liberties would be a prey to the means of defending ourselves against the ambition and jealousy of each other," *Doc. Hist.* v. 14, 146. For a discussion of the Federalist contrast between the union as one mode of organizing the relations between the American states and the balance of power characteristic of the contemporary European state system as the other, see Cathy D. Matson and Peter Onuf, *A Union of Interests: Political and Economic Thought in Revolutionary America* (Lawrence: University Press of Kansas, 1990), 134–41, 145–6; Peter Onuf and Nicholas Onuf, *Federal Union, Modern World: The Law of Nations in an Age of Revolutions 1776–1814* (Madison: Madison House, 1993), 130–3.

42. George Washington, "Sentiments on a Peace Establishment," 1 May 1783, *The Writings of George Washington, from the Original Manuscript Sources, 1747–1799,* ed. John C. Fitzpatrick, 39 vols. (Washington, D.C.: U.S. Government Printing Office, 1931–44), 26, 374–97; Hamilton, "Report on a Military Peace Establishment," *PAH* 3, 378–97.

43. Lawrence D. Cress, "Republican Liberty and National Security: American Military Policy as an Ideological Problem, 1783 to 1789," *WMQ*, 3d ser. 38 (1981), 91–4.

44. *The Federalist* 29, *Doc. Hist.* v. 15, 318–19; George Nicholas, Virginia ratifying convention, *Doc. Hist.* v. 10, 1314. In the Virginia convention Madison said that "the only possible way to provide against standing armies, is, to make them unnecessary. The way to do this is to organize and discipline our militia, so as to render them capable of defending the country against external invasions, and internal insurrections," ibid., 1302.

45. See the statements by James Wilson, Pennsylvania ratifying convention, *Doc. Hist.* v. 2, 577–8; Alexander White, Winchester *Virginia Gazette,* 29 February 1788, *Doc. Hist.* v. 8, 441; Edmund Randolph, Virginia ratifying convention, *Doc. Hist.* v. 10, 1289; An American 4 [Tench Coxe], *Doc. Hist.* v. 13, 435.

46. *The Federalist* 29, *Doc. Hist.* v. 15, 320–1.

47. Virginia ratifying convention, *Doc. Hist.* v. 9, 955; Edmund Randolph, ibid., 984.

48. "Philadelphiensis" 4 [Benjamin Workman], *Doc. Hist.* v. 14, 420; "On the New Constitution," *Doc. Hist.* v. 15, 486. See also Nason, Massachusetts ratifying convention, Elliot, *Debates* 2, 137; "A Democratic Federalist," *Doc. Hist.* v. 13, 390–1; "Cincinnatus" 3; "Cincinnatus" 4, *Doc. Hist.* v. 14, 127, 181.

49. "Denatus," *Doc. Hist.* v. 10, 1603–4.

50. Ibid., 1605.

51. [Hamilton] *The Federalist* 29, *Doc. Hist.* v. 15, 320; [Hamilton] *The Federalist* 24, ibid., 42; "Aristides" [Alexander Contee Hanson], ibid., 532–3; [Hamilton] *The Federalist* 8, *Doc. Hist.* v. 14, 144.

52. Edmund Randolph, Virginia ratifying convention, *Doc. Hist.* v. 9, 981; [Hamilton], *The Federalist* 24; [Hamilton], *The Federalist* 29, *Doc. Hist.* v. 15, 42, 320.

53. [Hamilton], *The Federalist* 24, ibid., 42.

54. Francis Corbin, Virginia ratifying convention, *Doc. Hist.* v. 9, 1014–15. See also Henry Lee: "Regulars are to be employed when necessary; and the service of the militia will always be made use of. This, Sir, will promote agricultural industry and skill, and military discipline and science," Henry Lee, Virginia ratifying convention, ibid., 1074.

1. "Seventh Annual Address," *A Compilation of the Messages and Papers of the Presidents 1789–1908* I (Washington, D.C.: Bureau of National Literature and Art, 1908), 182–6. Although he had then left the government, the address was drafted by Hamilton; see *PAH* 19, 460–7.

2. "Seventh Annual Address," *Messages and Papers of the Presidents* I, 182–4.

3. Ibid., 184–6.

4. Samuel Flagg Bemis, *Jay's Treaty: A Study in Commerce and Diplomacy* (New Haven, Conn.: Yale University Press, 1962 rev. ed.), 318–45; Bemis, *Pinckney's Treaty: America's Advantage from Europe's Distress, 1783–1800* (New Haven, Conn.: Yale University Press, 1960 rev. ed), 218–19, 229–35, 267–83; Jerald A. Combs, *The Jay Treaty: Political Battleground of the Founding Fathers* (Berkeley: University of California Press, 1970), 137, 145–8; Bradford Perkins, *The Cambridge History of American Foreign Relations* I: *The Creation of a Republican Empire, 1776–1865* (Cambridge, U.K.: Cambridge University Press, 1993), 98, 100.

5. *Doc. Hist.* v. 14, 212.

6. Stanley L. Engerman and Robert E. Gallman, "U.S. Economic Growth, 1783–1860," *Research in Economic History* 8 (1983), 17–19; Cathy Matson, "The Revolution, the Constitution, and the New Nation," in *The Cambridge Economic History of the United States* I: *The Colonial Era*, ed. Stanley L. Engerman and Robert E. Gallman (Cambridge, U.K.: Cambridge University Press, 1996), 373–7; John J. McCusker and Russel R. Menard, *The Economy of British America, 1607–1789* (Chapel Hill: University of North Carolina Press, 1985), 373–77; John J. McCusker, "Estimating Early American Gross Domestic Product," *Historical Methods* 33 (2000), 155–62; Jacob Price, "Reflections on the Economy of Revolutionary America," in *The Economy of Early America: The Revolutionary Period, 1763–1790*, ed. Ronald Hoffman (Charlottesville: University Press of Virginia, 1988), 321–2; James F. Shepherd and Gary M. Walton, "Economic Change after the American Revolution: Pre- and Post-War Comparisons of Maritime Shipping and Trade," *Explorations in Economic History*, 2d ser. 13 (1976), 397–422.

7. McCusker, "Estimating," 10 and table 1. See also Matson, "Revolution, Constitution and, New Nation," 375–6; McCusker and Menard, *Economy of British America*, 373–7; McCusker, *How Much Is That in Real Money? A Historical Price Index for Use as a Deflator of Money Values in the Economy of the United States* (Worcester, Mass.: American Antiquarian Society, 1992), table D-1.

8. Douglass C. North, *The Economic Growth of the United States, 1790–1860* (New York: Norton, 1966); Claudia D. Goldin and Frank D. Lewis, "The Role of Exports in American Economic Growth during the Napoleonic Wars, 1793 to 1807," *Explorations in Economic History*, 2d. ser. 17 (1980), 6–25; Douglass C. North, Terry L. Anderson, and Peter J. Hill, *Growth and Welfare in the American Past: A New Economic History* (Englewood Cliffs, NJ: Prentice-Hall, 1983, 3d ed.), 69.

9. Matson, "Revolution, Constitution, and New Nation," 373–4.

10. North, *Economic Growth*, 26, 221.

11. Stanley Elkins and Eric McKittrick, *The Age of Federalism: The Early American Republic, 1788–1800* (New York: Oxford University Press, 1993), 382.

12. For Republican political economy and for the Republicans' visions for

the American republic, see above all Drew R. McCoy, *The Elusive Republic: Political Economy in Jeffersonian America* (Chapel Hill: University of North Carolina Press, 1980); McCoy, "An Unfinished Revolution: The Quest for Economic Independence in the Early Republic," in *The American Revolution: Its Character and Limits*, ed. Jack P. Greene (New York: New York University Press, 1987), 131–48; John R. Nelson, Jr., *Liberty and Property: Political Economy and Policymaking in the New Nation, 1789–1812* (Baltimore: Johns Hopkins University Press, 1987).

13. Bemis, *Jay's Treaty*, 265–78; Combs, *Jay Treaty*, 120–36; Elkins and McKitrick, *Age of Federalism*, 388–96; John C. Miller, *The Federalist Era, 1789–1801* (New York: Harper, 1960), 148–54; James Roger Sharp, *American Politics in the Early Republic: The New Nation in Crisis* (New Haven, Conn.: Yale University Press, 1993), 115–16; An Act to Provide for the Defence of Certain Ports and Harbors in the United States, Act of March 20, 1794, ch. IX, 1 *Stat.*, 345–6.

14. Perkins, *Cambridge History of American Foreign Relations* 1, 99.

15. Bemis, *Jay's Treaty*, 289–98.

16. Ibid., 371–3; Elkins and McKitrick, *Age of Federalism*, 410–12.

17. For Spain's policy and western reaction as well as Pinckney's Treaty, see Bemis, *Pinckney's Treaty*; Andrew R. L. Cayton, " 'Separate Interests' and the Nation-State: The Washington Administration and the Origins of Regionalism in the Trans-Appalachian West," *JAH*, 79 (1992), 39–67; Cayton, "Radicals in the 'Western World': The Federalist Conquest of Trans-Appalachian North America," in *Federalists Reconsidered*, ed. Doron Ben-Atar and Barbara B. Oberg (Charlottesville: University Press of Virginia, 1998), 77–96; James E. Lewis, Jr., *The American Union and the Problem of Neighborhood: The United States and the Collapse of the Spanish Empire, 1783–1829* (Chapel Hill, University of North Carolina Press, 1998), 12–24; Arthur P. Whitaker, *The Spanish-American Frontier: 1783–1795, The Westward Movement and the Spanish Retreat in the Mississippi Valley* (Gloucester, Mass.: Peter Smith, 1962).

18. U.S. Bureau of the Census, *Historical Statistics of the United States, Colonial Times to 1970. Bicentennial Edition* I (Washington, D.C., 1975), 24–37.

19. Cayton, "Radicals in the 'Western World," 95–6.

20. See for instance Miller, *Federalist Era*, 155–62; Thomas P. Slaughter, "The Tax Man Cometh: Ideological Opposition to Internal Taxes, 1760–1790," *WMQ*, 3d ser. 41 (1984), 590–1. Quotation from Gary J. Kornblith and John M. Murrin, "The Making and Unmaking of an American Ruling Class," in *Beyond the American Revolution: Explorations in the History of American Radicalism*, ed. Alfred F. Young (DeKalb: Northern Illinois University Press, 1993), 61.

21. Richard H. Kohn, "The Washington Administration's Decision to Crush the Whiskey Rebellion," *JAH* 59 (1972), 568–72; Act of March 3, 1791, ch. XV, 1 *Stat.* 199–214; Act of December 27, 1792, ch. XXXI, 1 *Stat.* 267–71. Accounts and discussions of the Whiskey Rebellion can be found in Elkins and McKitrick, *Age of Federalism*, 461–88; Miller, *Federalist Era*, 155–9; Sharp, *American Politics*, 92–8; Thomas P. Slaughter, *The Whiskey Rebellion: Frontier Epilogue to the American Revolution* (New York: Oxford University Press, 1986); *The Whiskey Rebellion: Past and Present Perspectives*, ed. Steven R. Boyd (Westport, Conn.: Greenwood Press, 1985).

22. Act of May 2, 1792, ch. XXVIII, 1 *Stat.* 264.

23. "A Proclamation" *Messages and Papers of the Presidents* 1, 158–60, quotation at 160; *PAH* 17, 24–58, quotation at 34.

24. Kohn, "Washington Administration's Decision," 581; Saul Cornell, *The Other Founders: Anti-Federalism and the Dissenting Tradition in America, 1788–1828* (Chapel Hill: University of North Carolina Press, 1999), 200–13.

25. "Resolutions, January 8, 1795"; "Manuscript Minutes, December 8, 1794," in *The Democratic-Republican Societies, 1790–1800: A Documentary Sourcebook of Constitutions, Declarations, Addresses, Resolutions, and Toasts,* ed. Philip S. Foner (Westport: Greenwood, 1976), 304, 101. See also "Resolutions Adopted Condemning Opposition of Citizens of Western Pennsylvania to the Excise, September 22, 1794"; "Resolutions Adopted on the Conduct of Citizens in Western Pennsylvania, August 20, 1794," in ibid., 147, 183; Elkins and McKitrick, *Age of Federalism,* 482–3.

26. Ibid., 696–700; Robert W. Coakley, "Federal Use of Militia and the National Guard in Civil Disturbances: The Whiskey Rebellion to Little Rock," in *Bayonets in the Streets: The Use of Troops in Civil Disturbances,* ed. R. Higham (Lawrence: University of Kansas Press, 1969), 23; Coakley, *The Role of Federal Military Forces in Domestic Disorders 1789–1878* (Washington, D.C.: Center of Military History United States Army, 1988), 69–77. For Fries's Rebellion see also the special issue of *Pennsylvania History* 66 (2000), 5–171.

27. Act of March 3, 1807, ch. XXXIX, 2 *Stat.* 443; Leonard Levy, *Jefferson and Civil Liberties, the Darker Side* (Cambridge, Mass.: Harvard University Press, 1963), 93–141, quotation at 137; Coakley, "Federal Use of Militia," 23–5; Coakley, *Role of Federal Military Forces,* 77–90; Forrest McDonald, *The Presidency of Thomas Jefferson* (Lawrence: University Press of Kansas, 1976), 148–52; Leonard D. White, *The Jeffersonians: A Study in Administrative History 1801–1829* (New York: Macmillan, 1951), 423–52.

28. Coakley, "Federal Use of Militia," 25–6; Barton C. Hacker, "The United States Army as a National Police Force: The Federal Policing of Labor Disputes, 1877–1898," *Military Affairs* 32 (1969), 255–64. See also Jerry M. Cooper, *The Army and Civil Disorder: Federal Military Intervention in Labor Disputes, 1877–1900* (Westport, Conn.: Greenwood Press, 1980).

29. *Historical Statistics* 2, 1141–3; John K. Mahon, "History of the Organization of United States Infantry," in *The Army Lineage Book 2: Infantry* (Washington, D.C.: United States Department of the Army, Office of Military History, 1953), 8–12, 58–9.

30. Kohn, *Eagle and Sword: The Federalists and the Creation of the Military Establishment in America, 1783–1802* (New York: Free Press 1975), 91–127, 174–89, 281; Francis Paul Prucha, *The Sword of the Republic: The United States Army on the Frontier 1783–1846* (Bloomington: Indiana University Press, 1969); Michael S. Fitzgerald, "Rejecting Calhoun's Expansible Army Plan: The Army Reduction Act of 1821," *War in History* 3 (1996), 161–85.

31. Kohn, *Eagle and Sword,* 286; Karl-Friedrich Walling, *Republican Empire: Alexander Hamilton on War and Free Government* (Lawrence: University Press of Kansas, 1999). For John Adams's and the Adams Federalists' opposition to the army buildup, see Ralph Adams Brown, *The Presidency of John Adams* (Lawrence: University Press of Kansas, 1975), 70, 85; Alexander DeConde, *The Quasi War: The Politics and Diplomacy of the Undeclared War with France 1797–1801* (New York: Charles Scribner's Sons, 1966), 112, 263–6; Stephen G. Kurtz, *The Presidency of John Adams: The Collapse of Federalism 1795–1800* (Philadelphia: University of Pennsylvania Press, 1957), 360, 366, 369–73, 384–5, 387, 389–90, 403–4, 407.

32. Kohn, *Eagle and Sword*, 91–107.

33. Ibid., 107–27; Prucha, *Sword of the Republic*, 17–40.

34. *Annals of Congress*, 4th Cong. 1st sess., 905–13, 1418–1423, 1428–30, quotation at 910; Kohn, *Eagle and Sword*, 186; J.C.A. Stagg, *Mr. Madison's War: Politics, Diplomacy, and Warfare in the Early American Republic, 1783–1830* (Princeton: Princeton University Press, 1983), 124–30. See also the House debate in February 1797, *Annals of Congress*, 4th Cong. 2d sess., 1944–63, 1966–82, 2066–74, 2079–89. Contrary to the claim advanced here, Lawrence Cress emphasizes the continuity of the anti-army argument throughout the 1790s; see *Citizens in Arms: The Army and the Militia in American Society to the War of 1812* (Chapel Hill: University of North Carolina Press, 1982), 132–4.

35. Kohn, *Eagle and Sword*, 186, 268–8.

36. "First Inaugural Address," *Messages and Papers of the President* 1, 323.

37. *Historical Statistics* 1, 8; *ibid.* 2, 1141–3.

38. For the army in the period up to the Civil War, see Prucha, *Sword of the Republic*, and Durwood Ball, *Army Regulars on the Western Frontier* (Norman: University of Oklahoma Press, 2001).

39. "First Annual Message," *Messages and Papers of the President* 1, 329; *The Writings of George Washington from the Original Manuscript Sources, 1747–1799*, ed. John C. Fitzpatrick, 39 vols. (Washington, D.C.: U.S. Government Printing Office, 1931–44), 26, 374–97

40. Washington, "First Annual Address," and Jefferson, "First Annual Message," *Messages and Papers of the Presidents* 1, 65, 329.

41. John Vining, *Annals of Congress*, 1st Cong., 3d sess., 1855.

42. *Annals of Congress*, 1st Cong., appendix, 2146–53.

43. *Journal of William Maclay, United States Senator from Pennsylvania, 1789–1791*, ed. Edgar S. Maclay (New York: Appleton, 1890), 241.

44. Act of May 8, 1792, ch. XXXIII, 1 *Stat.* 271–4; *Annals of Congress*, 1st Cong., 3d sess., 1851–75; ibid., 2d Cong., 1st sess., 418–24, 552–6, 474–80.

45. Fitzsimons, ibid., 1st Cong. 3d sess., 1852; Hillhouse, ibid., 3d Cong. 2d sess., 1216–17; ibid., 5th Cong. 2d sess., 1385.

46. Sedgwick, ibid., 3d Cong. 2nd sess., 1216.

47. Secondary accounts of the history of the militia can be found in John K. Mahon, *The American Militia: Decade of Decision, 1789–1800* (Gainesville: University of Florida, 1969); Mahon, *History of the Militia and the National Guard* (New York: Macmillan, 1983), 46–153.

48. Randolph quoted in Fitzgerald, "Rejecting Calhoun's Expansible Army Plan," 161; Lance Banning, *The Jeffersonian Persuasion: Evolution of a Party Ideology* (Ithaca, N.Y.: Cornell University Press, 1978), 299–300. For the War of 1812, see Donald R. Hickey, *The War of 1812: A Forgotten Conflict* (Urbana and Chicago: University of Illinois Press, 1990); C. Edward Skeen, *Citizen Soldiers in the War of 1812* (Lexington: University Press of Kentucky, 1999); Stagg, *Mr Madison's War*.

49. Banning, *Jeffersonian Persuasion*, 299 (quotation); Cress, *Citizens in Arms*, 176.

50. Michael S. Fitzgerald, " 'Nature Unsubdued': Diplomacy, Expansion and the American Military Buildup of 1815–1816," *Mid-America: An Historical Review*, 77 (1995), 5–32.

51. Fitzgerald, "Rejecting Calhoun's Expansible Army Plan," 161–85.

10: Congressional Insolvency

1. Since I have no interest in apportioning guilt, it matters little if the people were able but unwilling, or indeed unable, to pay the costs of the national government. What matters to my argument is that the people did not pay and that the existing structure of government made it difficult to extract money by means of coercion.

2. E. James Ferguson, *The Power of the Purse: A History of American Public Finance, 1776–1790* (Chapel Hill: University of North Carolina Press, 1961), 29–31.

3. David Hume juxtaposed modern habits with the practice of antiquity in his essay "Of Public Credit," in *Political Essays*, ed. Knud Haakonssen (Cambridge, U.K.: Cambridge University Press, 1994), 166–7.

4. John Brewer, *The Sinews of Power: War, Money and the English State, 1688–1783* (London: Unwin Hyman, 1989), table 2.1, 30; Richard Bonney, "The Eighteenth Century II: The Struggle for Great Power Status and the End of the Old Fiscal Regime," *Economic Systems and State Finance*, ed. Bonney (Oxford: Oxford University Press, 1995), 345.

5. The British system of public finance and taxation will be further discussed in chapter 11.

6. According to James Ferguson "the habit of resorting to currency emissions was so ingrained in the colonists that nothing else was seriously considered," *Power of the Purse*, 26. In much the same way Edwin J. Perkins remarks that the performance during the 1750s and early 1760s instilled in the colonial governments a confidence that "future challenges could be met with equal dispatch by employing similar strategies and policies." In fact, argues Perkins, the "outstanding financial performance" of the colonies contributed to the colonies' decision to break with Britain and risk war in 1776, *American Public Finance and Financial Services 1700–1815* (Columbus: Ohio State University Press, 1994), 94.

7. Accounts of the continental currency can be found in Ferguson, *Power of the Purse*, ch. 2–4, especially 25–6, 31–2, 44–7, 51–2, 65–7 and Perkins, *American Public Finance*, ch. 5, esp. 95–105. A brief account is in Robert A. Becker, "Currency, Taxation and Finance, 1775–1787," in *The Blackwell Encyclopedia of the American Revolution*, ed. Jack P. Greene and Jack R. Pole (Oxford: Blackwell, 1991), 364.

8. E. James Ferguson, "Currency Finance: An Interpretation of Colonial Monetary Practices," *WMQ*, 3d ser. 10 (1953), 167–75 and *passim*; Ferguson, *Power of the Purse*, 26–7. Although mostly used in war, currency finance methods were sometimes also used in peacetime but then on a much lesser scale and in a slightly different way.

9. Ferguson, *Power of the Purse*, 19, 26–30, 33–5, 46–7, 65–7; Perkins, *American Public Finance*, 96–9 and table 5.2.

10. Thus Benjamin Franklin wrote that the "general effect of the depreciation among the inhabitants of the states has been this, that it has operated as a *gradual tax* upon them, their business has been done and paid for by the paper money, and every man has paid his share of the tax according to the time he retained any of the money in his hands, and to the depreciation within that time. Thus it has proved a tax on money, a kind of property very difficult to be taxed in any other mode; and it has fallen more equally than many other

taxes, as those people paid most, who being richest had most money passing through their hands," quoted in Becker, "Currency," 368.

11. Perkins, *American Public Finance*, ch. 15, 324–48.

12. Ferguson, *Power of the Purse*, 35–40, 53–5, 68–9, 179–80.

13. Ibid., 252–3.

14. Roger H. Brown, *Redeeming the Republic: Federalism, Taxation, and the Origins of the Constitution* (Baltimore: Johns Hopkins University Press, 1993), 25–6.

15. Ferguson, *Power of the Purse*, 127–9, 235, 237–8.

16. Ibid., 57–64; E. Wayne Carp, *To Starve the Army at Pleasure: Continental Army Administration and American Political Culture, 1775–1783* (Chapel Hill: University of North Carolina Press, 1984), 171–87. "Mass expropriation" is the title of ch. 4 of Ferguson, *Power of the Purse*.

17. *The Federalist* 30, *Doc. Hist.* v. 15, 161.

18. William Blackstone wrote in his *Commentaries on the Laws of England* that "no subject of England can be constrained to pay any aids or taxes, even for the defence of the realm or the support of government, but such as are imposed by his own consent, or that of his representatives in parliament," *Commentaries on the Laws of England* 4 vols. (Oxford, 1775, 7th ed.) 1, 140.

19. This was the view of some quartermaster and commissary officers during the War of Independence. See Carp, *To Starve the Army at Pleasure*, 84.

20. The texts of the impost proposals can be found in *Doc. Hist.* v. 1, 140–1 and 146–8. Accounts of the proposals are in Ferguson, *Power of the Purse*, 109–76; E. James Ferguson, "The Nationalists of 1781–1783 and the Economic Interpretation of the Constitution," *JAH*, 56 (1969), 241–53; Merrill Jensen, *The New Nation: A History of the United States During the Confederation, 1781–1789* (New York: Knopf, 1950), 407–21; John P. Kaminski and Gaspare J. Saladino, "Introduction," *Doc. Hist.* v. 13, 13–22. For New York incomes from the impost, see Brown, *Redeeming the Republic*, 134–5; John P. Kaminski, "Adjusting to Circumstances: New York's Relationship with the Federal Government 1776–1788," in *The Constitution and the States: The Role of the Original Thirteen in the Framing and Adoption of the Federal Constitution*, ed. Patrick T. Conley and Kaminski (Madison: Madison House, 1988), 227–31.

21. Brown, *Redeeming the Republic*, 24–8 and table 2.

22. The preceding three paragraphs are based on ibid., 32–138. Brown focuses on Pennsylvania, South Carolina, Rhode Island, and Massachusetts (53–121) and provides sketches of the other nine states (122–38). Other useful works on individual states are John P. Kaminski, "Democracy Run Rampant: Rhode Island in the Confederation," in *The Human Dimensions of Nation Making: Essays on Colonial and Revolutionary America*, ed. James Kirby Martin (Madison: State Historical Society of Wisconsin, 1976), 243–69; Eric C. Papenfuse, "The Legislative Response to a Costly War: Fiscal Policy and Factional Politics in Maryland, 1777–1789," in *Sovereign States in an Age of Uncertainty*, eds. Ronald H. Hoffman and Peter J. Albert (Charlottesville: University Press of Virginia, 1981), 134–56; Robert A. Becker, "Salus Populi Suprema Lex: Public Peace and South Carolina Debtor Relief Laws, 1783–1788," *South Carolina Historical Magazine*, 80 (1979), 65–75. The first published work to argue that Shays's Rebellion was caused by heavy taxes and heavy handed tax administration was Ellen Shapiro and Forrest McDonald, "On the Late Disturbances in Massachusetts," in *Requiem: Variations on Eighteenth-Century Themes* (Lawrence: University

Press of Kansas, 1988), 59–83. Their view has been supported by Brown, *Redeeming the Republic*, 97–121 and by Perkins, *American Public Finance*, 173–86. Rhode Island, New York, New Jersey, Pennsylvania, North Carolina, South Carolina, and Georgia emitted paper money in the 1780s. Older accounts of the emissions are in Jensen, *The New Nation*, 313–26 and Forrest McDonald, *E Pluribus Unum: The Formation of the American Republic 1776–1790* (Indianapolis: Liberty Press, 2d ed. 1979 [1965]), 80, 97–9, 111–13, 146–8, 179–81, whereas a recent one can be found in Perkins, *American Public Finance*, 137–72.

23. H. James Henderson, "Taxation and Political Culture: Massachusetts and Virginia, 1760–1800," *WMQ*, 3d ser., 47 (1990), 93–5 and notes 4–5; Robert A. Becker, *Revolution, Reform, and the Politics of American Taxation, 1763–1783* (Baton Rouge: Louisiana State University Press, 1980), 9–10, 34–5, 37–8, 69–71, 106–7; Marvin L. Michael Kay, "The Payment of Provincial and Local Taxes in North Carolina, 1748–1771," *WMQ*, 3d ser. 36 (1969), 219–20.

24. Jack P. Greene, *The Intellectual Construction of America: Exceptionalism and Identity from 1492 to 1800* (Chapel Hill: University of North Carolina Press, 1993), 72–3, 100.

25. Perkins, *American Public Finance*, 88–95.

26. For British taxation see Patrick K. O'Brien, "The Political Economy of British Taxation, 1660–1815," *Economic History Review*, 2d ser. 41 (1988), tables 2 and 5; Brewer, *Sinews of Power*, 95, 99, and figures 4.2 and 4.3; J. V. Beckett and M. Turner, "Taxation and Economic Growth in Eighteenth-Century England," *Economic History Review*, 2d ser. 43 (1990), table 1, 380–1. It has been estimated that on the eve of independence four-fifths of the American population was employed in agriculture, John J. McCusker and Russell R. Menard, *The Economy of British America, 1607–1789* (Chapel Hill: University of North Carolina Press, 1985), 248. For the claim that American farmers found taxes hard to pay because of specie shortage, see Brown, *Redeeming the Republic*, 34, 37–8, 39–40. For a discussion of the use and effect of indirect taxation in America, see Becker, *Revolution, Reform, and American Taxation*, 42–3, 45–7, 77–80, and tables 8 and 9 in the appendix; Mark D. Kaplanoff, "The Hamiltonian Moment," paper presented at the 1998 meeting of the Society for Historians of the Early Republic (SHEAR), Harpers Ferry, West Virginia.

27. Brown, *Redeeming the Republic*, 48, 49, 71, 73, 74, 85–6, 96, 102, 141–3 and ch. 11, especially 157–67 and 189–90.

28. Kaplanoff, "Hamiltonian Moment."

29. Ibid. Accounts of the federal assumption of state debts can be found in Stanley Elkins and Eric McKitrick, *The Age of Federalism: The Early American Republic, 1788–1800* (New York: Oxford University Press, 1993), 114–23; Ferguson, *Power of the Purse*, 289–325; Perkins, *American Public Finance*, 199–234. A discussion of possible intellectual influences on Hamilton is in the introductory note to Hamilton's "Report Relative to a Provision for the Support of Public Credit," *PAH* 6, 51–65.

30. Jensen, *The New Nation*, 83–4, 388–9, 400, 426–7, quotations at 400 and 426.

31. This and the preceding paragraph are based on Curtis P. Nettels, *The Emergence of a National Economy, 1775–1815* (New York: Knopf, 1962), 90–6; Ferguson, *Power of the Purse*, 120–1, 124; Ferguson, "The Nationalists of 1781–1783," 241, 247–9, 259–61; Ferguson, "Political Economy, Public Liberty and

the Formation of the Constitution," *WMQ*, 3d ser. 40 (1983), 389–412; Janet A. Riesman, "Money, Credit, and Federalist Political Economy," in *Beyond Confederation: Origins of the Constitution and American National Identity*, ed. Richard Beeman, Stephen Botein, and Edward C. Carter II (Chapel Hill: University of North Carolina Press, 1987), 137–48.

32. Ferguson, *Power of the Purse*, 124, 289; Ferguson, "The Nationalists of 1781–1783," 247.

33. Ferguson, *Power of the Purse*, 221–3, 228–34.

34. "A Citizen of Philadelphia" [Pelatiah Webster], *Doc. Hist.* v. 2, 660; Benjamin Rush, Pennsylvania ratifying convention, *Doc. Hist.* v. 2, 457–8; "Demosthenes Minor," *Doc. Hist.* v. 3, 245; "A State Soldier" 5, *Doc. Hist.* v. 9, 650; James Wilson, "Speech at a Public Meeting in Philadelphia, 6 October 1787," *Doc. Hist.* v. 13, 343; David Ramsay, South Carolina House of Representatives, Elliot, *Debates* 4, 286.

35. Ferguson, *Power of the Purse*, 270.

36. *The Federalist* 34, *Doc. Hist.* v. 15, 262. See also *The Federalist* 36, ibid., 305.

37. [Pelatiah Webster] "A Citizen of Philadelphia," *Doc. Hist.* v. 2, 660. In this statement, Webster was referring to that part of the union's debt which had been assumed by Pennsylvania. "It is only by adopting the federal government that this enormous, unequal, and oppressive burthen can be taken off our shoulders, and the state rescued out of the hands of speculators, sharpers, and public defaulters." He was not speaking about federal assumption of *state* debts, however. For two more examples see "A Freeholder," *Doc. Hist.* v. 9, 754; "Marcus," *Doc. Hist.* v. 13, 383.

38. But see McDonald's argument about the crucial role of Dutch investment in domestic securities for appreciation to take place, something that was unlikely to occur should Congress default on the Dutch loans, Forrest McDonald, *Novus Ordo Seclorum: The Intellectual Origins of the Constitution* (Lawrence: Kansas University Press, 1985), 138–9; McDonald, *Alexander Hamilton: A Biography* (New York: Norton, 1979), 143.

39. Quotation from [Alexander Contee Hanson] "Aristides," *Doc. Hist.* v. 15, 538. The debt was described by the Federalists as "part of the price of our liberty and independence" and therefore as a debt "which ought to be regarded with gratitude and discharged with honor," Davie, North Carolina ratifying convention, Elliot, *Debates* 4, 19. But instead the poor state of public finance had led to "repeated but necessary breaches of public faith in regard to the payment of the federal domestic debt" (James Bowdoin, Massachusetts ratifying convention, Elliot, *Debates* 2, 82), which had "reduced to indigence" the individuals "who lent us money in the hour of our distress" (Davie, North Carolina ratifying convention, Elliot, *Debates* 4, 19). Regarding the French loan Madison asked the Virginia convention to "recollect our conduct to that country from which we have received the most friendly aid. How have we dealt with that benevolent ally? Have we complied with our most sacred obligations to that nation? Have we paid our interest punctually from year to year?" (*Doc. Hist.* v. 9, 1035). In short, then, the United States had a moral obligation to pay back money that individuals and governments had lent the union in good faith. If Congress should have the right to borrow money, then it should also have the means to honor the engagements. The public debt, said Thomas McKean, bound the union "in honor and conscience to pay the interest, until

they pay the principal, as well to the foreign as to the domestic creditor; it therefore becomes our duty to put it in their power to be honest" (Pennsylvania ratifying convention, *Doc. Hist.* v. 2, 537–8).

By 1787 Congress had been forced not only to default on the French and Spanish loans but also to take the desperate measure of further borrowing in Amsterdam to pay the interest on the Dutch loans. That act was regarded by the Federalists as a low-water mark of Congressional policies, a symbol of the absolute impotence of the national government. "This wretched resource of turning interest into principal, is the most humiliating and disgraceful measure that a nation could take," they claimed (Davie, North Carolina ratifying convention, Elliot, *Debates* 4, 19). It was an act that "should strike us with shame" (Alexander Hamilton, New York ratifying convention, Elliot, *Debates* 2, 366), and which had made the world look upon the United States as bankrupts. "They borrow money, and promise to pay: they have it not in their power, and they are obliged to ask of the people, whom they owe, to lend them money to pay the very interest. This is disgraceful and humiliating." Furthermore, the policy of paying compound interest was also ruinous. "No private fortune, however great,—no estate, however affluent,—can stand this most destructive mode" (Johnston, North Carolina ratifying convention, Elliot, *Debates* 4, 89). Francis Corbin believed that it was a policy that "would destroy the richest country on earth" and Madison called it "a ruinous and most disgraceful expedient" (Virginia ratifying convention, *Doc. Hist.* v. 9, 1009); ibid., 1035. See also James Wilson and Thomas McKean, Pennsylvania ratifying convention, *Doc. Hist.* v. 2, 481, 538; Hugh Williamson, "Speech at Edenton," *Doc. Hist.* v. 16, 206.

40. To raise the foreign loans Congress had mortgaged "the United States jointly, and each of them in particular, together with all their lands, chattels, revenues, and products, and also the imposts and taxes already laid and raised in the same, or in time to come to be laid and raised." To make matters worse, in accordance with the terms a failure to pay even one installment meant that the whole debt became immediately payable. Should this happen, "any of the property of any of the states, whether public or private, that can be most easily come at, will, in that case, be seized and applied for that purpose," James Bowdoin, Massachusetts ratifying convention, Elliot, *Debates* 2, 82; see also Dawes, ibid., 41. For claims that retribution was likely, see Thacher, ibid., 146. See also "A Jerseyman," "To the Citizens of New Jersey," *Doc. Hist.* v. 3, 150; "Connecticutensis," "To the People of Connecticut," ibid., 512–13; "A State Soldier" 5, *Doc. Hist.* v. 9, 650; Edmund Randolph, Virginia ratifying convention, *Doc. Hist.* v. 9, 1094; "Civis," "To the Citizens of South Carolina," *Doc. Hist.* v. 16, 25–6.

41. "A Landholder" 5, *Doc. Hist.* v. 14, 336.

II: Unlimited Taxation, Public Credit, and the Strength of Government

1. Art. VIII of the Articles of Confederation stated that "[a]ll charges of war, and all other expences that shall be incurred for the common defence or general welfare, and allowed by the united states in congress assembled, shall be defrayed out of a common treasury, which shall be supplied by the several states. . . . The taxes for paying that proportion shall be laid and levied by the authority and direction of the legislatures of the several states within the time

agreed upon by the united states in congress assembled." Art. I, sect. 8, of the Constitution, on the other hand, said that "[t]he Congress shall have Power To lay and collect Taxes, Duties, Imposts and Excises, to pay the Debts, and provide for the common Defense, and general Welfare of the United States; but all Duties, Imposts and Excises shall be uniform throughout the United States." In addition to the restriction on indirect taxes in this clause there are further restrictions in art. I, sect. 2, and art. I, sect. 9. The first of these, containing the infamous and opaque reference to slavery subsequently changed by the fourteenth amendment, said that "Representatives and direct Taxes shall be apportioned among the several States which may be included within this Union, according to their respective Numbers, which shall be determined by adding to the whole Number of free Persons, including those bond to Service for a Term of Years, and excluding Indians not taxed, three fifths of all other Persons." Art. I, sect. 9, declared that "No capitation, or other direct, Tax shall be laid, unless in Proportion to the Census or Enumeration herein directed to be taken" and that "No Tax or Duty shall be laid on Articles exported from any State."

2. "Centinel" 2, *Doc. Hist.* v. 13, 465; "Address of the Seceding Assembly-men," ibid., 296–7. See also "A Farmer," *Doc. Hist.* v. 17, 138. Because they repeatedly declared their approval of a federal impost it is difficult to see how Janet Riesman could come to the conclusion that Antifederalists generally believed that "imposts were inherently undemocratic," Riesman, "Money, Credit, and Federalist Political Economy," in *Beyond Confederation: Origins of the Constitution and American National Identity*, ed. Richard Beeman, Stephen Botein, and Edward C. Carter II (Chapel Hill: University of North Carolina Press, 1987), 153.

3. "A Federal Republican," *Doc. Hist.* v. 14, 263; "Federal Farmer," "An Additional Number of Letters to the Republican," *Doc. Hist.* v. 17, 356.

4. Nevertheless, individual Antifederalists made proposals that conformed to the army amendments. Thus, it was suggested that a majority of two-thirds, or three-fourths, of both houses be required for any law raising internal taxes to pass Congress, ibid., 359. An alternative restriction, which also had a parallel among the army amendments, was that the national government be given an unlimited right to tax in wartime only. In times of peace, the expenses of the government would be stable, and its power to tax could be limited accordingly, but in wartime Congress would need more resources, "A Georgian," *Doc. Hist.* v. 3, 239; Spencer, North Carolina ratifying convention, Elliot, *Debates* 4, 82. See also Patrick Henry, *Doc. Hist.* v. 9, 1068: "Let us have national credit and a national treasury in case of war. You never can want national resources in time of war."

5. For some examples see "Many Customers," *Doc. Hist.* v. 2, 308; "Instructions to the Spotsylvania Delegates, Virginia," *Doc. Hist.* v. 9, 611; George Mason, Virginia ratifying convention, ibid., 938, 940, 1156; Patrick Henry, ibid., 962; William Grayson, *Doc. Hist.* v. 10, 1186; Luther Martin, "Genuine Information" 6, *Doc. Hist.* v. 15, 377–8; Symmes, Massachusetts ratifying convention, Elliot, *Debates* 2, 73; Robert Lansing, New York ratifying convention, ibid., 217; Spencer, North Carolina ratifying convention, Elliot, *Debates* 4, 76; See also the account in Bernard Bailyn, "The Ideological Fulfillment of the American Revolution," in *Faces of Revolution: Personalities and Themes in the Struggle for American Independence* (New York: Knopf, 1990), 236.

6. Pennsylvania ratifying convention, *Doc. Hist.* v. 2, 598. The suggested

amendment was also printed in "Dissent of the Minority of the Pennsylvania Convention," *Doc. Hist.* v. 15, 19.

7. How eighteenth-century Americans regarded the difference between external and internal taxation has been the subject of historiographical controversy. It has been argued that the colonists opposed the Stamp Act because it levied an internal tax whereas they did not oppose Parliament's right to levy external taxes. Against this view it has been claimed that the colonists in fact rejected Parliament's power to tax the colonies per se. Recently, it has been wrongly suggested that the Antifederalists "were especially enraged by the proposal to entrust a national congress 'with every species of *internal* taxation,' " Thomas P. Slaughter, "The Tax Man Cometh: Ideological Opposition to Internal Taxes, 1760–1790," *WMQ*, 3d ser., 41 (1984), 567. For a review of the historiographical controversy, see ibid., 568–9. During the ratification struggle, it would seem that the opposition to internal taxation emanated mainly from Pennsylvania and New York, which were the two states that had any significant income from excises, Robert A. Becker, *Revolution, Reform, and the Politics of American Taxation, 1763–1783* (Baton Rouge: Louisiana State University Press, 1980), 42–3, 45–7. For two such examples see "An Old Whig" 6, *Doc. Hist.* v. 14, 218; "Brutus" 5, ibid., 426–7. It was only in these two states that the external-internal division did not overlap with the indirect-direct division, which would explain why Antifederalists in other states were comparatively quiet on the matter. But it is dubious if any conclusions can be drawn from this, because writings from Pennsylvania and New York so dominated Antifederalist rhetoric. However, it cannot be maintained that opposition against the excise was universal among the Antifederalists, nor that they expected that an excise on spirits, such as provoked the Whiskey Rebellion in 1794, "would only be a tax of last resort," which is done in Slaughter, "Tax Man," 584–90, quotation at 590.

8. Massachusetts, Maryland (defeated), South Carolina, New Hampshire, Virginia, New York, North Carolina, and Rhode Island. See Murray Dry, "The Debate over Ratification of the Constitution," in *The Blackwell Encyclopedia of the American Revolution*, ed. Jack P. Greene and Jack R. Pole (Oxford: Blackwell, 1991), table 2, 482.

9. Massachusetts ratifying convention, Elliot, *Debates* 2, 177.

10. South Carolina convention amendments, 23 May 1788, *Doc. Hist.* v. 18, 72; New Hampshire convention amendments, 21 June 1788, ibid., 188; New York convention recommendatory amendments, ibid., 301–3; "Address of the Minority of the Maryland Convention," *Doc. Hist.* v. 17, 244–5; Virginia convention amendments, 27 June 1788, *Doc. Hist.* v. 18, 203; North Carolina convention amendments, 2 August 1788, *Doc. Hist.* v. 18, 317.

11. See chapter 13.

12. Madison, Virginia ratifying convention, Doc. Hist. v. 9, 997; Charles Pinckney, South Carolina House of Representatives, Elliot, *Debates* 4, 305–6; Robert Livingston, New York ratifying convention, Elliot, *Debates* 2, 342. For other examples see Thomas McKean, Pennsylvania ratifying convention, *Doc. Hist.* v. 2, 538; "Peregrine," *Doc. Hist.* v. 9, 640; [Hamilton] *The Federalist* 22, *Doc. Hist.* v. 14, 438; "America" [Noah Webster], *Doc. Hist.* v. 15, 198–9; Rufus King and Sumner, Massachusetts ratifying convention, Elliot, *Debates* 2, 56, 64; Spaight and Whitmill Hill, North Carolina ratifying convention, Elliot, *Debates* 4, 82.

13. [Hamilton] *The Federalist* 21, *Doc. Hist.* v. 14, 414. See also [Hamilton] *The Federalist* 15, ibid., 327.

14. Robert Livingston, New York ratifying convention, Elliot, *Debates* 2, 343. See also John Marshall, Virginia ratifying convention, *Doc. Hist.* v. 9, 1120–1; Oliver Ellsworth, "Speeches in the Connecticut Convention," *Doc. Hist.* v. 15, 246–7; Rufus King, Massachusetts ratifying convention, Elliot, *Debates* 2, 56.

15. "An Impartial Citizen" 6, *Doc. Hist.* v. 8, 499; "Peregrine," *Doc. Hist.* v. 9, 640; Henry Lee, Virginia ratifying convention, ibid., 948; Francis Corbin, ibid., 1009; Edmund Randolph, ibid., 1017–18, 1020; John Marshall, ibid., 1121; James Madison, ibid., 1145–6; Edmund Randolph, "Letter on the Constitution," *Doc. Hist.* v. 15, 126–7; "Fabius" 8 [John Dickinson], *Doc. Hist.* v. 17, 248; Alexander Hamilton, New York ratifying convention, Elliot, *Debates* 2, 232–3; Robert Livingston, ibid., 222, 343–4, quotation at 344; John Jay, ibid., 380; James Iredell, North Carolina ratifying convention, Elliot, *Debates* 4, 146. The policy was unfair because coercion would affect those who were ready to pay taxes in the same way as those who refused to do so.

16. "An Impartial Citizen" 6, *Doc. Hist.* v. 8, 499; "Peregrine," *Doc. Hist.* v. 9, 640.

17. John Brooks, "Oration" July 4, 1787, *Doc. Hist.* v. 13, 160. See also [Hamilton] *The Federalist* 16, *Doc. Hist.* v. 14, 341; [Hamilton] *The Federalist* 23, *Doc. Hist.* v. 15, 5; [Hamilton] *The Federalist* 31, *Doc. Hist.* v. 15, 213; Alexander Hamilton, New York ratifying convention, Elliot, *Debates* 2, 233.

18. Defoe, *The Review*, quoted in John Pocock, *The Machiavellian Moment: Florentine Political Thought and the Atlantic Republican Tradition* (Princeton, N.J.: Princeton University Press, 1975), 455.

19. Forrest McDonald, *Alexander Hamilton: A Biography* (New York: Norton, 1979), 143.

20. David Hume, "Of Public Credit" in *Political Essays*, ed. Knud Haakonssen (Cambridge, U.K.: Cambridge University Press, 1994), 166–7.

21. See the discussion in chapter 3.

22. John Brewer, *The Sinews of Power: War, Money and the English State, 1688–1783* (London: Unwin Hyman, 1989), 38–40 and figure 2.1. The figures are for the years with the highest spending for both wars, not average annual spending.

23. Patrick K. O'Brien, "The Political Economy of British Taxation, 1660–1815," *Economic History Review*, 2d ser., 41 (1988), 1–32.

24. See references cited in n18 and n19, chapter 3.

25. Peter Dickson, *The Financial Revolution in England: A Study in the Development of Public Credit, 1688–1756* (London: St. Martin's, 1967), 9–16.

26. "L'exactitude scrupuleuse & inviolable avec laquelle ces intérêts ont tojours été payés, & l'idée qu'on a de l'assurance Parlementaire, ont établi le crédit de l'Angleterre, au point de faire des emprunts qui ont surpris et étonné l'Europe," Isaac de Pinto, *Traité de la circulation et du crédit* (1771), quoted in Dickson, *Financial Revolution in England*, 11. Similarly, Montesquieu wrote about England that "this nation would have secure credit because it would borrow from itself and pay to itself. It could happen that it would undertake something beyond the forces natural to it and would assert against its enemies an immense fictional wealth that the trust and the nature of its government would make real," *The Spirit of the Laws*, ed. Anne M. Cohler, Basia C. Miller, and Harold S. Stone (Cambridge, U.K.: Cambridge University Press, 1989), pt. 3, bk. 19, ch. 27, 327.

27. O'Brien, "Political Economy of British Taxation," 3–4. See also Brewer, *Sinews of Power*, 88–9.

28. Brewer, *Sinews of Power*, 122–5. For the tax increase, see n17, chapter 3.

29. Hume, "Of Public Credit," 173–7, quotation at 173.

30. Gore, Massachusetts ratifying convention, Elliot, *Debates* 2, 66; Corbin, Virginia ratifying convention, *Doc. Hist.* v. 9, 1011. See also John Marshall, ibid., 1019.

31. *The Federalist* 30, *Doc. Hist.* v. 15, 164. See also Alexander Hamilton, New York ratifying convention, Elliot, *Debates* 2, 352; Robert Livingston, ibid., 342. "Every nation, even the most wealthy, and the oldest nations, have found it necessary to recur to loans in time of war," Edmund Randolph said in the Virginia ratifying convention, *Doc. Hist.* v. 9, 1021. Similarly, Madison asked the convention if it was "possible a war could be supported without money or credit?" ibid., 997.

32. Choate, Massachusetts ratifying convention, Elliot, *Debates* 2, 79. See also Whitmill Hill, North Carolina ratifying convention, Elliot, *Debates* 4, 85: "Loans must be recurred to sometimes. In case of war they would be necessary. All nations borrow money on pressing occasions."

33. Virginia ratifying convention, *Doc. Hist.* v. 9, 1020.

34. See chapter 13.

35. Edmund Randolph, Virginia ratifying convention, *Doc. Hist.* v. 9, 1021; James Madison, ibid., 996–7; James Iredell, North Carolina ratifying convention, Elliot, *Debates* 4, 220; Alexander Hamilton, New York ratifying convention, Elliot, *Debates* 2, 352; [Hamilton] *The Federalist* 30, *Doc Hist.* 15, 163–4, quotation at 164.

36. Hill, North Carolina ratifying convention, Elliot, *Debates* 4, 83; Iredell, ibid., 92. In addition to the references cited in note 15, see Johnston, ibid., 78–9; James Iredell, ibid., 91–2, 220.

37. Madison, Virginia ratifying convention, *Doc. Hist.* v. 9, 996–7; Livingston, New York ratifying convention Elliot, *Debates* 2, 344; Hamilton, ibid., 352. See also the Virginian writing as "The State Soldier," who noted that the credit of the union, like the credit of an individual, "was only to be kept up by a prospect of being at some time or another able to pay the debts it had necessarily contracted—and that prospect could no way begin but by the establishment of some fund whereon the CONTINENT could draw with certainty," "The State Soldier" 1, *Doc. Hist.* v. 8, 305.

38. Virginia ratifying convention, *Doc. Hist.* v. 9, 1021.

39. Thomas Hartley, Pennsylvania ratifying convention, *Doc. Hist.* v. 2, 431–2. Thomas McKean was of the same opinion: "Those who lent us in our distress have little encouragement to make advances again to our government; but give the power to Congress to lay such taxes as may be just and necessary, and public credit will revive," ibid., 538.

40. Whitmill Hill, North Carolina ratifying convention, Elliot, *Debates* 4, 85. See also Johnston, ibid., 78; Edmund Randolph, Virginia ratifying convention, *Doc. Hist.* v. 9, 1021.

41. Choate, Massachusetts ratifying convention, Elliot, *Debates* 2, 79; Johnston, North Carolina ratifying convention, Elliot, *Debates* 4, 91; *The Federalist* 30, *Doc. Hist.* v. 15, 164.

42. Christopher Gore, Massachusetts ratifying convention, Elliot, *Debates* 2,

66–7; Ellsworth, "Speeches in the Connecticut Convention," *Doc. Hist.* v. 15, 274. See also Ellsworth, "Speeches in the Connecticut Convention," *Doc. Hist.* v. 15, 247.

43. One may ask why this was not the case with the Dutch republic, perhaps the most striking success story of early modern Europe. The answer, at least the one preferred by the Federalists, was that the dominance of Holland in the federation meant that the actions of Holland alone determined the credit rating of the union. This dominance also allowed Holland to force the other states to comply with the union's demands.

12: The Costs of Government

1. New York recommendatory amendments, *Doc. Hist.* v. 18, 302.

2. "Brutus" 8, *Doc. Hist.* v. 15, 335–6.

3. John Brewer, *The Sinews of Power: War, Money and the English State, 1688–1783* (London: Unwin Hyman, 1989), 89, 91, 95, 99; J. V. Beckett, "Land Tax or Excise: The Levying of Taxation in Seventeenth- and Eighteenth-Century England," *English Historical Review*, 100 (1985), 305–6 and table 2; J. V. Beckett and M. Turner, "Taxation and Economic Growth in Eighteenth-Century England," *Economic History Review*, 2d ser., 43 (1990), 380–1, 383–8, table 1, figures 1 and 3a-3d; Patrick K. O'Brien, "The Political Economy of British Taxation, 1660–1815," *Economic History Review*, 2d ser., 41 (1988), 3, 6–7, 14–17, tables 2 and 4.

4. Beckett, "Land Tax or Excise," 305–6 and table 2; Beckett and Turner, "Taxation and Economic Growth," 383–8, figures 1 and 3a-3d, table 1; Brewer, *Sinews of Power*, 95, 99, 101–10, 113, 128–9, figures 4.3 and 4.4; O'Brien, "Political Economy of British Taxation," 14–17, 28 and table 4. For some examples of anti-excise rhetoric, see Paul S. Boyer, "Borrowed Rhetoric: The Massachusetts Excise Controversy of 1754," *WMQ*, 3d ser., 21 (1964), 328–51. The standard account of the controversy surrounding Walpole's excise scheme is Paul Langford, *The Excise Crisis: Society and Politics in the Age of Walpole* (Oxford: Oxford University Press, 1975). In this work, Langford is not very interested in the rhetorical aspect of the conflict. However, the symbolic dimensions are brought out very clearly in the prints reproduced in Langford, *Walpole and the Robinocracy* (Cambridge, U.K.: Chadwyck-Healey, 1986), part of *The English Satirical Print, 1600–1832* series.

5. Colin Brooks, "Public Finance and Political Stability: The Administration of the Land Tax, 1688–1720," *The Historical Journal*, 17 (1974), 283.

6. Beckett, "Land Tax or Excise," 295, 301; Brewer, *Sinews of Power*, 101; Brooks, "Public Finance and Political Stability," 281–300, quotation at 283; O'Brien, "Political Economy of British Taxation."

7. Beckett and Turner, "Taxation and Economic Growth," 381, 383, 387, 391; O'Brien, "Political Economy of British Taxation," 12, 17–22, 26–7. O'Brien compares Parliamentary conflicts to shadow-boxing at 26.

8. See the discussion of eighteenth-century works in Herbert G. Sloan, *Principles and Interest: Thomas Jefferson and the Problem of Debt* (New York: Oxford University Press, 1995), 88–90; J. G. A. Pocock, "Machiavelli, Harrington and English Political Ideologies in the Eighteenth Century," *WMQ*, 3d ser., 22, 549–83.

9. For the contemporary view, see Sloan, *Principles and Interest*, 91–6.

10. *Spirit of the Laws*, ed. Anne M. Cohler, Basia C. Miller and Harold S. Stone (Cambridge, U.K.: Cambridge University Press, 1989), pt. 2, bk. 11, ch. 6, 164.

11. *Commentaries on the Laws of England* (Oxford, 1775, 7th ed.), vol. 1, 335.

12. Bernard Bailyn, *The Ideological Origins of the American Revolution* (Cambridge, Mass.: Harvard University Press, 1967), 65, 100–1, Dickinson's *Letters from a Farmer in Pennsylvania* quoted at 101.

13. Quoted in Edmund S. Morgan and Helen M. Morgan, *The Stamp Act Crisis: Prologue to Revolution* (Chapel Hill: University of North Carolina Press, 1953), 95.

14. Virginia ratifying convention, *Doc. Hist.* v. 9, 1064.

15. Amos Singletarry, Massachusetts ratifying convention, Elliot, *Debates 2*, 101; "Centinel" 8, *Doc. Hist.* v. 15, 231–2.

16. Quoted in Herbert J. Storing, *What the Antifederalists Were For* (Chicago: Chicago University Press, 1981), 31.

17. Patrick Henry, Virginia ratifying convention, *Doc. Hist.* v. 9, 959.

18. The first article's eighth section gave Congress, among other things, the power to tax and the final paragraph of the section also gave Congress the power "To make all laws which shall be necessary and proper for carrying into execution the foregoing powers, and all other powers vested by this constitution in the government of the United States, or in any department or officer thereof." Article VI stated that "This constitution and the laws of the United States which shall be made in pursuance thereof; and all treaties made, or which shall be made, under the authority of the United States, shall be the supreme law of the land; and the judges in every state shall be bound thereby, anything in the constitution or laws of any state to the contrary notwithstanding."

19. "An Old Whig" 6, *Doc. Hist.* v. 14, 216. The same point was made in "Brutus" 1, *Doc. Hist.* v. 13, 416; "Brutus" 5, *Doc. Hist.* v. 14, 424–6 and "A Farmer," *Doc. Hist.* v. 17, 142. Long excerpts from "Brutus" 5 were quoted verbatim by Williams in the New York ratifying convention, Elliot, *Debates 2*, 330–1.

20. "Dissent of the Minority of the Pennsylvania Convention," *Doc. Hist.* v. 15, 22.

21. John Smilie, Pennsylvania ratifying convention, *Doc. Hist.* v. 2, 408; Patrick Henry, Virginia ratifying convention, *Doc. Hist.* v. 9, 1045–6; "Federal Farmer," "Letters to the Republican," *Doc. Hist.* v. 14, 37; "An Old Whig" 6, ibid., 216, 217–18; "Brutus" 5, ibid., 425–6; "Dissent of the Minority of the Pennsylvania Convention," *Doc. Hist.* v. 15, 22; "Brutus" 6, ibid., 111–12; "A Farmer," *Doc. Hist.* v. 17, 142; Spencer, North Carolina ratifying convention, Elliot, *Debates 4*, 75. See also William Findley, Pennsylvania ratifying convention, *Doc. Hist.* v. 2, 503; "A Columbian Patriot" [Mercy Otis Warren], "Observation on the Constitution," *Doc. Hist.* v. 16, 280.

22. [Hamilton] *Federalist 32–3, Doc. Hist.* v. 15, 217–19; [Hamilton] *Federalist 34*, ibid., 259; Oliver Ellsworth, "Speeches in the Connecticut Convention," 7 January, ibid., 274; "A Freeman" 3 [Tench Coxe], *Doc. Hist.* v. 16, 51; Parsons, Massachusetts ratifying convention, Elliot, *Debates 2*, 93; Alexander Hamilton, New York ratifying convention, Elliot, *Debates 2*, 364.

23. John Smilie, Pennsylvania ratifying convention, *Doc. Hist.* v. 2, 408. See also "Centinel" 1, *Doc. Hist.* v. 13, 333; "A Federal Republican," *Doc. Hist.* v. 14,

264; "Federal Farmer," "An Additional Number of Letters to the Republican," *Doc. Hist.* v. 17, 294.

24. "Brutus" 6, *Doc. Hist.* v. 15, 114–15. See also "Brutus" 1, *Doc. Hist.* v. 13, 414 and "Centinel" 4, *Doc. Hist.* v. 14, 320.

25. John Smilie, Pennsylvania ratifying convention, *Doc. Hist.* v. 2, 408. See also "Dissent of the Minority of the Pennsylvania Convention," *Doc. Hist.* v. 15, 22; "Federal Farmer," "Letters to the Republican," *Doc. Hist.* v. 14, 35.

26. "Federal Farmer," "Letters to the Republican," *Doc. Hist.* v. 14, 28.

27. "Federal Farmer," "An Additional Number of Letters to the Republican," *Doc. Hist.* v. 17, 356.

28. For the House of Commons, see Brewer, *Sinews of Power*, 159–61; Jack N. Rakove, *Original Meanings: Politics and Ideas in the Making of the Constitution* (New York: Knopf, 1996), 209–11.

29. William Grayson, Virginia ratifying convention, *Doc. Hist.* v. 10, 1185. See also Bodman, Massachusetts ratifying convention, Elliot, *Debates* 2, 60.

30. "Federal Farmer," "Letters to the Republican," *Doc. Hist.* v. 14, 35–6.

31. "An Old Whig" 6, *Doc. Hist.* v. 14, 216.

32. Melanchton Smith, New York ratifying convention, Elliot, *Debates* 2, 334.

33. Quoted in "Centinel" 2, *Doc. Hist.* v. 13, 460–1.

34. "An Old Whig" 1, *Doc. Hist.* v. 13, 377–8. The remark was made in the context of a discussion about the possibility of the states taking the initiative to amend the Constitution after adoption.

35. John Smilie, Pennsylvania ratifying convention, *Doc. Hist.* v. 2, 409–10.

36. Melanchton Smith, New York ratifying convention, Elliot, *Debates* 2, 312–13. The people, "Centinel" wrote, would soon tire of living under two governments and "would be apt to rid themselves of the weaker," "Centinel" 2, *Doc. Hist.* v. 13, 465. See also James Monroe, Virginia ratifying convention, *Doc. Hist.* v. 10, 1111.

37. "A Federal Republican," *Doc. Hist.* v. 14, 263–4 ("multiplicity"); "An Old Whig" 6, ibid., 217; "Centinel" 2, *Doc. Hist.* v. 13, 465; "An Officer of the Late Continental Army," *Doc. Hist.* v. 2, 212; "Centinel" 4, *Doc. Hist.* v. 14, 320 ("presidential court"); "A Plebeian," *Doc. Hist.* v. 17, 161 ("federal town").

38. Patrick Henry, Virginia ratifying convention, *Doc. Hist.* v. 10, 1218.

39. "Blessings of the New Government," *Doc. Hist.* v. 13, 345.

40. Massachusetts ratifying convention, Elliot, *Debates* 2, 102; "Philadelphiensis" 3, *Doc. Hist.* v. 14, 351; "Philadelphiensis" 11, *Doc. Hist.* v. 17, 364; "A Columbian Patriot" [Mercy Otis Warren], "Observations on the Constitution," *Doc. Hist.* v. 16, 274.

41. Williams, New York ratifying convention, Elliot, *Debates* 2, 340. For other claims that the supporters of the Constitution contemplated the introduction of a stamp duty see "A Son of Liberty," *Doc. Hist.* v. 13, 482, and Luther Martin, "Genuine Information" 6, *Doc. Hist.* v. 15, 376.

42. "Brutus" 6, *Doc. Hist.* v. 15, 113.

43. "The Impartial Examiner" 1, *Doc. Hist.* v. 8, 421.

44. "A Farmer," *Doc. Hist.* v. 17, 139.

45. In addition to the complaints by Singletarry, "Philadelphiensis," and Warren cited previously, see also the complaint that arose from the Antifederalist interpretation of the Constitution's declaration that "all Duties, Imposts and Excises shall be uniform throughout the United States." Some took this to

mean that land taxes would be levied at a flat rate per acre regardless of the land's productivity. Thus a man "who has 100 acres of the richest land will pay as little as a man who has 100 acres of the poorest land," George Mason, Virginia ratifying convention, *Doc. Hist.* v. 9, 1157. See also Lancaster, North Carolina ratifying convention, Elliot, *Debates* 4, 212. For complaints about stamp taxes see references cited in note 41.

46. Virginia ratifying convention, *Doc. Hist.* v. 10, 1218. For a further discussion of opposition to a federal excise, see later.

47. Williams, New York ratifying convention, Elliot, *Debates* 2, 340; "Cato" 5, *Doc. Hist.* v. 14, 184; "Cato" 6, ibid., 430; "Dissent of the Minority of the Pennsylvania Convention," *Doc. Hist.* v. 15, 30. See also the discussion in Montesquieu's *Spirit of the Laws*, pt. 2, bk. 13, ch. 14, 222, often referred to by Antifederalists, e.g., Williams, New York ratifying convention, Elliot, *Debates* 2, 340. For further Antifederalist remarks on poll taxes see George Mason, Virginia ratifying convention, *Doc. Hist.* v. 9, 1156–7; "A Farmer," *Doc. Hist.* v. 17, 139; Widgery, Massachusetts ratifying convention, Elliot, *Debates* 2, 44, 105–6; "Strictures on the Proposed Constitution," *Doc. Hist.* v. 13, 245; "A Son of Liberty," ibid., 481; "Cato" 6, *Doc. Hist.* v. 14, 430–1.

48. "Brutus" 7, *Doc. Hist.* v. 15, 239. See also "Federal Farmer," "Letters to the Republican," *Doc. Hist.* v. 14, 35–6; "Brutus" 5, ibid., 427.

49. "Cincinnatus" 5, *Doc. Hist.* v. 14, 309–10. The passage on federal assumption reads as follows: "It will be expected, that the new government will provide for this [i.e. the state debts] also; and such expectation is founded, not only on the promise you hold forth, of its reviving and supporting public credit among us, but also on this unavoidable principle of justice, that is the new government takes away the impost, and other substantial taxes, from the produce of which the several states paid the interest of their debt, or funded the paper with which they paid it. The new government must find ways and means of supplying that deficiency, or in other words of paying the interest in hard money, for in paper as now, it cannot, without a violation of the principles it boasts, attempt to pay."

50. "Cincinnatus" 6, *Doc. Hist.* v. 14, 360–1. See also "Centinel" 2, *Doc. Hist.* v. 13, 465–6.

51. See for instance "A Farmer," *Doc. Hist.* v. 17, 139.

52. Boyer, "Borrowed Rhetoric," 328–51.

53. Luther Martin, "Genuine Information" 6, *Doc. Hist.* v. 15, 377.

54. "Brutus" 6, *Doc. Hist.* v. 15, 113–14.

55. "Federal Farmer," "An Additional Number of Letters to the Republican," *Doc. Hist.* v. 17, 352. The Congressional power to tax was "perfectly independent of, and supreme over, the state governments; whose intervention . . . is entirely destroyed," "Dissent of the Minority of the Pennsylvania Convention," *Doc. Hist.* v. 15, 22. For the meaning of "consolidated government," see Rakove, *Original Meanings*, 181–3.

56. "Cato Uticensis," *Doc. Hist.* v. 8, 74. Luther Martin also pointed out that there was no guarantee that revenue officers would be citizens of the state in which they collected, see "Genuine Information" 6, *Doc. Hist.* v. 15, 377; Martin, "Speech in the Maryland Assembly," 29 November, 1787, *Doc. Hist.* v. 14, 290.

57. Symmes, Massachusetts ratifying convention, Elliot, *Debates* 2, 73–4. He also painted a scene of the future state of America, in "an age or two," when "Congress shall have become tyrannical." Then "these vultures, their

servants, will be the tyrants of the village, by whose presence all freedom of speech and action will be taken away."

58. Barell, Massachusetts ratifying convention, Elliot, *Debates* 2, 160.

59. Luther Martin, "Genuine Information" 6, *Doc. Hist.* v. 15, 377.

60. "Cato Uticensis," *Doc. Hist.* v. 8, 75; "A Son of Liberty," *Doc. Hist.* v. 13, 481–2. See also George Mason, Virginia ratifying convention, *Doc. Hist.* v. 9, 1157.

61. "Cato Uticensis," *Doc. Hist.* v. 8, 75. In this context see also the following remarks in a discussion of jury trials. Suppose "that a constable, having a warrant to search for stolen goods, pulled down the clothes of a bed in which there was a woman, and searched under her shift—suppose, I say, that they commit similar, or greater indignities, in such cases a trial by jury would be our safest resource, heavy damages would at once punish the offender, and deter others from committing the same: but what satisfaction can we expect from a lordly court of justice, always ready to protect the officers of government against the weak and helpless citizen," "A Democratic Federalist," *Doc. Hist.* v. 13, 390. "If any of the Federal officers should be guilty of the greatest oppressions, or behave with the most insolent or wanton brutality to a man's wife or daugther, where is this man to get relief?" George Mason, Virginia ratifying convention, *Doc. Hist.* v. 10, 1404.

62. Patrick Henry, Virginia ratifying convention, ibid., 1215.

63. Roger H. Brown, *Redeeming the Republic: Federalism, Taxation, and the Origins of the Constitution* (Baltimore: Johns Hopkins University Press, 1993), 34, 37–8, 39–40; George Mason, Virginia ratifying convention, *Doc. Hist.* v. 9, 937–8. See also ibid., 1156–7.

64. Luther Martin, "Genuine Information" 6, *Doc. Hist.* v. 15, 377.

65. For the link between knowledge and convenience, see Patrick Henry, Virginia ratifying convention, *Doc. Hist.* v. 9, 962; George Mason, ibid., 940; William Grayson, ibid., *Doc. Hist.* v. 10, 1186; "Federal Farmer," "An Additional Number of Letters to the Republican," *Doc. Hist.* v. 17, 358–9; Spencer, North Carolina ratifying convention, Elliot, *Debates* 4, 76.

66. George Mason, Virginia ratifying convention, *Doc. Hist.* v. 9, 937–8.

67. "Philadelphiensis" 5, *Doc. Hist.* v. 15, 46. See also "Philadelphiensis" 11, *Doc. Hist.* v. 16, 364–5; Spencer, North Carolina ratifying convention, Elliot, *Debates* 4, 76; Patrick Henry, Virginia ratifying convention, *Doc. Hist.* v. 10, 1464–5.

68. Luther Martin, "Genuine Information" 8, *Doc. Hist.* v. 15, 436. Martin continued "by *whom* their property is to be *seized upon* and *sold* in this *scarcity* of *specie at a sheriffs sale*, where nothing but *ready cash* can be received for a *tenth part* of its *value*, and *themselves* and their *families* to be consigned to *indigence* and *distress*."

69. "Cincinnatus" 6, *Doc. Hist.* v. 14, 361.

70. "A Son of Liberty," *Doc. Hist.* v. 13, 482.

71. Nason, Massachusetts ratifying convention, Elliot, *Debates* 2, 186. See also John Humble, "Adress of the Lowborn," *Doc. Hist.* v. 2, 206: "And although it appears to us that a *standing army*, composed of the purgings of the jails of Great Britain, Ireland and Germany, shall be employed in collecting the *revenue* of this our king and government; yet, we again in the most solemn manner declare, that we will abide by our present determination of nonassistance and passive obedience; so that we shall not dare to molest or disturb those military gentlemen in the service of our royal government. And (which is not improb-

able), should any of those soldiers when employed on duty in collecting the *taxes*, strike off the arm (with his sword) of one of our *fellow slaves*, we will conceive our case remarkably fortunate if he leaves the other arm on." For further examples, see "Address of the Seceding Assemblymen," *Doc. Hist.* v. 13, 296; "Cato" 3, ibid., 476; "Philadelphiensis" 4, *Doc. Hist.* v. 14, 420.

72. "Dissent of the Minority of the Pennsylvania Convention," *Doc. Hist.* v. 15, 30. See also "Centinel" 1, *Doc. Hist.* v. 13, 332–3.

73. "Cincinnatus" 6, *Doc. Hist.* v. 14, 362.

13: A Government for Free

1. Mark D. Kaplanoff, "The Hamiltonian Moment," paper presented at the 1998 meeting of the Society for Historians of the Early American Republic (SHEAR), Harpers Ferry, West Virginia.

2. Roger H. Brown, *Redeeming the Republic: Federalism, Taxation, and the Origins of the Constitution* (Baltimore: Johns Hopkins University Press, 1993). For page references see note 27, chapter 9.

3. [Hamilton] *The Federalist* 12, *Doc. Hist.* v. 14, 237.

4. Oliver Ellsworth, "Speeches in the Connecticut Convention," 7 January, *Doc. Hist.* v. 15, 275.

5. [Hamilton] *The Federalist* 12, *Doc. Hist.* v. 14, 237.

6. James Wilson, Pennsylvania ratifying convention, *Doc. Hist.* v. 2, 481.

7. George Nicholas, Virginia ratifying convention, *Doc. Hist.* v. 9, 999.

8. *Spirit of the Laws*, ed. Anne M. Cohler, Basia C. Miller, and Harold S. Stone (Cambridge, U.K.: Cambridge University Press, 1989), pt. 2, bk. 13, ch. 7, 217.

9. David Hume, "Of Taxes," *Political Essays*, ed. Knud Haakonsen (Cambridge, U.K.: Cambridge University Press, 1994), 162–3.

10. Writing about British customs duties, William Blackstone said that these "customs are then, we see, a tax immediately paid by the merchant, although ultimately paid by the consumer. And yet these are the duties felt least by the people; and if prudently managed, the people hardly consider that they pay them at all. For the merchant is easy, being sensible he does not pay them for himself; and the consumer, who really pays them, confounds them with the price of the commodity," *Commentaries on the Laws of England* (Oxford, 1775, 7th ed.), I, 316–17.

11. James Wilson, Pennsylvania ratifying convention, *Doc. Hist.* v. 2, 576.

12. Federalists tried ceaselessly to drum this into the minds of their opponents. See James Wilson, Pennsylvania ratifying debate, *Doc. Hist.* v. 2, 558; "Connecticutensis," "To the People of Connecticut," *Doc. Hist.* v. 3, 514; James Wilson, "Speech at a Public Meeting in Philadelphia," 6 October, *Doc. Hist.* v. 13, 342–3; [Hamilton] *The Federalist* 21, *Doc. Hist.* v. 14, 417; Oliver Ellsworth, "Speeches in the Connecticut Convention," 7 January, *Doc. Hist.* v. 15, 276; "A Citizen of New Haven" [Roger Sherman], ibid., 282; "Aristides" [Alexander Contee Hanson], "Remarks on the Proposed Plan," ibid., 545; Hugh Williamson, "Speech at Edenton," *Doc. Hist.* v. 16, 207; "Publicola" [Archibald Maclaine], "To the Freemen of North Carolina," ibid., 441; Rufus King, Massachusetts ratifying debate, Elliot, *Debates* 2, 57 Sumner, ibid., 63–4; Robert Livingston, New York ratifying convention, Elliot, *Debates* 2, 211; Charles Pinckney, South Carolina House of Representatives, Elliot, *Debates* 4, 260; Johnston, North Carolina ratifying convention, Elliot, *Debates* 4, 77–8; Archibald Ma-

claine, ibid., 189–90. In *The Federalist* 30, however, Hamilton asked how anyone could "pretend that commercial imposts are or would be alone equal to the present and future exigencies of the Union? Taking into account the existing debt, foreign and domestic, upon any plan of extinguishment, which a man moderately impressed with the importance of public justice and public credit could approve, in addition to the establishments, which all parties will acknowledge to be necessary, we could not reasonably flatter ourselves, that this resource alone, upon the most improved scale, would even suffice for its present necessities. Its future necessities admit not of calculation or limitation; and upon the principle, more than once adverted to, the power of making provision for them as they arise, ought to be equally unconfined. I believe it may be regarded as a position, warranted by the history of mankind, that *in the usual progress of things, the necessities of a nation in every stage of its existence will be found at least equal to its resources*," *Doc. Hist.* v. 15, 162. In other places, Hamilton thought better of such bold assertions.

13. [Hamilton] *The Federalist* 36, *Doc. Hist.* v. 15, 306.

14. Oliver Ellsworth, "Speeches in the Connecticut Convention," *Doc. Hist.* v. 15, 276; [Hamilton] *The Federalist* 12, *Doc. Hist.* v. 14, 239.

15. "Publicola" [Archibald Maclaine], "To the Freemen of North Carolina," *Doc. Hist.* v. 16, 441. See also James Wilson, Pennsylvania ratifying convention, *Doc. Hist.* v. 2, 480–2, 558–9; Thomas Dawes, Massachusetts ratifying convention, Elliot, *Debates* 2, 42; Francis Dana, ibid., 42; Theodore Sedgwick, ibid., 60–1; Increase Sumner, ibid., 64; Francis Corbin, Virginia ratifying convention, *Doc. Hist.* v. 9, 1011–12.

16. New York ratifying convention, Elliot, *Debates* 2, 342.

17. James Wilson, Pennsylvania ratifying convention, *Doc. Hist.* v. 2, 558.

18. Ibid., 481.

19. [Hamilton] *The Federalist* 12, *Doc. Hist.* v. 14, 237; Oliver Ellsworth, "Speeches in the Connecticut Convention," *Doc. Hist.* v. 15, 276.

20. Edmund Randolph, Virginia ratifying convention, *Doc. Hist.* v. 9, 1027.

21. *Federalist* 36, *Doc. Hist.* v. 15, 305–6. See also Robert Livingston, New York ratifying convention, Elliot, *Debates* 2, 346; [Madison] *Federalist* 45, *Doc. Hist.* v. 15, 479. It seems probable that this was the idea behind the Federalist argument, that in the unlikely event that Congress would have to resort to internal taxes, the state governments would first get the chance to collect them on behalf of Congress. Obviously, this argument is diametrically opposed to the Federalists' commonly vented contempt for the requisition system. Madison is best known for making this argument in ibid., but other Federalists did so as well. See Oliver Ellsworth and Roger Sherman, "Letter to Governor Samuel Huntington," *Doc. Hist.* v. 13, 471; James McHenry, "Speech in Maryland's State House of Delegates," *Doc. Hist.* v. 14, 283; "A Citizen of New Haven" [Roger Sherman], *Doc. Hist.* v. 15, 282; "A Freeman" [Tench Coxe], *Doc. Hist.* v. 16, 50–1; Gilbert Dench, Massachusetts ratifying convention, Elliot, *Debates* 2, 44.

22. Alexander Hamilton, New York ratifying convention, Elliot, *Debates* 2, 364.

23. "America" [Noah Webster], *Doc. Hist.* v. 15, 198; [Hamilton] *The Federalist* 36, ibid., 304.

24. John Marshall, Virginia ratifying convention, *Doc. Hist.* v. 9, 1127. Similarly, Madison asked "where is the evil of different laws operating in different States, to raise money for the General Government? Where is the evil of such

laws? There are instances in other countries, of different laws operating in different parts of the country, without producing any kind of oppression." Madison then points to England and Scotland as a good example of this, Virginia ratifying convention, ibid., 1148–9.

25. *The Federalist* 34, *Doc. Hist.* v. 15, 260–1; Alexander Hamilton, New York ratifying convention, Elliot, *Debates* 2, 350–1.

26. *The Federalist* 34, *Doc. Hist.* v. 15, 259–63, quotation at 262.

27. Jack N. Rakove, *Original Meanings: Politics and Ideas in the Making of the Constitution* (New York: Knopf, 1996), 196.

28. Robert Livingston, New York ratifying convention, Elliot, *Debates* 2, 341.

29. [Hamilton] *The Federalist* 36, *Doc. Hist.* v. 15, 305.

30. [Hamilton] *The Federalist* 34, ibid., 262.

31. Oliver Ellsworth, "Speeches in the Connecticut Convention," *Doc. Hist.* v. 15, 274.

32. Hugh Williamson, "Speech at Edenton," *Doc. Hist.* v. 16, 206; "Connecticutensis," "To the People of Connecticut," *Doc. Hist.* v. 3, 513; Gorham, Massachusetts ratifying convention, Elliot, *Debates* 2, 106; "A Slave," *Doc. Hist.* v. 13, 481; "A Friend of Society and Liberty," *Doc. Hist.* v. 18, 283.

33. James Wilson, Pennsylvania ratifying convention, *Doc. Hist.* v. 2, 481; [Hamilton] *The Federalist* 21, *Doc. Hist.* v. 14, 417. See also "Philanthrop," "To the People," *Doc. Hist.* v. 3, 469.

34. "Connecticutensis," "To the People of Connecticut," *Doc. Hist.* v. 3, 513.

35. Johnston, North Carolina ratifying convention, Elliot, *Debates* 4, 78; James Iredell, ibid., 92; Whitmill Hill, ibid., 86. See also Iredell, ibid., 220–1.

36. George Nicholas, Virginia ratifying convention, *Doc. Hist.* v. 9, 999; "Connecticutensis," "To the People of Connecticut," *Doc. Hist.* v. 3, 513; Ellsworth, "Speeches in the Connecticut Convention," *Doc. Hist.* v. 15, 275.

37. George Nicholas, Virginia ratifying convention, *Doc. Hist.* v. 9, 999; Ellsworth, "Speeches in the Connecticut Convention," *Doc. Hist.* v. 15, 275.

38. George Nicholas, Virginia ratifying convention, *Doc. Hist.* v. 9, 1000.

39. Curiously, this essay is also held to be at the same time both stunningly innovative *and* representative of the general Federalist view.

40. Yeates, Pennsylvania ratifying convention debates, *Doc. Hist.* v. 2, 436. See also George Nicholas, Virginia ratifying convention debates, *Doc. Hist.* v. 10, 1327: "we trust to the fellow-feeling of our Representatives, and if we are deceived, we then trust to altering our Government. It appears to me, however, that we can confide in their discharging their powers rightly, from the peculiarity of their situation, and connection with us."

41. "America" [Noah Webster], *Doc. Hist.* v. 15, 195; Hancock, Massachusetts ratifying convention debates, Elliot, *Debates,* 2, 175; James Madison, Virginia ratifying convention debates, *Doc. Hist.* v. 10, 1417.

42. Johnston, North Carolina ratifying convention, Elliot, *Debates* 4, 89.

43. [Madison], *The Federalist* 56, *Doc. Hist.* v. 16, 130. See also the speech by James Marshall in the Virginia convention, *Doc. Hist.* v. 9, 1121–22. The authorship of *Federalist* 56 was later claimed by both Madison and Hamilton, but is now generally attributed to the former. That the authorship was contested suggests that both men believed it to express their feelings on the matter. Its argument is certainly more in tune with what Hamilton wrote elsewhere in *The Federalist* than with what is traditionally described as the Madisonian theory of representative government.

44. *The Federalist* 35, *Doc. Hist.* v. 15, 272; *The Federalist* 36, ibid., 303 (quotation). In *Federalist* 56 Madison made a very similar remark about militia regulation: "With regard to the regulations of the militia, there are scarcely any circumstances in reference to which local knowledge can be said to be necessary. The general face of the country, whether mountainous or level, most fit for the operations of infantry or cavalry, is almost the only consideration of this nature that can occur. The art of war teaches general principles of organization, movement and discipline, which apply universally," *Doc. Hist.* v. 16, 132, n2. This passage replaced a paragraph in the newspaper version and so only exists in the book version of *The Federalist*.

45. *The Federalist* 36, *Doc. Hist.* v. 15, 304.

46. Virginia ratifying convention, *Doc. Hist.* v. 9, 1147–8. See also Madison's remarks in *Federalist* 56, *Doc. Hist.* v. 16, 130.

47. Pennsylvania ratifying convention, *Doc. Hist.* v. 2, 409.

48. [Hamilton] *The Federalist* 27, *Doc. Hist.* v. 15, 95–6.

49. [Hamilton] *The Federalist* 21, *Doc. Hist.* v. 14, 417. Federalists often denounced the Antifederalist claim that the federal revenue would only be collected if backed by military force. Congress was composed of the representatives of the people and there was no reason to believe that the people would refuse to pay the taxes they levied, "One of the People," *Doc. Hist.* v. 2, 190; Virginia *Independent Chronicle*, 28 November, *Doc. Hist.* v. 14, 244; "Publicola" [Archibald Maclaine], "An Address to the Freemen of North Carolina," *Doc. Hist.* v. 16, 440; James Wilson, Pennsylvania ratifying convention, *Doc. Hist.* v. 2, 558. Should there ever be need to levy internal taxes at all, there was no reason to doubt that "the force of civil institutions will be adequate to the purpose," James Wilson, "Speech at a Public Meeting in Philadelphia," 6 October, *Doc. Hist.* v. 13, 343. In any case, should the national government ever transgress the limits of propriety and actually levy oppressive taxes, it would not be able to enforce them by force. In the government devised by the Federalists, force of arms would always be on the side of the people. See the discussion in chapter 8.

50. Wilson, ibid., 342–3. In the Pennsylvania convention Wilson described the impost as "the easiest, most just and most productive mode of raising revenue," *Doc. Hist.* v. 2, 481.

51. Hamilton, New York ratifying convention, Elliot, *Debates* 2, 365; George Nicholas, Virginia ratifying convention, *Doc. Hist.* v. 9, 1000.

52. Sedgwick, Massachusetts ratifying convention, Elliot, *Debates* 2, 60–1. "Some gentlemen have said, that Congress may draw their revenue wholly by direct taxes; but they cannot be induced so to do; it is easier for them to have resort to the impost and excise," Dawes, ibid., 42. See also Francis Dana, ibid., 42; Sumner, ibid., 64; James Wilson, Pennsylvania ratifying convention, *Doc. Hist.* v. 2, 480–2, 558–9; Frances Corbin, Virginia ratifying convention, *Doc. Hist.* v. 9, 1011–12; "Publicola" [Archibald Maclaine], "To the Freemen of North Carolina," *Doc. Hist.* v. 16, 441.

53. [Hamilton] *The Federalist* 36, *Doc. Hist.* v. 15, 306.

54. "Centinel" 5, *Doc. Hist.* v. 14, 348.

14: The Federalists and the Uses of Fiscal Power

1. *PAH* 17, 429.

2. *PAH* 19, 53.

3. Ibid., 57, 24, 54, 55.

4. Ibid., 17–18, 29–30, 35.

5. Ibid., 35–6.

6. Stanley Elkins and Eric McKittrick, *The Age of Federalism: The Early American Republic, 1788–1800* (New York: Oxford University Press, 1993), 114–23; E. James Ferguson, *The Power of the Purse: A History of American Public Finance, 1776–1790* (Chapel Hill, University of North Carolina Press, 1961), 289–329; Edwin J. Perkins, *American Public Finance and Financial Services 1700–1815* (Columbus: Ohio State University Press, 1994), 199–234; Forrest McDonald, *Alexander Hamilton: A Biography* (New York: Norton, 1979), 143–88.

7. Davis Rich Dewey, *Financial History of the United States* (New York: Augustus Kelley, 1968, 12th ed), 112–13, 124–5, 128–38; U.S. Bureau of the Census, *Historical Statistics of the United States, Colonial Times to 1970: Bicentennial Edition* (Washington, D.C., 1975) 2, 1118; Perkins, *American Public Finance,* 324–48.

8. *Historical Statistics* 2, 1106, 1115.

9. Roger H. Brown, *Redeeming the Republic: Federalism, Taxation, and the Origins of the Constitution* (Baltimore: Johns Hopkins University Press, 1993), table 2; *Historical Statistics* 2, 1104.

10. Ibid., 1106.

11. Frederick Dalzell, "Taxation with Representation: Federal Revenue in the Early Republic" (Unpublished Dissertation, Harvard University, 1993), 84–106. I am indebted to Bernard Bailyn for drawing Dalzell's work to my attention.

12. William D. Barber, " 'Among the Most *Techy Articles of Civil Police'*: Federal Taxation and the Adoption of the Whiskey Excise," *WMQ,* 3d ser., 25 (1968), 64; Frederick Dalzell, "Prudence and the Golden Egg: Establishing the Federal Government in Providence, Rhode Island," *New England Quarterly,* 65 (1992), 355–88, quotations at 370 and 386.

13. Joseph B. Felt, "Statistics of Taxation in Massachusetts, Including Valuation and Population," *Collections of the American Statistical Association,* 1 (1847), 474; Van Beck Hall, *Politics without Parties: Massachusetts, 1780–1791* (Pittsburgh: Pennsylvania State University Press, 1971), 97 n3; Charles J. Bullock, "Historical Sketch of the Finances and Financial Policy of Massachusetts from 1780 to 1905," *Publications of the American Economic Association* 8: 2, 3d ser. (1907), 22.

14. *North Carolina Session Laws,* Dec. 1785, ch. IX, 130; Nov. 1786, ch. IX, 12; Nov. 1787, ch. II, 1–2; Nov. 1790, ch. XVI, 10–11.

15. It is of course well known that the state governments had trouble collecting the taxes they levied. For this reason, this investigation does not show how much the states actually received in taxes or how much the people actually paid. Nevertheless, taxes levied is a fair measure of tax *pressure* because once taxes were levied they were almost never rescinded, but remained a charge on the tax payer. Furthermore, it may well be a greater psychological strain to lack the means to pay taxes, and therefore to accumulate debt, than to actually pay a high tax.

16. Mark D. Kaplanoff, "Hamiltonian Moment," paper presented at the annual meeting of the Society for Historians of the Early Republic (SHEAR), Harpers Ferry 1998; Oliver Wolcott, "Direct Taxes: Communications to the House of Representatives, December 14, 1796," *American State Papers* (Washington D.C.: Gales and Seaton, 1832–59) 5, 437.

17. Brown, *Redeeming the Republic*, 236.

18. Quoted in Barber, " 'Among the Most *Techy Articles*'," 74. See also Adams to Trumbull, ibid., 83.

19. Hamilton to Madison, Oct. 12, 1789, *PAH* 5, 439.

20. Madison to Hamilton, Nov. 19, 1789, ibid., 525.

21. *The Papers of James Madison*, ed. William T. Hutchinson et al. (Chicago and Charlottesville: University of Chicago Press and University of Virginia Press, 1979) 12, 455.

22. Thomas P. Slaughter, "The Tax Man Cometh: Ideological Opposition to Internal Taxes, 1760–1790," *WMQ*, 3d ser. 41 (1984), 586–91, quotation at 590.

23. See chapter 10. This is also noted by Barber, " 'Among the Most *Techy Articles*,' " 61–2.

24. *PAH* 6, 99; Dewey, *Financial History*, 105–7; W. Elliot Brownlee, *Federal Taxation in America: A Short History* (Cambridge, U.K.: Cambridge University Press, 1996), 17–18.

25. *Historical Statistics* 2, 1106.

26. Bradford Perkins, *The Cambridge History of American Foreign Relations* I: *The Creation of a Republican Empire, 1776–1865* (Cambridge, U.K.: Cambridge University Press, 1993), 81–146; *Historical Statistics* 2, 1106.

27. Dalzell, "Taxation with Representation," 315–16, see also 328–9 and 334.

28. Dewey, *Financial History*, 109–10.

29. Dalzell, "Taxation with Representation," 311–28.

30. Quoted in ibid., 322.

31. Lance Banning, *The Jeffersonian Persuasion: Evolution of a Party Ideology* (Ithaca, N.Y.: Cornell University Press, 1978), 246–70; Ralph Adams Brown, *The Presidency of John Adams* (Lawrence: University Press of Kansas, 1975), 190–3; Dalzell, "Taxation with Representation," 328–36; Elkins and McKittrick, *Age of Federalism*, 726–43; Stephen G. Kurtz, *The Presidency of John Adams: The Collapse of Federalism 1795–1800* (Philadelphia: University of Pennsylvania Press, 1957), 366, 371, 359–6, 385–7, 404; James Roger Sharp, *American Politics in the Early Republic: The New Nation in Crisis* (New Haven, Conn.: Yale University Press, 1993), 226–49.

32. Quoted in Banning, *Jeffersonian Persuasion*, 274.

33. Dalzell, "Taxation with Representation," 303–38, quotation at 305.

34. *An Inquiry into the Nature and Causes of the Wealth of Nations* 2, ed. Andrew Skinner and W. B. Todd (Oxford: Oxford University Press, 1976), 573–4.

35. See the very similar conclusion reached by Perkins, *American Public Finance*, 217–19.

36. "Second Inaugural Address," *A Compilation of the Messages and Papers of the Presidents, 1789–1908* I (Washington, D.C.: Bureau of National Literature and Art, 1908), 379.

Conclusion

1. Francis Hopkinson, "An Ode," *Doc. Hist.* v. 18, 247.

2. The words are Alexander Hamilton's, *The Federalist* 12, *Doc. Hist.* v. 14, 237.

3. Jack N. Rakove, *Original Meanings: Politics and Ideas in the Making of the*

Constitution (New York: Knopf, 1996), 288–338. The passage about the Civil War amendments, but especially the Fourteenth, as "the most Madisonian elements of the American Constitution," appears on 337–8. Obviously, the Constitution is just as much a failure if it is regarded as an attempt to put an end to the democratization of American government, as the Constitution never managed to restore the principle of deference or break the trend toward greater popular influence in government.

4. Michael Mann, *The Sources of Social Power 2: The Rise of Classes and Nation-States, 1760–1914* (Cambridge, U.K.: Cambridge University Press, 1993), 375–80 and tables 11.3 and 11.4. An account of the transformation of the British state can be found in P. Harling and P. Mandler, "From 'Fiscal-Military' State to Laissez-Faire State, 1760–1850," *Journal of British Studies,* 32 (1993), 44–70.

5. These are the words of John M. Murrin, "The Great Inversion, or Court versus Country: A Comparison of the Revolutionary Settlements in England (1688–1721) and America (1776–1816)," in *Three British Revolutions: 1640, 1688, 1776,* ed. J.G.A. Pocock (Princeton, N.J.: Princeton University Press, 1980), 425.

6. Mann, *Sources of Social Power 2,* 377 and table 11.4.

7. *The Federalist* 27, *Doc. Hist.* v. 15, 97.

INDEX

despotic power, 49
despotism
  in military strength, 74, 108, 112,
    280n.42
  in ratification debate, 42–44, 67,
    244n.49
  of taxation, 185
determinism
  economic (see economic
    determination)
  social, 33–36, 238n.9
dialogue, as collective reasoning, 21–
    24
Dick Act (1903), 144
diplomatic relations, after U.S.
    independence war, 130–134,
    139–142, 145–146
direct rule
  in early modern Europe, 49,
    248n.8, 248n.10
  by national governments, 94–95
  by princes, 42–44, 249n.12,
    244n.49
direct taxation, 157–158, 165, 173,
    182, 188–189, 193–194, 198–
    199, 202–203, 212–216, 224–
    225, 296n.26, 311n.52
disarmament
  Congress's power for, 92, 272n.22
  of peacetime militia, 134,
    280n.36, 285n.80
discipline
  of militia, 91–92, 107–114, 123–
    127, 142–144, 271n.20–
    272n.23, 289n.44
  by standing armies, 108, 111, 113,
    281n.46–n.47, 282n.55,
    282n.57, 283n.73–285n.80
discussion
  print (see print discourse)
  public (see public debate)
division of labor
  impact on militia, 113–114, 127–
    128, 143, 285n.80, 289n.54
  in ratification debate, 26, 236n.40–
    n.42
  taxation and, 56–57, 198–199,
    215, 251n.38–252n.39, 296n.26
domestic police, 105, 107, 114, 197,
    285n.80

draft(s), military, for American
    Revolution, 80
Dutch loans, 161, 297n.38, 303n.43
duties, customs
  fiscal power and, 149–150, 154–
    155, 165, 186, 194, 308n.10; as
    dependent, 210–211, 213–216
  military power and, 73–75, 84–
    86, 217

economic determination
  in colonial America, 56–57,
    251n.38
  postwar, 132–134
  public financing and, 158–162,
    297n.39
  in ratification debate, 35–36,
    238n.9, 239n.14
  through trade, 84–88, 265n.53,
    266n.56, 266n.59–267n.65
egalitarianism, 38
electorates
  British reform of, 68, 257n.34
  in early modern Europe, 53–54
  European vs. colonial American,
    5, 68–70, 258n.43
elitists
  democrats vs., 34–35, 238n.9
  in Europe, 49, 52–54
  Federalists as, 33–36, 83, 238n.9
  ratification influence, 24–27, 33–
    36, 236n.39–n.40, 236n.42
Ellsworth, Oliver, 121
Embargo Acts, 137
England. See Great Britain
Enlightenment thought, 37–39
enlistment, military
  during American Revolution, 77–
    80, 260n.15, 261n.20
  during peacetime, 82–83, 91–92,
    94, 270n.12–n.13, 271n.19,
    272n.24
"enlistment bounty," 79
escalation, logic of, 67
Europe and European states
  autonomy evolution in, 49–55,
    250n.23
  country ideology impact on, 66–
    68, 257n.34

peacetime armies
Antifederalist view of, 90–95,
270n.12, 270n.14, 271n.16,
271n.19, 272n.23, 273n.34; as
government force, 105–108,
111, 113–115, 128, 279n.28,
280n.39, 280n.42, 283n.71–
n.73
for citizen obedience, 108, 110–
111, 113, 281n.46–n.47,
282n.55, 282n.57, 282n.61–
n.63, 283n.73–285n.80
citizen-soldiers in, 108–109, 111–
114, 127–128, 283n.65,
283n.71–285n.80, 289n.54
Congress's power for, 89–94,
268n.1–n.5, 271n.16, 273n.26,
273n.34
constitutional debate about, 90–
95, 268n.4–n.5, 269n.8–
270n.14, 271n.19–273n.26,
273n.31
constitutional limitations on, 91–
92, 270n.12–n.14, 271n.19,
272n.24
despotism with, 49, 74, 108, 112,
280n.42
discipline of, 91–92, 107, 114, 142–
144, 271n.20–272n.23
enlistment for, 82–83, 91, 111–
114, 270n.12–n.13
Federalist view of, 90–95, 97–100,
225, 269n.10, 273n.26,
273n.34, 275n.50, 275n.58,
276n.65; unrestricted power for,
115–128, 134–138, 286n.16,
288n.41, 289n.44, 289n.54
in government by consent, 120–
123, 287n.34–288n.41
Great Britain's need for, 95–97,
274n.40, 274n.44
law enforcement by, 102–105,
110, 278n.10, 278n.14,
278n.17, 282n.57, 282n.61
military rule by, 109–110,
282n.55, 282n.57
for national defense, 97–99,
275n.52, 275n.57–n.58,
276n.61, 276n.65
objectives for, 81–86, 262n.26,
263n.33

as tax collectors, 109, 111–112,
281n.49–n.52
as threat to liberty, 99–102, 107,
110–113, 134–138, 277n.1,
277n.3, 280n.39, 282n.63
for trade interests, 81–87, 89–100,
122, 262n.26, 263n.33, 266n.59–
267n.65, 288n.37
Pennsylvania Convention
on peacetime armies, 271n.19,
272n.23–n.24, 273n.26,
274n.47, 275n.57, 282n.55,
282n.61
on taxation, 216, 306n.55,
308n.12, 310n.40
Person, Thomas, 17–18
personal liberty
as human right, 62, 65, 69, 100
peacetime armies as threat to, 99–
102, 107, 110–113, 277n.1,
277n.3, 280n.39, 282n.63
personal security
as human right, 62, 65, 69, 97
military for, 105, 107, 114, 197,
285n.80
persuasion, in ratification debate,
26–28, 32, 236n.39–n.40,
236n.42
Philadelphia Convention (1787)
legitimacy of, 16–18, 24, 216
on peacetime armies, 90–95,
268n.4–n.5, 269n.8–270n.14,
271n.19–273n.26, 273n.31
as root of debate, 3–4, 6, 11
on taxation, 73–75, 149, 154,
158, 181
on war making power, 74–76
"Philadelphiensis," on ratification,
22–23, 266n.56
Pinckney's Treaty, 130
plebeian. *See* common people
pluralism, 36, 38, 51, 250n.23
police, peacetime armies as, 102–
105, 110, 278n.10, 278n.14,
278n.17, 281n.46–n.47,
282n.57, 282n.61
political ideology(ies)
country, 37–38, 40–45, 61, 66–
68, 243n.46
in European state expansion, 34,
37, 40, 131, 145–146

Quakers, 283n.73
Quasi-War, 138, 144, 209, 215–216, 229

radicalism
  American, 34, 37
  British, 66, 105, 178, 257n.34
Randolph, Edmund, 22
ratification debate
  conclusions about, 219–229, 313n.3
  European vs. American contexts of, 47–58
  interpretation of, 15–70
  meaning of, 28–30; as elusive, 31–46
  peacetime armies in, 120–123, 287n.34–288n.41
  political ideologies in, 32–33, 68–70, 238n.5, 238n.8, 239n.14, 241n.39
  progressive interpretation of, 33–37, 238n.8, 239n.14
  public debate significance to, 15–30
  roots of, 3–11
  state expansion ideologies in, 59–70
  taxation in, 73–76, 163–174, 191–192, 215–216, 221, 298n.1, 299n.4, 302n.32, 302n.39
ratification struggle, 11, 15, 27–30, 33, 36
reason and reasoning
  by elitist vs. commoner, 24–27, 236n.39–n.40, 236n.42
  individual vs. collective, 21–24, 28
  in ratification debate, 18–21, 27–28
reason of state doctrine, 39
referendums, for ratification process, 17–18, 234n.11
regular troops. *See* military, professional
religion
  military preservation of, 62, 68, 95–96
  as military service objection, 113, 115, 283n.73

representation
  constitutional debate on, 5, 73–74, 91
  in country ideology, 41–42
  as taxation issue, 200–204, 212, 310n.40, 310n.43, 311n.44, 311n.49
Republican party
  army reform by, 142–144
  in ratification debate, 9, 29, 193
  on taxation, 212, 214, 216–217
republicanism, classical, in ratification debate, 33, 37–39, 241n.34–n.35
requisition system
  for peacetime armies, 91–94, 269n.10, 273n.34
  in public financing, 155, 158, 163, 166–167, 172, 298n.1
  taxation and, 182, 184
resource extraction. *See* extractive capacity/powers
respect, of government, 110–111, 282n.61–n.62
revenue
  from commerce (*see* trade)
  in early modern European states, 48–50, 176
  efficient administration of, 171–172, 174 (*see also* administration)
  for military (*see* fiscal-military state)
  in ratification debate, 73–76
  taxes for (*see* taxation)
Revolution of 1800, 216–218
revolutionaries, Antifederalists as, 40, 43–45, 245n.54, 245n.58
Revolutionary War, American
  influence on ratification, 38–39, 217, 240n.32, 341n.35
  influence on state building, 9, 11, 43, 55–58
  militia recruitment for, 76–81, 123–124, 260n.15, 261n.20
  as response to British state expansion, 68–70, 258n.43
  rhetoric of, 38–40, 241n.35, 244n.50–n.52

278n.17, 282n.57, 282n.61, 286n.16, 287n.22
as threat for taxation returns, 156, 172
Virginia Convention
on peacetime armies, 90–91, 97, 269n.9, 270n.12, 270n.14, 271n.16, 271n.20–272n.21, 273n.31, 275n.55, 275n.58, 283n.65, 284n.78, 289n.44, 289n.54
on public financing, 154–155, 302n.37
on taxation, 179, 185, 187, 202, 217, 307n.61, 309n.24, 310n.43
on U.S. Constitution, 22, 73, 227
virtue, 37, 45
volunteer militia, in American Revolution, 77–80, 97, 123–124, 260n.15, 261n.20

Walpole, Robert, 96, 274n.44
war(s)
early modern European state formation and, 47–49, 246n.2–247n.5
fiscal powers for, 74–76, 163–164, 206–207
influence on state building, 8–9, 44–45, 245n.58
military protection during, 98–99, 275n.55, 276n.61
unlimited taxation during, 163–174, 298n.1, 299n.4, 301n.26, 302n.31–n.32, 302n.37, 302n.39
war making power
in Articles of Confederation, 73, 88, 267n.65

of Congress: fiscal power, 74–76, 163–164, 206–207; as impotent, 73–88; peacetime objectives, 81–86, 262n.26, 263n.33; professional military, 81–83, 262n.24–n.27; revolutionary militia recruitment, 76–81, 260n.15, 261n.20; taxation debate, 74–76; trade jurisdiction, 73–76, 84–88, 265n.53, 266n.56, 266n.59–267n.65
War of 1812, 135, 138, 144–145, 152, 210, 214, 229
War of Independence. See Revolutionary War
Washington, George, 78, 80, 123, 214, 261n.20, 263n.33
on postwar military use, 129–130, 132, 142
West Indies, as British maritime interest, 85, 87, 267n.63
western expansion, in U.S.
Congress' inability to protect, 220, 222–223, 225
military protection for, 122, 129, 134, 138–142, 287n.34, 287n.36
Whiskey Rebellion, 130, 135–138, 206, 209, 212, 216
Wilson, James, 106, 121, 136, 195, 268n.5, 274n.47, 279n.28, 280n.39
Workman, Benjamin, 22–23

XYZ Affair, 216

Yorktown Convention, 154, 158, 273n.31